International Conference on Big Data Analytics, Data Mining and Computational Intelligence 2019 and International Conference on Theory and Practice in Modern Computing 2019

Held at the Multi-Conference on Computer Science and Information Systems (MCCSIS 2019)

Porto, Portugal
16 - 19 July 2019

Editors:

Ajith P. Abraham
Jorg Roth

ISBN: 978-1-5108-9238-5

Printed from e-media with permission by:

Curran Associates, Inc.
57 Morehouse Lane
Red Hook, NY 12571

Some format issues inherent in the e-media version may also appear in this print version.

Printed by Curran Associates, Inc. (2019)

For permission requests, please contact International Association for Development of the Information Society (IADIS) at the address below.

International Association for Development of the Information Society (IADIS)
Rua Sao Sebastiao Da Pedreira
No. 100, 30, 1050-209
Lisbon, Portugal

Phone: 351 21 3151373
Fax: 351 21 3151244

secretariat@iadis.org

Additional copies of this publication are available from:

Curran Associates, Inc.
57 Morehouse Lane
Red Hook, NY 12571 USA
Phone: 845-758-0400
Fax: 845-758-2633
Email: curran@proceedings.com
Web: www.proceedings.com

MULTI CONFERENCE ON COMPUTER SCIENCE AND INFORMATION SYSTEMS

MCCSIS 2019

16-19 JULY PORTO, PORTUGAL

Proceedings of the International Conferences

Big Data Analytics, Data Mining and Computational Intelligence 2019
Theory and Practice in Modern Computing 2019

Edited by
Ajith P. Abraham
Jörg Roth

iadis
international association for development of the information society

INTERNATIONAL CONFERENCES ON

BIG DATA ANALYTICS, DATA MINING AND COMPUTATIONAL INTELLIGENCE 2019

and

THEORY AND PRACTICE IN MODERN COMPUTING 2019

part of the

MULTI CONFERENCE ON COMPUTER SCIENCE AND

INFORMATION SYSTEMS 2019

PROCEEDINGS OF THE INTERNATIONAL CONFERENCES ON

BIG DATA ANALYTICS, DATA MINING AND COMPUTATIONAL INTELLIGENCE 2019

and

THEORY AND PRACTICE IN MODERN COMPUTING 2019

Porto, Portugal
JULY 16 - 18, 2019

Organised by

iadis
international association for development of the information society

Co-Organised by

isep Instituto Superior de Engenharia do Porto

Volume Editors:
Ajith P. Abraham and Jörg Roth

Computer Science and Information Systems Series Editors:
Piet Kommers and Pedro Isaías

Associate Editor: Luís Rodrigues

TABLE OF CONTENTS

THEORY AND PRACTICE IN MODERN COMPUTING

SHORT PAPERS

BIG DATA ANALYTICS, DATA MINING AND COMPUTATIONAL INTELLIGENCE

THEORY AND PRACTICE IN MODERN COMPUTING

POSTERS

BIG DATA ANALYTICS, DATA MINING AND COMPUTATIONAL INTELLIGENCE

DOCTORAL CONSORTIUM

FOREWORD

These proceedings contain the papers and posters of the 4th International Conference on Big Data Analytics, Data Mining and Computational Intelligence 2019 and the 8th International Conference on Theory and Practice in Modern Computing 2019, which were organised by the International Association for Development of the Information Society and co-organised by ISEP – Instituto Superior de Engenharia do Porto, from 16 - 18 July, 2019. These conferences are part of the Multi Conference on Computer Science and Information Systems 2019, 16 - 19 July, which had a total of 926 submissions.

The aim of the Big Data Analytics, Data Mining and Computational Intelligence (BigDaCI) 2019 is to serve as a forum to present current and future work as well as to exchange research ideas in this field.

BigDaCI'19 invites authors to submit their original and unpublished work that demonstrate current research using big data analytics, computational intelligence and other intelligent computing techniques and their applications in science, technology, business and commerce.

Submissions were accepted under the following areas and topics:

- Big Data Algorithms and Architectures
- Computational Intelligent Frameworks for Big Data Processing
- Data Mining Topics and Applications
- Big Data Applications
- Multi-Agent Systems: Models, Architectures and Applications

The International Conference on Theory and Practice in Modern Computing (TPMC 2019) provides a forum for research and developments in the field of computing foundations and technology. Modern computing comes not only with efficient concepts and their application, but also it often addresses networking and mobility topics. Hence, the view in TPMC ranges from fundamentals like new or improved algorithms to very recent and modern applications like ubiquitous scenarios or even everyday computing.

Submissions were accepted under the following four main topics

- Design Foundations
- Mobility Communication and Services
- Realization Aspects
- Networking and Grid Approaches

These conferences received 152 submissions from more than 22 countries. Each submission has been anonymously reviewed by an average of five independent reviewers, to ensure that accepted submissions were of a high standard. Consequently, only 24 full papers were approved which means an acceptance rate of 16%. A few more papers were accepted as short papers, reflection papers, posters and doctoral paper. An extended version of the best papers will be published in the IADIS International Journal on Computer Science and Information Systems (ISSN: 1646-3692) and also in other selected journals, including journals from Inderscience.

Besides the presentation of full, short and reflection papers, posters and one doctoral paper, the conferences also included one keynote presentation and one tutorial from an internationally distinguished researcher. We would therefore like to express our gratitude to Dr. Boris Stilman, University of Colorado Denver, USA & STILMAN Advanced Strategies, USA for accepting our invitation to be the keynote speaker and tutorial presenter.

This volume has taken shape as a result of the contributions from a number of individuals. We are grateful to all authors who have submitted their papers to enrich the conference proceedings. We wish to thank all members of the organizing committee, delegates, invitees and guests whose contribution and involvement are crucial for the success of the conference.

Last but not the least, we hope that everybody had a good time in Porto, and we invite all participants for the next years´ edition of these conferences.

Ajith P. Abraham, Machine Intelligence Research Labs (MIR Labs), USA
Big Data Analytics, Data Mining and Computational Intelligence 2019 Program Chair

Jörg Roth, University of Applied Sciences Nuremberg, Germany
Theory and Practice in Modern Computing 2019 Program Chair

Piet Kommers, University of Twente, The Netherlands
Pedro Isaías, The University of Queensland, Australia
MCCSIS 2019 General Conference Co-Chairs

Bertil Marques, ISEP, Portugal
MCCSIS 2019 Local Organising Chair

Porto, Portugal
July 2019

PROGRAM COMMITTEE

BIG DATA ANALYTICS, DATA MINING AND COMPUTATIONAL INTELLIGENCE

PROGRAM CHAIR

Ajith P. Abraham, Machine Intelligence Research Labs (MIR Labs), USA

THEORY AND PRACTICE IN MODERN COMPUTING

PROGRAM CHAIR

Jörg Roth, University of Applied Sciences Nuremberg, Germany

MCCSIS GENERAL CONFERENCE CO-CHAIRS

Piet Kommers, University of Twente, The Netherlands
Pedro Isaías, The University of Queensland, Australia

MCCSIS LOCAL ORGANISING CHAIR

Bertil Marques, ISEP, Portugal

BIG DATA ANALYTICS, DATA MINING AND COMPUTATIONAL INTELLIGENCE

COMMITTEE MEMBERS

Abdel-Badeeh Salem, Ain Shams University, Egypt
Agapito Ledezma, Universidad Carlos III de Madrid, Spain
Alessandro Giuliani, University of Cagliari, Italy
Ambra Molesini, Università di Bologna, Italy
Andrei Olaru, University Politehnica of Bucharest, Romania
Andres Castillo, Pontificial University of Salamanca, Spain
Anirban Kundu, West Bengal University of Technology, India
Audrone Lupeikiene, VU Institute of Data Science and Digital Technology, Lithuania
Boris Kovalerchuk, Central Washington University, USA
Carson K. Leung, University of Manitoba, Canada
Christos Kalloniatis, University of the Aegean, Greece
Christos Makris, University of Patras, Greece
Daniel Pop, University of the West Timisoara, Romania
Daniela Briola, Università Degli Studi di Milano Bicocca, Italy
Dariusz Krol, Wrocław University of Science and Technology, Poland
David Pelta, Universidad de Granada, Spain
Devesh Agrawal, Uber, USA
Domenico Talia, Università della Calabria, Italy

THEORY AND PRACTICE IN MODERN COMPUTING

COMMITTEE MEMBERS

KEYNOTE LECTURE

CHECKMATE THE ENEMY: ADVERSARIAL REASONING FOR DEFENSE SYSTEMS

Dr. Boris Stilman,
University of Colorado Denver, USA
& STILMAN Advanced Strategies,
USA

ABSTRACT

Linguistic Geometry (LG) is a type of game theory scalable to solving complex real world problems that are considered intractable by conventional approaches. Modern applications of LG, related to defense, generate, in real time, courses of action that are highly creative and even exceed the level of those developed by human commanders. Currently, those applications considered vital for the US national defense. This talk will consist of two surveys. In the first survey, going backward in time, I will review applications of LG, from modern battles to the ancient ones. I will introduce participants to several advanced applications; especially those developed for DARPA and US Army and to major experiments utilized those applications. I will also establish link between LG and legendary ancient battles of Alexander the Great and Hannibal. In the second survey, going forward in time, I will cover development of LG beginning from the 18th century to the foundation of STILMAN Advanced Strategies in 1999. Within this survey, I will introduce participants to the results in solving chess endgames and positions and to the elements of the theory of LG with the focus on the hierarchy of pictorial constructs, a trajectory, a zone, and a translation, represented as a hierarchy of formal languages. I will conclude this talk by introducing the hypothesis that LG is one of the ancient algorithms based directly on the Primary Language of the human brain crucial for development of human intelligence.

TUTORIAL

DISCOVERIES ON DEMAND: DISCOVERING THE ALGORITHM OF DISCOVERY

Dr. Boris Stilman,
University of Colorado Denver, USA
& STILMAN Advanced Strategies,
USA

ABSTRACT

I will introduce participants to the hypothesis that there exists a universal meta-algorithm, the Algorithm of Discovery (AD), the ultimate tool utilized by our brain for discovering new algorithms and perfecting the existing ones. The AD should be based directly on the Primary Language of the human brain (as suggested by J. von Neumann). One of the goals of our research is to understand the AD to the level, which will permit its computer modeling by producing discoveries on demand. Our approach to understanding the AD is to replay manually past discoveries by applying the simulated AD. In this tutorial, I will demonstrate application of the simulated AD for obtaining a major result in Linguistic Geometry (LG), a type of game theory that permits constructing intelligent strategies for opposing games. This result is related to discovering an algorithm for constructing (not searching) intelligent strategies for a class of opposing games and, simultaneously, prove optimality of those strategies. Prior knowledge of the issues included in the tutorial is not required.

Full Papers

NOVEL LEARNING STRATEGY BASED ON GENETIC PROGRAMMING FOR CREDIT CARD FRAUD DETECTION IN BIG DATA

Ibtissam Benchaji, Samira Douzi and Bouabid El Ouahidi
IPSS. Faculty of Sciences, University Mohammed V, Rabat, Morocco

ABSTRACT

Due to the growing volume of monetary transactions on the internet, credit card fraud poses many challenging issues for banks and financial institutions, thus forcing them to continuously improve their fraud detection systems. However, current fraud detection techniques are far from accurate and fail to minimize the false alarm rates, which can cause inconvenience and dissatisfaction for customers in e-banking system. Furthermore, there are several factors that decrease the performance of Fraud Detection Systems (FDS), such as skewed distribution, concept drift, supports real time detection, large amount of data etc. In this paper, we address the highly imbalanced class issue faced by a FDS when working with big data and propose a novel method of generation of data set's minority class based on K-means clustering method and genetic algorithm to improve classification performance in credit card fraud detection. In our experiments, we apply the proposed approach to synthetic unbalanced credit card fraud data set to demonstrate its effectiveness by means of the most appropriate performance measures for fraud detection purposes.

KEYWORDS

Big Data, Fraud Detection, Imbalanced Dataset, K-means Clustering, Genetic Programming

1. INTRODUCTION

As the improvement of technology and the advent of new payment solutions has brought many new benefits to the society and established credit card as the most popular payment mode for both online and offline purchases, it has also resulted unfortunately in an increase of card fraud activities.

Automatic credit card fraud detection is a challenging machine learning problem and different techniques have been proposed to deal with it (Aleskerov, E. et al, 1997; Whitrow, C. et al, 2009; Sánchez, D. et al, 2009; Bhattacharyya, S. et al, 2011; Jha, S. et al, 2012; Sahin, Y. et al, 2013; Dal Pozzolo, A. et al, 2014; Bahnsen, A. C. et al, 2015). However, several aspects must be considered at the same time when building a system for card fraud detection. For instance, the data distribution evolves over time because of seasonality and new attack strategies. On the other hand, the system has to respond in very short times to become useful in real scenarios. Another critical aspect is the skewness of the data since legitimate transactions far outnumber the fraudulent ones. In fact, Class distribution is extremely unbalanced in credit card transactions, because frauds are typically less than 1% of the overall transactions, as shown in (Dal Pozzolo, A. et al, 2014 ; Krivko, M., 2010). Such imbalanced sets require additional precautions because the prediction accuracy of standard machine learning techniques, especially for the minority class which is the class of interest, tends to be lower. Thus, misclassifying the minority class has much higher cost compared to misclassifying a majority class instance. Notice that, when the system predicts a transaction as fraudulent when in fact it is not (false positive), the financial institution has an administrative cost, as well as a decrease in customer satisfaction. On the contrary, when the system does not detect a fraudulent transaction (false negative), the amount of that transaction is lost.

In this paper, we address primarily the last issue and propose the generation method of imbalanced data set's minority class, by using K-means clustering method and genetic algorithm, thus new mimicked minority class samples can be obtained through crossover on the basis of cluster, which are then merged with training data into an augmented training set so that the effectiveness of a classifier can be improved. We provide the obtained results to support and validate our findings.

This work is organized as follows. In Section 2, related work is analyzed and discussed. In Section 3, we present the organization of our proposed methodology. Section 4 describes the dataset used in this work and discusses the obtained results. Finally, Section 5 concludes the paper and proposes ideas for future research.

2. RELATED WORK

As introduced, the major challenge to be addressed when designing a Fraud Detection System is handling the class imbalance. A dataset is called imbalanced when the number of negative (majority) instances outnumbers the amount of positive (minority) class instances. Figure 1 illustrates the class distribution of Credit Card Dataset used in our experiments.

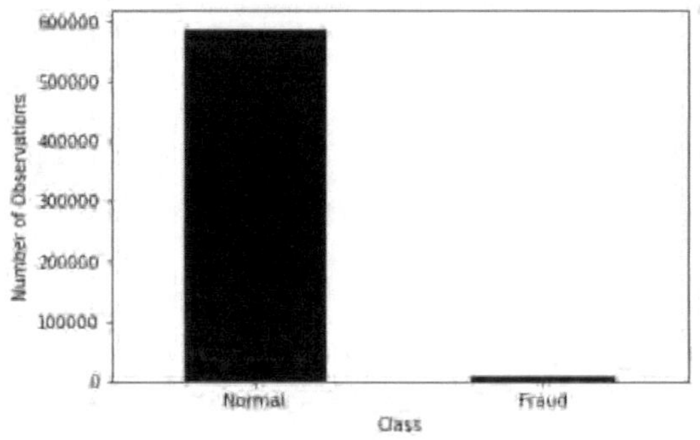

Figure 1. Class distribution of Credit Card Data Set

Hence, standard machine learning algorithms that maximize overall accuracy tend to classify all observations as majority class instances and perform poorly in terms of predictive accuracy on the minority class (low recall). In real world applications, classification accuracy of the smaller class is critically important because the minority class usually is the class of great interest such as cases of fraud. Thus, misclassifying the minority class has much higher cost compared to misclassifying a majority class instance.

In this regard, various approaches have been proposed to address the imbalanced datasets issue and improve the performance of predictive modeling. These approaches could be mainly divided into two categories. The first category solves the problem at data level, that is, data resample techniques are performed to directly alter the original dataset which is not balanced by removing samples from the majority class (undersampling) or replicating training samples of the minority class (oversampling) (Dal Pozzolo, A. et al, 2015). Advanced oversampling methods like SMOTE (Chawla, N. et al, 2002) generate synthetic training instances from the minority class by interpolation, instead of sample replication. However, these techniques present significant drawbacks, such as undersampling may lose some potential information, and oversampling may lead to overfitting.

The second main type of approaches that considers classification of imbalanced data sets at algorithm level is known as Cost based learning or Ensemble learning (Cieslak, D. A. et al, 2012). Ensemble methods include bagging and boosting strategies that aim to combine several weak classifiers as one strong classifier which can improve the classification performance of imbalanced dataset. The ideas of Bagging (Bootstrap Aggregating) (Breiman, L., 1996) is to split the majority class into multiple sub sets, and for each sub set, training a basic weak classifier together with the minority class, then integrate these classifiers into a strong classifier. The AdaBoost (Adaptive Boosting) (Freund, Y. and Schapire, R. E., 1996) talks about the misclassified samples that generated by the former basic classifier will be augmented by assigning weights. The weighted data sets will be send to next basic classifier to reduce the total bias error. AdaBoost is equivalent to resampling the data space (Sun, Y. et al, 2007), which are applicable to most classification systems without changing their learning methods. Besides, it could eliminate the extra learning cost for exploring the optimal class distribution and representative samples (Ali, A. et al, 2015). Moreover, compared with the method of eliminating samples from data set, it reduces the information loss, overfitting risk and bias error of a certain classification learning method (He, H. and Garcia, E. A., 2009).

Instead of these approaches, the present paper focuses on generating new samples for minority class with respect to the original set, using clustering and genetic operators, which is a novel approach of oversampling the minority fraudulent data that aims to improve the performance of imbalanced data classification when designing an effective Fraud Detection System.

3. PROPOSED METHODOLOGY

In this paper we propose a new oversampling approach for improving classification effectiveness in credit card fraud detection based on k-means cluster and genetic algorithms. Firstly, we apply the k-means algorithm to split minority class of fraud instances into clusters according to their similarities. The goal of this clustering method is to have in each cluster samples that are as much similar as possible which can guarantee that new samples of whole minority class have better coverage and representation. Thus, by means of crossover and mutation operators we generate in each cluster new synthetic minority class instances that mimic the original minority class examples as closely as possible and merge them with the original dataset into an augmented training set. Figure 2 shows the big picture of the proposed method.

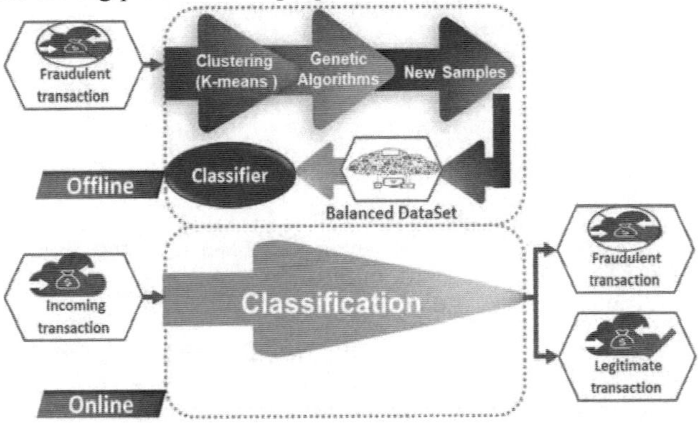

Figure 2. The illustration of credit card fraud detection system

3.1 K-means Clustering Method

Clustering is a process of partitioning a set of samples into a number of groups without any supervised training. The goal of this technique is to categorize the records of a dataset in such a way that similar records are grouped together in a cluster and dissimilar records are placed in different clusters. The most popular clustering algorithm is k-means because of its simplicity and efficiency (Zhang, J. et al, 2013; Jain, A.K, 2010).

K-means algorithm groups N objects into K clusters maintaining high intra group similarity and low inter group similarity of the objects. The K-means algorithm places a data object into a group by finding closest cluster center using a distance measure. This measure calculates similarity distance between each data objects and centroids. Among many available distance measures, Euclidean distance is the widely used measure for distance calculation between objects and centroids (Bawane, V. S. and Kale, S. M., 2015).

Given a set of n data points D = { $x_1, x_2, x_3, \ldots, x_n$ } in R^d and an integer K , the K-means problem is to determine a set of K centroids C = { $c_1, \ldots, c_k$ } in R^d so as to minimize the following error function :

$$J = \sum_{j=1}^{k} \sum_{i=1}^{n} \left\| x_i^{(j)} - c_j \right\|^2$$

The K-Means Clustering algorithm is composed of the following steps:

1. Select k points at random as cluster centers.

2. Assign objects to their closest cluster center according to the Euclidean distance function.
3. Calculate the centroid or mean of all objects in each cluster.
4. Repeat steps 2, 3 and 4 until the same points are assigned to each cluster in consecutive rounds.

As K-Means algorithm requires the number of clusters as input, we will use the elbow method to get the optimal number of clusters. The idea of the elbow method is to run k-means clustering on the dataset for a range of K values and for each value of K calculates the mean distance between data points and their cluster centroid. Since increasing the number of clusters will always reduce the distance to data points, increasing K will always decrease this metric, to the extreme of reaching zero when K is the same as the number of data points. Thus, the elbow method plots the mean distance to the centroid as a function of K and the "elbow point," where the rate of decrease sharply shifts, can be used to roughly determine K, as depicted in Figure 3.

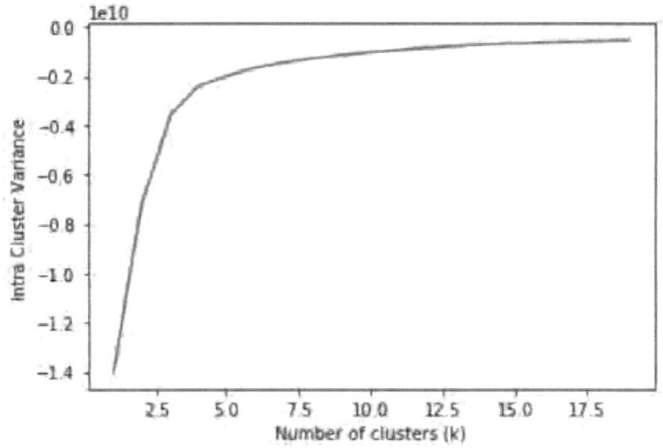

Figure 3. Elbow Method for selection of optimal "K" clusters applied to our DataSet

In Figure 3, it can be observed that an elbow point occurs at K=4. Hence, for values larger than K=4, the difference in SSE (Sum of Squared Errors) starts to decrease and diminishes gradually. Hence, we will choose to have 4 clusters and provide this value as input to the K-Means algorithm.

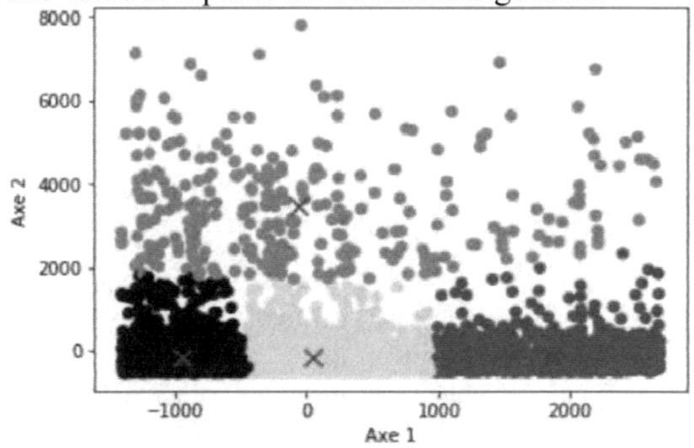

Figure 4. Fraud Data repartition using K-Means Algorithm

In the proposed paper, K-Means Clustering is applied on the dataset taken for study to split minority class of fraud instances into 4 clusters according to their similarities. New mimicked samples can be created from samples that are as much similar as possible in each cluster through genetic operators. Thus, every cluster can obtain certain proportion of new samples, which can guarantee that new samples of whole minority class have better coverage and representation. Figure 4 presents the scatter plot of the 4 clusters formed.

3.2 Genetic Algorithms

Genetic algorithms were inspired from Darwin's theory of evolution and were pioneered by John Holland (Holland, J. H., 1992). A genetic algorithm can be defined as a search algorithm based on the mechanics of natural selection and natural genetics (Goldberg, D., 1983). Genetic algorithms have at least the following elements in common: Populations of chromosomes, selection according to fitness, crossover to produce offspring, and random mutation of a new offspring (Ben Amor, H. and Rettinger, A., 2005). In a broader usage of the term, a genetic algorithm is any population-based model that uses selection and recombination operators to generate new sample points in a search space. Figure 5 and Figure 6 depicts a schematic view of different steps involved.

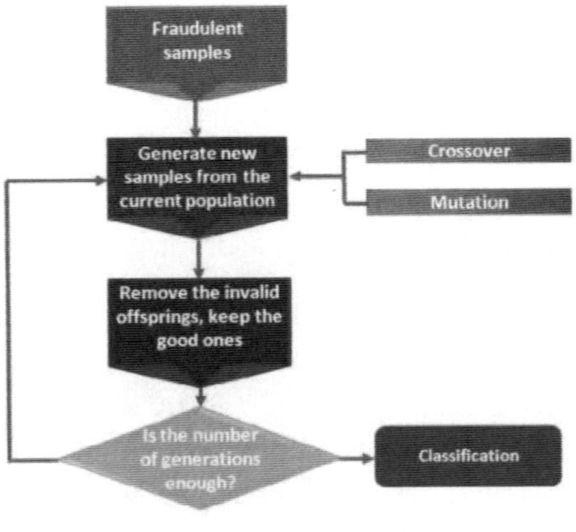

Figure 5. GA Flow

In further details, the genetic algorithm starts with the cluster's samples which act as the parents of the current generation. New synthetic individuals are generated from these samples by the crossover and mutation operators. New individuals will inherit the individual's characteristic of parent's generation, rather than simple duplication. The less fit individuals of this generation are eliminated and the fitter members are selected as the parents for the next generation. This procedure is repeated until a pre-specified number of generations have passed, and the augmented training data set until then is balanced. Thus, binary classifier is more effective in detecting fraudulent transactions.

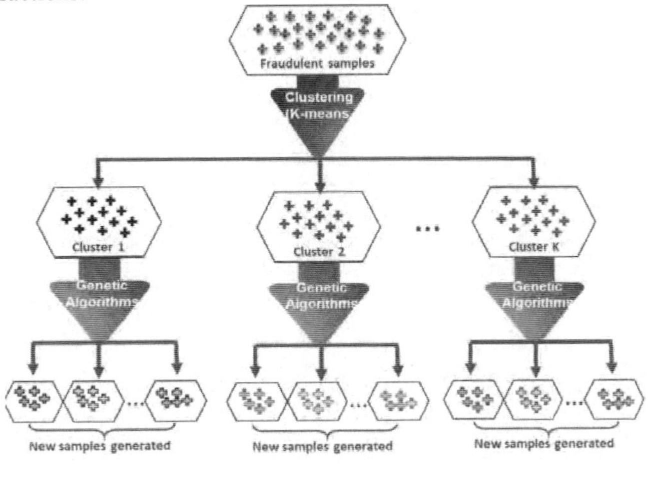

Figure 6. GA generation process

Here are steps of algorithm:

1. With k=4, fraudulent class C_f is divided into four clusters by means of K-means algorithm, the Ith cluster can be expressed as C_f^i with $1 \le i \le 4$.

2. The fitness value is calculated in each population C_f^i and is sorted out.

3. Carry out random pairing to individual m_i inside the C_f^i, the amount of pairing group is $\frac{m_i}{2}$.
4. Each pair of individuals of the population C_f^i can suffer crossover based on a given crossover probability.
5. After crossover, each individual can be mutated, based on a given mutation probability.

This process is repeated the number of times necessary to achieve the desired size of fraudulent population and obtain a balanced training dataset.

4. EXPERIMENTAL RESULTS

This section describes the dataset and provides the evaluation metrics used in this work. The results of the experiments of the proposed method are then presented.

4.1 Dataset Description

Datasets provide a way to train and verify the efficacy of the proposed techniques and therefore play crucial role for driving the research. One of the difficulties with studying Credit card fraud detection is that considered highly confidential and not disclosed to public (Lopez-Rojas, E. A., and Axelsson, S., 2016; Dal Pozzolo, A. et al, 2014). Hence, researchers have suggested using synthetic data that is modeled after a real data set such that it contains similar patterns. For this work, we use data produced by BankSim, a simulation tool specifically designed to emulate fraud data (Vaughan, G., 2018; Lopez-Rojas, E. A., and Axelsson, S., 2014). The data produced by BankSim is freely available on Kaggle.

BankSim uses a Multi Agent-Based Simulation approach based on a sample of aggregated real transaction data provided by one bank in Spain. The original bank data consists of thousands of records of transactional data from November 2012 to April 2013. BankSim mimics this original bank data using several agents of three different categories: merchants, customers, and fraudsters. These agents interact over a sequence of simulated days, resulting in a log of purchase transactions that closely resemble the original bank data.

The dataset used in this work contains transactions corresponding to card purchases made during 180 simulated days and consists of 594,643 different transactions, among which 7,200 (≈1,2%) are labeled as "Fraud", while the remaining 587,443 are labeled as "Geniune". Raw data include information about the transactions that are processed. Table 1 describes the feature vector of a transaction message.

Table 1. Feature vectors description

Name	Description
Step	The day the transaction took place from 1 to 180
Customer ID	A number identifying the customer account involved in the transaction
Age Category	A categorical value putting the customer into one of 8 different age groups
Gender	A categorical variable indicating the gender of the customer
Zip Code of account	The zip code associated with the customer
Merchant ID	A number identifying the merchant involved in the transaction
Zip Code of Merchant	The zip code of the merchant
Category purchase	A categorical variable indicating what type of good or service was purchased
Amount of purchase	The total amount that the transaction cost
Fraud status	A binary variable indicating if the transaction was fraudulent of not

4.2 Performance Metrics

In order to evaluate our approach, the performance of Random Forest classifier is measured based on accuracy, sensitivity, specificity and precision. These evaluation metrics are used based on their relevance in evaluating imbalanced binary classification problem.

$$Accuracy = \frac{TP + TN}{TP + FP + TN + FN} \qquad Sensivity = \frac{TP}{TP + FN}$$

$$Specificity = \frac{TN}{FP + TN} \qquad Precision = \frac{TP}{TP + FP}$$

True positives (TP) are cases classified as positive which are actually positive. True negative (TN) are cases classified rightly as negative. False positive (FP) are cases classified as positive but are negative cases. False negative (FN) are cases classified as negative but are truly positive. Sensitivity (Recall) gives the accuracy on positive (fraud) cases classification. Specificity gives the accuracy on negative (legitimate) cases classification and precision gives the accuracy in cases classified as fraud (positive).

In this study, 70% of the dataset is used for training while 30% is set aside for validating and testing. Accuracy, sensitivity, specificity and precision are used to evaluate the performance of the Random Forest classifier. The accuracy of the classifier for the original imbalanced dataset and balanced dataset by means of application of our proposed approach are presented in Table 2.

Table 2. Accuracy results for balanced and imbalanced set

Metrics	RF Classifier	
	Imbalanced Set	Balanced Set
Accuracy	0.9537	0.9769
Sensitivity	0.8572	0.9514
Specificity	0.9341	0.9696
Precision	0.7605	0.8786

An observation of the metric table shows that there is significant improvement from the balanced dataset distribution for accuracy, sensitivity and specificity of RF classifier. This shows that applying our strategy on a highly imbalanced dataset greatly improves the performance of binary classification.

5. CONCLUSION

The credit card fraud detection is becoming important topic of research, as different types of attacks are increasing at an alarming rate. The goal of our work is to deal with the problem of class imbalance and improve fraud detection accuracy on new incoming transactions. Given a training set, an augmented set is produced, containing more examples of the minority class through the generation of mimicked examples by means of genetic operators. While we have presented our strategy in the context of credit card fraud detection, it is quite general and can be extended to other application domains characterized by significant class imbalance rates.

To validate our work, we performed experiments on publicly available credit card fraud detection data, where the minority class is severely underrepresented. Experiments show that a classifier trained on the balanced set outperforms the same classifier trained on the original data, especially as far the sensitivity is concerned, resulting in an effective fraud detection mechanism.

Besides the class imbalance problem, fraud detection algorithms also need to account for the fact that the class conditional distribution changes over time. As future work, we would like to devise a strategy to exploit the temporal information of customer expending behaviors and fraud patterns using Deep Learning architectures.

REFERENCES

Aleskerov, E. et al, 1997. CARDWATCH: a neural network based database mining system for credit card fraud detection. *In Proceedings of the IEEE/IAFE Computational Intelligence for Financial Engineering (CIFEr).* New York City, NY, USA, pp. 220-226.

Ali, A. et al, 2015. Classification with class imbalance problem: A Review. *In Int. J. Advance Soft Compu. Appl,* Vol. 7, No. 3.

Bahnsen, A. C. et al, 2015. Example-dependent cost-sensitive decision trees. *In Expert Systems with Applications,* Vol. 42, No. 19,pp 6609–6619.

Bawane, V. S. and Kale, S. M., 2015. Clustering algorithms in MapReduce: a review. *In National Conference on Recent Trend in Computer Science and Engineering.*

Ben Amor, H. and Rettinger, A., 2005. Intelligent exploration for genetic algorithms: Using self-organizing maps in evolutionary computation. *In proceedings of the 2005 conference on Genetic and evolutionary computation,* pp 1531–1538.

Bhattacharyya, S. et al, 2011. Data mining for credit card fraud: A comparative study. *In Decision Support Syst,* Vol. 50, No. 3,pp 602–613.

Breiman, L., 1996. Bagging Predictors. *In Journal of Machine Learning,* Vol. 24, No. 2,pp 123–140.

Chawla, N. et al, 2002. SMOTE: Synthetic minority over-sampling technique. *In Journal of Artificial Intelligence Research,* Vol. 16, No. 1,pp 321-357.

Cieslak, D. A. et al, 2012. Hellinger distance decision trees are robust and skew-insensitive. *In Data Mining and Knowledge Discovery,* Vol. 24, No. 1,pp 136–158.

Dal Pozzolo, A. et al, 2014. Learned lessons in credit card fraud detection from a practitioner perspective. *In Expert Systems with Applications,* Vol. 41, No. 10,pp 4915–4928.

Dal Pozzolo, A. et al, 2014. Using HDDT to avoid instances propagation in unbalanced and evolving data streams. *In Proc. International Joint Conference on Neural Networks (IJCNN).* Beijing, China, pp 588–594.

Dal Pozzolo, A. et al, 2015. When is undersampling effective in unbalanced classification tasks?. *Machine Learning and Knowledge Discovery in Databases.* Cambridge, U.K, pp 200-215.

Freund, Y. and Schapire, R. E., 1996. Experiments with a New Boosting Algorithm. *In Proceedings of the Thirteenth International Conference on International Conference on Machine Learning.* Bari, Italy, pp. 148-156.

Goldberg, D., 1983. Computer-Aided Gas Pipeline Operation Using Genetic Algorithms And Rule Learning. *In University of Michigan, Ann Arbor.*

He, H. and Garcia, E. A., 2009. Learning from imbalanced data. *In IEEE Transactions on Knowledge and Data Engineering.* Vol. 21, No. 9,pp 1263–1284.

Holland, J. H., 1992. Adaptation In Natural And Artificial Systems. *In University of Michigan Press.*

Jain, A.K, 2010. Data clustering: 50 years beyond k -means. *In Pattern Recognition Letters,* Vol. 31, No. 8,pp 651–666.

Jha, S. et al, 2012. Employing transaction aggregation strategy to detect credit card fraud. *In Expert Systems with Applications,* Vol. 39, No. 16,pp 12650–12657.

Krivko, M., 2010. A hybrid model for plastic card fraud detection systems. *In Expert Systems with Applications,* Vol. 37, No. 8,pp 6070–6076.

Lopez-Rojas, E. A., and Axelsson, S., 2014. BankSim: A bank payment simulation for Fraud detection research. *In The 26th European modeling and simulation symposium*, pp 144–152.

Lopez-Rojas, E. A., and Axelsson, S., 2016. A review of computer simulation for fraud detection research in financial datasets. *In 2016 future technologies conference*, pp 932–935.

Sahin, Y. et al, 2013. A cost-sensitive decision tree approach for fraud detection. *In Expert Systems with Applications,* Vol. 40, No. 15,pp 5916–5923.

Sánchez, D. et al, 2009. Association rules applied to credit card fraud detection. *In Expert Systems with Applications,* Vol. 36, No. 2,pp 3630–3640.

Sun, Y. et al, 2007. Cost-sensitive boosting for classification of imbalanced data. *In Pattern Recognition,* Vol. 40, No. 12,pp 3358–3378.

Vaughan, G., 2018. Efficient big data model selection with applications to fraud detection. *In International Journal of Forecasting.*

Whitrow, C. et al, 2009. Transaction aggregation as a strategy for credit card fraud detection. *In Data Mining and Knowledge Discovery. 18, pp. 30-55.*

Zhang, J. et al, 2013. A parallel clustering algorithm with mpi-mkmeans. *In Journal of Computers,* Vol. 8, No. 1.

TRANSFORMATION OF SYSTEMS OF INTERACTIVE SIMULATION OF CONFLICT SITUATIONS INTO SYSTEMS BASED ON DECISION PATTERNS

Andrzej Najgebauer
Military University of Technology, Faculty of Cybernetics, Institute of Computer and Information Systems
00-908 Warsaw, Kaliskiego 2 Street, Poland

ABSTRACT

The simulation can be observed as a type of intelligence, where software there is a mind and hardware there is a body. The limitations of such intelligence are concerned. The researches cover the process of construction, testing and experimentation with the simulation system, towards knowledge extraction. The technological line of conflict analysis with different computer tools utilization is presented. The central part of the line there is an interactive simulation environment for the analysis (and/or training) of military operations. The idea of interactive simulation for land operations and its exemplification there is presented. The necessity and requirements for computer environment were described. Possible directions and solutions of these environments are presented. On the basis of own methodology for simulation system designing and development, simulation systems MSCombat (as prototype) and Złocień, SWDT as professional systems were built and tested. The methodology consists of eight phases - the general description of a conflict, the conflict model as non-coalition 3-person game, the model of battle process - the multidimensional stochastic process, the decision model - the multiple stage stochastic optimization problem, the computer environment for simulation of combat process, the experiments, monitoring and visualization phase, the post-simulation analysis.. In the environment it is possible to examine different approaches and models because the construction is modular and object-oriented. The chosen phases of analysis, definition, modelling and implementation of professional system are presented in the paper. The directions of transformation of the simulation environment into the artificial intelligence are proposed.

KEYWORDS

Interactive Simulation, Decision Support, Decision Patterns, Systems Analysis and Modelling

1. INTRODUCTION

The simulation as mentioned, can be observed as a type of intelligence, where software there is a mind and hardware there is a body (Penrose R., 1989). The limitations of such intelligence should be concerned. A military conflict can be concerned as a complex adaptive system (Ilachinski J, 1996). The author formulated some hypotheses, that military conflict can be characterized by:

- non-linear interaction of combat components (measure --> counter-measure --> counter-countermeasure--> ...)
- hierarchical structure of command and control
- decentralized control
- self-organization (long range order)
- non-equilibrium order
- adaptation
- collectivism

The main conclusion of these consideration is:

there exists commander's battlefield intuition as ability to perceive some patterns - that is the basis of thinking about an extraction of decision rules in military conflicts. Some very important concepts of combat modelling are presented in (Dockery at al, 1993).

We would like to test the hypotheses, so it is required to conduct very sophisticated researches. The researches cover the process of construction, testing and experimentation with the simulation system, towards knowledge extraction. The technological line of conflict analysis with different computer tools utilization is presented. The central part of the line there is an interactive simulation environment for the analysis (and/or training) of military operations. The fundamental questions of the analysis and computer support of the conflict analysis were put:

- How to identify the real conflict situation?
- How to reflect the situation?
- How to determine the best decisions?
- What type of criteria should we take into account?
- What a sense do the decisions have under uncertainty conditions?
- How to decompose the complex situations into local type situations?
- What type of local conflict models should we use in the situation?
- Do any patterns of behavior exist in a decision situation?
- How to reflect uncertainty and surprise in a conflict situation?
- How to show the dynamics and changes in a situation?
- Where are the limits of the computer simulation and our belief in efficacy of that type of conflict analysis?

The answers for the questions consist in the specific methodology of the analysis and computer support proposed.

The phases of the methodology are as follows:

- the general description and identification of a conflict
- the conflict model as non-coalition n-person game (as the start point)
- the model of battle process - the multidimensional stochastic process
- the decision model - the multiple stage stochastic optimisation problem with risk criteria
- the computer environment for simulation of combat process
- the experiments, monitoring and visualization phase
- the post-simulation analysis

The transition between the stochastic model and simulation model is realized during the implementation phase. Many characteristics of the military conflict modelled are random variables or stochastic processes. So it is necessary to use random generators with different distributions. The direction of transformation of the simulation environment into the artificial intelligence is proposed. The simulation system can be defined as a formal system and it undergoes the same limits like another formal system. The famous German mathematician – Hilbert formulated e.g. Entscheidungsproblem, which consists in the question:

Does exist the automatic procedure, which allows to resolve all the mathematical problems, belonging into the wide, well defined class? (Hilbert, 1900, 1928).

The thesis of Church and Turing and also the Gödel's theorem, that everyone formal system, consisting of natural number arithmetic isn't complete, so contains indeterminate formulas (1931) show us the limits of computer simulation as formal system.

The modern battle-winning forces must be adequately trained and equipped. The changes in defense climate in recent years have placed greater emphasis on the use of modelling and simulation to explore training and justify chosen solutions. In fact, since reality is infinitely complex, especially a conflict situation, all human decision-making is based on models. In most cases these are mental models that we construct but they are rarely fully defined and usually qualitative in nature. The analytical model, in contrast, is fully defined, open to examination and challenge, and to maximum extent possible, quantitative (G.P. Hawkins, 2000). The essence of the analytical process is to bring together in a systematic and auditable way a range of data, assumptions and judgements relevant to the problem and to demonstrate their implications and interrelationships. Analytical models and closed constructive models offer speed, controllability, repeatability, flexibility and relatively low cost, and are usually the preferred option. Unfortunately the real situations are very complicated and it is necessary to use simulation models, which are more flexible in examining procurement options or different concept of operations. This type of analysis is repeatable.

Simulations in military domain can be divided into three types:

- Live – real people operating real equipment, platforms or systems, usually on tactical or weapons ranges.
- Virtual – real people operating simulated systems. The latter may include any mix of equipment, system or platform simulators, rigs or testbeds, computer presentations/visualizations or prototypes of the same, factories and production lines, and/or constructive models of forces or force elements.

- Constructive – simulated people operating simulated equipment, or systems. Computer models represent the actions of people and/or equipment using mathematical equations and/or logical algorithms.

Distributed interactive simulation is a technology develop by military experts to facilitate the integration and use of multiple simulations and simulators in a distributed collaborative computing environment. Synthetic environments extend the modelling and simulation concept by integrating consistent sets of models, simulations, people and real equipment within a common representation of the world. The consistent set is assembled from three types of components:

- a framework (architecture, standards, communications) with which all components must comply, so that they can interoperate.
- a world, reflecting the properties of the real environment, usually a "battlespace", including physical feature (such as terrain), phenomena (such as weather and smoke) and an operational context/scenario.
- participants i.e. equipment/systems (and/or their components), individuals, force elements and/or whole forces.

Synthetic environments can be constructed and operated at many levels of representation, aggregation and fidelity ranging from geopolitical analysis down to component-level action support and cost modelling.

In the paper I am focused on land operations (division and brigade). The commanders and their staffs should be trained, so it is proposed the construction specific computer environment on the basis of operational game model:

$$\Gamma_S = < \mathbf{N}, M_{SW}, SC_W > \tag{1}$$

where: N – a set of participants, the component of the set is determined by their role (head, trainee, observer, analyst, expert, opposing forces commander), personal data, team structure, if group participant;
M_{SW} – campaign process model, which can be described by $S(t)$ (Najgebauer, 1999a) and set of complementary parameters
SC_W - scenario of combat, which is defined as initial state of campaign process $S(t_0)$, termination time T^Y ($Y=A,B,C,...$-participant of game notation) and mission from higher level T^Y, $\mathbf{S}_{Sat}(T^Y)$, ($Y=A,B,C,...$)

The phases of game construction (Najgebauer, 1999a):

- Conceptual phase – the aim of game is determined.
- Data gathering – collecting of the conflict situation data, possible actions or counteractions, probable events on the battlefield..
- The situation model – verbal or mathematical model of the situation, possible relations, manoeuvre models, combat and logistics models, criteria of decision estimation
- The transformation of the situation model into operational game – the simplification, type of simulation, time procedures, methods of state update:
- guidelines, exercise team and service team determination, initial conditions, evaluation method determination, the method of combat success justification, the method of activity trace, the method of documentation, mission ordering, publication of guidelines.
- Game testing – the game designer examines the procedures and results of the game.
- Operational phase – scenario preparation and the experiment realisation.

2. THE ANALYSIS AND PROBLEM DEFINITION

The main subject of interests there are decision-making processes in armed conflict situations and the subject of evaluation there is decision–maker, who makes the decisions. The decision-making process in armed conflict is very complex, because of uncertainty, incomplete information and rate of combat.

The conflict situations cause many decisions problems. It is possible to support a commander in the process realising the analysis of probable moves and expected results of these moves. The attention is focused on valid reflection of decisions, made by commanders, who take part in the exercises. Computer simulations of the situation can support the commander in the complex process. The computer environment should be carefully designed to flexible and precise reflection of conflict situation and decision-makers interaction.

The interaction process in computer environment is one of decision updating method, when the decision-maker tries to react on changeable conditions of combat. In (Najgebauer, 1999a) the general decision procedure was proposed as a multistage decision problem. The results of decisions can be observed. The strategies of decision-makers (players) are formulated on the basis of a combat process model that is defined as a multivariate stochastic process. The stochastic model expresses the uncertainty in a conflict situation. There exists the possibility of observation of the battlefield and making decisions on the basis of these measurements. The general combat process presented below is a simplification of much more widely described process for the professional system Złocień. However there are much more sophisticated models are described and applied in the computer environments, which were built by my team. The simplification is used for the purpose of synthetic presentation of transformation problem and the way of modelling in the paper.

2.1 General Combat Process

Let $\{S(t), t \in [0,T]\}$ be the multidimensional stochastic process (Najgebauer, 1999a,), where:

$$\{S(t) = (S_{1Y}(t), S_{2Y}(t), S_{3Y}(t), S_{4Y}(t), S_{5Y}(t), S_{6Y}(t), S_{1PW}(t), S_{2PW}(t)), t \in [0,T], Y = A,B \} \quad (2)$$

$S_{1Y}(t)$ - number of combat units of side Y (A, B)(they are ready to fight), $S_{1Y}(t) \in \{0, 1, 2, ..., M^Y\}$, $S_{2Y}(t)$ - combat potential of side Y, $S_{2Y}(t)=(S^1_{2Y}(t),S^2_{2Y}(t))$ $S_{2Y}(t)\in\{\{0,\bar{S}^1_{2Y}\}\times\{0,\bar{S}^2_{2Y}\}\}$, $S^1_{2Y}(t)$ - combat potential of side Y in an attack, $S^2_{2Y}(t)$ - combat potential of side Y in a defence, $S_{3Y}(t)$ - state of readiness, $S_{3Y}(t) \in \{0, 1\}$, $S_{4Y}(t)$ - efficacy degree of logistics system, $S_{4Y}(t) \in \{1, 2, 3, 4\}$, the levels of combat potential renewal in a period of time, $S_{5Y}(t)$ - surveillance level, $S_{5Y}(t) \in \{1,2,...,7\}$, the levels of enemy recognition, $S_{6Y}(t)$ - combat units placement, $S_{6Y}(t)=\left(S^1_{6Y}(t),S^2_{6Y}(t),\cdots,S^i_{6Y}(t),\cdots,S^{H^Y}_{6Y}(t)\right)$, $S^i_{6Y}(t)\in H^Y=\{1,2,3,4,5,6\}$, $S_{1PW}(t)$- the set of battlefield routes, $S_{1PW}(t)\subset L=\{l_1,l_2,\cdots,l_k,\cdots,l_K\}$, $S_{2PW}(t)$- weather at the time t, $S_{2PW}(t) \in \{1,2,3,4,5,6,7\}$- set of numbers of different types of weather.

2.2 Terrain Model

The terrain model is discrete and can be expressed as follows:

$$Z=< G, \{\varphi_l\}_{l=1,2,3,} \{\varnothing\}> \quad (3)$$

where $G=<W,U>$- Berge graph, W – set of vertices , U – set of arcs , $U \subset W \times W$
$\varphi_1 : W \rightarrow C$ – function, which describes a location of the zone, represented by vertex $w \in W$, $C \subset R^3$, C describes the whole battlefield area of the conflict, φ_2: $W \rightarrow 2^L$ function, which describes an assignment of roads to node w (these roads are accessible for mobility in a zone w), L- set of all road numbers in a battlefield, φ_3: $W \times J^{A(B)} \rightarrow 2^{TU}$ – assignment function of formation type subset to node w, TU – set of all possible types of combat units formation, φ_4: $W \times J^{A(B)} \rightarrow R^n$ – the determination of maximal velocities of combat units on roads of battlefield, $n=|L|$. Arcs of the graph represent possibility of close transition between zones. The process is discrete in states and continuous in time (DC). Combat actions, decisions and their realizations, natural phenomena and so on causes the transitions between states. The phase space X of the process $S(t)$ can be represented as follows:

$$\mathbf{X} = [\{0,1,...,M\}\times\{0,1,...,\overline{S^1_{2Y}}\}\times\{0,1,....,\overline{S^2_{2Y}}\}\times\{0,1\}\times\{1,2,3,4\}\times$$
$$\times\{1,2,3,4,5,6,7\}\times\{0,1\}\times\times(\mathbf{H}^M)^Y]^2\times 2^{\mathbf{L}}\times\{1,2,3,4,5,6,7\} \quad (4)$$

Each element of the battle system, which represents one of the sides or the battlefield, can be represented as an object. The transitions of the combat process are connected with events on the battlefield and their time is random variable. One of the important sources of randomness on the battlefield there is random result of the local clash. We have proposed many stochastic models of the local conflict in a sense of locality as a closed combat process between two elementary combat units (process of combat units resource destroying). There are applied three models of local combat in the environment built for initial analysis. Now is built and developed new model of distributed interactive simulation system for CAX. So I propose the set of requirements, which should be realised to better (more adequate) reflection of conflict situation.

2.3 Computer Assisted Exercises - Design of the Experimental Environment

The process of designing environments for interactive distributed simulation can be presented in the form of diagrams (Figure 1, Figure 2).

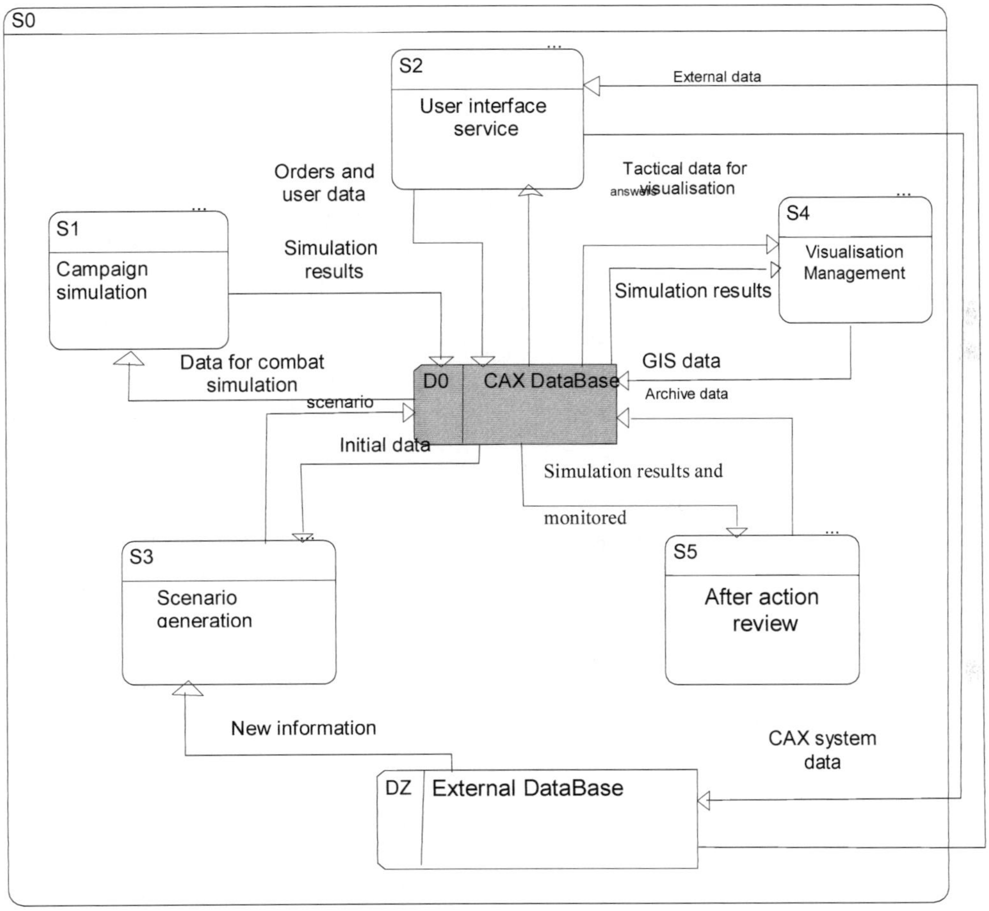

Figure 1. Data Flow Diagram of main process – "Computer Assisted Exercises"

The next step there is particular analysis of the components, separated on the 1st level. For example it is presented one of the main processes in the CAX system – simulation of campaign.

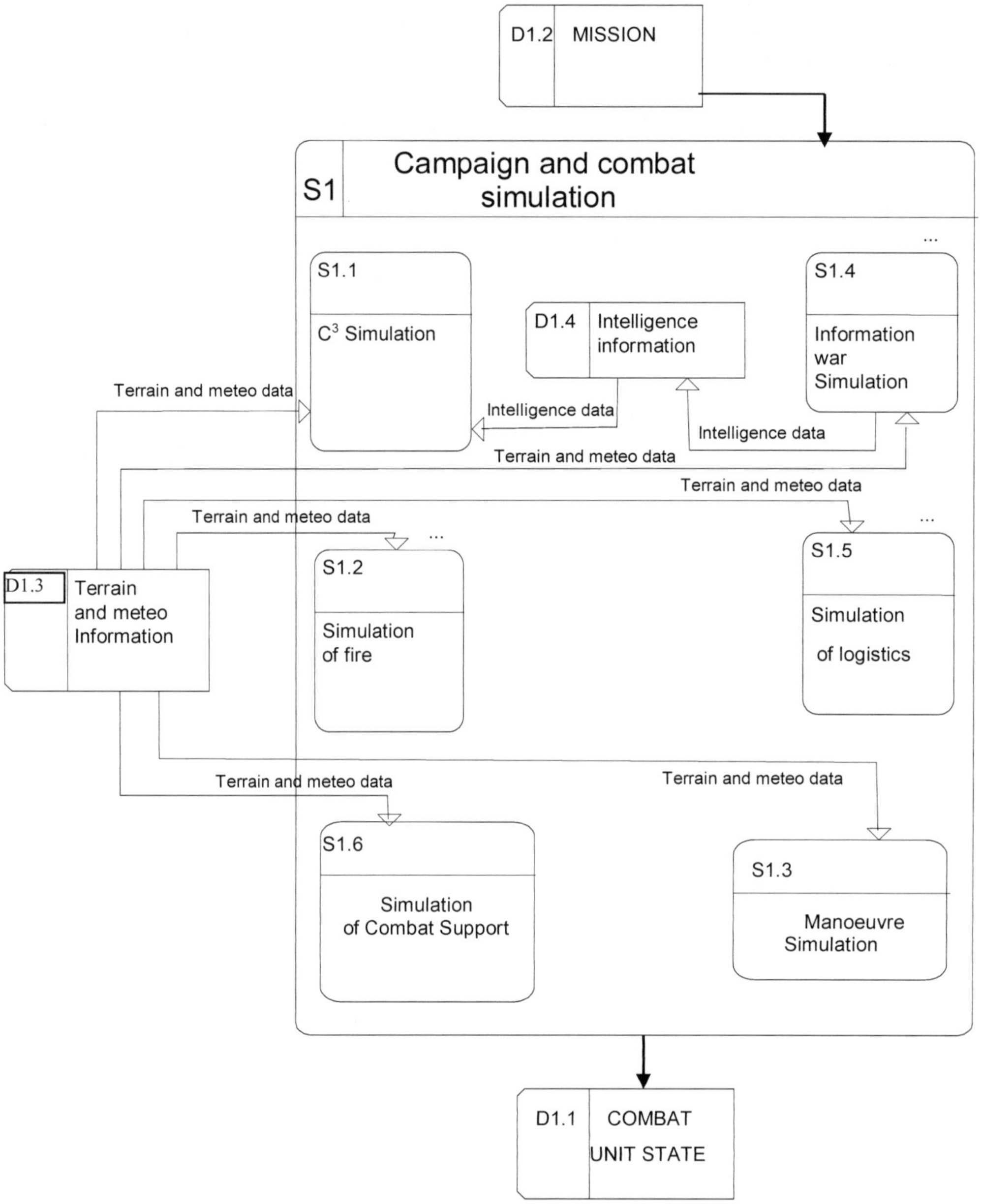

Figure 2. Data Flow diagram of campaign simulation process (2nd level)

The two-level analysis is only an example of the designing process. Each of the components is described by formal model. In the case the conflict models should take into account:

- different forms of combat (defence, attack,...), the mobility of combat units (different combat rate), terrain conditions, overtaking of possible sides during combat actions, direct-fire and it results, „inertia" of combat units, collaboration and synchronisation of neighbours troops, supply limits, the results of reconnaissance, the decision delays, C2 possibility.

Moreover, these models should:

- reflect an uncertainty conditions, show the interaction of decision-maker, enable different survivability of own and enemy forces on depending on enemy action (force and direction), present deviation of combat unit trajectory as a result of counteraction of enemy, enable an observation of temporary results, present changes of combat characteristics , have stability in a sense of invariant rules describing the whole process, enable an evaluation of their sensitivity, enable an implementation on the computer, have possible the least complexity, enable the testing in a computer environment, enable the flexible changes of components if necessary.

The local combat models should answer for the question: what state of combat units will be after combat?

Logistics models should supply an information: about movement of combat units on the, battlefield, connected with presentation of different strategies of resource supplying to combat units, about logistics characteristics for combat models.So the next model in the evolutionary process of professional simulation system designing there is (Najgebauer at al, 2002):

$$SPW(t) = \langle S_A(t), S_B(t), R(t), S_O(t) \rangle \tag{5}$$

where: $S_A(t), S_B(t)$ status vectors of the conflict sides; $R(t) = (R_1(t), R_2(t), ..., R_{Ln}(t))$ - vector of states of other conflict participants (e.g. state of civilian population, state of guerrillas, etc.);

$S_O(t) = (Z_1(t), Z_2(t))$ - the state of the conflict environment describing: field conditions, meteorological conditions, engineering conditions, contamination, electromagnetic conditions, etc. It should be stressed that the states presented above will be random variables (for a fixed time t; in general, they will be stochastic processes). Randomness of the state for side A (own forces) may result from e.g. disturbances of the communication system, which causes that the information provided to the commander is incomplete. The randomness of the state for side B (enemy army) results from the fact that our information about this state comes from the recognition, which gives incomplete and uncertain information. The randomness of a state concerning the environment (weather, terrain) results from both uncertainty of the results transmitted from the reconnaissance (e.g. about the terrain) as well as from forecasts e.g. meteorological, which are of a random nature.

3. THE IMPLEMENTATIONS

One of sophisticated examples of interactive simulation environments can be our prototype MSCombat and real simulation system Złocień and SWDT, which are object oriented and base on the stochastic model *S(t)* (2) the first one and $SPW(t)$ (5) battlefield model the second and third one. Many of their features can indicate the directions of development such environments. Primarily the environment was built to test possible solutions in simulation of land operations. The main point of view there was a technology. However many experiments for not so complicated situations were conducted and conclusions are very interesting. The main direction in the technological process there is High-Level Architecture rules utilisation, because one of most important requirements for Polish environments there is possibility of co-operation with NATO-countries simulation systems. This time the HLA is becoming the standard of communication and synchronisation of simulation environments. HLA consists of a number of interrelated components. The three that define HLA are: (1) the HLA rules, which define interoperability and what capabilities a simulation must have to achieve it within HLA; (2) the Object Model Template, which is a semi-formal methodology for specifying simulation and federation object classes, attributes, and interactions; and (3) the Interface Specification, a precise specification of the functional actions that a simulation may invoke, or be asked to perform, during an HLA exercise. The HLA Run-Time Infrastructure (RTI) is a software embodiment of the Interface Specification that implements the actions defined therein to be invocable by a simulation, provided as a set of services.

The deterministic and discrete time driven simulator SWDT models two-face land conflict of military units on the company/battalion level. The simulator is implemented in JAVA language as an integrated part of some system for CAXes. SWD-T is being used according to the following steps: the variant verification (via simulation) and the variant recommendation. Moreover, it can be also used for: (1) optimization of military units' command chains, (2) evaluation of the military operational rules and improving the command and control procedures, (3) research of military equipment's parameters which modify results of military actions, (4) verification quality of battlefield processes models (shooting, target searching, movement, etc.).

SWDT is a discrete time – driven simulator and models a two-face land conflict of military units on the company/battalion level. The inner models concern the couple processes of firing interaction and movement executed by a single military unit. These two complementary models use a terrain model described by a network of square areas which aggregates movement characteristics with 200m×200m granularity. The course of each process depends on many factors among them: terrain and weather conditions, states and parameters of weapons the units are equipped, type of executed units activities (attack, defence), distance between opponent units.

4. THE EXERCISES AND AFTER ACTION REVIEW

The professional system (Najgebauer at al, 2002, Najgebauer, 2004) consists of a number of software applications, which should be mentioned:

- Combat Simulator - the main part of the software responsible for simulating the situation on the battlefield. It implements all models of units, combat models and other types of operations, task interpreters, report generators, terrain model together with meteorological, engineering, radio electronic and contamination situation.
- Procedures for playing exercises - a package of procedures for playing exercises is an extension of the simulator that allows you to play the course of previously performed exercises.
- Calibration parameters editor - software used to modify the values of calibration parameters of models of actions and behaviours of active simulation objects (military units, elements of the battlefield). You can modify the default values of parameters (associated with each new scenario).
- Operational database - is embedded in Oracle database server (OLTP class). The database model has been defined using ORM technique for the object-oriented model of the information structure of the Złocień system. The database contains definitions of all ready-made scenarios together with all related elements. The operational base also includes elements related to the exercise being played according to the scenario. They include: descriptions of tasks set during the game, reports and periodically or incidentally recorded states of simulated elements.
- Map database - is embedded in Oracle database server (OLTP class). It contains tables describing such elements as point objects (e.g. bridges), linear objects (e.g. road sections, river sections), surface objects (forested areas, reservoirs), which were loaded from data available in VPF format, DTED height grid, as well as data describing squares converted on this basis (200x200 size, about 12.5 million squares in total) on which the combat simulator is based.

The analysis scheme is as follows: (1) the construction of different alternatives of combat, (2) the experimenting with monitoring of chosen characteristics (many replications); (3) the statistical analysis due to pattern of action and reaction recognition for different parameters of battlefield, (4) the comparison of battle results for different local combat models.

A scenario for the specific analysis can be presented as follows:

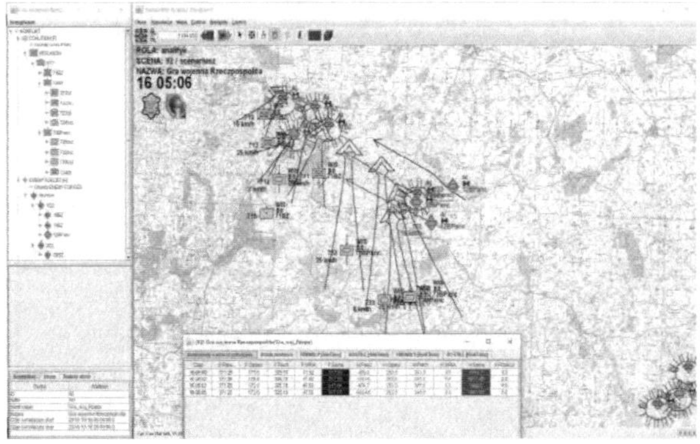

Figure 3. SWDT scenario and simulation of combat (own sources)

Table 1. Selected combat simulation results for the scenario (Figure 3)

Time	Side	Unit	Armt/mun	Code	Status
0	0	711bz	SPW	BWP-1	31
0	0	711bz	SPW	KBKAK	310
0	0	711bz	SPW	RPG-7	60
0	0	711bz	SPW	HS-2S1	8
...	...	...	...	....	....
0	0	711bz	MPS	ON	30960
0	0	712bz	SPW	BWP-1	31
0	0	712bz	SPW	KBKAK	500
0	0	712bz	SPW	RPG-7	60
0	0	712bz	SPW	HS-2S1	8
0	0	712bz	AMO	NB-PG-15W-73mm	1224
0	0	712bz	AMO	NB-OG-15W-73mm	816
0	0	712bz	AMO	NB-7.62x39mm	60000
....	....	.....	.....	......	......
....	....	.....	.....	......	......
2100	1	203bz	MPS	ON	20367
2100	1	204bcz	SPW	T-80U	31
2100	1	204bcz	AMO	NB-3WBM6-125mm	1640
2100	1	204bcz	AMO	NB-7.62x54mm	82000
2100	1	204bcz	AMO	NB-NSW-12.7x108mm	8200
2100	1	204bcz	MPS	ON	65337
2160	0	712bz	AMO	NB-BK-6M-122mm	0
2160	0	712bz	MPS	ON	0
2160	0	713bz	SPW	BWP-1	0
2160	0	713bz	SPW	KBKAK	211
2160	0	713bz	SPW	RPG-7	41
2160	0	713bz	SPW	HS-2S1	1
2160	0	713bz	AMO	NB-PG-15W-73mm	0
2160	0	713bz	AMO	NB-7.62x54mm	0
2160	0	713bz	AMO	PK-9M14-125mm	0

A lot of data are generated during the simulation process (tab.1) and then the set of data is the main source of knowledge extracted in the process of after action review (described below) towards the learning and generalization some decision procedures.

After Action Reviews are conducted during training exercises as logical predetermined events (based on the exercise scenario) are completed and at the conclusion of the exercise to assist the commander in answering such questions as:

(1) What went right (or well) and wrong (or badly) during the exercise?
(2) What went better than expected during the exercise?
(3) How does the unit improve?

The After Action Review Analyzer is a tool which enables checking selected game characteristic values off-line, after simulation. The characteristic are divided into a few categories as follows: state/resource levels of units (weapons, personnel, materials, potential), losses distribution of units regarding weapons, personnel, materials, potential (time distribution, structural distribution, time-structural distribution), schedule for units recognized by other units, task realization degree, real action speed, relation between real action speed and normative one. AAR Analyzer allows presentation of simulation results using tables and graphs. The tool can help in the process of data collecting for the learning of artificial intelligence based applications.

5. THE TRANSITIONS OF DISTRIBUTED INTERACTIVE SIMULATIONS TOWARDS DECISIONS PATTERNS

The transformation of interactive simulation environment into expert system there is multi-direction task. I wouldn't like to present complete transformation, however it could be very interested to obtain these decision patterns in a conflict situation. The pattern can be defined as an ordered pair of vectors:
$\xi = < \alpha, \beta >$, where: α - vector of input magnitudes of the conflict situation, which fully identify the current state of the controlled system of $A(B)$-decision maker , β - vector of possible actions and its evaluations (risk, cost, effectiveness and so on).
One of possible pattern acquisition there is an assortment of tendency model: $X(t) = f(t) + x(t)$ - model of chosen characteristics, side $A(B)$ losses in a moment t, probability of wining in a moment t, $f(t)$- trend function (linear, lognormal, logistic,...); $x(t)$ - random trend variation.

The scheme of model trend assortment is as follows: registration of characteristic realisation, estimation of trend model parameters, statistical verification of models, choice of the best model verified.

Another way there is rough set approach, where an information system: $IS=<OBJ, A, \{VAL_a\}_{a \in A}>$ OBJ - universe of objects, A - set of attributes, VAL_a - domain of $a \in A$

Let's try to find any dependency between groups of attributes P and Q: (1) $R(P)$ - an equivalence relation between objects from the set P point of view, so we have $(OBJ, R(P))$ - approximation space, $R^*(P)$- collection of equivalence classes of $R(P)$ -objects with the same value of attributes belonging to P; (2) lower and upper approximation in the space $(OBJ, R(P))$: $INT(Y)=\cup\{X \in R^*(P): X \subseteq Y\}$ $UPP(Y)= \cup\{X \in R^*(P): X \cap Y \neq \emptyset\}$ *IF* $INT(Y) \neq UPP(Y)$ *then Y is rough set,*

(3) Let $R^*(Q)$ be a partition of $(OBJ, R(P))$ and $R^*(Q)=\{Y_1, Y_2, Y_3,... Y_m\}$ a measure of dependency is $\sum_i (card(INT(Y_i))/card(OBJ))$.A rule with respect to a value V of the decision attribute d: $r = (a_{i,1}=V_{i,1}),...,(a_{i,n}=V_{i,n})\}$, where $A_r=(a_{i,k})_{k=1,...,n} \subseteq A$, $r: (a_{i,1}=V_{i,1}) \wedge ... \wedge (a_{i,n}=V_{i,n}) \rightarrow (d=V)$ - decision rule. Quite interesting problem of knowledge generalization there is looking for fast response of local combat (Najgebauer et al. 2001). The local combat is defined as a clash of two formations, which consists in direct fire of two sides under optical visibility. The main purpose of local combat model construction is obtainment of answer for the question - how is resource decrease process running and how is fighting formations' location changing, when we know the state of the process before the battle?

The simulation process is time-consuming and the time of running depends on accuracy and the "granularity" of combat model. The proposal consists in construction of specific tool, which allows us to generate combat result very quickly. The generated combat result for the initial conditions determined (as a scenario) should provide an information about time of combat and the evaluation of formation's state.

The tool there is procedure of service of multidimensional table $GW = [gw_{ij...k}]_{I \times J \times ... \times K}$ The element of the table $gw_{ij...k}$ there is vector of probability distributions (empirical) and / or regression function of output magnitudes. The input magnitudes are processes, which have many states. The particular element of a table can be identify by an index $(i,j, ...k)$ which describes number of an input magnitudes state. This generator can be used as: a tool for quick receiving of local combat result; an element of knowledge base for decision support system and simulation system; a method of comparison of different combat models; a method of evaluation of payoff in a theory game model (in armed conflict).

The most sophisticated idea was realized in the expert decision support system (Najgebauer, 2007), where the key term were decision situation and decision pattern situation: we can apply those elements for the decision situation vector definition, which contains knowledge about the terrain, military potential distribution in a combat formation and assigned tasks formulating a template for recognition process. We define a decision situations space and a set of patterns. We propose the measures of similarity and distance between the current decision-making situation and the model situation. On the basis of the selected closest (most similar) model situation to the current decision situation, a course of action of our own forces is build (Jędrzejowicz at al, 2011, Carlos Ramirez at al (eds), 2012). Some decision processes are based on approach in (Prekopa, 1995).

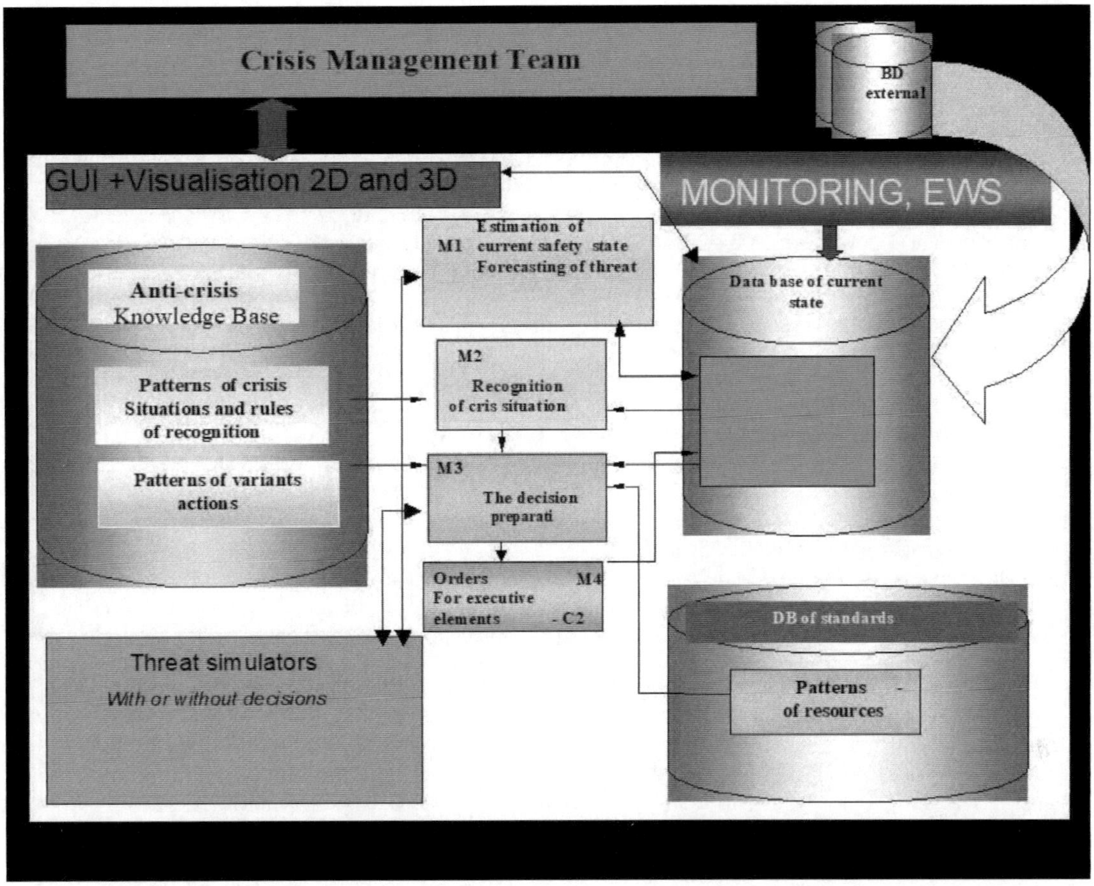

Figure 4. The idea of knowledge-based DSS (own sources- system "Guru" (Najgebauer at al, 2007)

6. CONCLUSION

Modelling and simulation with computer simulation environment presented have many applications within the defence and other than war processes. The principle domain of application is (see Clarke 1995, Hawkins 2000 as well): (1) as a training device for use at the individual, command team, and strategic levels, (2) as a tool for the conduct of campaign and mission rehearsal, and the analysis of operations, (3) as a device to assist the development of defence policy and doctrine, and the formulation of the equipment programme, (4) as a tool for testing the military equipment. The environment proposed is built as an opened system and can be developed and improved. The characteristics of battle process are being monitored during the simulation process and their statistical analysis allows combat actions predicting for different conflict situations (Figure 4) (see Carlos Ramirez (ed) 2012). The transition from interactive simulation environment into intelligent framework is being successfully realised and the collected data during simulations are big data set for learning the AI platform. Some interesting results are presented as the concept of CAST logic and stochastic PERT analysis to support military joint operation planning (see at Al-Begain K et al(eds), 2010). These methods were implemented in the computer package presented in the paper. By using the method and computer tool an exemplified military joint operation is considered. The system was built as a prototype knowledge-based decision support system and was tested in many computer assisted exercises organised in Polish Armed Forces (2007-2016). Author of the paper took part as an expert in the Strategic Defence Review and used described tools for the analysis of Armed Forces capabilities and also in the process of predicting of Armed Forces structure development.

REFERENCES

Al-Begain K., Fiems D., W. Knottenbelt (Eds.) 2010. *ASMTA 2010*, Chapter: Antkiewicz R, Gąsecki A, Najgebauer A, Pierzchała D, Tarapata Z, „Stochastic PERT and CAST Logic Approach for Computer Support of Complex Operation Planning", LNCS 6148, pp. 159--173. Springer, Heidelberg (2010).

Antkiewicz R., Kulas W., Najgebauer A., Pierzchała D., Rulka J., Tarapata Z., Wantoch-Rekowski R, 2007.: The Automation of Combat Decision Processes in the Simulation Based Operational Training Support System, *Proceedings of the 2007 IEEE Symposium on Computational Intelligence in Security and Defense Applications (CISDA)* 2007, ISBN 1-4244-0698-6, Honolulu (Hawaii, USA), April 1-5, 2007.

Carlos Ramirez (ed.) 2012. *Advances in Knowledge Representation*, INTECH, Rijeka, Croatia 2012. Chapter: Antkiewicz R, Chmielewski M, Drozdowski T, Najgebauer A, Rulka J., Tarapata Z, Wantoch-Rekowski R, Pierzchała D., Knowledge-Based Approach for Military Mission Planning and Simulation.

Clarke T.L., 1995- "Distributed Interactive Simulation Systems for Simulation and Training in the Aerospace Environment". SPIE Optical Engineering Press, USA, Orlando,1995.

Dockery J., Woodcock A.E.R., (1993 - *The Military Landscape, Mathematical Models of Combat*, Published by Woodhead Publishing Ltd., Cambridge, England, 1993.

Hawkins G.P., 2000, - *The UK MoD Requirement for Modelling and Simulation, Simulation for Military Planning, British Crown* Copyright 2000. London.

Ilachinski J., 1996 - *Land Warfare and Complexity, Part I: Mathematical Background and Technical Sourcebook*, Centre for Naval Analyses, Alexandria, Virginia, USA, 1996.

Jędrzejowicz P., Nguyen N.T., Hoang K. (eds) 2011. *Computational Collective Intelligence. Technologies and Applications. ICCCI 2011,* Chapter: Antkiewicz R., Najgebauer A., Rulka J., Tarapata Z., Wantoch-Rekowski R. (2011) Knowledge-Based Pattern Recognition Method and Tool to Support Mission Planning and Simulation. Lecture Notes in Computer Science, vol 6922. Springer, Berlin, Heidelberg

Najgebauer A. (PM) et al. 2007. *Technical reports on "Automated decision support tools - expert system" – "GURU".* Military University of Technology, Warsaw 2005-2007.

Najgebauer A. 2004. Polish Initiatives in M&S and Training. Simulation Based Operational Training Support System (SBOTSS) Zlocien, *Proceedings of the ITEC'2004*, London, UK, April 20-22 2004

Najgebauer A. et. al. 2002. *Technical Project of Simulation System for Supporting Operational Training, Volume I-VI*, Faculty of Cybernetics, MUT, Warsaw 2002. (Najgebauer A. – principal designer in the phase of research and development and PM in the phase of deployment process).

Najgebauer A., 1999a "Decision Support Systems for Conflict Situations. Models, Methods and the Interactive Simulation Environments" (in Polish). Ed. Bulletin WAT. Warsaw 1999, Poland. (294 p.). ISBN 83-908620-6-9

Najgebauer A., Nowicki T., Rulka J. 2001, "The Method of Construction and Learning of Local Combat Generator". *Proceedings of Modelling & Simulation Group Conference on Future Modelling and Simulation Challenges, NATO Modelling&Simulation Group Conference in The Netherlands*, Breda, 2001, November.

Najgebauer A., Pierzchała D., Rulka J., 1999b, "The Simulation Researches of Decision Processes in a Conflict Situation with Opposite Objectives". *Proceedings of SCS International Conference ESM'99* June 1-4 1999, Warsaw Poland. (pp. 591-598).

Penrose R. 1989. *The Emperor's New Mind. Concerning Computers, Minds, and the Laws of Physics.* Oxford University Press 1989

Prekopa A., 1995 -*Stochastic Programming* Kluwer Academic Publisher, Dordrecht/Boston/London, ISBN 0-7923-3482-5.

A KNOWLEDGE BASED TWO-STAGE CASCADE MODEL FOR TEST-QUESTION/ANSWER RETRIEVAL

Yilu Wei, Daifeng Li and Andrew David Madden
School of Information Management, Sun Yat-sen University, GuangZhou, China

ABSTRACT

Test-question/answer retrieval task has raised higher requirements in terms of accuracy, coverage and semantic understanding. We design a cascade model with two-stage training processes: The first stage uses 41,532 user test-question click records and 207,660 unclick records, which are collected from a designed test-question-answer experimental platform, to generate 200,000 pairwise training dataset to train a deep learning model, which could improve generalization ability. The second stage combines the output of the first stage with structural knowledge as new features to train a logistic regression for selecting the results from the candidates with higher accuracy, the training dataset is generated by manually annotating 20,000 test-question samples. The structural knowledge is also manually extracted from the samples for generating a small knowledge graph, and on this condition, we design knowledge features. Experimental results show that the proposed model outperforms the state-of-the-art algorithms, among which the cascading model contributes 3% improvement and the knowledge features contribute 1% improvement.

KEYWORDS

Deep Learning, Test-Question/Answer Retrieval, Knowledge Feature, Cascade Model

1. INTRODUCTION

In recent years, vertical domain search services have become more and more popular in China. One of the most popular domains is education. China has 200 million primary, secondary and college students who create strong demand for educational resources. Various search applications have been developed to address the students' needs for knowledge and answers. For example, Zuoyebang (https://www.zybang.com/) allows students of all disciplines to search for test-questions. Students can input their questions in the form of text, voice or images, and the system provides answers. Unlike traditional information retrieval tasks or relevance models, test-question searching has unique requirements, which are described below:

- Strong generalizability: Test-questions are often expressed in a diverse and complex manner. Some results have the same meaning as the target query, but are expressed in a different manner, so traditional term-matching based relevance models (Salton et al. 1975) do not work.
- Semantic understanding for high accuracy: A relevance model without semantic understanding may lead to serious misinterpretations (Gómez-Adorno et al. 2013). For example, "Length and width are known. How should area be calculated" versus "Length and width are known. How should perimeter be calculated" are very different, but it is hard to distinguish them without semantic understanding.
- Interpretable model: Deep Learning is hard to interpret, thus increasing the incidence of errors and bad cases. For test-question/answer tasks, errors are usually unacceptable because minor differences may lead to irrelevant answers. Proper understanding arising from correct interpretations is particularly important for test-question retrieval.

Much research has focused on improving the generalizability of existing relevance models, and improving their capacity for semantic understanding (Xiao et al. 2018, P. S. Huang et al. 2013). However, researchers have seldom conducted specific domain optimization using procedures such as combining users' behavior records with domain structural knowledge to design an interpretable model. Not only is it hard to design a complete model for accurate semantic understanding, it is also hard to generalize it to handle lots of complex semantic representations in reality. To achieve this, we designed a knowledge-based two-stage cascading model, the main innovations of which are listed as below:

- The framework was designed to take into account both generalizability and accuracy. In the first stage, generalizability was improved by using a large-scale users' online behavior log. In the second stage, structural knowledge was used to obtain results that are more accurate.
- The first stage was achieved by use of a deep learning framework with pairwise strategy (Timur et al. 2019) which detected users' preference patterns from a training dataset based on 200,000 pairwise data. A multi-layer deep neutral network was designed on the framework. We selected word embedding (Danchen et al. 2018) to vectorize the input so that we could obtain the maximum fuzzy matching segment of title towards query.
- We designed knowledge features and used pointwise strategy to improve the capability of semantic understanding and to acquire results that are more accurate.

2. THE FRAMEWORK OF THE PROPOSED MODEL.

We designed a two-stage cascading model to handle the test-question/answer retrieval task. The framework is shown in Figure 1:

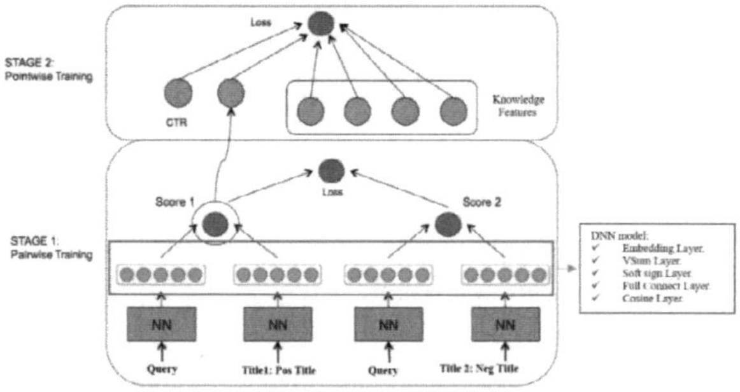

Figure 1. Framework of the two-stage cascading model

2.1 Stage 1: Deep Neural Network Model with Pairwise Learning Strategy

According to previous studies (Sunil et al. 2017, Jun et al. 2015), users' preferences and clicking behaviors show a strong semantic correlation. In this case, the dataset contains 200,000 pairwise training data, and we adopted a pairwise strategy. When different users entered the same query, we selected two candidate results, labelled Title 1 and Title 2. If the number of clicks on Title 1 was greater than that on Title 2 we classed Title 1 as a good title and Title 2 as a poor title, and a pairwise based partial order is generated. To eliminate the influence of ranking position COEC (Click Over Expected Clicks) was used (Zhang et al. 2007).

Score 1 is the relevance score between the query and Title 1, while Score 2 is the relevance score between the query and Title 2. A loss function is used to determine whether Score 1 is greater than Score 2. If Score 1 > Score 2, then we consider that the DNN model has a correct understanding of relevance; If Score 1 <= Score 2, the learned model has biases in understanding the relevance, and needs to be optimized through a back-propagation algorithm. The DNN model consists of 5 layers which are described in Figure 2.

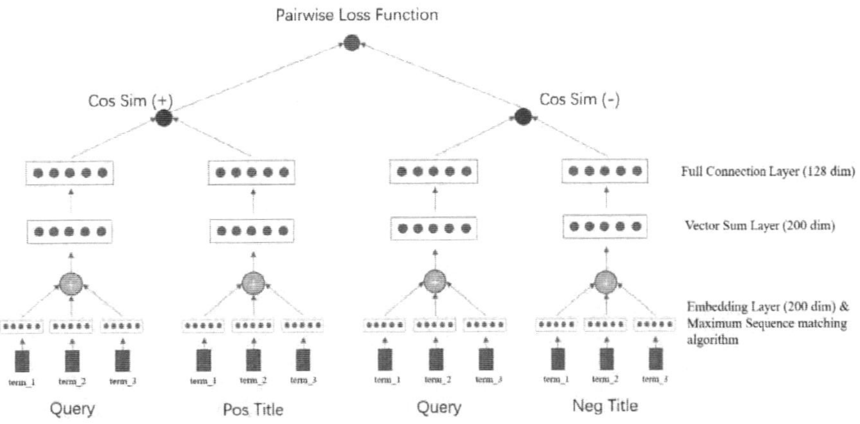

Figure 2. Framework of DNN with pairwise strategy

2.1.1 Input Format and Embedding Layer

For pairwise strategy, assume the input query = {q_term$_1$, q_term$_2$, q_term$_3$, ... q_term$_q$}, the positive title is posTitle = {p_term$_1$, p_term$_2$, p_term$_3$, ... p_term$_p$}, the negative title is negTitle = {n_term$_1$, n_term$_2$, n_term$_3$, ... n_term$_n$}. In the embedding layer, we use word2vec to vectorize each term of query, posTitle and negTitle, which can be seen in formulas (1), (2), and (3):

$$q\_term_i \xrightarrow{Embedding} Vq_i = \{q_{i1}, q_{i2}, \dots \dots, q_{ik}\} \quad (1)$$

$$p\_term_i \xrightarrow{Embedding} Vp_i = \{p_{i1}, p_{i2}, \dots \dots, p_{ik}\} \quad (2)$$

$$n\_term_i \xrightarrow{Embedding} Vn_i = \{n_{i1}, n_{i2}, \dots \dots, n_{ik}\} \quad (3)$$

where i is the ith term of query, posTitle or negTitle. q_{ij}, p_{ij}, n_{ij} are the value of jth dimension. k is the dimension of vector (which is set to 200 here). The configuration of the embedding layer can be seen below:

embedding_layer = {**type:** "embedding",
learn strategy: "word2vec",
parameter: "embedding param",
input: [query, posTitle, negTitle],
output: [query embedding, posTitle embedding, negTitle embedding]}

2.1.2 Vector Sum Layer

In Vector Sum Layer, we use formulas (4), (5), and (6) to obtain vector representation of query and title, which are listed below:

$$q\_v = \sum_{i=1}^{q} Vq_i = \{ \sum_{i=1}^{q} q_{i1}, \sum_{i=1}^{q} q_{i2}, \sum_{i=1}^{q} q_{i3}, \dots \dots \sum_{i=1}^{q} q_{ik} \} \quad (4)$$

$$p\_v = \sum_{i=1}^{p} Vp_i = \{ \sum_{i=1}^{p} p_{i1}, \sum_{i=1}^{p} p_{i2}, \sum_{i=1}^{p} p_{i3}, \dots \dots \sum_{i=1}^{p} p_{ik} \} \quad (5)$$

$$n\_v = \sum_{i=1}^{n} Vn_i = \{ \sum_{i=1}^{n} n_{i1}, \sum_{i=1}^{n} n_{i2}, \sum_{i=1}^{n} n_{i3}, \dots \dots \sum_{i=1}^{n} n_{ik} \} \quad (6)$$

where q_v represents the sum of query term vector, p_v represents the sum of posTitle term vector and n_v represents the sum of negTitle term vector. The configuration of Vector Sum Layer can be seen as below:

vector_sum_layer = {**type:** "vector sum",
parameter: "vector_sum param",
input: [query embedding, posTitle embedding, negTitle embedding],
output: [query emb sum, posTitle emb sum, negTitle emb sum]}

In addition, we designed a maximum sequence-matching algorithm to find the most related pattern of title towards query. The algorithm is displayed below:

```
Main:
    For each term q_termi in a query:
    PairSet < String t_patterni, Double scorei, >= Func(q_termi, query, title);
    End
  Assign variable New_title as the t_pattern with maximum score.
  //New_title is a segment of the title, and it has the highest similarity with the query.

PairSet < String t_pattern, Double score> Func(q_term, query, title):
//Find all possible sequence matching patterns and their scores between query and title.
  Find all indexes that q_term appears in title as index = [ind(1), ind(2), ind(3)];
  Array<PairSet<String, Double>> arr = null;
  If no index is found, return <null, 0.0>
  Else:
    For i in index:
      score = 1;
      t_pattern = "q_term" ;
      For j in `seq indexOf(q_term, query) + 1 -> query.length`:
        If (indexOf(query[j], title) begin from indexOf(q_term, title) is not null):
          score += Dis_score(indexOf(query[j], title - indexOf(q_term, title));
            //function Dis_score considers that if the distance between two adjacent terms of a query in the
                        title is big, the score will be small.
          t_pattern += " " + query[j];
        fi
      End
      Arr.append(t_pattern, score);
    End
        Find PairSet from arr with maximum score, and return the PairSet.
```

Algorithm 1. Maximum sequence-matching algorithm for finding the most suitable title segment for the target query

2.1.3 Fully Connected Layer

We assign a 128-dimension vector of neurons in a fully connected layer, and map the 200-dimension embedding vector into the 128-dimension vector (Hinton et al. 2006). In the fully connected layer, all queries share the same parameter distributions and all titles share the same parameter distributions. In the embedding layer, we use a pre-training strategy to obtain the vectored representation of each term. The configuration of fully connected layer can be seen below:

full_connect_layer = {**type:** "full connect",
learning strategy: "full connection",
parameter: "full connect param",
input: [query emb sum, posTitle emb sum, negTitle emb sum],
output: [query fc, posTitle fc, negTitle fc]}

2.1.4 Cosine and Loss Function Layer

In the cosine layer, we use a cosine function to calculate the cosine similarity (Metzler et al. 2005) between query and posTitle, and between query and negTitle. In the loss function layer, we select Hinge Loss function. The detail of the network design is shown below:

cos_sim_layer = {**type:** "cosine sim",
input: [{query fc, posTitle fc}, {query fc, negTitle fc}]
output: [pos_cos_sim_score, neg_cos_sim_score]}

loss_layer = {**type:** "HingeLoss",
input: [pos_cos_sim_score, neg_cos_sim_score, label]
output: loss}

network = {embedding layer, vector sum layer, full connect layer, cos_sim_layer, loss_layer}

2.2 Stage 2: Knowledge Feature Design for Accurate Semantic Understanding

Scores obtained from Stage 1 were used to improve generalizability. In addition, we added features to improve the model's capacity for semantic understanding. Added features included entity-attribute (which was extracted from the condition description of a question), and the target solution of the question. We manually extracted entity-attribute and entity-action from the samples to generate a small knowledge graph that covers 7 disciplines (Chinese, math, chemistry, physics, biology, history and geography). The knowledge graph contains 2,582 entities, 6,336 attributes and 1,213 actions. For math related questions, we defined three patterns to identify different target solutions. These are summarized below:

Pattern 1: "求" (request) + [entity][attribute] | [entity] | [attribute] + "?" | " "

Pattern 2: [entity][attribute] | [entity] | [attribute] + "怎么求" (how to find out) | "?" | " "

Pattern 3: [entity][attribute] | [entity] | [attribute] + "是" | "重" | "有" (is | has) | " " + "多少" (how much) + [unit] | " " + "?" | " "

We use the extracted entity-attribute-action to build the knowledge graph, then use the knowledge graph to generate knowledge features. The main principle is that we use the knowledge graph and a NLP parse method to extract entities, attributes, attribute values and actions for both query and title. We then analyze whether query and title describe the same entity with the same attribute or action, for the same attribute, and whether they have the same value. The comparison results can be seen as knowledge features, and gets assigned to a sequence of feature slots. Details of the knowledge feature generation can be seen below in Figure3.

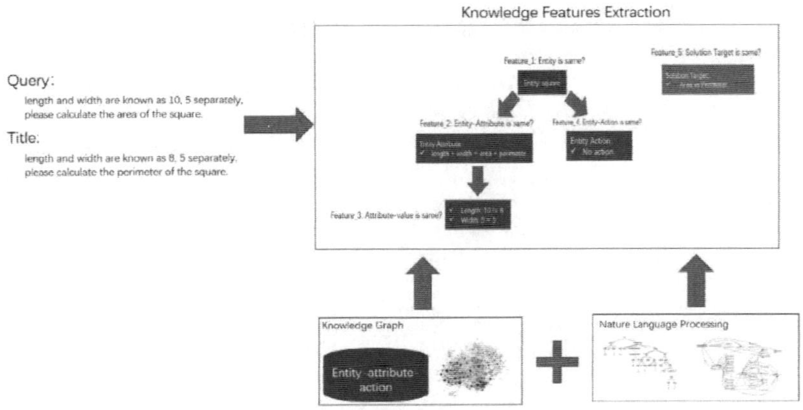

Figure 3. Examples of knowledge extraction features.

3. DATA

Table 1. Data Format of test-question/answer searching records

Userid	Query	Title	Answer	Rank	Click
1	using 30 stamps with a length of 3cm and a width of 2.5cm	Use 30 stamps that have a length of 3cm and a width of 2.5cm to form a square. What is the length of the square' s sides?	Using 30 stamps with a length of 3cm and a width of 2.5cm to form a square without gaps, the area of every stamp is calculated first, and then the total area of the square. After that, the square root of the area is just the length of sides.	2	1
2	Oxygen production equation with hydrogen peroxide	How to write equation for oxygen production from hydrogen peroxide	$2H_2O_2{=}MnO_2{=}2H_2O{+}O_2\uparrow$	3	1
3	When a car suddenly starts, passengers will move backward, because they are under the force of inertia	"When a car suddenly starts, passengers will move backward, because they are under the force of inertia". Why is this sentence wrong?	It should not be "under the force of inertia", because inertia is an inherent property of objects. The original sentence should be changed to: when a car suddenly starts, passengers will move back because they have inertia.	1	1

The experimental dataset, which mainly comprises records relating to users' searching and clicking behavior in the test-question/answer domain, is collected from a vertical domain experimental platform. We crawled 325,415 questions from websites, which cover 7 disciplines, and then built the test-question-answer platform by using a term-matching cosine algorithm. Participants were invited to use the platform and provided clicking data, allowing us to collect 41,532 records relating to user searching and clicking, and 20,7660 unclicked records for pairwise comparison. The format of each record is described in Table 1.

The format used to label the 20,000 samples from the 41,532 records is shown in Table 2. For each sample, the following were manually extracted: entity-attribute; entity-action; target from query; result. Queries and titles were then compared from two perspectives: target matching (same/not same/unknown) and relevance (Rel). Relevance is on a scale from 0 to 2, where 2 is the most relevant. We also used patterns defined above to formalize the math-related solution target.

Table 2. Manual labeling format of the selected records

id	Query	Target	Title	Entity -Attribute -Action	Target	Target matching (same/not same/unknown)	Rel
1	using 30 stamps with a length of 3cm and a width of 2.5cm	NULL	Use 30 stamps that have a length of 3cm and a width of 2.5cm to form a square. What is the length of the square' s sides?	**Entity:** square **Attribute:** length, width **Unit:** [cm]	How much is the length of the side? [Pattern 3]	Unknown	2
2	Oxygen production equation with hydrogen peroxide	Oxygen productio n equation	How to write the equation for oxygen production from hydrogen peroxide	**Entity:** hydrogen peroxide **Action:** oxygen production **Entity:** oxygen	equation for oxygen production	Yes	2
3	When a car suddenly starts, passengers will move backward, because they are under the force of inertia	NULL	"When a car suddenly starts, passengers will move backward, because they are under the force of inertia" . Why is the sentence wrong?	**Entity:** inertia **Action:** move backward	Why is the sentence wrong?	Unknown	2

4. RESULTS AND DISCUSSION

We selected 80% of the 41,532 data as a training dataset. The remaining 20% were used as test data. Two baselines were selected: LR (Logistic Regression) with pointwise strategy and LR + DNN with point-pairwise strategy. Neither baseline considers knowledge features. The experimental results are shown in Figure 4:

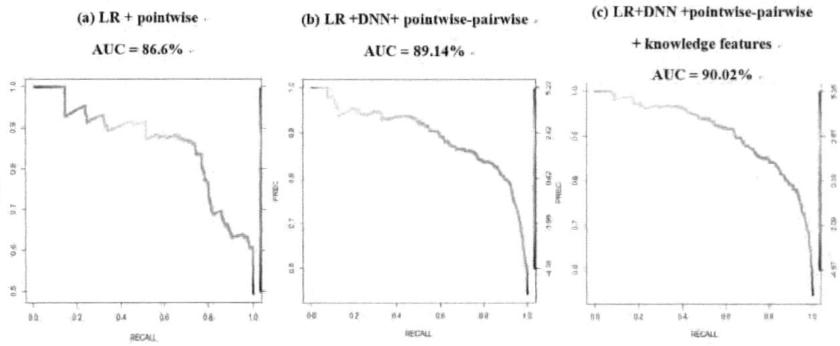

Figure 4. Experimental results of the proposed model

In the graphs shown in Figure 4, the abscissa represents Recall, and the ordinate represents Precision. The Area Under Curve (AUC) of LR + pointwise strategy is 86.6%. This is improved upon by both LR + DNN (AUC=89.14%), and LR + DNN with knowledge features (AUC=90.02%). Another important benefit of the proposed model is that it fluctuates less than the other models, making it a more useful predictor.

When we set a threshold of 30% on recall, the precision of the three models was 92%, 94% and 97% respectively. We also selected several cases to further illustrate the performance of the proposed model, as shown in Table 3.

Table 3. Case Studies of the proposed model with recall at 30%

Query	LR	LR + DNN	LR + DNN + Knowledge Features
How many usages does “Ji” have?	How many usages does “De” have?	How many usages does “De” have?	What is the specific usage of “Ji ” in Chinese?
Why should diazo reaction be carried out at low temperatures?	Why should diazo reaction be carried out at low temperatures?	Why does diazo reaction not need to be carried out under strong acid conditions?	What is diazo reaction? Why should it be carried out at low temperatures?
In a circle with a diameter of 4cm, draw the largest square.	Draw the largest circle in a square with a length of 4cm.	Draw the largest square in a circle.	Here is a circle with a diameter of 4cm. Please draw the largest square in the circle and calculate its area.

As can be seen in Table 3, the proposed model performs better on cases where query and title have the same meaning but are expressed in different ways. By taking into consideration entities related to knowledge points , the model can identify important differences and make correct judgement, while other state-of-art algorithms still depend on term matching similarity. Currently, knowledge features can only contribute a 1% improvement, because the construction of the knowledge graph is still at an early stage. With continuous construction of the knowledge graph, the model will be improved significantly.

For parameter assignment, we set learning rate at 0.02, batch at 128, margin of hinge-loss at 0.1, and sampling-rate of shuffle at 0.1. The training curve can be seen below in Figure 5.

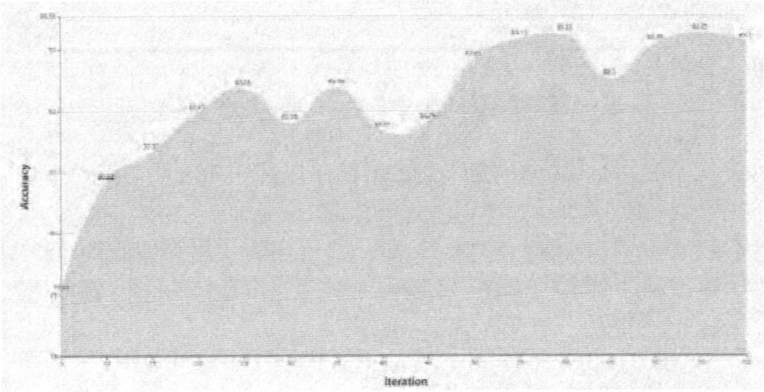

Figure 5. Accuracy statistics of training process

5. CONCLUSION

In this research, we used a two-stage cascading model with knowledge features to optimize a test-question/answer search task. In Stage 1, we used a log of 41,532 clicked records and 207,660 unclicked records to generate a 200,000 pairwise dataset. This was used to train a DNN model to recognize semantic correlation through users’ preference patterns, thus further improving generalizability. In stage 2, we designed and incorporated knowledge features to improve semantic understanding by the model, of different questions. The combination of Stages 1 and 2 could not only accurately interpret semantic information relating to the questions, but also improved generalizability using the large-scale user log. One challenge in information retrieval is generalizing from a precise semantic model. The proposed model helps to address that challenge.

In future, we would like to design more complete and accurate knowledge features, and create a domain knowledge graph for test-questions/answers. In addition, we are seeking to incorporate LR and DNN into a unified framework to realize collaborative learning, which can achieve a dynamic balance between generalizability and accurate semantic understanding.

ACKNOWLEDGEMENT

This work was supported by Chinese National Youth Foundation Research (Grant No: 61702564), Talent Scientific Research Foundation of Sun Yat-sen University (20000-18831102).

REFERENCES

Danchen Zhang, Daqing He, 2018. Can Word Embedding Help Term Mismatch Problem? - A Result Analysis on Clinical Retrieval Tasks. *International Conference on Information*. Sheffield, UK, pp 402-408.

Gómez-Adorno, H., Pinto, D. and Vilarino, D., , 2013. A Question Answering System for Reading Comprehension Tests. *Mexican Conference on Pattern Recognition,* Spring, Berlin, Heidelberg, pp 354-363.

Hinton G. E, Salakhutdinov R. R, 2006. Reducing the dimensionality of data with neural networks. *Science*, Vol. 313, No. 5786, pp 504-507.

P.-S.Huang, X.He, J.Gao, et al, 2013. Learning deep structured semantic models for web search using clickthrough data. *Proceedings of the 22nd ACM international conference on Conference on Information and Knowledge Management*. San Francisco, USA, pp 2333-2338.

Jiafeng Guo, Yixing Fan, Qingyao Ai, W. Bruce Croft, 2016. A deep relevance matching model for Ad-hoc retrieval. *proceedings of the 25th ACM International conference on Conference on Information and Knowledge Management*. Indianapolis, USA, pp 55-64.

Jun Yu, Dacheng Tao, Meng Wang, Yong Rui, 2015. Learning to Rank Using User Clicks and Visual Features for Image Retrieval. *IEEE Transactions on Cybernetics*, Vol. 45, No. 4, pp 767-779.

G.Salton, A.Wong, and C.-S.Yang, 1975. A vector space model for automatic indexing. *Communications of the ACM*, Vol. 18, No. 11, pp 613–620.

Sunil Mohan, Nicolas Fiorini, Sun Kim, Zhiyong Lu, 2017. Deep Learning for Biomedical Information Retrieval: Learning Textual Relevance from Click Logs. *Proceeding of the 16th Biomedical natural language processing*. Vancouver, Canada, pp 222-231.

Timur Osadchiy, Ivan Poliakov, Patrick Olivier, et al, 2019. Recommender system based on pairwise association rules. *Expert Systems with Applications*, Vol. 115, pp 535-542.

Xiao Bai, Erik Ordentlich, Yuanyuan Zhang,et al, 2018. Scalable Query N-Gram Embedding for Improving Matching and Relevance in Sponsored Search. *Proceedings of the 24th ACM SIGKDD International Conference on Knowledge Discovery and Data Mining*. London, UK, pp 52-61.

W. Zhang, R. Jones, 2007. Comparing click logs and editorial labels for training query rewriting. *16th International World Wide Web Conferences*. Banff, Canada, pp 2-5.

REVIEWING DATA ACCESS PATTERNS AND COMPUTATIONAL REDUNDANCY FOR MACHINE LEARNING ALGORITHMS

Imen Chakroun, Tom Vander Aa and Tom Ashby
ExaScience Life Lab, IMEC, Leuven, Belgium

ABSTRACT

Machine learning (ML) is probably the first and foremost used technique to deal with the size and complexity of the new generation of data. In this paper, we analyze one of the means to increase the performances of ML algorithms which is exploiting data locality. Data locality and access patterns are often at the heart of performance issues in computing systems due to the use of certain hardware techniques to improve performance. Altering the access patterns to increase locality can dramatically increase performance of a given algorithm. Besides, repeated data access can be seen as redundancy in data movement. Similarly, there can also be redundancy in the repetition of calculations. This work also identifies some of the opportunities for avoiding these redundancies by directly reusing computation results. We document the possibilities of such reuse in some selected machine learning algorithms and give initial indicative results from our first experiments on data access improvement and algorithm redesign.

KEYWORDS

Increasing Data Locality, Data Redundancy and Reuse, Machine Learning

1. INTRODUCTION

Machine learning algorithms and their implementations typically are computationally intensive and also operate on large data sets. To learn, an ML algorithm needs to look at the training points (which together make up the training set). In supervised learning, the training set consists of data points for which the outcome to be learned is known: the points are labelled. Based on the training points, the algorithm builds a model by setting model parameters (also known as weights) so that the resulting model represents the underlying structure of the data. The model is evaluated on the test points to evaluate its accuracy. An algorithm and/or model may have extra parameters that are set by the user rather than learned from the data. These extra parameters are called hyperparameters. A particular algorithm being run on a particular data set to make a model is called a learner. To distinguish between particular hyperparameter settings for a learner we refer to a learner instance per hyperparameter tuple. The train and test steps are typically performed several times for different types of model and different model hyperparameters e.g. by dividing between training and test sets.

The reuse distance of a data location is the number of surrounding loop iterations that occur in between accesses to it. During the training phase, most machine learning algorithms have to read each data point in the training set at least once. Such a full traversal of the training set is called an epoch. Once a learner is trained, the resulting fixed model can be used in an operational testing phase to make predictions for previously unseen points. In the next sections we will investigate the potential for performance improvements. Unless otherwise stated, we are dealing with the training algorithms for a given learner rather than its use to classify unlabeled data in an operational environment. This is because the reuse available in the operational phase is often a) very little or zero and b) rather simple to exploit.

The remainder of this paper is as follows: in Section 2 an analysis of data and computational redundancy is given for the stochastic gradient descent along with experimental results. In Section 3, the instance based leaners class of models are presented together with empirical gains obtained when coupling these modes together. Section 4 deals with data reuse in logistic regression and support vector machines. We draw some conclusions is Section 5. The experiments presented in this paper have been conducted on a node from a 20 nodes cluster equipped with dual 6-core Intel(R) Westmere CPUs with 12 hardware threads each, a clock speed 2.80GHz and 96 GB of RAM. The implementations are all sequential (executed on one core) and C++ is used as a programming language. The results from the experiments are very much initial results given as an indication as to how some of the reuse and redundancy outlined in this document could be used.

2. RELATED WORK

To the best of our knowledge, no similar research work centered on analyzing data access patterns and identifying locality and redundancy for ML algorithms exist. Indeed, conventional contributions dealing with reducing data access overheads in ML suggest using distributed approaches [SHARED,CYCLADES]. In this case the focus is on single machine settings. We think however that such a review is a first step towards improving the performance and the efficiency in HPC settings.

3. STOCHASTIC GRADIENT DESCENT

The training or fitting of many ML models is based on optimisation techniques, with many approaches based on gradient based optimisation, using either first or second order gradients. Due to the expense of gradient calculations for complex models on large data sets, an approximation is often used, hence we consider these algorithms here. Stochastic Gradient Descent (SGD) is a quite popular algorithm. It is an optimization method that attempts to find the values of the model coefficients (the parameter or weight vector) that minimizes the loss function when they cannot be calculated analytically. SGD has proven to achieve state of-the-art performance on a variety of machine learning tasks [bottou_2012,sgdBPMF]. With its small memory footprint, robustness against noise and fast learning rates, SGD is indeed a good candidate for training data-intensive models. SGD is a variety of the gradient descent (GD) method [gradient_descent] with a major difference in the number of updates per visited data point. For SGD, only a random element from the training data is considered every iteration to perform the update of the weights vector. A template of both methods is described in *Algorithm 1* where the input parameter n defines the number of points to consider in the gradient computation and hence the algorithm. For SGD, n is equal to 1 while for GD the n is equal to the size of the complete training set.

```
Data: T, a training set
M, an initial guess for the model parameters
n, the batch size for calculating the gradient
for The required number of epochs do
    for Each batch B of size n in T do
        for Each training point t in B do
            Compute the gradient g of the loss function for M with respect to t
            Add g to the combined gradient G
        end
        Update model parameters M by a step in direction G
        Update algorithm parameters such as step size etc.
    end
end
```

Algorithm 1. (Stochastic) Gradient descent algorithm template

The main data touched in both algorithms is the training set, the model and the calculated gradient. The reuse distance for any training point in both algorithms is $|T|$, the size of the training set. Similarly, any calculated gradient g is used directly in the same iteration (reuse distance 0), and the model is reused every iteration (reuse distance 1). The learning rate parameter is updated as frequently as the weight vector for each algorithm.

Gradient descent-like optimization is often used with several learners. The data traversal and the number of data touches is largely determined by the optimization algorithm used *regardless of the model being trained.* Hence, one intuitive idea for a data reuse-aware coding is to fold different models together and train them simultaneously using the same optimization method, thus re-using the stream of data. A second approach we propose is a cache efficient SGD where the gradient is computed using new training points that have just been loaded from the large memory, along with others that are still in the cache memory.

3.1 Cache-Efficient SGD

The basic idea of a cache efficient SGD is to also consider recently visited points in the computation of the gradient. The list of recently visited points is kept in a vector potentially saved in the cache memory. The technique relies on the fact that computing the differentiated loss function on larger sized batches that come from cache is almost a free operation compared to loading new training points from the main memory. Indeed, as an example of how effective caches can theoretically be, let us assume a simple computation where access to main memory takes 40 cycles and access to the cache memory take 4 cycles (such as on Intel(R) Westmere CPUs [Intel]). If the model uses 100 data elements 100 times each, the program spends 400,000 cycles on memory operations if there is no cache and only 40,000 cycles if all data can be cached. The principle of the sliding window can be applied to every level of the memory hierarchy though, in a nested fashion, thereby extending simple SW-SGD to cover more complex hierarchies. The application of SW-SGD could be complicated somewhat by the features of the cache that is being used to store the training points.

From machine learning and optimization prospective, using extra points in a gradient calculation should provide some extra smoothing similar to the extra points used in mini batch SGD (MB-GD). Ideally the smoothing would be as effective as that in MB-GD and achieve lower noise whilst having the same data touch efficiency as 1-point SGD. The cache efficient SGD does not introduce any parameters to the algorithm and it should be possible to apply the fundamental idea of this work to many SGD algorithmic variants.

The cache efficient SGD was experimented with a classification problem of the MNIST [MNIST] dataset containing 60,000 training and 10,000 testing images. It have also been tested on other gradient descent optimization algorithms [SGDvariant]such as Momentum, Adam, Adagrad, etc. The model to train is a neural network with 3 layers and 100 hidden units each. All the results are averaged from 5-fold cross-validation runs. A preliminary set of experiments was conducted in order to determine the best hyper-parameters (learning rate, batch size) of the algorithm. These best hyper-parameters have been used in a second experiments where the aim here to prove that using the data reuse optimization helps accelerating the convergence and that it is orthogonal to the other gradient algorithms. We experimented with three scenarios for every algorithm: (1) only a batch of B new points (B being the best batch size from the preliminary experiments), (2) B new points + B points from the previous iteration and (3) B new points + 2 * B points from the previous iteration.

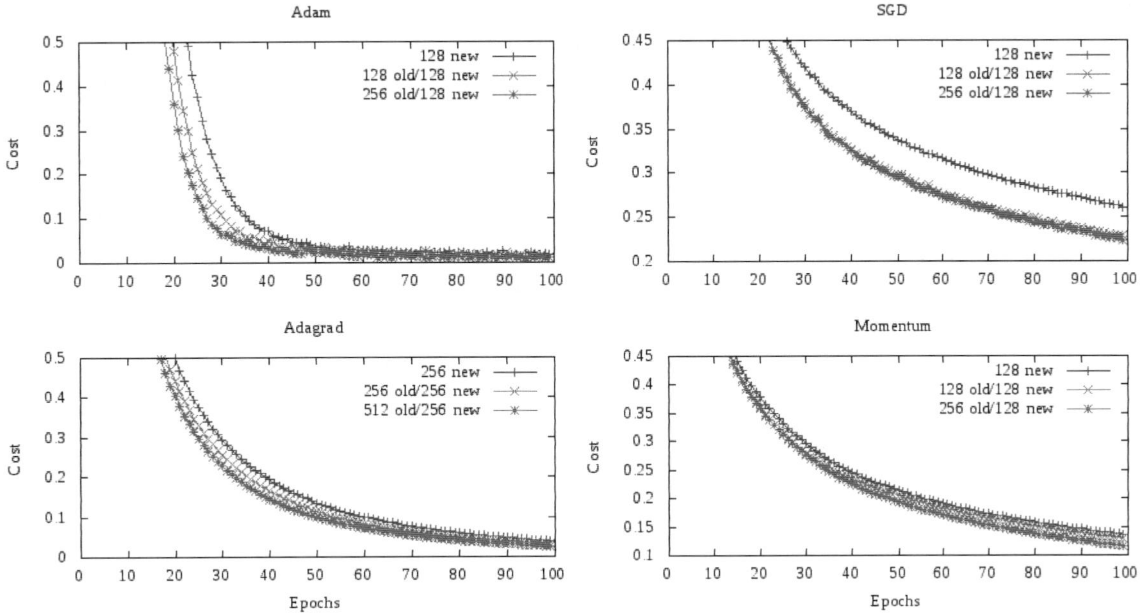

Figure 1. Comparing different sizes of batches for different optimizers.

In Figure 1, different sizes of batches are compared for different optimizers. For all algorithms, adding cached data points to the computation of the gradient improves the convergence rate. It is important here to highlight that, for the Adam algorithm for example, using a batch of size 256 and 512 new points is less efficient than using 128 new points as the first set of preliminary experiments showed that 128 is the best batch size. The added value here is therefore brought by the characteristic of considering old visited points in the computation and not because of a bigger batch size.

Further possible direction can be explored in this context such as loading different batches of points and to computing their gradients at the same time. Hence (1) future vectorisation opportunities are available, (2) the reuse distance is reduced for each point and as a consequence the temporal and spatial locality are increased.(3) matrix product best practices such as a cache blocking could be used where possible.

4. INSTANCE-BASED LEARNERS

In this section, we zoom in data and computation reuse possibilities in Instance-based class of learners (IBL), also known as memory-based learners. IBL is a class of ML algorithms that do not construct a model as in usual classification methods. They are called instance-based because they construct the hypotheses directly from the training points themselves, and the learner is ``memorising" the training set. In several of these methods no training phase takes place (with the possible exception of a search for the best value of some hyperparameter) and the predictions are made by measuring similarities between points to predict and points from the training data set. The similarity measure and way of combining input from the training points defines the different types of instance-based learners.

4.1 K-Nearest Neighbours

The principle behind the k -nearest neighbour (k -NN) method is to find the k training samples closest in distance to the new point, and predict the label from these. The distance can, in general, be any metric but the standard Euclidean distance is definitely the simplest and most used technique (if the attributes are all of the same scale). An unknown instance point is classified by a majority vote of its neighbours. For a classification problem, the output of k-NN is a class membership while for a regression problem, the output of k -NN is the average of the values of its k nearest neighbours. The algorithm template of the k -NN technique is given in Algorithm 2, but note that this is the classification phase, not the training phase as this instance based learner is not trained.

```
Data: RT, the set of remembered training points
P, the set of points to predict
for all i points in P (1) do
    for all j remembered training points in RT (2) do
        d = compute_distance(i, j)
        if d ≤ the k closest distances then
            Add j to the list of k nearest neighbours of i
            (Remove further away members from the list if necessary)
        end
    end
    for all j in the list of k nearest neighbours of i do
        Add class of j to the running vote count for i
    end
    Return the class of i based on the majority vote
end
```

Algorithm 2. Algorithm template of the k nearest neighbours method (classification)

The data accessed here are the points in RT and the points in P. The point from P being classified is reused directly in each iteration of loop level 2, with a reuse distance of one. The reuse of training points from RT is carried by loop level 1, with reuse distance RT. Each execution of loop level 2 is an epoch. There is some reuse in the handling of the list of k nearest neighbours for any point, but this is likely to be a trivial amount of data and computation compared to handling RT and computing distances. The only simple way to improve reuse is to shorten the reuse distance for elements of RT by calculating distances to multiple prediction points simultaneously; an appropriate batch size can be calculated based on cache sizes available.

4.2 Parzen-Rosenblatt Window

The second instance-based ML algorithm considered here is the Parzen-Rosenblatt window (PRW) density estimation method which has been introduced by Emanuel Parzen and Murray Rosenblatt respectively in [Parzen] and [Rosenblatt]. Its basic idea for predicting the probability density function P(x) is to place a window function f at x and determine what are the contribution of each training point x_i to the window. The approximation to the probability density function value P(x) is computed using a kernel function that returns a weighted sum of the contributions from all the samples x_i to this window. PRW has two important hyperparameters, the window bandwidth and the kernel function. A great number of bandwidth selection techniques exist such as [Jones1996, Sheather2004]. For the kernel function, different variants exist: Gaussian, Epanechnikov, Uniform, etc. The Gaussian probability density function is the most popular kernel for Parzen-window density estimation because it has no sharp limits as the kernels listed above, it considers all data-points and produces smooth results with smooth derivatives.

Data: RT, the set of remembered training points
P, the set of test points to predict
for *all i test points in P (1)* **do**
    for *all j remembered training points in RT (2)* **do**
        $s = compute\_similarity(i, j)$
        Add s to the running total for the C, the class of j
    end
    Return the class of i based on the class with the highest total weight C
end

Algorithm 3. Algorithm template of the Parzen-Rozenblatt Window method

From an implementation point of view, as sketched in the Algorithm template 3, computing PRW implies evaluating a large number of kernel-functions at a large number of data points. Given that the kernel function similarities are often based on Euclidean distance, the similarity with *k*-NN is obvious. The data reuse and distances involved are hence the same as for *k*-NN. The same optimizations are also applicable for the *k*-NN method as mentioned above.

4.3 Coupling Instance Based learners

Similar to other various machine learning algorithms, Parzen-Rozenblatt window and *k*-NN exhibit very similar data access pattern and share a large volume of the computations in different steps of the ML process: training, optimization, sampling, etc.

From a machine learning perspective, the Parzen window method can be regarded as a generalization of the *k* -nearest neighbour technique. Indeed, rather than choosing the *k* nearest neighbours of a test point and labelling the test point with the weighted majority of its neighbours' votes, one considers all points in the voting scheme and assigns their weight by means of the kernel similarity function. From a computation perspective, these algorithms similarly loop over all the points and sometimes calculate the same underlying distances (typically Euclidean). Therefore, the idea here is to run these two learners jointly on the same input data whilst producing different models. A proof of concept has been made on a subset of the Chembl public data set [CHEMBL] with 500K compounds and 2K targets. Our objective here was to give a first estimation of the amount of compute time that can be saved using the aforementioned optimization.

Table 1. Comparing the elapsed time when running PRW and k-NN separately and jointly

	Load time (s)	Test time (s)
PRW+*k*-NN separately	7.545	2695.45
PRW+*k*-NN jointly	3.726	1601.035

In Table 1, the results are represented for two scenarios: both learners are run separately and the total elapsed time is accumulated and both learners run jointly. The elapsed times are in seconds. Two steps are considered: the time for loading the training and testing sets and the time for the testing step (recall here that in instance-based learners no actual training phase occurs).

The preliminary experimental results clearly show the added value of increasing data reuse when computing PRW and k-NN on the same pass over the data. The computing time is indeed almost divided by two.

5. LOGISTIC REGRESSION AND SUPPORT VECTOR MACHINE

Logistic Regression (LR) and Support Vector Machine (SVM) are two closely related approaches for fitting linear models for binary classification. The optimum placement of the hyperplane dividing the two classes is determined by the loss function, which determines the per training point contribution to the total cost of any given model parameters, or the gradient of the cost which can then be used for optimisation. Optimisation is made easier by the fact that the loss function is convex.

In terms of the access to data, the two approaches are essentially the same. For a given batch of training points, the distance of the point to the model hyperplane is calculated with an inner-product per training point to produce a scalar, which is then fed into the differentiated loss function (to calculate the gradient). For the purpose of discussion, we assume an Euclidean distance and the associated inner-product. Algorithm 4 describes the procedure (the bias term is omitted for clarity).

Data: A batch of training samples B
An initial guess for the hyperplane model M
for *all training points t in B (1a)* **do**
  for *all vector indices i in t and M (2)* **do**
    Multiply scalars t_i and M_i
    Accumulate in p (the inner product)
  end
  Accumulate the gradient $f'(p)$ in g (the batch gradient)
end
for *all weights in model M (1b)* **do**
  update the weight based on weight decay, training schedule step size and the entry in g
end
Return M

Algorthim 4. Pseudo-code for updating a linear model with a mini-batch gradient descent

The reuse in a single batch update for these algorithms is relatively limited. Each training point t in the batch is accessed only once. The majority of accesses to the model M is carried by loop (1a); there is one inner-product per training point. This leads to a reuse distance of $|M|$. These loops can be easily rearranged to carry out the inner-products simultaneously so that there is one traversal over the model for those operations. The update of the weights in loop (1b) is, in the basic algorithm, dependent on the gradient calculated in loop (1a), so these two calculations are effectively sequentialised.

If these two algorithms are to be run on the same training set note that they can be quite tightly coupled. The training points can be presented to both models in the same order, meaning that the common visit to a training point can be combined so that the data only needs to be touched once. Indeed, the inner-product of the training point with the different hyperplane models can be done at the same time so that there is direct reuse in a feature-by-feature way of the training point.

5.1 Jointly Training Logistic Regression and SVM

In this section, an experimental investigation is conducted to explore the impact of exploiting the data reuse opportunities related to logistic regression and the support vector machine collectively trained by SGD. Note that the algorithms are not being changed in any way, this is pure leveraging of available reuse. Recall that LR and SVM are very closely related approaches in terms of data accesses especially when they are trained by optimization algorithms based on gradient calculation. In this case, only the computation of the cost functions are different. However, these two functions are applied in the exact same order and at the same time during the model training. By training two learners we are adding an outer loop over them to Algorithm 4. We then perform interchange of the mini-batch loop and the learner loop to be able to exploit reuse.

We have empirically compared the impact of training LR and SVM using the SGD optimization algorithm on two different sized benchmarks also used in state of the art related work [bottou2010]. The benchmark dataset is extracted from the Pascal challenge on large scale hierarchical classification [pascal_dataset] which is a text classification challenge. The ALPHA data set is composed of 250,000 training point and 250,000 test points. The DNA data set is composed of 4,038,390 train points and 2,500,000 test points. In Table 2, we report the elapsed time in seconds for running SVM and LR separately and jointly on the aforementioned datasets.

Table 2. Comparing the elapsed time when running LR and SVM separately and jointly

	Alpha dataset		DNA dataset	
	Train time (s)	Test time (s)	Train time (s)	Test time (s)
SVM + LR separately	49.9833	24.6442	338.559	155.2869
SVM + LR jointly	45.6416	22.0608	279.708	115.644

The obtained results show that reducing the data traversal decreases the total execution time and that the gain increases with the size of the data used. Indeed, with the DNA dataset the total training and testing time is reduced by around 20% compared to the time measured when the two models are run separately more than the time gained with the alpha dataset. It is important here to highlight that the output predictions are exactly the same with the two scenario because the essence of the models are not modified. It should also be noted that these are very early results, and that the benefit of combining the models is not yet as large as initially expected.

6. CONCLUSION

In this research paper we have highlighted various access patterns with reuse and computations containing redundancy for a set of ML algorithms that we think are most used and useful. For each of these we investigated the potential for performance improvements by identifying the reuse distances for the data used and the computations that could be grouped mainly between different learners. This work is intended as a starting point for further work on improving the performance of learners as implemented on supercomputing clusters and applied to big data volumes.

ACKNOWLEDGMENTS

This project has received funding from the European Union's Horizon 2020 research and innovation programme under grant agreement No 801051

REFERENCES

[Parzen] Parzen, Emanuel. On Estimation of a Probability Density Function and Mode. The Annals of Mathematical Statistics 33 (1962), no. 3, 1065–1076.

[Rosenblatt] Rosenblatt, Murray. Remarks on Some Nonparametric Estimates of a Density Function. The Annals of Mathematical Statistics 27 (1956), no. 3, 832–837.

[bottou_2012]. Bottou, Léon. Stochastic Gradient Tricks. Neural Networks, Tricks of the Trade, Reloaded , pages 430-445, 2012.

[bottou_2010] Bottou, Léon. Large-Scale Machine Learning with Stochastic Gradient Descent. Proceedings of the 19th International Conference on Computational Statistics (COMPSTAT'2010). Paris, France, 2010, pages 177-187.

[sgdBPMF] S. Ahn et al. Large-scale distributed bayesian matrix factorization using stochastic gradient MCMC. Proceedings of the 21th ACM SIGKDD International Conference on Knowledge Discovery and Data Mining, 2015.

[CHEMBL] A. Bento et al. The ChEMBL bioactivity database: an update. Nucleic Acids Res., vol. 42, pp. 1083–1090, 2014.

[SHARED] S. Sallinen et al. "High Performance Parallel Stochastic Gradient Descent in Shared Memory," 2016 IEEE International Parallel and Distributed Processing Symposium (IPDPS), Chicago, IL, 2016, pp. 873-882.

[CYCLADES] P. Xinghao et al. "CYCLADES: Conflict-free Asynchronous Machine Learning" . eprint arXiv:1605.09721 05/2016.

[gradient_descent] https://en.wikipedia.org/wiki/Gradient_descent.

[Intel] http://www.7-cpu.com/cpu/Westmere.html

[Jones1996] Jones, M et al. A brief survey of bandwidth selection for density estimation, Journal of American Statistical Association, vol 91, 401-407, 1996.

[Sheather2004] Sheather, S. J. Density estimation. Statistical Science, 19, 588–597, 2004.

[pascal_dataset] http://lshtc.iit.demokritos.gr/node/1.

[MNIST] LeCun, Y et al. (1998). Gradient-based learning applied to document recognition. Proceedings of the IEEE, 86, 2278-2324.

[SGDvariant]http://sebastianruder.com/optimizing-gradient-descent/index.html#gradientdescentoptimizationalgorithms

AN ETL PATTERN FOR LOG CONFIGURATION AND ANALYSIS

Bruno Oliveira[1], Óscar Oliveira[1], Telmo Matos[1], Vasco Santos[1] and Orlando Belo[2]
[1]*CIICESI, School of Management and Technology, Porto Polytechnic, Felgueiras, Portugal*
[2] *ALGORITMI R&D Centre, University of Minho, Campus de Gualtar, Braga, Portugal*

ABSTRACT

In many scenarios, such as the ones related to Data Warehousing Extract-Transform-Load (ETL) processes, logging techniques are usually applied for capturing event metrics across system levels for system auditing and system recovery. The diversity of strategies and architectures of the toolset used to support the ETL implementation introduces another layer of complexity, both for system development and audit. Although a valuable system diagnosis resource for the development team, logging is generally underestimated, being used only when the system reveals unexpected behaviours and not to drive the ETL system evolution. We believe that the use of logs for steering ETL development and maintenance can improve significantly global system quality. However, this approach is only effective if flexible and efficient logging systems exist. In this paper, we describe a Log Pattern used in a pattern-oriented approach for ETL systems development, which provides a configurable and flexible component for using to drive ETL development and maintenance phases.

KEYWORDS

Data Warehousing, ETL Systems, Logging, Log Pattern, ETL Patterns, Process Mining, Graph Databases

1. INTRODUCTION

Data Warehouses (DW) store massive and integrated data that represents an organizational view of transactional data needed for understanding corporative business activities. Extract-Transform-Load (ETL) (Kimball and Caserta, 2014) is one of the key components of a DW, which is responsible for ensuring data integrity and properties correctness. Such properties represent the foundations for data analysis, meaning that any inadequacy in the ETL system may compromise system capability for supporting decision-making processes. The ETL component is responsible for controlling how data is extracted, cleaned, transformed and loaded according to the DW requirements, usually dealing with huge amounts of data collected from several business sources with their own requirements, technology, and availability.

When dealing with an ETL process development, most designers and software architects plan the work to be done considering, beforehand, the toolset to be used to support the implementation, either choosing existing tools, developing their own or following a programmable approach based often on a set of ad-hoc procedures. This means that the initial plan and prototypes designed are in most cases algorithms developed based on a technical programming language or software architecture. This approach is by nature error-prone, hard to understand and to communicate, limiting the process reusability and the system evolution. Also, most of the initial efforts done using software modelling languages (e.g., Unified Modelling Language[1]) are ignored by ETL developers because are not well suited for representing all ETL specificities and are viewed as an extra effort that is hard to reuse at physical phases due to the disparities between the representations. Additionally, the maintenance cycle is also challenging since several problems can occur as more business areas are assimilated by the DW system, or the execution requirements are becoming more demanding. Thus, the system evolution must be considered to follow the natural evolution and growth of the data we need to hand (Mannimo and Zhiping, 2006).

[1] http://www.uml.org/

The use of a Pattern-Oriented Approach (POA) was proposed by (Oliveira and Belo, 2012) as a way for simplifying and decoupling process components for ETL development and maintenance. In POA, the most commonly used tasks – designed as patterns – are identified and used as preconfigured components for supporting ETL development. This approach covers all ETL development phases, as follows:

1. Conceptual phase – ETL Conceptual representation based on patterns, usually, using Business Process Model and Notation (BPMN).
2. Logical phase - The conceptual model is enriched using a domain specific language (DSL) to represent the specificities of each pattern.
3. Physical phase - The logical model is translated to physical primitives, representing, at least, a skeleton of the target system with the possibility to be executed by existing ETL tools.

As an integral part of the pattern configuration, ETL metadata can be used to support error handling and logging strategies. Thus, Error Handling (Throwable) and Log patterns can be used as patterns' subsystems, encapsulating all the logic behind error and log handling. These two components represent a crucial resource for capturing ETL metadata, and so monitoring all the process stages and handling unexpected exceptions or errors that can occur. All this contributes to improve or correct the logic of an ETL process (Belo et al., 2017).

Based on the POA for the ETL development, we present in this paper the Log Pattern as a configurable and flexible component, that let creating logging strategies, that, alongside to the traditional system audit and recovery use, allows in conjunction with other technologies to streamline the ETL development and maintenance. With flexible logging mechanisms, several log analysis approaches can be exploited and used to drive the ETL development. As an example, we explored the current development on graph databases, e.g., neo4j[2], used to provide efficient and flexible data analytic tools (even for large datasets) that can be used as new resources for ETL development and maintenance. The rest of this paper is organized as follows. Section 2 presents the concept of pattern and how logging techniques can be encapsulated within the POA. Section 3 presents the use of logging following the POA and how generated data can be used to drive the ETL development and maintenance. Conclusions and future work directions are presented in the last Section.

2. LOG PATTERN

Tracking ETL system activities is an important task that can be used for identifying inconsistent states, errors or performance bottlenecks. During the ETL workflow execution, several events related to audit or error scenarios are generated. They are stored using transaction log files that are used for providing useful insights about system behaviour considering a specific time window. Logging is a very important component of every ETL system and can be used for several purposes, namely; maintaining consistency and system reliability, monitoring some tasks for ensuring process quality and performance measures, and for identifying bottlenecks and errors that can influence the ETL process operationally. Additionally, log mechanisms can also support recovery mechanisms for handling critical failures and providing a way to roll back data repositories to a consistent state.

The POA frames the ETL development in three main phases: conceptual, logical and physical (Belo et al., 2014). The result of each phase is an input for the next one, representing an incremental development process for building an ETL system. At the conceptual phase, patterns are represented using the BPMN. Basically, patterns are represented as simple "boxes" (activities) used in a workflow context while a subset of the BPMN constructs is used for expressing data and control flow requirements (El Akkaoui et al., 2012). Figure 1 presents an ETL process conceptual model using the POA approach. As the basis for the presented ETL process, a DW repository built to support the decision-making processes from a Movie Rent Company was used. This conceptual model presents the necessary tasks to migrate Movie data from two relational databases to a target DW Movie dimension. As we can see, the process presented in Figure 1 starts with two Change Data Capture (CDC) patterns used to extract only the data changes from Movie data in each one of the involved data sources. For clarity reasons, the ETL patterns are identified using the "#" character surrounding their name initials. Next, a BPMN parallel gateway is used to indicates that both patterns are independent of each other, meaning that it can be executed in parallel (if the implementation tool used to allow that).

[2] https://neo4j.com/

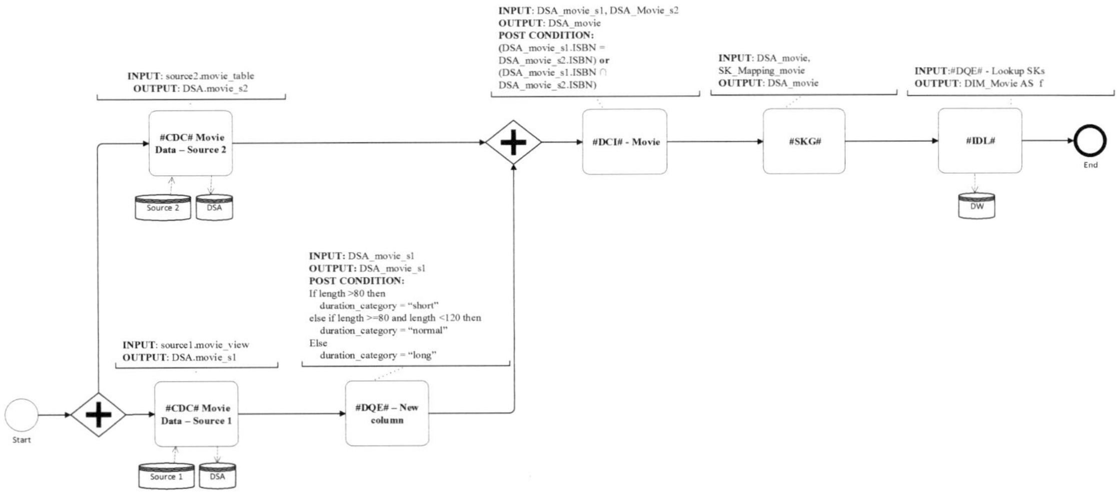

Figure 1. An ETL process used for populating the "Movie" dimension

In some cases, we use BPMN Data Stores artefacts in patterns for improving process readability, representing the type of source that we use – when the data source for a given pattern is the same for the next ones, data source artefacts are omitted. For clarity reasons, we added to each pattern a text annotation artefact, using a specific documentation structure for documenting each BPMN task (Akkaoui et al., 2009). The "input" and "output" keywords (respectively) describe the data handling performed in the data sources (using *sourceName.objectName* format) for data extraction and load; and "POST CONDITION" keyword for representing the assumptions that should be guaranteed after pattern application. Next, a Data Quality Enhancement (DQE) pattern was used for adding a new column (based on specific rules) that is missing in the Movie's data extracted from Source 1. After data extraction from each data source, the Data Conciliation and Integration (DCI) pattern is used to integrate and consolidate data from the two sources, i.e., for identifying common records existent between the two sources and solve potential conflicts. Next, a Surrogate Key Generator (SKG) pattern is used to generate new surrogate keys for the new records extracted from each data source. Finally, an Intensive Data Loading (IDL) pattern is used to load new data from the Data Staging Area (DSA) to the target DW Movie dimension.

Even in such a simple ETL scenario, logging techniques can be very useful for identifying problems or even possible improvements. Undesirable and unpredictable problems that compromise the system adequacy are often difficult to detect and correct due to a large amount of data involved and to the workflow complexity. Logging is the most used strategy for system monitoring for detecting those problems. As an example, some ETL black points (Belo et al., 2017), which are typical ETL performance bottlenecks, are being analysed using logs for system efficiency, for reducing system execution time, and decreasing the consumption of computational resources. Additionally, ETL execution usually generates a massive number of logs registering all events in a strict format, i.e., process information and errors with several degrees of severity and detail. Moreover, logs can arrive from diverse sources, each of them with its own format, making it hard to effectively use all this information. This foster the need for flexible logs implementations, as the log information needed at one time, can later be irrelevant or unnecessary. The flexibility of logs can proportionate an alternative use for their use as they can help to drive the ETL development and maintenance.

For enabling a simple log capturing over the process presented in Figure 1, we enrich the conceptual model for providing the logic we need for describing with more detail the behaviour of each pattern, and how to generate logging events as a result of their execution. For that, a domain specific language (Oliveira and Belo, 2015) can be used for reducing ambiguities that are regularly associated with BPMN conceptual models. In Figure 2 we can see a DSL excerpt using JavaScript Object Notation (JSON), representing the configuration applied to the CDC pattern instance represented in the "#CDC# Movie Data – Source 1" BPMN task.

```
{
	"use": {
		"pattern": "CDC",
		"type": "Extraction",
		"name": "Movie Data - Source 1"
	},
	"source": {
		"data": "source1.movie_view",
		"type": "relational"
	},
	"target": {
		"data": "DSA.ContainerSpSource",
		"type": "relational"
	},
	"fieldMapping": {(...)},
	"options": {(...)},
	"log": [
		{
		  "level":"Process",
		  "type":"Audit",
		  "event": "onComplete",
		  "target": {
		      "data":"DSA.MovieProcessLog",
		      "type":"relational"
		  }
		  "fieldMapping":[
		      {
		         "from":"#executionKey",
		         "to":"#target.executionID"
		      },
		      (...)
		  ]
		}
	]
}
```

Figure 2. A DSL example of configuring a CDC pattern instance

The DSL covers all the general requirements of each pattern, providing a powerful way to configure its behaviour. The pattern configuration starts with the "USE" keyword followed by the pattern name. Next, a set of blocks delimited by "{}" (braces) are used for describing the pattern input ("source"), output ("target"), the field mapping between source and target repositories ("fieldMapping") and the specific configuration properties ("options") that should be applied to each pattern (e.g. for identifying the core metadata used to support the logic for data extraction). We also present a configuration excerpt for the Log pattern component, identifying the rules for capturing the system's events. Several log configurations can be used for the same pattern, which can vary in granularity and scope, triggering the events associated to pattern's internal tasks or by associated to process level like the one presented in the provided example. In any case, several properties can be configured: The "level" property identifies the scope applied to the log activities, which can be "Process", "Pattern" or "Group Pattern" level. The Process level is associated to the scope in which the pattern is used, the Pattern level refers to the pattern's internal activities and Group Pattern level is valid when a set of patterns is placed within a group (which can be identified using BPMN subprocesses);

- The "type" property identifies the log events that should be generated. Basically, a set of log entries will be generated based on Audit or Throwable events. The Audit type covers audit activities that are automatically registered while the Throwable events cover error/exception scenarios that can occur while ETL is executing.
- The "event" property describes the event that will be used to capture activities. For example, the "onComplete" event is triggered when the pattern completes its execution. Figure 3 presents an example of events categorized in Audit and Throwable.
- The "Target" block allows for describing how log data will be stored. In the example provided in Figure 2, "data" and "type" properties describe the target database table and the type of the log provider used. The "fieldMapping" property describes the log schema using a set of predefined elements that can be used and mapped to the log structure used. Several log elements can be used, e.g., log unique identifier ("Log Key"), activities that originated log events ("Activity") or date fields for identifying the start ("StartDate") and end ("EndDate") dates. The "#" character is used to refer to predefined or declared elements ("target" prefix is used to refer to the target repository previously declared).

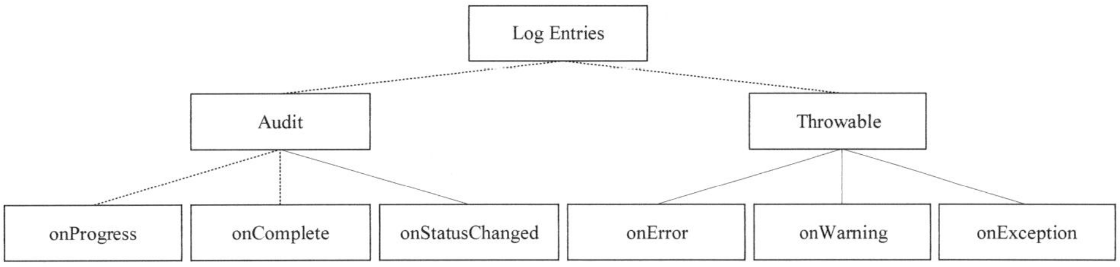

Figure 3. Log events taxonomy according to event nature

The configuration presented in Figure 2 shows some configurations examples for the pattern log component. The rules supporting all these configurations are supported by an extensible meta-model responsible for regulating the POA (Oliveira and Belo, 2016). Assuming that each activity presented in Figure 1 has a similar log configuration to the one presented in Figure 2 (which can also be configured at the process level). Table 1 presents a possible log table (simplified to ease reading) generated based on multiple process executions. To achieve the physical log file, a translation process from the specifications presented should be carried out using a specific ETL tool (Oliveira and Belo, 2018). In this case, the Pentaho Data Integration was used for executing the skeletons generated by a specific parser (the mapping to physical primitives is beyond the scope of this paper).

Table 1. Log table sample data for the process from Figure 1

ExecutionID	Activity	StartDate	Duration	Order	Processed Records
1	#CDC# Movie Data – Source 1	2019-02-12 11:10:54	311	1	120K
1	#CDC# Movie Data – Source 2	2019-02-12 11:10:54	261	2	64K
1	#DQE# – New column	2019-02-12 11:16:05	1212	1.1	120K
1	#DCI# - Movie	2019-02-12 11:36:17	245	3	60K
1	#SKG#	2019-02-12 11:40:22	151	4	60K
1	#IDL#	2019-02-12 11:42:53	210	5	60K
(…)	(…)	(…)	(…)	(…)	(…)

The configuration of "fieldMapping" property in the "log" block from the Figure 2 configuration, allows for the inclusion of the fields need to build the log file. Additional fields (omitted from Figure 2) were also considered for the log file presented in Table 1, namely:

- The "ExecutionID" column, identifying process execution. Each time the process executes, a new ExecutionID is used;
- The "Activity" column, identifying the activity (a pattern or a pattern internal task) that triggered the event;
- The "StartDate" and "Duration" columns for storing the start date and execution time in seconds for a given activity;
- The "Order" column, representing the position for each log entry activity within the process context, which can be used for ETL debugging. The values for "Order" field are organized hierarchically;
- The "ProcessedRecords" column, identifying the number of records processed by a given activity.

With the log catalogues generated by the pattern log component, ETL events timeline and data lineage can be identified, allowing for the detection of bottlenecks, execution errors, among other things. Thus, the ETL process can be analysed to identify design flaws, providing a way to apply strategies for minimizing process problems and consequently improve data quality and reduce the ETL resources that usually are needed for subsequent data loads.

3. ETL LOGGING ANALYSIS

Nowadays the volume of event log generated from business processes is becoming increasingly high. Although being a valuable resource, this information is often underestimated. Log data has been used in many scenarios to discover several problems in process mining, leading to the system overall performance. In (Uskenbayeva et al., 2015), structured event logs were proposed to build new business processes models with process mining techniques. More recently (Belo et al., 2017), data generated by the ETL process were used to discover black points, which cause additional processing times. The author proposes the analysis of event logs for helping the system administrator to recognize and eliminate these bottlenecks by means of a process mining approach. In (Rozinat et al., 2009), the authors proposed the enhancement of the behaviour of a multi-agent robotic system through the analyses of the log data collected using a process mining tool (ProM[3]).

Analysis of business process or process mining using a graph-oriented database is a relatively new approach. This technology is growing considerably in popularity and applications such as risk management (Rawat, 2017), fraud detection (Akoglu et al., 2015) or social network analysis (Jensen and Neville, 2003). Graph databases (Ian Robinson, Jim Webber, 2015), supported by graph theory, brings another way to work with data, where several characteristics of the model can be identified, suggesting new ways to improve the overall system architectures (Díaz-Pace et al., 2018; Joishi and Sureka, 2014). Logging is a common strategy for mining events, being able to discover specificities in the workflow process that can compromise the overall system. In our approach, we use a graph-oriented model as a use case for the Log Pattern. An intrinsic advantage in a graph-based modelling for process mining lies on the use of graph mining techniques where identification of frequent subgraphs within graph data sets can be discovered (Kashyap et al., 2016; Washio and Motoda, 2003). Additionally, recent advances in graph databases allow effective analytics on a large volume of highly-related data, where traditional approaches, e.g., raw data or relational database, are not suitable.

Considering the flexibility provided by the Log Pattern (described in section 2), the generated log structures can be used as an object for the application of more oriented process mining techniques, based on specific data analysis requirements. For example, a process mining approach for log analysis using graphs is presented to trace system activities. The graph representation specificities show the flexibility of the presented approach to adapt log files metadata. The generated log pattern can be mapped onto a connected graph, streamlining the ETL development and maintenance. Figure 4 presents a view of the resulting graph after mapping the log file described in Table 1.

Figure 4. A simple graph model of a log sample data (from Table 1)

[3] http://www.promtools.org/doku.php

The conversion from the log file to the presented graph is made identifying the patterns and respective patterns instances. The presented graph has two types of nodes: patterns representing the nature of each activity (green nodes) and the activities used in the BPMN model, representing specific instances of each one of the patterns presented (red nodes). Relations (edges) between nodes are represented as associations and denotes the "IS_INSTANCE_OF" or "CALL" regarding the pattern or the (pattern) instance, respectively.

However, the most complex transformation procedure is related to the activities clustering based on each ETL execution. Basically, the large log data set is grouped in smaller sets of similar data based on the "ExecutionID" column. That way, distinct graphs can be created, allowing the application of data profiling techniques associated with each ETL execution. Figure 4 represents only a single execution, storing its details in each data object using specific properties such as: "ExecutionID", "Duration" and "ProcessedRecords" (extracted from the Table 1). In fact, this is just one among many possibilities to represent a graph using the data provided in the Table 1. Different representations can open different possibilities for new perspectives and insights, which can be adjusted according to analysis requirements.

The analysis of the connected data stored in the graph (Figure 4), allows for understanding anomalies and also for discovering and better perceiving the log data (Chen et al., 2008; Kashyap et al., 2016; Yu, 2018). Such analysis implies data profiling techniques for analysing the structure, contents and log metadata. A series of techniques for collecting statistics and new data insights revealing the process workflow over time, contributing to the understanding of process flaws, identify hidden patterns more easily and potentially improving process performance.

Table 2 presents a node analysis over the pattern instances, representing the ratio between the duration (in seconds) and the number of records processed by the respective pattern (for better reading, we multiplied the values of the ratios by 100). Even for a simple case like the one presented, the ETL designer can analyse and tissue important considerations. Looking at the results, it is possible to observe that the most critical pattern is the "#DQE# – New column" with a ratio of 1. Analysing the ratios and the workflow, we could process the "#DQE# – New column" pattern instance after the "#DCI# – Movie" pattern, because as there few input records, would reduce the computational time of all ETL system. This workflow restructuration is possible considering that each pattern is decoupled for the remaining ones, i.e., the change in one pattern will not affect the behaviour of the remaining pattern.

Table 2. The ratio between pattern execution duration and the number of processed records

Activity	Ratio
#CDC# Movie Data – Source 1	0.25
#CDC# Movie Data – Source 2	0.4
#DQE# – New column	1
#DCI# – Movie	0.2
#SKG#	0.25
#IDL#	0.35

4. CONCLUSIONS

In this paper, we presented and discussed a Log pattern for facilitating ETL systems implementation. We can use this pattern component not only at the ETL development phase but also for overcoming well-known problems that usually occur when redesigning an ETL process. We present the Log Pattern under POA that allows for, due to its flexibility, configuring target log structures according to different analytic lenses, improving ETL systems development and maintenance. The graphs application scenario presented, is just an approach for log mining, revealing interesting results that achieved by the Log pattern specification described under a POA approach. The log data mapping to a graph enables the use of graph mining techniques, allowing for the representation of several specificities inherent to graphs modelling. We believe that a flexible approach that can be easily reconfigured and readapted at workflow context makes ETL components more independent each other, which facilitates ETL evolving processes phases that can be used identify undesired situations that can be at least minimized.

We concluded that besides the discovery of the traditional ETL "black points" that reduce the efficiency of an ETL system, the Log Pattern flexibility provide means to deeper analysis. The next step of this research is to fully exploit the graph modelling advantages to further improve the ETL development and maintenance to attain improved system performance, reliability and quality.

REFERENCES

Akkaoui, Z. El, Zimanyi, E., El Akkaoui, Z., Zimanyi, E., 2009. Defining ETL worfklows using BPMN and BPEL. Proceeding ACM twelfth Int. Work. Data Warehous. Ol. Dol. 09 41–48.

Akoglu, L., Tong, H., Koutra, D., 2015. Graph based anomaly detection and description: A survey, Data Mining and Knowledge Discovery.

Belo, O., Cuzzocrea, A., Oliveira, B., 2014. Modeling and Supporting ETL Processes via a Pattern-Oriented, Task-Reusable Framework. In: Proceedings - International Conference on Tools with Artificial Intelligence, ICTAI.

Belo, O., Dias, N., Ferreira, C., Pinto, F., 2017. A process mining approach for discovering ETL black points. In: Advances in Intelligent Systems and Computing. pp. 426–435.

Chen, C., Yan, X., Zhu, F., Han, J., Yu, P.S., 2008. Graph OLAP: Towards online analytical processing on graphs. Proc. - IEEE Int. Conf. Data Mining, ICDM 103–112.

Díaz-Pace, J.A., Tommasel, A., Godoy, D., 2018. Can Network Analysis Techniques Help to Predict Design Dependencies? An Initial Study. Proc. - 2018 IEEE 15th Int. Conf. Softw. Archit. Companion, ICSA-C 2018 64–67.

El Akkaoui, Z., Mazón, J.-N.N., Vaisman, A., Zimányi, E., Akkaoui, Z. El, Mazón, J.-N.N., Vaisman, A., Zimányi, E., Zineb El Akkaoui, Mazón, J.-N.N., Vaisman, A., Zimányi, E., Akkaoui, Z. El, Mazón, J.-N.N., Vaisman, A., Zimányi, E., 2012. BPMN-Based Conceptual Modeling of ETL Processes. Lect. Notes Comput. Sci. (including Subser. Lect. Notes Artif. Intell. Lect. Notes Bioinformatics) 7448, 1–14.

Ian Robinson, Jim Webber, E.E., 2015. Graph Databases, Joe Celkos Complete Guide to NoSQL.

Jensen, D., Neville, J., 2003. Data mining in social networks. pp. 287–302.

Joishi, J., Sureka, A., 2014. Performance Comparison and Programming Process Mining Algorithms in Graph-Oriented and Relational Database Query Languages. In: Proceedings of the 19th International Database Engineering & Applications Symposium on - IDEAS '15. ACM Press, New York, New York, USA, pp. 192–197.

Kashyap, N.K., Pandey, B.K., Mandoria, H.L., Kumar, A., 2016. Graph Mining Using gSpan: Graph-Based Substructure Pattern Mining. Int. J. Appl. Res. Inf. Technol. Comput. 7, 132.

Kimball, R., Caserta, J., 2014. The Data Warehouse ETL Toolkit, Igarss 2014.

Mannimo, M., Zhiping, W., 2006. A framework for data warehouse refresh policies. Decis. Support Syst. 42, 121–143.

Oliveira, B., Belo, O., 2012. BPMN Patterns for ETL Conceptual Modelling and Validation. 20th Int. Symp. Methodol. Intell. Syst. Lect. Notes Artif. Intell. 7661 LNAI, 445–454.

Oliveira, B., Belo, O., 2015. A domain-specific language for ETL patterns specification in data warehousing systems, Lecture Notes in Computer Science (including subseries Lecture Notes in Artificial Intelligence and Lecture Notes in Bioinformatics).

Oliveira, B., Belo, O., 2016. An Ontology for Describing ETL Patterns Behavior. In: Francalanci, C., Helfert, M. (Eds.), An Ontology for Describing ETL Patterns Behavior. SciTePress, Lisboa, pp. 102–109.

Oliveira, B., Belo, O., 2018. From ETL Conceptual Design to ETL Physical Sketching using Patterns. In: Proceedings of the 20th International Conference on Enterprise Information Systems - Volume 1: ICEIS,. pp. 262–269.

Rawat, D.S., 2017. Analysis of Fraudulent in Graph Data base for Identification & Prevention. IJIRST –International J. Innov. Res. Sci. Technol. 4, 42–49.

Rozinat, A., Zickler, S., Veloso, M., van der Aalst, W.M.P., McMillen, C., 2009. Analyzing Multi-agent Activity Logs Using Process Mining Techniques. In: Distributed Autonomous Robotic Systems 8. Springer Berlin Heidelberg, Berlin, Heidelberg, pp. 251–260.

Uskenbayeva, R., Kurmangaliyeva, B., Shynybekov, D., Temirbolatova, T., 2015. Application process mining techniques to optimize the business process models based on information systems issuing licenses and permits e-license: Practical research. In: 2015 54th Annual Conference of the Society of Instrument and Control Engineers of Japan (SICE). IEEE, pp. 298–300.

Washio, T., Motoda, H., 2003. State of the art of graph-based data mining. ACM SIGKDD Explor. Newsl. 5, 59.

Yu, F., 2018. Data Profiling: A Holistic View of Data using Neo4j [WWW Document]. F. Eng. Neo4j. URL https://neo4j.com/blog/data-profiling-holistic-view-neo4j/

DRIVING MODEL OF BIG DATA GOVERNANCE IN URBAN COMMUNITY SAFETY SERVICE

Zhao-Ge Liu and Xiang-Yang Li
School of Management, Harbin Institute of Technology
Room 601, No. 13, Fayuan Street, Nangang District, Harbin, 150001, China

ABSTRACT

Community is the basic unit of public safety management. A good community safety service is the key of improving community safety level. At the era of data explosion, big data based decision making has been widely adopted to facilitate community safety service. To achieve big data sharing and service value increasing, big data governance is the prime mode. Current big data governance studies lack an integrated model for comprehensively solving different data sharing problems. Models have dual advantages including supporting organizational synergy and supporting resource reuse. This paper puts forward a kind of driving model of big data governance in urban community safety service, integrating scenario-based driven, data-based driven and model-based driven approaches. The scenario-driven part of driving model provides the overall solutions for big data governance. The data-based driven level provides big data governance with objective evidence. The model-based level provides effective operational modes to the problem solving in big data governance. Through a use case, the rationality and effectiveness of the driving model are verified.

KEYWORDS

Community, Public Safety, Safety Service, Big Data Governance, Driving Model

1. INTRODUCTION

Urban community safety can be understood from two perspectives, which are state and degree. From the first perspective, researchers define community safety as the state that the risks of incidents threatening community residents' safety can be controlled (Wei and Lovegrove, 2013; Elbasyouny and Elbassiouni, 2013). From the second perspective, community safety is similar to community safety risk, which refers to the stable degree of external environment, including the community living conditions, community management mechanism and public service capacity. Safety service can be understood as all kinds of measures applied to guarantee safety. At the background of data explosion, it is concerned by both academia and industry that how to realize the mechanism innovation of community safety service by integrating, sharing and using the big data resources in community safety management. To solve this important problem, big data governance becomes the prime mode.

As a part of generalized information governance plan, big data governance is to make policies including data optimizing, privacy protecting and data realization relevant to big data. Big data governance framework includes three dimensions that are big data categories, big data governance principles and industries and functions of big data governance (Soares, 2014). Division of big data categories can help solve relevant problems such as data tracing, data right and data processing (George et al., 2016). Big data governance principles can be understood as major problems which need to be solved in big data governance. Tradition information governance principles such as organization, meta-data management, safety and privacy, data quality, business process integration, master data integration and information life cycle management can also be used in big data governance (Liu et al., 2016). Big data analysis is driven by specific scenes which contain certain industries and functions. Big data analysis can be applied to various industries and functions such as marketing, risk management, customer service, data sharing, information technology and human resource management (Martin et al., 2017).

To sum up, existing studies of big data governance have basically established the general framework of big data governance and provide simple solutions to common problems in big data sharing. At different fields using big data based decision making methods, a lot of advanced technical achievements has emerged. However, existing studies are scattered and incomplete in the solving of complex governance problems. The solving process of integrative problems lack systematization. Specially, most of big data sharing and governance problems involve problems of different levels such as regulation, mater data and meta-data. It's difficult to solve the problems effectively only using single governance methods. For example, the data privacy and security problem involves problems including the regulation in organizational level and data structure in meta-data level.

Model driven decision making activities have dual advantages including supporting organizational synergy and the reuse of knowledge resource. Specifically, at the background of complex system, models can establish the relationship among various work or activities. Model driven method has been applied to many fields, and a lot of advanced methods have been proposed (Hidayet and Geylani, 2014). This paper proposes a kind of driving model of big data governance with certain degree of universality and hierarchy, which includes three levels that are scenario-driven level, data-driven level and model-driven level, separately realizing solution generating, data analyzing and process supporting.

2. THE BASIC CONTENTS OF BIG DATA GOVERNANCE IN URBAN COMMUNITY SAFETY SERVICE

According to the framework of big data governance and surveys on successful big data organizations (Hidayet, and Geylani, 2014), this paper generalizes the problems of big data governance in urban community safety service into three aspects that are data demand-supply, data sharing and data processing, coming with the basic contents of big data governance that are data demand-supply planning, data sharing strategy planning and multi-source data processing.

Data demand-supply planning, DDSP. Data demand-supply problem is pretty complex, involving specific fields such as data right, data lifecycle and data transaction. Data demand-supply planning is to make improvement projects according to the factors causing complexity to guarantee that the demand-supply plans are reasonable, rational and legal. Data demand-supply plans are designed according to three indicators that are reasonable data demands, rational choosing of data supply and legal data transfer. Among them, Reasonable data demands mean that all the specific requirements for data demands can be basically realized with regulation and techniques. For example, the time and space ranges of sharing data should be reasonable, or the data supply organizations may not be willing to supply the data. Rational choosing of data supply parties refers to choosing the data supply parties with acceptable data quality and data cost. For example, investigate and test the data quality of supply parties, and decide whether regulating supply parties or choosing other supply parties according to test results. Legal data transfer means that the processes of data supply of supply parties, data receiving of demanding parties and the data sharing among the different parties need to be consistent with existing laws and data right claims, in order to effectively support the activities of relevant stakeholders.

Data sharing strategy planning, DSSP. In terms of specific data demand-supply plan/network, data sharing strategy planning is to design strategies to make big data sharing extent meets the demands of data demanding parties. DSSP involves the contents of two levels that are organization and technique. At the level of organization, DSSP aims to design data sharing strategies through the games between demand and supply parties. At the level of technique, SEA pays more attention to the problem that how to facilitate data sharing with secure and reliable technical approaches.

Multi-source data processing, MSDP. Multi-source data processing is to solve the data processing problems at technical level. Specifically, MSDP includes multisource data processing, heterogeneous data processing and mixed conditions. MSDP takes the basic mode of data integration, which includes 4 parts that are pattern alignment, entity linking, conflict resolution and relationship inferring. Pattern alignment is used to find the actual same data with different semantic expression. For example, different governments often don not have the same description of community feature data. Entity linking technique is used to provide a similarity calculation method for discovering the actual same entity with different features, which is the key of big data integration. The key of entity linking technique lies on finding similar entities and processing.

Conflict resolution technique is applied to reduce the problems including mode heterogeneity, semantic conflict and data redundancy produced in the process of big data integration and fusion. The conflict resolution technique is corresponded with pattern/ontology alignment technique, but pays more attention to the conflict problems in big data integration. Relationship inferring technique infers possible relationship to create value for achieving system functions using the techniques above.

3. DRIVING MODEL CONSTRUCTION OF BIG DATA GOVERNANCE IN URBAN COMMUNITY SAFETY SERVICE

According to the contents of big data governance, a kind of driving model of big data governance is proposed, as shown in Figure. 1. In the solving of big data governance problems, descriptive information, process data, and relevant models are all important. Descriptive information can help structure complex problems and express them, and further drive the overall strategy planning. Process data analysis can provide objective evidence for decision making. Process models provide a series of standard procedures of governance problem solving. Effectively using models can improve efficiency and effectiveness. Integrating the three types of resources, the driving model of big data governance includes three levels that are scenario-driven level, data-driven level and model-driven level. The hierarchical driving model can integrate scenario-driven, data-driven and model-driven methods, separately realizing solution generating, data analyzing and process supporting.

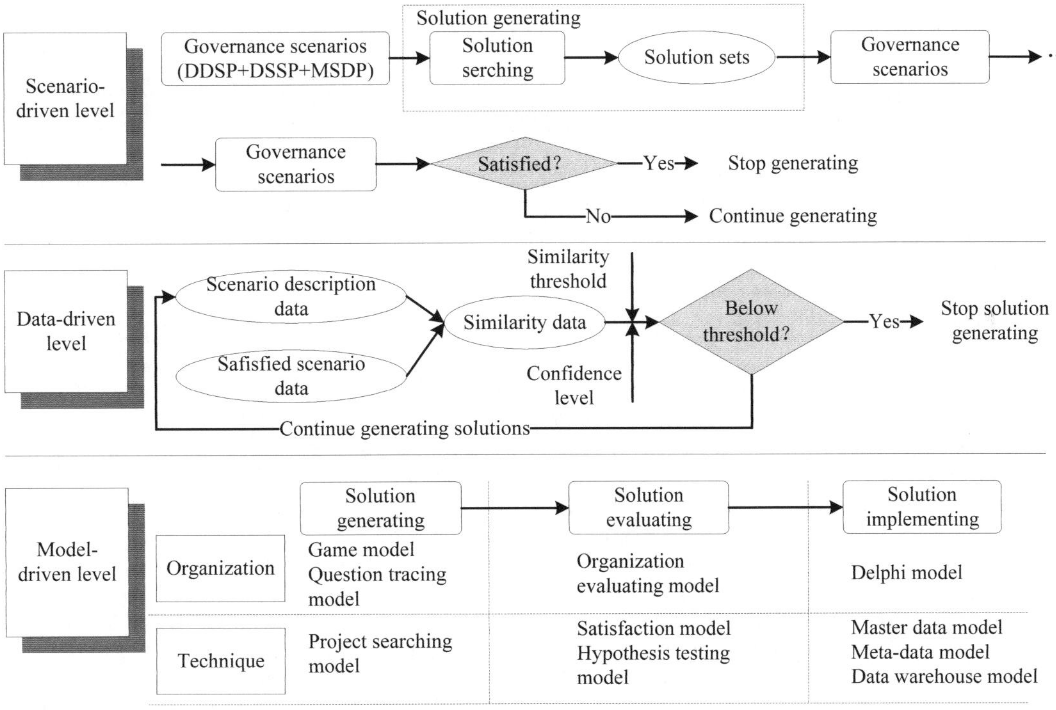

Figure 1. Driving model of big data governance in urban community safety service

Scenario-driven level, SDL. In big data governance, governance scenario refers to all kinds of problem description information. The major problems existing in current big data governance can thus be obtained by scenario analyzing. In scenario-driven level, the overall solving solutions are provided. The structured integration of related information gives a clear problem description, and the solution searching module intellectually generates guiding solutions. Via the continuous problem description and problem solving, the original problems are solved step by step. For example, in terms of the multi-source data processing problem, data integration techniques are identified that can effectively solve it. As a result, the data integration techniques are considered as overall solution. The multi-source data processing problem is originally solved in the new governance scenarios, but data demand-supply and data sharing problems are still remained in the new governance scenarios. Consequently, solutions need to be continuously induced to solve the problems. Finally, an originally general plan is generated as the results of SDL, which actually includes a set of solutions.

Data-driven level, DDL. Data-driven level provides big data governance with the objective evidence to make decisions of problem solving. It supports decision making with the input data, process data and output data at each decision making point. In the generation of solutions, the similarity between real scenarios and satisfied scenarios can be calculated with Euclidean distance. Consequently, the intellectually decision making can be achieved based on giving similarity thresholds and confidence level.

Model-driven level, MDL. Model-driven level provides big data governance with effective and standard procedures of the solving of big data governance problems. It realizes the generating, evaluating and implementing of solutions by calling and using relevant algorithms. For example, in terms of data sharing strategies in solution generating processes, the stakes of all stakeholders need to be coordinated. Further, the data sharing extent can be improved at the level of organization. In this process, the game model among multi-agents is used.

4. CRUCIAL TECHNIQUES OF BIG DATA GOVERNANCE IN URBAN COMMUNITY SAFETY SERVICE

The solutions of big data governance problems can be generated with the driving model of big data governance. In this part, the crucial techniques involved are discussed based on big data governance driving model. In fact, big data governance driving model is to gradually solve problems by scenario identifying and solution searching. Consequently, scenario identifying and solution searching become the most important parts in the driving model. Among them, scenario identifying is to figure out the problems, which is realized by using field knowledge. The knowledge here includes the experience knowledge contained in historical cases, the structured knowledge contained in rules, universal recognition of people, and so on. In this section, we take examples of mess map and case-based reasoning to illustrate the technical theories of scenario identifying and solution searching.

4.1 Scenario Identifying Technique and Mess Map

Scenario identifying technique is used to reduce the uncertainty of current scenarios by continuously mining the reasons causing governance problems. Mess map is a kind of question tracing technique, which can help find the reasons and describing the scenarios. As a tool of dealing with conflict opinions and data, mess map can help stakeholders in complex problems to form unified opinions in terms of social messes, which refer to fuzzy social problems that don't have direct solutions. The basic thinking of mess map is that the problems can be solved if the sources of problems can be traced by tracing reasons from the results of problems. Mess map provides the integral framework of analyzing problems by visual expression forms. It helps find the solutions by cross-organization coordination and communication.

Specially, mess map includes a kind of question tracing algorithm, which is a kind of procedure level technique that drives the operation of mess map. The leading departments of question tracing jointly achieve problem solving by man-machine interaction, as shown in Figure. 2. In the figure, U_{ij} refers to the uncertainty in the jth stage of question tracing in terms of question i. If $U_{ij}=0$, the uncertainty is reduced completely, which means the solutions have been obtained.

4.2 Experience Learning Technique and Case-Based Reasoning

Experience learning technique is another kind of method to obtain solutions of problems, which solves problems by reusing historical experience. Case-based reasoning (simplified as CBR) is a typical kind of experience learning technique. The most obvious features of CBR are structuring experience and programming experience learning processes. It supports the intelligent generating of solutions and doesn't involve man-machine interaction, which improves the objectivity of experience learning. The key of CBR is similarity calculation of scenarios, it refers to extract experience embedded in cases to guide practice by sorting the cases that have similar governance scenarios. In the solution generating of big data governance, it's necessary to match the scenarios of problems between current and case scenarios. The calculation method of similarity is as follows.

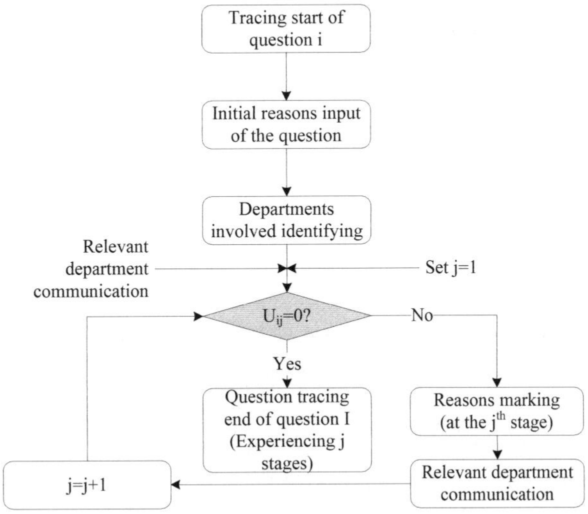

Figure 2. Question tracing alogorithm

Set ca_0 as real case, which means the case with a set of scenario features. Set me_{0j} as the value of the real case in feature *j*. In CBR, the similarity is calculated through the calculation of Euclidean distance or Manhattan distance of two cases.

Distance of scenario features. $\forall i \in [1,m]$, $\forall j \in [1,n]$, the distance between in scenario feature j can be represented in (1).

$$dis_{0ij} = \left| me_{0j} - me_{ij} \right| \tag{1}$$

Distance of cases. $\forall i \in [1,m]$, set dis_{0i} as the distance of two cases, it is calculated by integrating all of the distances of scenario features between the two cases, which can be represented in (2).

$$dis_{0i} = (\sum_{j=1}^{n} (w_j \times dis_{0ij})^p)^{\frac{1}{p}} \tag{2}$$

Among them, p denotes the norm. If p=1, the dis_{0i} represents the Euclidean distance. If p=2, the dis_{0i} represents the Manhattan distance. w_j denotes the weight of scenario feature j, and $\sum w_j = 1$.

Similarity of cases. The similarity LIK_{0i} between two cases can be converted from the distance of the cases, which can be represented in (3).

$$LIK_{0i} = \frac{1}{1 + \alpha \times dis_{0i}} \quad (i = 1, 2, \mathrm{L}\ , m) \tag{3}$$

Among them, $\alpha \in [0,1]$ is the similarity coefficient. Generally, the value is set as 1.

It is worth to note that the case here can be divided as local cases and external cases according to case sources. Cases coming from different places have different applicability. Practice surveys need to be carried on to decide whether adopting the experience or not.

5. USE CASE

In this section, a use case of big data governance in S city in China is illustrated to verify the rationality and effectiveness the proposed driving model. Specifically, the technique of solution searching here is CBR. In this section, we take position data contained in social media data as example, to realized the current governance scenarios and generate corresponding solutions. According to spot surveys, the scenario is generalized into 18 detailed types, as shown Table 1.

Table 1. Scenario feature of big data governance in the use case

Scenario feature type	Scenario feature	Feature value	Feature weight
Governance problems	Data precision	0.65	0.25
	Data precision threshold	0.85	0.20
	Data precision state	Error (0)	0.20
	Master data	Social media text (1)	0.20
	Meta-data	Position (1)	0.15
	Whether authorized or not	Not (0)	0.35
	Protected data	Name (0)	0.30
	Protection technique	Access control (1)	0.15
	Privacy risk	0.52	0.12
	Risk threshold	0.75	0.08
Governance solutions	Level number of Access authority	5	0.40
	Access control regulation	No (0)	0.30
	Technical security level	5	0.30
Governance environment	Big data management department	Yes (1)	0.28
	Maturity of big data governance	2nd level (2)	0.24
	Big data management platform	Yes (1)	0.21
	Level number of big data governance	3	0.15
	Scores of techniques	0.61	0.12

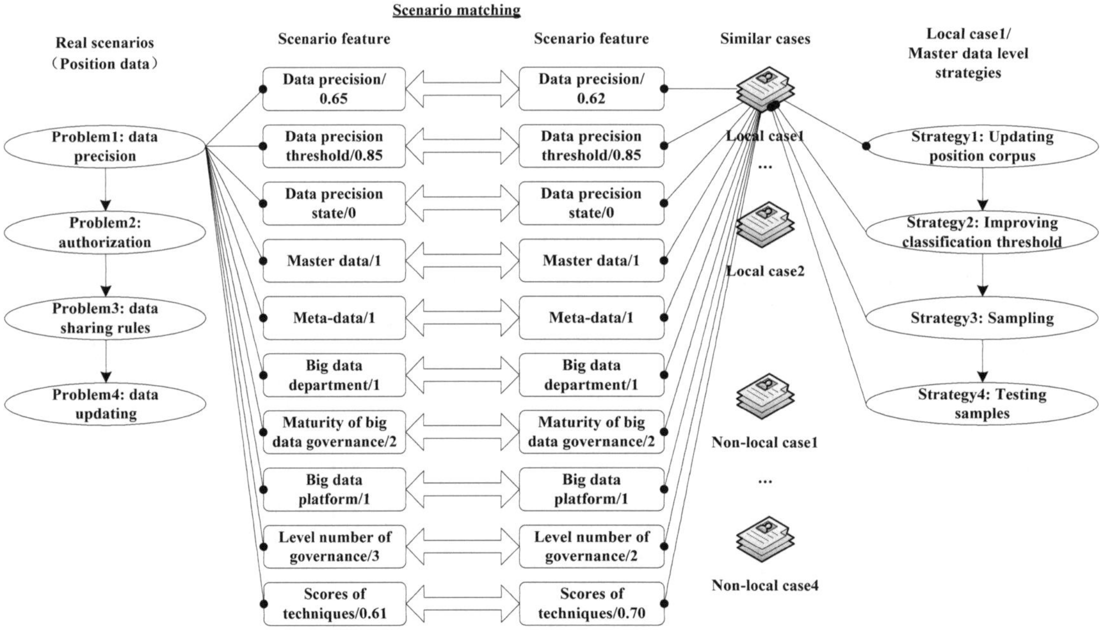

Figure 3. Scenario matching and solution genrating processes of big data governance in use case

Using CBR technique to search for solutions of big data governance. According to eq(1) to eq(3), the similarity degrees between current scenarios and case scenarios can be obtained. The scenario matching process is shown in Figure. 3. Finally, specific strategies of big data governance are extracted from historical cases.

6. CONCLUSION

At the background of data explosion, big data governance has become the prime model to integrate, share and use the big data resources in community safety service, and further realize the mode innovation of services. Most big data governance problems involve various problems of different levels including regulation, master data and meta-data. In terms of this field problem, this paper puts forward a kind of driving model of big data governance with certain universality and hierarchy. The main contributions are as follows. Firstly, the basic contents of big data governance are extracted, including three kinds of contents that are data demand-supply planning, data sharing strategy planning and multi-source data processing. Secondly, the driving model of big data governance is proposed, including three levels that are scenario-driven level, data-driven level and model-driven level, separately realizing solution generating, data analyzing and process supporting. Thirdly, the critical techniques of big data governance driving in urban community safety service are discussed. Mess map and case-based reasoning are taken as examples to illustrate the technique theories of scenario identifying and solution searching. Of course, there are spaces which need further exploration, mainly reflecting as the connection of big data governance driving model with other models such as scenario models and reference models, and the empirical test of the driving model.

ACKNOWLEDGEMENT

This work is supported by the Major Research Project of Nation Natural Science Foundation of China named "Big data Driven Management and Decision-making Research" (No. 91746207), the General Program of Nation Natural Science Foundation of China (No. 71774043) and the Emergency Management Major Research Project of Nation Natural Science Foundation of China (No. 91024028).

REFERENCES

Elbasyouny, K., Elbassiouni, M. Y., 2013. Modeling and Analyzing Traffic Safety Perceptions: An Application to the Speed Limit Reduction Pilot Project in Edmonton, Alberta. *In Accident Analysis and Prevention*, Vol 51, pp 156-167.

George, G. et al, 2016. Big Data and Data Science Methods for Management Research. *In Academy of Management Journal*, Vol 59, pp 1493-1507.

Hidayet, B. S., Geylani, K., 2014. A Model Driven Architecture for the Development of Smart Card Software. *In Computer Languages Systems &Structures*, Vol. 40, No. 2, pp 53-72.

Liu, X. et al, 2016. A Structured Analysis of Unstructured Big Data by Leveraging Cloud Computing. *In Marketing Science*, Vol 35, pp 363-388.

Martin, K. D. et al, 2017. Data Privacy: Effects on Customer and Firm Performance. *In Journal of Marketing*, Vol 81, pp 36-58.

Soares, S., 2014. *Data Governance Tools: Evaluation Criteria, Big Data Governance, and Alignment with Enterprise Data Management.* MC Press, Canada.

Wei, F., Lovegrove, G., 2013. An Empirical Tool to Evaluate the Safety of Cyclists: Community Based, Macro-level Collision Prediction Models Using Negative Binomial Regression. *In Accident Analysis and Prevention*, Vol 61, pp 129-137.

DEEP LEARNING: APPLICATION OF THE LSTM MODEL IN THE CATEGORIZATION OF TWEETS ON VIOLENCE IN THE CITY OF BELÉM

Jonatã Paulino da Costa, Aurea Milene Teixeira Barbosa dos Santos, Eulália Carvalho da Mata, Marcelino Silva da Silva, Priscila Siqueira Aranha and Carlos Renato Lisboa Francês
UFPA – Unniversidade Federal do Pará
Rua Augusto Corrêa, 0 –Guamá–CEP 66075-110-Belém-Pará-Brazil

ABSTRACT

Twitter has more than 313 million users, is considered a subjective social network of content generation on the Internet, not only used to disclose personal information, but shares opinions and information about events and events in general, being a great source of research for the discovery of knowledge among relevant data. In this context, the present work presents a study on the implementation (application) of the Recurrent Neural Network LSTM for the analysis and classification of tweets that are related to crime and not crime. The set of data that is the object of the survey comes from an account of a newspaper in the city of Belém, containing 20000 records in a period of two months. The results obtained with the use of RNR LSTM proved to be quite satisfactory, reaching accuracy in some cases of 90% correctness.
Based on the results of this research, we observed the effectiveness of this method in the analysis of feelings in comparison with other algorithms such as Nayve Bayes, Convolutional Neural Networks used in the literature. Because it is a network that uses a Long-Term Memory technique, it can adapt to large time intervals, such as Twitter texts.

KEYWORDS

Deep Learning, Twitter (Tweets), Python, Embeddings, Categorization, Analysis of Feelings

1. INTRODUCTION

The internet has evidently revolutionized the world and people as a whole. With the advancement of technology, people are using their computers or mobile devices more often to access the web and establish their social networks. According to a survey carried out by the Regional Center for the Development of the Information Society (CETIC, 2014), in 2014, 94.2 million Brazilians had Internet access, 76% of whom used it to participate in social networks, indicating that virtual communication is increasingly common and present in the lives of Brazilians. Comments are openly shared as suggestions and feedback on particular things, product, merchandise, political affairs and crimes, such as murder, femicide and other types of crimes (Kaur, 2014). Most of these comments, being publicly shared, can be easily accessed from the web (Schuller, 2014).

Social Networks are networks formed from interactions between people, groups or institutions motivated by common interests or goals that relate through digital media. In Social Networks there are opinions, personal information or events in general. Among the tools that allow the creation of social networks is Twitter that has more than 313 million monthly active users (TWITTER, 2017).

Twitter emerged in 2006, a social network with an unusual premise - each post, called tweet, should not exceed the limit of 140 characters. Due to its growing popularity, the network has gradually become more efficient and accessible, becoming of paramount importance, giving its users the power to create and share ideas and information instantly, without barriers. Twitter is a subjective network of content generation on the Internet, according to the region and the culture of the population inserted in the context. Another factor that influences is related to the use given to this network by its users. They not only use it to disclose personal information as originally intended, but also to share opinions and information on facts and events in general (Naaman, 2010).

This usage feature makes Twitter a people-based news feed (Zhao, 2009), making it a very important tool for two types of user profiles: those who seek information and those who want to spread their information widely (Java, 2007). The combination of these factors makes Twitter an important source of opinions and feelings about events and events that can be analyzed and subsequently used in several areas such as politics, social and even business marketing, as verified by (Li, 2011).

With the emergence of Computational Intelligence techniques, in particular Deep Learning, it is now possible to analyze several texts, including social networks. These techniques give us quite satisfactory results according to the effectiveness of the implemented model.

In this research, the Twitter social network was used where data from @doldiarionline (referring to a local newspaper in the city of Belém) were collected to train a classifier and to be able to categorize if a tweet contains a crime report or not, in a binary way. To classify the tweets, a Recurrent Neural Network (RNN) with LSTM extension (Long-Short Term Memory) was applied. The selection of this network was based on the observation of the works in the literature as (lucca, 2013), which employs this same technique of analysis and demonstrates satisfactory results for classification. This network is also used in applications involving handwriting recognition (Doetsch, 2014), handwriting generation (Graves, 2013), language translation (Luong, 2015), acoustic modeling of speech (Sak, 2014), synthesis of speech (Fan, 2014), audio analysis (Marchi, 2014), video analysis (Zhu, 2017).

The importance of this classification is due to the discovery of knowledge among the relevant data of the social network (Twitter), providing an understanding of the cause and effect relationships in relation to the various issues that refer to crimes such as homicide, femicides, homophobia, and many other types. Such phenomenon is influenced by parameters of the real world society. You can also search for social networking information by distributing projects.

The article is organized in the following sections: Section 2 discusses Recurrent Neural Networks LSTM; Section 3 presents the methodology; section 4 discusses the experiment and the results and in section 5 the final considerations.

2. RECURRENT NEURAL NETWORKS LSTM

These networks use a specific mechanism in their hidden layers, called memory cells. This allows the RNN LSTM to be able to 'remember' the information it has stored even after several iterations occur. It can understand not only the words in the text, but also the order in which they are found (Ghazi, 2019).

There is a dependence of the sequence with which the data occur in time dimension, and the variation occurs in time, where the sense of time in this context means position, sequence, that is, $t + 1$, $t + 2$. An example of its operation is that when the phrase "The house" is read, the letter A follows to the matrix the front where is the word house, that is, the letter A comes from the previous matrix and combines with the matrix the front where is the word house and so on. This way when working with longer sentences your memory is not lost, and when the network reaches the end of the reading there will be an understanding of the complete sentence, just like our brain, where we take into account what happened before (DEEP LEARNING BOOK, 2019).

There are several LSTM drive architectures. A common architecture is composed of a cell (the memory part of the LSTM unit) and three "regulators", commonly called ports, of the information flow inside the LSTM unit: an input port, an output port, and a forgetfulness port. Some variations of the LSTM drive do not have one or more of these gates or perhaps have other gates. For example, blocking recurring units (GRUs) do not have an exit port (Sercu, 2017).

There are connections inside and outside the LSTM ports, some of which are recurrent. The weights of these connections, which need to be learned during training, determine how the doors operate. In Figure 1, we can see an LSTM unit with its internal processes.

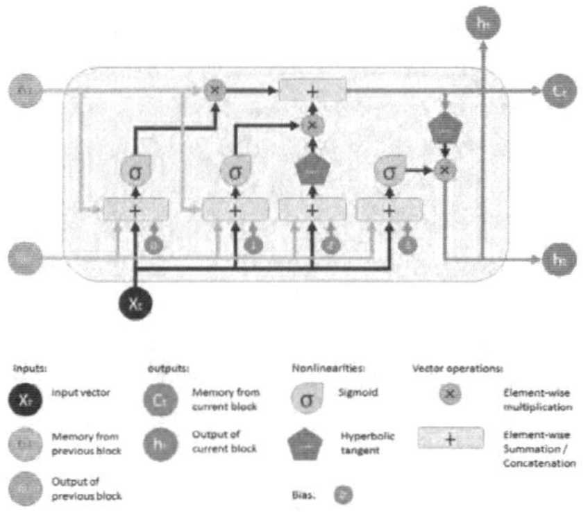

Figure 1. Unit LSTM

The processes are detailed step by step in the items below for a more detailed understanding.

a) Cell State: Partially solves the vanishing problem. In the cell state there is no function, the gradient can flow through the cell state besides passing through the sums and multiplications that ponder what will enter the cell. There is permission to fix all times, partially solving the problem. If we read very long times we can have problems, but there are some adaptations that can read a thousand, five thousand ten thousand times.

b) Forget Gate LSTM: Gates are the multiplicative units. The Forget Gate is responsible for forgetting internal state information that comes from the previous state that will be discarded. This gate is a sigmoid that varies between 0 and 1. At value 1 the intact internal state is maintained. At value 0 the internal state is discarded, it is totally cleaned based on the previous state and also on the input. All operations work with the same idea, that is, based on what is known based on what is being received now, if it determines what to do, the internal state discarded, 1 internal state intact.

c) Input Gate: It is who decides what is going to be inserted as information in the cellular state, which will enter again. Besides forgetting something, there needs to be an update. In this case there is another sigmoid operation, 1 enters all information, 0 does not enter any information. At the moment a $\hat{C}$ is created that is a candidate to a new cellular state and based on that there is an update soon after.

d) Output Gate: It is who determines what new information will be passed to the next time and to exit the Network in its internal state, and if there is a new time, is what will be sent to this new time, also based on the input and the previous state.

Figure 2 illustrates the processes that were respectively cited above.

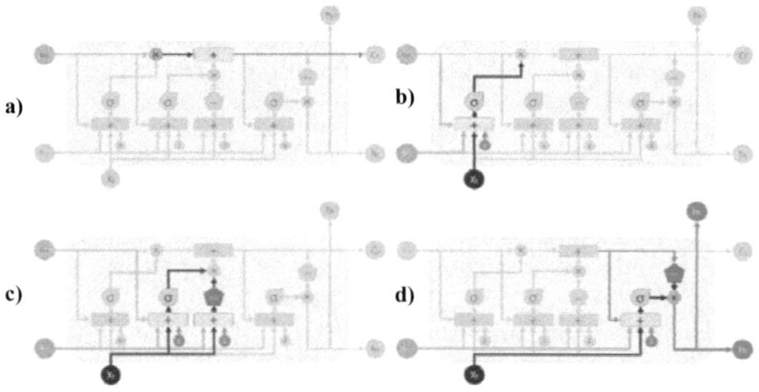

Figure 2. LSTM processes

3. METHODOLOGY

The approach proposed in the preparation of this work follows the following steps: (i) data collection in the social network Twitter, (ii) pre-processing of the data, in order to remove noises and irrelevant terms; (iii) extraction of characteristics of texts for entry into the Network; (iv) Experiments and results through the training of the Neural Network to classify existing categories on the basis of crime or non-crime.

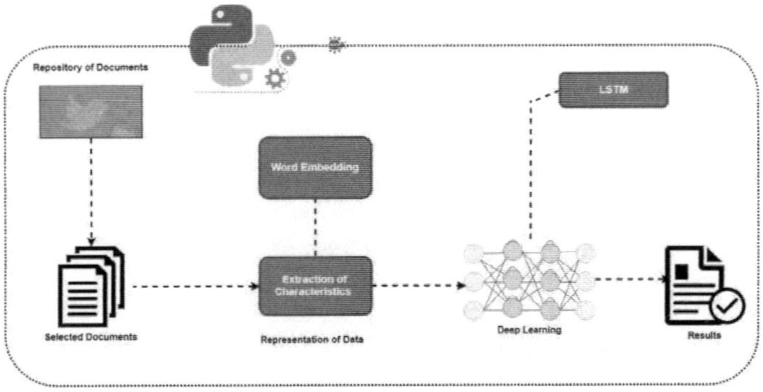

Figure 3. Methodology Flowchart

3.1 Data Collect

The data collection stage for this work was done on twitter, in a period of 2 months on interspersed days, with 3,200 tweets being extracted each day. 20,000 tweets were collected with publications that related to crimes that happened in the city of Belém and others that had no relation with crimes.

3.2 Preprocessing

Preprocessing is the step performed immediately after data collection. This step consisted of separating the tweets into tokens, soon afterwards they removed all the mentions like URLs and emoticons of each of them. Subsequently, the tokens are normalized, that is, they undergo transformations. After normalization, stopwords were removed and soon after the elimination of stemming.

Of a total of 20,000 tweets collected, 1,500 tweets were separated to be labeled in crime and 1,500 tweets to be labeled in non-crime, serving as a basis for learning the Network. This separation and labeling of data in crime, not crime, is given as a supervised model, and in this type of model the Neural Network makes decisions based on the experiences contained in predefined examples (labels) that serve as a sample for its learning. This information has been used explicitly so that the Neural Network can be able to show expected results at the exit of the Network. This labeled base served for the training and learning of the Neural Network. Table 1 shows an example of the database labeled.

Table 1. Table Example of Tweets that Have Been Labeled in crime and naocrime for Network Training

Tweets	Labels
A woman is found dead inside the cemetery	crime
Thieves attack ALEPA to steal copper cables	crime
Remains of four people are found in the interior	crime
Man arrested on charges of raping two children	crime
Fernanda Gentil is tight with language in Russia: It's easy	non-crime
20 years after the defeat, 98's selection finally has revenge	non-crime
Dol wants to know: do you think spanking educates you?	non-crime
Ex-BBB Marcos Harter will be a candidate for federal deputy	non-crime

3.3 Extraction of Characteristics

After the preprocessing step and extraction of the raw data characteristics, an LSTM Recurrent Neural Network was used, where these networks according to the state of the art are widely used for text classification (Poria, 2016), given its effectiveness when it comes to solving problems related to time series. Figure 7 shows the network architecture.

The model for conducting the experiments consists of an architecture that contains four layers: the first is the input layer that receives the documents in time intervals, the second layer is the embedding layer that brings an array with the pre-trained vector representation of the word vocabulary. The third layer is an LSTM layer, where these vector representations enter, and the cell output of the LSTM Network is then fed into a densely connected layer and finally a softmax activation function with two categorical outputs. The number of outputs (units, nodes or neurons) is the dimension of the representational space of the layer, that is, the amount of freedom that the network can learn by an internal representation.

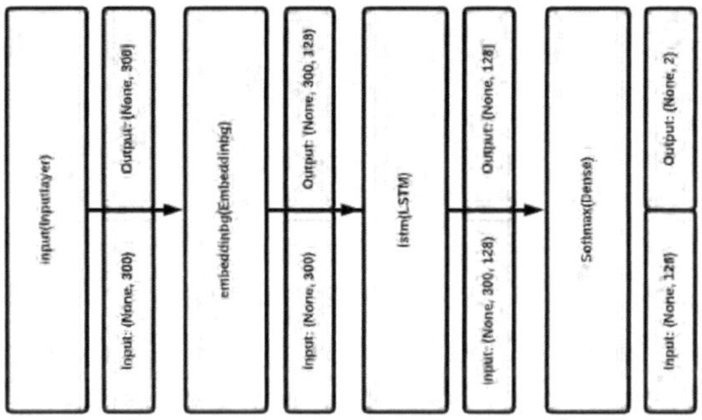

Figure 4. Network Architecture

4. EXPERIMENTS AND RESULTS

The experiments will be presented and the results obtained after the evaluation of the proposed method.

In this step the model was trained and evaluated using a set of hyper parameters with the objective of obtaining better results in the classification of the categories of tweets, crime or non-crime. Table 2 describes the main hyper parameters used in the Neural Network.

Table 2. Configuration of Hyper Parameters

Hyper parameters	description	value
word embeddings	Layer size word embeddings	50
batch_size	Number of samples to be used for each gradient update	30
max_fatures	Reflects the maximum number of words in the dataset maintained in the vocabulary	5000
max_sequence_length	It limits the maximum of the sequences that will be used in the training, the size of the sequences in the dataset are varied, so it is necessary to limit this size and will be used from the beginning to the end of the training	300

4.1 Neural Network Performance

To evaluate the performance of the model, the tweeter tests are not included in the training data set, where the model is presented as a performance indicator after the insertion of the new tweeters as shown in table 3, where we see the Input, which are the entries of new tweets, the description, where the model indicates the due class referred to the Input and finally the percentage of hit that is reached by the model.

A binary_crossentropy loss function, an adam optimizer, and the f1-score metric were used in this network. The metric f1-score is one of the most suitable metrics for unbalanced databases, which is the case of the base used in this work. The data were divided into 20% for the tests, 80% for training. Sixty iterations were performed with the model.

Observing the graphs of figure 5 and figure 6, where a comparison between the training data and the validation data is shown, we can see that the model presented efficient results based on 90% peak accuracy at the end of 60 seasons. When the model is submitted to new tweeters.

Table 3. Table Demonstration Percentage of Correctness of new Description Tweet

Input	Description	Probability
Woman is killed with two head shots	crime	88%
Roberto Carlos show in Belem will be held on Saturday	non-crime	88%
Seven people were murdered at dawn in Belem	crime	89%
Some church members held a fraternization party	non-crime	89%

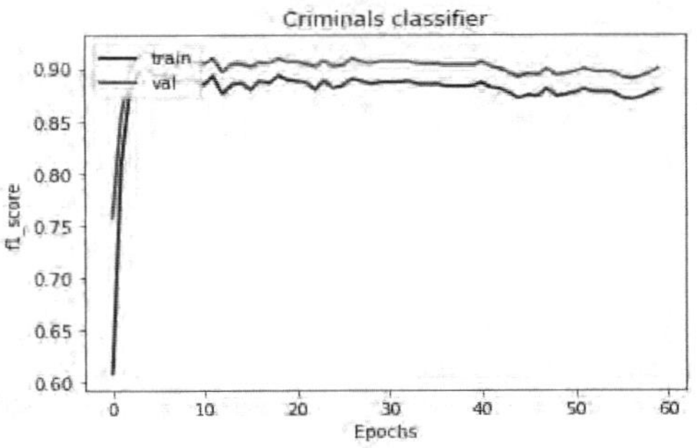

Figure 5. Graphic f1-score of the Model

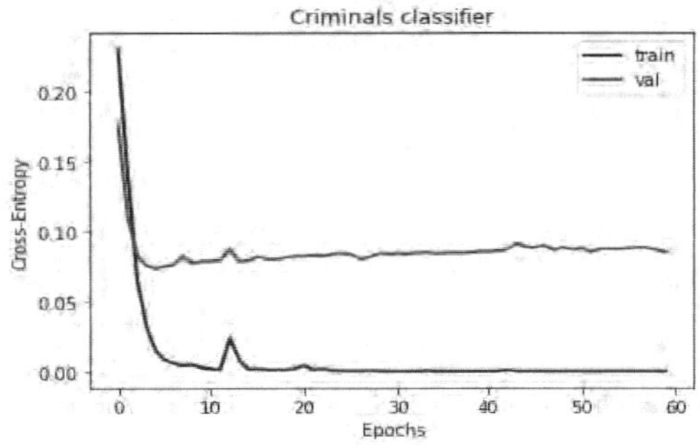

Figure 6. Graphic Crossentropy of the Model

5. CONCLUSION

In the present research was developed and analyzed the application of a Recurrent Neural Network LSTM for the categorization of tweeters in crime or non-crime in the city of Belém. For the development of the same it was necessary to make collections of twitters that had relations with crimes and those that did not had no relation to crimes to have a substantial sampling of the problem domain, thus generating the data set for training and testing, this stage was one of the most laborious because of the need for manual labeling of all used tweets, considering that for the context of the research there is no reference indicating a pre-existing basis.

The results obtained were quite satisfactory, presenting a great advantage in detecting these feelings by means of the classification method, with 90% accuracy, demonstrating that the Recurrent Neural Network LSTM is an efficient method in the proposal of this work. Since the purpose of the research was to demonstrate the potential of the use of the recurrent neural networks LSTM in the context of the classification of tweets related to crime.

In future works, comparisons and evaluations will be carried out with other learning methods used in the literature of feelings analysis in social networks, such as Naíve Bayes and Convolutional Neural Networks to show which would be the best method to categorize tweets related to crimes, as well as change of metrics by analyzing their performance.

Another contribution of this research will be to use the best method of categorizing social networks to create a database of crimes in cities that do not have an organized public database with data on crime, a situation that is recurrent in several Brazilian cities. The creation of this base will enable the obtaining of important information in the understanding of the society, besides assisting in studies and demands to combat the decrease of crime.

ACKNOWLEDGEMENT

A UFPA (Universidade Federal do Pará), PPGEE, CAPES, CNPq.

REFERENCES

CETIC (2014). Apresentac ̧ao dos principais resultados tic domicílios: Acesso em 10 fev 2019.

Data Science Academy (2019). Long short-term memory (lstm). Acesso em: 11 fev. 2019.

Doetsch, P., Kozielski, M., and Ney, H. (2014). Fast and robust training of recurrent neural networks for offline handwriting recognition. In 2014 14th International Conference on Frontiers in Handwriting Recognition, pages 279–284. IEEE.

Fan, Y., Qian, Y., Xie, F.-L., and Soong, F. K. (2014). Tts synthesis with bidirectional lstm based recurrent neural networks. In Fifteenth Annual Conference of the International Speech Communication Association.

Ghazi, M. M., Nielsen, M., Pai, A., Cardoso, M. J., Modat, M., Ourselin, S., Sørensen, L., Initiative, A. D. N., et al. (2019). Training recurrent neural networks robust to incomplete data: Application to alzheimer's disease progression modeling. Medical image analysis, 53:39–46.

Graves, A. (2013). Generating sequences with recurrent neural networks. arXiv preprint arXiv:1308.0850.

Java, A., Song, X., Finin, T., and Tseng, B. (2007). Why we twitter: understanding microblogging usage and communities. In Proceedings of the 9th WebKDD and 1st SNA-KDD 2007 workshop on Web mining and social network analysis, pages 56–65. ACM.

Kaur, A. and Gupta, V. (2014). N-gram based approach for opinion mining of punjabi text. In International Workshop on Multi-disciplinary Trends in Artificial Intelligence, pages 81–88. Springer.

Li, Y.M. and Li, T.-Y. (2011). Deriving marketing intelligence over microblogs. In Proceedings of the 2011 44th Hawaii International Conference on System Sciences, HICSS '11, pages 1–10, Washington, DC, USA. IEEE Computer Society.

Lucca, G., Pereira, I. A., Prisco, A., and Borges, E. N. (2013). Uma implementac ̧ao do algoritmo naıve bayes para classificac ̧ao de texto. Centro de Ciencias Computacionais-Universidade Federal do Rio Grande (FURG).

Luong, M.-T. and Manning, C. D. (2015). Stanford neural machine translation systems for spoken language domains. In Proceedings of the International Workshop on Spoken Language Translation, pages 76–79.

Marchi, E., Ferroni, G., Eyben, F., Gabrielli, L., Squartini, S., and Schuller, B. (2014). Multi-resolution linear prediction based features for audio onset detection with bidirectional lstm neural networks. In 2014 IEEE international conference on acoustics, speech and signal processing (ICASSP), pages 2164–2168. IEEE.

Naaman, M., Boase, J., and Lai, C.-H. (2010). Is it really about me?: Message content in social awareness streams. In Proceedings of the 2010 ACM Conference on Computer Supported Cooperative Work, CSCW '10, pages 189–192, New York, NY, USA. ACM.

Poria, S., Cambria, E., and Gelbukh, A. (2016). Aspect extraction for opinion mining with a deep convolutional neural network. Knowledge-Based Systems, 108:42–49.

Sak, H., Senior, A., and Beaufays, F. (2014). Long short-term memory recurrent neural network architectures for large scale acoustic modeling. In Fifteenth annual conference of the international speech communication association.

Schuller, B., Steidl, S., Batliner, A., Epps, J., Eyben, F., Ringeval, F., Marchi, E., and Zhang, Y. (2014). I (special session)******** the interspeech 2014 computational paralinguistics challenge: Cognitive & physical load. In Fifteenth Annual Conference of the International Speech Communication Association.

Sercu, T., Saon, G., Cui, J., Cui, X., Ramabhadran, B., Kingsbury, B., and Sethy, A. (2017). Network architectures for multilingual speech representation learning. In 2017 IEEE International Conference on Acoustics, Speech and Signal Processing (ICASSP), pages 5295–5299. IEEE.

Twitter (2017). Twitter milestones: a selection of memorable moments.

Zhao, D. and Rosson, M. B. (2009). How and why people twitter: The role that micro-blogging plays in informal communication at work. In Proceedings of the ACM 2009 International Conference on Supporting Group Work, GROUP'09, pages 243–252, New York, NY, USA. ACM.

Zhu, X., Wang, Y., Dai, J., Yuan, L., and Wei, Y. (2017). Flow-guided feature aggregation for video object detection. In The IEEE International Conference on Computer Vision (ICCV).

A STUDY ON BIG DATA FRAMEWORKS AND MACHINE LEARNING TOOL KITS

Imad Sassi and Samir Anter
Computer Science Laboratory of Mohammedia (LIM)
FST Mohammedia, University of Hassan II, Casablanca, Morocco

ABSTRACT

Big Data is an extremely large amount of structured and unstructured data, gathered from a wide range of sources which often require a fast processing and real time analysis. In this new context, the performances of the traditional techniques are limited. However, to handle these bulky quantities of data, new technologies emerged, called Big Data technologies. In fact, the characteristics of Big Data made the exploration process of these data a painful task. This process is called Big Data Analytics. One of the important challenges of Big Data is to search new technologies or to improve and extend the existing platforms, infrastructures and standard techniques to manage the Big Data. Hadoop / MapReduce paradigm and the Spark framework are among the most prominent solutions for large-scale parallel distributed data processing alongside Machine Learning techniques, in particularly, Deep Learning for performing powerful statistical and predictive analysis. In this paper, we first, give an overview, a classification and a comparison of main Big Data technologies. Then, we focus in particular on Machine Learning platforms and libraries, especially those for Deep Learning. The results show that Spark is a general-purpose computation engine thanks to its very generalized solutions.

KEYWORDS

Big Data, Hadoop, Spark, Machine Learning, Deep Learning

1. INTRODUCTION

We currently live in an era marked by the importance of the data. It should be known that in 2019, at every minute, 4 million Google queries sent, 350000 tweets, 7 million snapshots sent on Snapchat, 216 million photos liked on Facebook and 2.4 million photos liked on Instagram and 400 hours of videos uploaded to YouTube. Today, there is more than 4.2 billion internet users who generate and disseminate data. All the signals suggest that the massive production of data is only in its early infancy. Consequently, the advent, since the early 2000s, of the notion of "Big Data" with which multiple challenges, related to the volume, the variety and the velocity, have emerged (Chen et al., 2014). As a result, scientists and companies are now focusing not only on data storage but especially on designing solutions to understand and demystify this huge amount of data to extract value. It is the exploitation of the potential of these data that is promising. Indeed, several Big Data technologies have emerged and their use by large companies, especially the giants of the Web, has become a necessity. These technologies include those that optimize processing time on giant databases such as NoSQL (Han et al., 2011) (Not Only SQL) databases (e.g., MongoDB (Chodorow, 2013), Cassandra (Carpenter, & Hewitt, 2016)). Also, among these technologies, the server infrastructures make it possible to distribute the processing on thousands of nodes. This is called Massively Parallel Processing. The Hadoop paradigm is undoubtedly the best known of them (White, 2012). It combines the Hadoop Distributed File System (Shvachko et al., 2010), the NoSQL HBase database (George, 2011) and the MapReduce framework (Dean, & Ghemawat, 2008). Moreover, others Big Data technologies, aimed at moving towards more real-time processing, have emerged (e.g., Storm (Leibiusky et al., 2012), Samza (Noghabi et al., 2017)). Others offer a hybrid system for batch and stream processing such as Apache Spark (Zaharia et al., 2010). There are also complementary technologies for data collection like Kafka (Kreps et al. 2011), data integration like Flume (Hoffman, 2015), coordination and workflow such as Zookeeper (Junqueira, & Reed, 2013) or the system deployment like Ambari (Wadkar, & Siddalingaiah, 2014). To process a large amount of data, there are analytical application tools also called Big Data Analytics. One of the most used and certainly the most powerful solutions of Big Data Analytics is Machine Learning (Mitchell et al., 1990). In this area, several libraries and platforms are implemented and can be easily integrated into Big Data frameworks. Apache Mahout (Lyubimov, & Palumbo, 2016), Spark's MLlib (Meng et al., 2016) and Python Scikit-learn (Pedregosa et al., 2011) are examples. Deep Learning (LeCun et al., 2015) is, certainly, one of the most promising Machine Learning techniques, whose software transpositions have produced results that surpass, in a number of use cases, traditional algorithmic approaches. Various tools for Deep Learning, are currently available and are used in different applications areas. Among these, TensorFlow (Abadi et al., 2016), Caffe (Jia et al., 2016) and Deeplearning4j (Team, 2016).

Our main contributions can be summarized as follows: (i) a review and analysis of the main Big Data technologies and the challenges they face; (ii) a classification of its frameworks according to the processing mode (i.e. batch or streaming); (iii) a comparison of these main Big Data frameworks based on several criteria, presenting their advantages and disadvantages. The rest of the paper is organized as follows: In section 4, Big Data Machine Learning tools, mainly those of Deep Learning, are studied and discussed. Sections 5 and 6 conclude the paper and discuss directions for future work.

2. BIG DATA SYSTEM

2.1 Big Data Definition

The definitions of Big Data are diverse. One of the well-known definitions was proposed by International Data Corporation (IDC), which defines Big Data as follows: "Big Data Technologies describes a new generation of technologies and architectures, designed to economically extract the value from very large volumes of a wide variety of data, allowing a high speed of capture, discovery and / or analysis" (Gantz, & Reinsel, 2011). It is an extension of Douglas Laney's "3Vs" model, which indicates that challenges and opportunities for growth are three-dimensional data, namely increasing volume, velocity and variety.

2.2 Big Data Value Chain

Generally, in a specific Big Data system, there are four phases: data generation, data acquisition, data storage and data analysis. These phases compose what is called a Big Data value chain, as shown in "Figure 1".

2.2.1 Big Data Generation

The first phase of the Big Data system is the Big Data generation. It's about how data is generated. There are diverse and complex data generated from various longitudinal and / or distributed data sources.

2.2.2 Big Data Acquisition

The second phase of the Big Data system is Big Data acquisition, which includes data collecting, data transmission and data pre-processing (Lyko et al., 2016).

2.2.3 Big Data Storage

This phase of the Big Data system includes not only the storage, but also the management of large-scale datasets. In addition to analyzing or interacting with stored data, storage systems must provide several interface, quick query and other programming models (Siddiqa et al., 2017).

2.2.4 Big Data Analysis

Big Data analysis is the last and most important step in the Big Data system value chain. Big Data analysis is the process of using analytical tools, algorithms and methods to inspect, transform and model data to uncover hidden potential of Big Data. This is called Big Data Analytics.

To be able to process and analyze Big Data, several frameworks and tools are developed. In the next section, we present the main Big Data technologies. We also present, in the same section, a comparative study of these frameworks (Chintapalli et al., 2016; Gradvohl et al., 2014; Zhang et al., 2017).

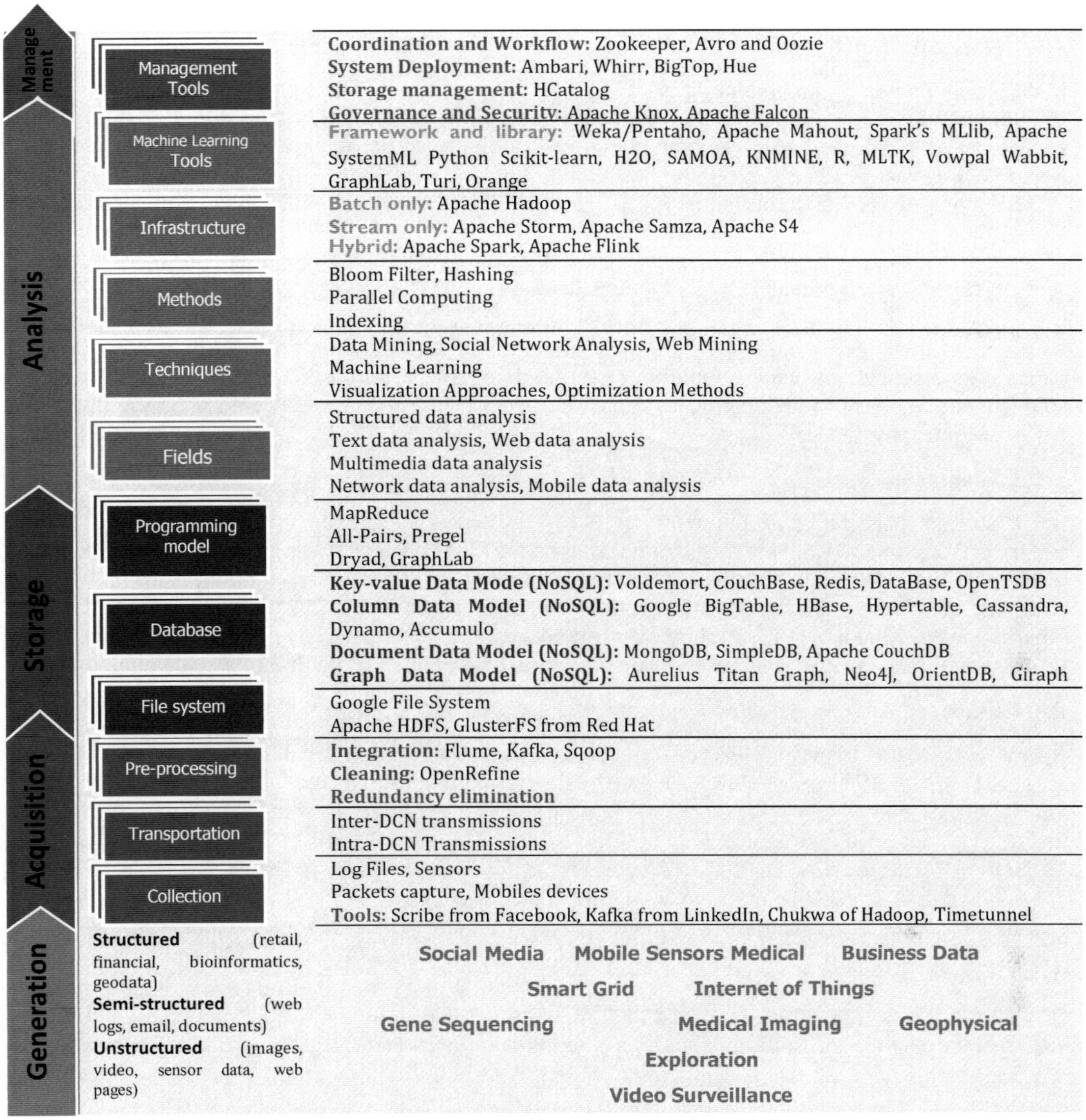

Figure 1. Big Data System value chain

3. TECHNOLOGIES AND TOOLS FOR BIG DATA ANALYTICS

3.1 Stream vs Batch Processing Frameworks

Depending on the processing time, Big Data analysis can be classified into two paradigms: Stream processing and Batch processing. Stream processing is suitable for applications where the data requires rapid processing and analysis and whose analytical results need to be returned in a very short time. Storm is one of the main frameworks of this processing mode. However, Batch processing is generally used for applications that do not require a high response time. In this processing mode, the data is first stored and then analyzed. MapReduce, actually, is the dominant model of Batch processing.

In the following, we will discuss the main Big Data frameworks for batch and stream processing and we will focus, in particular, on open source frameworks.

3.1.1 Hadoop/MapReduce

MapReduce is a parallel programming model for very large amounts of data processing developed by Google in 2003 with a specific file management system (Google File System) (Ghemawat et al., 2003). The basic strategy of MapReduce is to divide and conquer. The divide and conquer method is implemented in two steps: Map step and Reduce step.

Hadoop is an open source framework developed in 2008 to better generalize the use of massively parallel storage and processing of MapReduce and Google File System. It is widely used to perform Big Data analysis that support large volume of data distributed applications. Hadoop consists of many components and several related projects including YARN (Vavilapalli et al., 2013), Pig, Hive, Sqoop and HBase.

3.1.2 Dryad

Dryad is a framework for running applications on multiple servers (Isard et al., 2007). Programs based on this solution can be ported to multiple nodes. It is a clustered platform for large-scale clustering. It is based on dataflow graph processing.

3.1.3 Spark

Spark is the next generation paradigm for Big Data processing. Its main goal is to extend Hadoop to a general framework that adopts Resilient Distributed Datasets (RDDs) (Zaharia et al., 2012) in memory computation technique and to offer fault tolerance without replication.

Spark includes seven main components: Spark core of data engine, Spark Cluster Manager (includes Hadoop, Apache Mesos (Hindman et al., 2011) and built-in Standalone cluster manager), Spark SQL, Spark Streaming (Zaharia et al., 2013), Spark Machine Learning Library, Spark GraphX and Spark programming tools.

3.1.4 Flink

It is an open source framework that offers batch and stream processing capabilities for distributed Big Data (Carbone et al., 2015). It provides data distribution, communication and fault tolerance for distributed computing.

3.1.5 Storm

It is a distributed, scalable and fault-tolerant open source framework designed for stream processing used for real-time analytics, distributed Machine Learning and many other cases (Leibiusky et al., 2012).

3.1.6 Samza

It is an open source framework for distributed stream processing. It uses Kafka for messaging and YARN for fault tolerance, processor isolation, security and resource management (Noghabi et al., 2017).

3.1.7 S4

S4 is a pluggable, distributed, scalable, fault-tolerant plug-in platform for processing continuous unbounded streaming data (Neumeyer et al., 2010). Since 2011, it has become an Apache Incubator project.

Table 1. summarizes the results of a comparative study presenting the most important characteristics, advantages and disadvantages of the main Big Data frameworks.

4. BIG DATA MACHINE LEARNING TOOLS

The major problem of Big Data is not the collection and the storage, but the evaluation of these data. Among the techniques used to extract knowledge from raw data, Machine Learning techniques are the most dominant. It is a branch of Artificial Intelligence that aims to build systems that learn from the received data. Building a system begins by training the machine from a known set of data. Once the system is trained, it must be confronted to the real world and evaluated regularly so that it corrects itself and improves with each new received data. This principle of Machine Learning explains its renewed interest with the appearance of Big Data.

Table 1. Big Data Frameworks Comparison

	Batch vs Streaming	Characteristics and comparison with other frameworks	Advantages	Disadvantages
Hadoop/ MapReduce	Batch	efficiency of programming model (MapReduce) better in terms of material costs than some alternatives Database: HDFS languages: JAVA, PIG LATIN, HiveQL	scalability -robustness - fault tolerance -handling of huge datasets	problem of speed of execution and processing - limited SQL support - inefficient iterative algorithms
Spark	Batch and Streaming	run a more general directed acyclic graph (DAG) with more operators than MapReduce -complete the MapReduce feature with a rich set of transformations - supports memory processing unlike MapReduce whose use storage allows Intermediate data logging - easy integration with Hadoop ecosystem tools - exploits main memory unlike Storm - RDD units are larger than Storm tuples - more resource consumption than MapReduce	scalability - fault tolerance -polyvalence -flexible computing -facility and speed of use - ingestion from various platforms (Kafka, Flume, Kinesis) - high-level streaming abstraction (DStream) - richness of the ecosystem of libraries (MLlib)	Its execution cost more compared to disk-based systems
Flink	Batch and Streaming	integrates with YARN and HDFS - unlike Spark, Flink does not require manual optimization or adjustment - Unlike Flink, Spark users can control persistence and partition scheme on nodes -Flink performs iterations as cyclic data flows unlike Spark which executes them by loop unrolling	Low latency -high throughput and real entry-by-entry processing - excellent Streaming Windows flexibility for streaming model	remains a young project that does not have tools around yet - large scale deployments are not as common as other processing frameworks
Storm	Streaming	Unlike Spark, Storm is very difficult to develop applications with and has limited resources available in the market - have a very wide language support more than most processing frameworks - easily integrates with existing Big Data technologies	distributed, scalable and fault-tolerant processing - provides competitive performance - real-time Machine Learning - high speed and scalability	does not provide message control guarantees - it is not suitable for applications requiring clusters of several thousand nodes
Samza	Streaming	offers high-level abstractions that are easier to use than other systems such as Storm - unlike Storm, it does not have the same language flexibility - only supports JVM languages.	ability to store state using fault-tolerant control checkpointing system - Kafka direct write capability eliminates backpressure problems	use of a Kafka-like queuing system appears to be restrictive -does not provide accurate recovery of aggregate status in failure
S4	Streaming	many competitive properties - automatically manage communication, scheduling and distribution across nodes -process continuous unbounded streams of data	scalability -robustness - fault-tolerant - effectiveness in cluster management	no support for dynamic load balancing -only supports partial fault tolerance

We present below, the main Big Data Machine Learning projects, including the Deep Learning tools.

4.1 Machine Learning Tools

4.1.1 Mahout

It is a very rich and complete library of Machine Learning which covers in particular the algorithms of classification and clustering. It distributes its computational algorithms using the Map/Reduce paradigm (Lyubimov, & Palumbo, 2016).

4.1.2 Spark MLlib

This is a scalable Machine Learning library built in Apache Spark designed for high quality algorithms 100 times faster than MapReduce. It offers tools for feature extraction, transformation and basic statistics (Meng et al., 2016).

4.1.3 Python Scikit-learn

It is an open source Machine Learning library. It provides a simple and effective solutions to learning problems. Scikit supports preprocessing, classical algorithms, feature and model selection algorithms (Pedregosa et al., 2011).

4.1.4 SystemML

Apache SystemML provides automatic generation of optimized runtime plans ranging from single node computing, in memory, to distributed computations on Hadoop and Spark (Pansare et al., 2018).

4.1.5 WEKA

WEKA (Waikato Environment for Knowledge Analysis) is one of the most widely used Java-based Machine Learning software developed at the University of Waikato, New Zealand (Holmes et al., 1994).

4.1.6 H2O

H2O is an open source, in-memory, distributed, fast and scalable predictive analytics and Machine Learning platform (Cook, 2016).

4.2 Deep Learning Tools

In this section, we discuss the most popular Deep Learning tools and libraries.

4.2.1 TensorFlow

It is a complete Python library. It is made open source by Google in November 2015. It is a set of mathematical functions and calculation methods to develop Machine Learning functions (Abadi et al., 2016).

4.2.2 Caffe

It is a Deep Learning library designed to easily express all types of models such as CNN and RNN in a friendly python-based API and run them using an efficient back-end expressed in C++ and CUDA (Jia et al., 2014).

4.2.3 Deeplearning4j

DeepLearning4J (DL4J) is a Deep Learning library developed in Java language (and JVM languages) to solve problems involving huge amounts of data in a reasonable amount of time (Team, 2016).

4.2.4 Torch

Torch (called Torch7) is an open source Deep Learning library developed by Ronan Collobert. Torch uses C / C ++ libraries as well as CUDA for GPU (Collobert et al., 2002).

5. DISCUSSION

With the advent of Big Data, several technologies have emerged, including NoSQL databases and Massively Parallel Processing frameworks. Scientists and companies can choose, depending on their needs, their use case and application requirements, between a vast array of Big Data frameworks for batch processing only, for stream processing only or for a hybrid processing. Hadoop and its MapReduce processing framework is an excellent choice for batch processing model. This one is best suited for handling very large data sets that are not time-sensitive. It offers excellent compatibility and integration with other frameworks and Big Data technologies. In addition, in terms of the cost of the necessary components, Hadoop is inexpensive and efficient for many applications. For stream processing requiring very strict latency, Storm and Samza are a very good choice. Both support many programming languages. Storm is used when unique processing guarantees are needed, it offers competitive performance. Spark’s comparison with Storm Streaming shows Spark's performance on Storm. Indeed, Spark is a versatile computation engine thanks to its very general solutions. It offers a complete and unified framework because it can be used in batch processing, stream processing, interactive processing as well as iterative processing. This is the right choice for Big Data processing for different data sets of different nature (e.g., text, image, video, graphics) as well as different sources (batch mode or real time). Unlike Storm, which is very difficult to develop with limited resources on the market, Spark is simple, flexible, integrates very well with the Hadoop ecosystem and can primarily handle many types of problems. Spark, offering the possibility to use both modes of processing simultaneously, has many other advantages especially speed, simplicity, scalability, additional modules proposed and easier integration with other tools of the Hadoop ecosystem, but also the possibility of using Machine Learning tools. Apache Spark, is without doubt, a common framework for different types of data processing. For example, real-time data analytics, structured data processing, graph processing, etc. Alongside the explosion of Big Data, several innovations in Machine Learning have emerged, including Mahout, Spark MLlib, Python Scikit-learn and others. Generally, MLlib's dependence on Spark's iterative batch and streaming approaches, as well as its use of in-memory computation, allows tasks to run much faster than those using Mahout.

6. CONCLUSION AND FUTURE WORK

The amount of digital data circulating around the world is considerable and will continue to increase in the years to come. The main driver of this growth is the digitization of human life, represented by two main components: connected computing and technology and the Internet of Things. Big Data technologies are fortunately there to help manage the large amounts of data transiting through its ecosystem, but also to explore new data, including those characterized by the speed of the flows it generates. In this work, we studied the major Big Data technologies by referring to the Big Data system value chain. We also evaluated the main batch and stream processing platforms based on several criteria. Much work remains to be done to increase the performance of Big Data technologies to meet the challenges it faces. In this direction, Deep Learning is at the forefront of Machine Learning with great promise. It has demonstrated that it is extremely promising for many areas of Big Data Machine Learning. Cloud computing is also a fertile area of Big Data. It is a highly achievable technology that attracts a large number of researchers to develop it and try to apply it to Big Data issues. From an algorithmic point of view, it's very natural to think about improving or extending the performance of traditional Machine Learning algorithms to make them more suitable for the context of large-scale data or to search for new algorithms that may be good solutions for Big Data Analytics.

REFERENCES

Abadi, M. et al, 2016. TensorFlow: A System for Large-Scale Machine Learning. In *12th {USENIX} Symposium on Operating Systems Design and Implementation ({OSDI}16)* (pp. 265-283).

Carbone, P. et al, 2015. Apache flink: Stream and batch processing in a single engine. *Bulletin of the IEEE Computer Society Technical Committee on Data Engineering*, 36(4).

Carpenter, J. et al, 2016. *Cassandra: The Definitive Guide: Distributed Data at Web Scale.* " O'Reilly Media, Inc.".

Chen, M. et al, 2014. Big data: A survey. *Mobile networks and applications*, 19(2), 171-209.

Chintapalli, S. et al, 2016. Benchmarking streaming computation engines: storm, flink and spark streaming. In *Parallel and Distributed Processing Symposium Workshops, 2016 IEEE International* (pp. 1789-1792). IEEE.

Chodorow, K., 2013. *MongoDB: The Definitive Guide: Powerful and Scalable Data Storage.* " O'Reilly Media, Inc.".

Collobert, R. et al, 2002. *Torch: a modular machine learning software library* (No. REP_WORK). Idiap.

Cook, D., 2016. *Practical machine learning with H2O: powerful, scalable techniques for deep learning and AI.* " O'Reilly Media, Inc.".

Dean, J., and Ghemawat, S., 2008. MapReduce: simplified data processing on large clusters. *Communications of the ACM*, 51(1), 107-113.

Gantz, J., and Reinsel, D., 2011. Extracting value from chaos. *IDC iview*, 1142(2011), 1-12.

George, L., 2011. *HBase: the definitive guide: random access to your planet-size data.* " O'Reilly Media, Inc.".

Ghemawat, S. et al, 2003. The Google file system.

Gradvohl, A. L. S. et al, 2014. Comparing distributed online stream processing systems considering fault tolerance issues. *Journal of Emerging Technologies in Web Intelligence*, 6(2), 174-179.

Han, J. et al, 2011. Survey on NoSQL database. In *2011 6th international conference on pervasive computing and applications* (pp. 363-366). IEEE.

Hindman, B. et al, 2011. Mesos: A platform for fine-grained resource sharing in the data center. In *NSDI* (Vol. 11, No. 2011, pp. 22-22).

Hoffman, S., 2015. *Apache flume: Distributed log collection for hadoop*. Packt Publishing Ltd.

Holmes, G. et al, 1994. Weka: A machine learning workbench.

Isard, M. et al, 2007. Dryad: distributed data-parallel programs from sequential building blocks. In *ACM SIGOPS operating systems review* (Vol. 41, No. 3, pp. 59-72). ACM.

Jia, Y. et al, 2014. Caffe: Convolutional architecture for fast feature embedding. In *Proceedings of the 22nd ACM international conference on Multimedia* (pp. 675-678). ACM.

Junqueira, F., and Reed, B., 2013. *ZooKeeper: distributed process coordination*. " O'Reilly Media, Inc.".

Kreps, J. et al, 2011. Kafka: A distributed messaging system for log processing. In *Proceedings of the NetDB* (pp. 1-7).

LeCun, Y. et al, 2015. *Deep learning*. nature, 521(7553), 436.

Leibiusky, J. et al, 2012. *Getting started with storm*. " O'Reilly Media, Inc.".

Lyko, K. et al, 2016. Big data acquisition. In *New Horizons for a Data-Driven Economy* (pp. 39-61). Springer, Cham.

Lyubimov, D., and Palumbo, A., 2016. Apache Mahout: Beyond MapReduce. *CreateSpace Independent Publishing Platform*.

Meng, X. et al, 2016. Mllib: Machine learning in apache spark. *The Journal of Machine Learning Research*, 17(1), 1235-1241.

Mitchell, T. et al, 1990. *Machine learning. Annual review of computer science*, 4(1), 417-433.

Neumeyer, L. et al, 2010. S4: Distributed stream computing platform. In *Data Mining Workshops (ICDMW), 2010 IEEE International Conference on* (pp. 170-177). IEEE.

Noghabi, S. A. et al, 2017. Samza: stateful scalable stream processing at LinkedIn. *Proceedings of the VLDB Endowment*, 10(12), 1634-1645.

Pansare, N. et al, 2018. Deep Learning with Apache SystemML. *arXiv preprint arXiv*:1802.04647.

Pedregosa, F. et al, 2011. Scikit-learn: Machine learning in Python. *Journal of machine learning research*, 12(Oct), 2825-2830.

Shvachko, K. et al, 2010. The hadoop distributed file system. In *MSST* (Vol. 10, pp. 1-10).

Siddiqa, A. et al, 2017. Big data storage technologies: a survey. *Frontiers of Information Technology & Electronic Engineering*, 18(8), 1040-1070.

Team, D., 2016. *Deeplearning4j: Open-source distributed deep learning for the jvm*. Apache Software Foundation License, 2.

Vavilapalli, V. K. et al, 2013. Apache hadoop yarn: Yet another resource negotiator. In *Proceedings of the 4th annual Symposium on Cloud Computing* (p. 5). ACM.

Wadkar, S., and Siddalingaiah, M., 2014. Apache ambari. In *Pro Apache Hadoop* (pp. 399-401). Apress, Berkeley, CA.

White, T., 2012. *Hadoop: The definitive guide*. " O'Reilly Media, Inc.".

Zaharia, M. et al, 2010. Spark: Cluster computing with working sets. *HotCloud*, 10(10-10), 95.

Zaharia, M. et al, 2012. Resilient distributed datasets: A fault-tolerant abstraction for in-memory cluster computing. In *Proceedings of the 9th USENIX conference on Networked Systems Design and Implementation* (pp. 2-2). USENIX Association.

Zaharia, M. et al, 2013. Discretized streams: Fault-tolerant streaming computation at scale. In *Proceedings of the twenty-fourth ACM symposium on operating systems principles* (pp. 423-438). ACM.

Zhang, K. et al, 2017. A Comparison of Distributed Machine Learning Platforms. In *2017 26th International Conference on Computer Communication and Networks (ICCCN)* (pp. 1-9). IEEE.

EMOTION ANALYSIS OF TWEETS USING DEEP LEARNING TECHNIQUES

Sahil Bhatnagar, Sagar Malik and Niladri Chatterjee
Indian Institute of Technology, Delhi, India

ABSTRACT

Microblogging is one of the most prominent forms of communication among internet users today. These services offer users a tool to share opinions on a plethora of issues and aspects of their lives, and hence, they are rich data sources for textual analysis, and offer vast potential to gain insight into the way people communicate. We examine the task of emotion analysis of twitter data and design a neural network architecture for the task of classifying each tweet into one of five emotion categories: joy, sadness, anger, laughter and fear. We also show a method to automatically collect and tag a corpus of data for emotion analysis. Our experiments showed that our models outperform current state of the art techniques for the proposed problem.

KEYWORDS

Emotion Analysis, Deep Learning, LSTM, Twitter

1. INTRODUCTION

Microblogging sites are a source of varied opinions and emotions, with millions of messages constantly exchanged on a vast spectrum of domains. The active user base of Twitter alone stands at over 330 million users (Statista, 2018). People express opinions about their life, the products or services they use, of problems they face and on social, religious and political issues. Many of these opinions have emotions associated with them, and understanding these emotions has vast applications for different organizations. For example, a company might want to know how people respond to their current marketing campaign, social organizations and NGOs may want to understand how people feel about present social issues or political parties may want to understand what people think of their policies and/or candidates. Given the vast number of users on microblogging sites, and especially on Twitter, who express their thoughts and opinions on the above issues, it is an important avenue for a range of organizations to mine and analyze the emotions of the users. Additionally, emotion analysis of text can serve as a step in the pipeline for other complex tasks, such as accessibility frameworks involving text-to-speech, where having knowledge of the emotion of the sentence can lead to more nuanced speech output.

Emotions expressed by humans have been classified into multiple types, from Ekmans list of 6 basic emotions to the more comprehensive Plutchik's Wheel of Emotions (Plutchik, 1989). In our paper, we condense the emotions analyzed into 5 categories: happiness, sadness, anger, laughter and fear (Chin et al., 2016). Thus, our problem is fundamentally a multi-class classification task. The fundamental pipeline for the task is as described in figure 2.

For our task, we restricted the data to the category of political tweets. We collected a corpus of over 18000 tweets evenly distributed among the top 2016 US presidential election candidates: Donald Trump, Hillary Clinton, Bernie Sanders and Ben Carson, which we automatically tagged using methodology described later. For experiments involving Hindi, we use a corpus of around 20000 Hindi tweets evenly distributed amongst various Indian political leaders and parties. We perform some basic linguistic analysis and describe some basic pre-processing and data cleaning techniques that we applied. We then describe and analyze deep learning techniques to model the classification problem, and proceed to create a model which outperforms present state-of-the-art techniques in the domain of emotion analysis of tweets.

We have organized the rest of this paper into 7 following sections. In section 2, we do survey current literature and discuss previous works on sentiment and emotion analysis of tweets. In section 3, we discuss our technique to automatically collect and annotate tweets. In section 4, we describe our pre-processing steps and analyze the resulting corpus. In section 5, we present our baseline neural network model. In section 6, we present our new state of the art long short term memory (LSTM) neural network model. In section 7, we analyze the results, compare the different models and give insights into the same. We conclude and discuss some avenues of future research in section 8.

1.1 Contributions

The contributions of our paper are as follows:

- We present a scalable, automated method of collecting and annotating tweets with their respective emotion. This allows us to collect arbitrary large corpora of data for emotion analysis tasks
- We devise a model which allows us to solve the problem for tweets of any language
- We perform experimental evaluation of our model prove the efficacy of our solution and show that it performs better than previous work

2. LITERATURE SURVEY

Sentiment analysis at different levels of granularity has been worked on and is a significant field of interest for NLP researchers. Recently, there has been a lot of research on sentiment analysis of microblogging data in particular. Some of the popular early work has been done by Go et al. (2009), Bermingham and Smeaton (2010) and Pak and Paroubek (2010). Much of their work has been done to classify tweets into 3 basic categories of sentiments, positive, negative and neutral. The fundamental models used are built using Naive Bayes, MaxEntropy and SVMs. Many researchers have used distant learning methods to curate the datasets, for example, using tweets with emoticons to serve as noisy labels to the data. For the feature space, Go et al. (2009) used a combination of unigrams and bigrams based feature spaces along with features derived from POS tags. Pak and Paroubek (2010) used similar features, but differed in the way they curated their dataset and their use of entropy measures to choose more discriminative n-gram features. Barbosa and Feng (2010) additionally used Twitter specific syntax features like hashtags, links and exclamation tags in addition to using prior polarity of words (derived from various sentiment lexicons) and their POS tags. Agarwal et al. (2011) furthered the ideas of Barbosa and Feng (2010) by using real valued polarity lexicon like WordNet, and gave an in-depth analysis of the effect of various features. Their conclusions stated that tweet syntax features only marginally improved classification accuracy, while the most important features were the prior-polarity of parts-of-speech.

Fundamentally, the above works focus on feature engineering, which is different to our approach of learning the features automatically while training our model on large distantly supervised tweet corpora. Tang et al. (2014) have worked on techniques to automatically learn sentiment specific word embeddings (SSWE) and have developed a corresponding deep learning model "Coooolll". Severyn and Moschitti (2015) performed sentiment analysis using deep convolutional neural networks.

In the explicit domain of emotion classification, Alm et al. (2005) worked on emotion analysis of story text, and created features using WordNet lexicon, POS tags, punctuation and bag of words. Microsoft (2015) has publicly published some of their work on the task of emotion classification using deep learning on annotated data from the Mechanical Turk. Their model was a relatively simple 3-layer deep neural network used along with word embeddings obtained from the public domain such as GloVe (Pennington et al., 2014). Thomas et al. (2014) used a multinomial Naive Bayes approach using unigram features for the identification of emotions in the text to one of seven classes, as defined in the ISEAR (Scherer and Wallbott, 1994) dataset. Razek and Frasson (2017) built individual models for each emotion using a Dominant Meaning tree model, and chooses the emotion with the highest score for a given sentence representation.

3. AUTOMATED CORPUS COLLECTION

We used a combination of Twitter API and web-scraping techniques to collect tweets. We only considered tweets which contained keywords such as "Donald Trump", "Trump", "Hillary", "Clinton", "Sanders", "Modi",

"BJP", "Gandhi", "Congress" etc. in order to restrict them to the primary subjects. The tweets scraped in English were primarily concerned with the 2016 US elections and the candidates, whereas for Hindi, recent tweets in the run up to the 2019 Indian Parliamentary elections about various key figures have been considered.

Multiple studies have been done on the correlation of the emojis used in a tweet and the corresponding emotion of the text. There has been a strong correspondence between the emotion intended and the use of emojis is (Novak et al., 2015). Additionally, since tweets are restricted in length, they generally comprise of only 1 sentence, or a couple of related sentences. Hence, the emojis used can be expected to correspond to the emotion of the tweet at large. Thus, we used a distant supervision model of using the emojis to assign emotion classes to each tweet. We collected millions of tweets of which around 100,000 contained emojis. Of those, around 44000 of them contained emojis which were associated with an emotion in our lexicon. Figure 1 gives the lexicon we used to annotate the tweets with the corresponding emotion. When considering Hindi tweets, the lexicon stayed the same except for the emotions associated with the National Flag emojis.

Figure 1. The lexicon used to automatically tag tweets to emotion classes (Chin et al., 2016)

In tweets which contained more than one emoji, we assigned the emotion which was associated with the maximum number of emojis in that tweet. In the cases of a tie, we rejected that tweet.

4. CORPUS ANALYSIS AND PROCESSING

The distribution of emotions in the dataset is given in table 1. For the ISEAR data, there are 1076 sentences for each of the 7 emotion classes (Scherer and Wallbott, 1994).

Table 1. Confusion matrix generated on a randomized blind test set of 4728 tweets

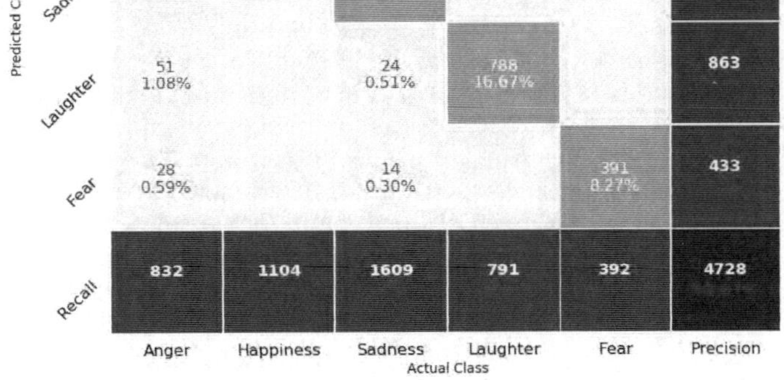

Table 2. Per emotion count of tweets for either dataset

Language	Joy	Fear	Sadness	Anger	Laughter
English	2843	2439	6740	12241	7316
Hindi	5164	2889	3249	8043	2573

Before passing the tweets in the neural network architecture, some basic preprocessing steps were performed (Garg and Chatterjee, 2014). These are crucial in order to reduce the size of the vocabulary while keeping only relevant words. The following were the steps to clean and process the tweets:

- *Tokenization* - The most important of these steps is tokenizing the tweet, for which we used the nltk (Bird et al., 2009) TweetTokenizer. This allowed us to get tokens while maintaining the integrity of URLs, @mentions and hashtags, along with punctuation like exclamation marks.
- *Stopword Removal* - We then removed stopwords which generally do not play a role in determining sentiments, like articles and some prepositions.
- *Filtering* - We removed URLs, @mentions and numbers using specially constructed regexes, and also removed punctuation like quotes, commas etc
- *Lemmatization* - We used the nltk's WordNet lemmatizer to reduce words. This played a significant role by reducing the size of the vocabulary by almost 15%. We couldn't apply this step for Hindi, since reliable lemmatizers aren't readily available for the language.

5. MODELS

Instead of working on hand-crafted features to perform emotion analysis we abstracted that task to neural networks in addition to word embeddings which capture semantic meaning of words. In the first sub-section, we describe a basic neural network architecture and associated models with their potential shortcomings. In the second sub-section, we describe the architecture of the LSTM based deep-learning model that outperformed the standard models. For all models, a masking layer was used to pad shorter tweets/sentences with a token word in order to keep all sentences of the same size.

5.1 Neural Networks

The first step in the architecture is to represent words in a vector space format. We used pre trained embeddings from the Global Vectors for Word Representation (GloVe) (Pennington et al., 2014) project to represent each word in a 100-dimensional vector. Further, in order to get a vector representation of the sentence constituted by the words i.e. the sentence vector, we tried 2 different approaches.

- *Mean of vectors of words in a sentence* - Since word-vectors also represent in some way, the sentiment behind every word, taking the mean across all the words describes the overall emotion vector for the sentence (Arora et al., 2016).
- *Element-wise max across the word vectors* - If we assume that underlying emotions of words are also captured by the word embedding, with different emotions being mapped to different dimensions, then taking the max of the dimensions may give us the emotion vector of the sentence.

Once a sentence vector is obtained, it was passed into a Neural Network with 5 Dense Layers. The models obtained were much faster than other deep learning models with considerably smaller number of learning parameters and had fairly high accuracy. The problem while taking the mean across all the words is that equal importance is given to all the words in a sentence whereas some words can be neutral while others can strongly represent an emotion like anger or laughter. The models does not capture the relationships between the words of a sentence. Therefore, the semantic meaning of the sentence gets lost if a sentence contains both positive and negative words. To overcome the above challenges, we use LSTM models.

5.2 Long-Short Term Memory Neural Networks

LSTM networks can be applied to get appropriate semantic meaning of the sentence as it effectively detects the keywords while attenuating less important words in the sentence automatically by switching on and off the gates within the LSTM cells. LSTMs being a special kind of Recurrent Neural Network are able to resolve long term dependencies (Hochreiter and Schmidhuber, 1997).

For training the network, we use the backpropagation algorithm with an adaptive learning rate (Kingma and Ba, 2014). The LSTM layer is further stacked with dense layers and finally, to obtain a probability vector we use a softmax classifier given below:

$$P(y = j \mid x) = \frac{e^{x^T w_j}}{\sum_{k=1}^{k} e^{x^T w_k}}$$

The outline of the neural network architecture is illustrated in the figure given below.

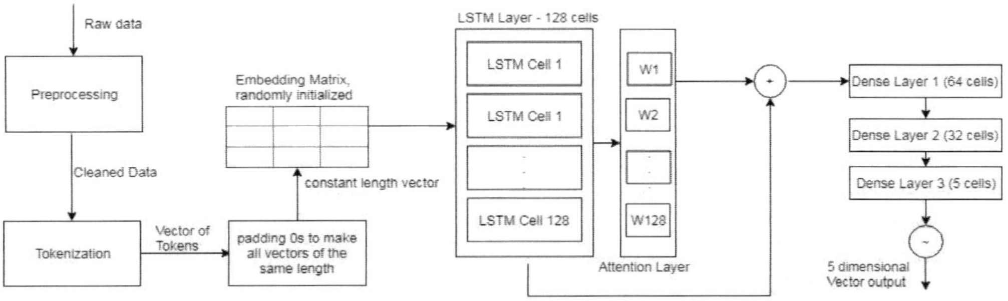

Figure 2. Neural Network architecture corresponding to the LSTM based model

To obtain word embeddings required for the LSTM models we used the following 2 different approaches.

- *Using pre-trained Embeddings*: We used the GloVe Embedding which is already pre-trained on twitter data (Pennington et al., 2014), thus we had vector representation of nearly all the words of our collected English dataset. Therefore, our model could not only have a representation for all words in our training set, but also handle most new words in the test or validation set.
- *Training an Embedding Layer*: To make our approach more generic we used an embedding layer instead of using pre-trained embeddings. We uniquely indexed the words in the training data and then passed the resultant sentence vector into the embedding layer on which further layers of the models were stacked. The embedding matrix gets trained along the network. We observed the variation in the model's performance with the number of unique words in our training data. Since our embedding matrix was trained on limited number of words, on encountering a new word in test set, we assign a default index of the embedding matrix to these words. Given that the model is learning word representation while training, it is able to learn local context of the words in the data instead of relying on the universal meaning. This idea is extremely powerful, since it allows us to use the same technique to work with different languages and contexts, hence allowing us to abstract away the differences in language structures and semantics.

Finally, we added an attention layer stacked immediately after the LSTM. An attention mechanism allows the model to gain a finer understanding of the different parts of the sentence/tweet, potentially allowing for clearer identification of emotions in the different parts.

6. BASELINE ACCURACY

In order to understand how well our model performs, we determine the following benchmarks

- Probabilistic baseline - Since the task is a 5-class classification, random probability to get a correct result is 20%.
- Skewed probabilistic baseline - In light of the fact that the data is skewed and the dominant class accounts for almost 40% of the data, a naive classifier giving the dominant class as the only answer would result in about 40% accuracy.
- Past research - We will evaluate and compare the results of contemporary models such as the one proposed by Microsoft (2015) on our dataset, as well as evaluate our models (with minimal modifications) on the standardized ISEAR (Scherer and Wallbott, 1994) dataset and compare the results with those achieved by Thomas et al. (2014) and Razek and Frasson (2017). For comparing results on the Hindi data, we evaluated the model proposed by Microsoft (2015) on our data and compared the results.

7. EXPERIMENTS

We performed two basic experiments with our neural network architectures. The first was a 5-class emotion analysis as described in the introduction, where we classify the dominant emotion of a tweet into one of the following five emotions-*joy, sadness, anger, laughter and fear*. We split the tweets according to language and into 3 sets; train, verify and test. The training and test sets were made by using a 80-20% split of the dataset for each language. Further, 20% of the total training set was used as a verification set to train and improve the model, and comprised of a total of 17534 tweets for the Hindi set, and 26842 tweets for the English set. The remainder of tweets were used to test the developed models, and results were measured using the accuracy measure, as well as per-class precision and recall via a confusion table. The division of the tweets was done randomly after shuffling the dataset. The ADAM optimization algorithm was used for training.

The second experiment was performed using the ISEAR dataset in order to compare the performance of fundamental neural network architecture. Thus, using the same architecture as proposed, we trained a new model based on the exact same architecture with the minor modification of having a 7-node final layer instead of a 5-node layer in order to perform a 7-class emotion analysis. In order to make a direct comparison to the models proposed by Thomas et al. (2014) and Razek and Frasson (2017), we used the same train-test split of the dataset as they had in their experiments.

8. RESULTS

The first trend noticed was that accuracy of models increased with the number of unique words considered (Table 3). This could be explained as some words that may not be frequent in the dataset may change the overall sentiment of the sentence and to the fact that the models couldn't capture the sentiment of new unseen words in the test data set. The variation was less when a pre-trained embedding was used instead of training an Embedding layer. The best neural network model had an accuracy of 86.8%. Such high accuracy could be attributed to the embedded sentiment data in the pre-trained GloVe embeddings (Pennington et al., 2014). Hence, the computed sentence vector must also be carrying some of this meaning.

Table 3. Accuracy obtained using the basic Neural Network

Neural Network Model (Sec 5.1)	Accuracy
Mean Model (1000 words)	82.07%
Mean Model (2000 words)	82.5%
Mean Model (3000 words)	83.2%
Mean Model (all words)	**86.8%**
Max Model	84.9%

Table 4. Comparison of accuracy: English Dataset

Model	Accuracy
Microsoft (2015)	89.47%
Neural Network	86.8%
LSTM Model	90.06%
LSTM Model w/ Attention	**92.48%**

Table 5. Comparison of accuracy: Hindi Dataset

Model	Accuracy
LSTM	86.36%
LSTM w/ attention	**88.50%**

The LSTM models outperformed above models because these models also learnt the semantic relationship between the words in a sentence. Implicit relationships between words and their corresponding parts of speech as well as their usage in specific context and their spatial relationship with other words are captured by the

LSTM model, which are otherwise lost using the simple Neural Network strategy (Hochreiter and Schmidhuber, 1997). As expected from previous research, the implicit incorporation of the above features led to better accuracy using the LSTM model. The accuracy of the models may further be increased by increasing the size of the dataset and thus reducing the probability of discovering new words. The model trained in less than 5 minutes on an Nvidia Tegra K80 gpu, thus it is relatively lightweight in terms of resources required to train.

Table 6. Per emotion count of tweets for either dataset

Model	Joy	Fear	Sadness	Anger	Laughter
Microsoft (2015)	0.92	0.91	0.90	0.77	0.93
LSTM w/ attention	**0.96**	**0.94**	**0.94**	**0.80**	**0.95**

We also plot the confusion matrix, from which we see that the model possesses very high precision and recall for almost all classes. As compared to the study conducted by Microsoft (2015), our model outperforms them consistently across all emotions by at least 3 percentage points in the f-score measure. The LSTM model inherently develops a better understanding of sentence context as compared to other simple neural network or bag of words models, which is why we believe we see such higher per-class precision and recall.

The second experiment on the ISEAR (Scherer and Wallbott, 1994) dataset, finds our results convincingly better than those obtained by Thomas et al. (2014) and Razek and Frasson (2017). This shows the general ability of our model to outperform manual feature extraction based methods of emotion analysis.

Table 7. Comparison of per-class F-score: ISEAR Dataset

Model	Joy	Fear	Sadness	Anger	Guilt	Disgust	Shame
Razek and Frasson (2017)	0.58	0.56	0.67	0.66	0.50	0.47	0.55
LSTM w/ attention	**0.96**	**0.81**	**0.90**	**0.80**	**0.78**	**0.89**	**0.78**

Table 8. Comparison of per-class Accuracy: ISEAR Dataset

Model	Joy	Fear	Sadness	Anger	Guilt	Disgust	Shame
Thomas et al. (2014)	78.3%	83.06%	**79.16%**	68.94%	80.67%	69.76%	78.84%
LSTM w/ attention	**92.82%**	**87.08%**	70.0%	**73.87%**	**90.71%**	**81.01%**	**80.36%**

Finally, we analyze our LSTM based models on the Hindi dataset we collected. The relatively high accuracy obtained verifies our claim that our proposed architecture can also work with tweets in a different language too. Note that models depending on pre-trained embeddings would not easily work with such a task. Similarly, hand-crafted features would potentially be different and hence, not scalable to train on multiple languages.

9. CONCLUSION

In our paper, we have successfully designed a strategy to automatically collect twitter corpus and tag it using distant learning techniques, thus allowing us to continuously extract any amount of data to train and test our models. Further, we used it to collect corpus to train different deep learning techniques to perform emotion analysis on tweets, with the LSTM approach, as expected, giving the best results. Additionally, we can see that the results obtained beat current state-of-the-art techniques.

For future work, we plan on augmenting our embedding layers, using both pre-trained embeddings like GloVe and using them to initialize our layer, as well as incorporating different linguistic features like POS tags to better train the embedding. Finally, we think working on mixed language tweets would prove an interesting challenge.

REFERENCES

Apoorv Agarwal, Boyi Xie, Ilia Vovsha, Owen Ram-bow, and Rebecca Passonneau. 2011. Sentiment analysis of twitter data. In *LSM '11 Proceedings of the Workshop on Languages in Social Media*, pages 30–38, Portland, Oregon.

Cecilia Ovesdotter Alm, Dan Roth, and RichardSproat. 2005. Twitter sentiment analysis with deep convolutional neural networks. In *HLT '05 Proceedings of the conference on Human Language Technology and Empirical Methods in Natural Language Processing,* pages 579–586, Vancouver, British Columbia, Canada.

Sanjeev Arora, Yingyu Liang, and Tengyu Ma. 2016. A simple but tough-to-beat baseline for sentence embeddings.

Luciano Barbosa and Junlan Feng. 2010. Robust sentiment detection on twitter from biased and noisy data. In *Proceedings of the 23rd international conference on computational linguistics: posters,* pages36–44. Association for Computational Linguistics.

Adam Bermingham and Alan F Smeaton. 2010. Classifying sentiment in microblogs: is brevity an advantage? In *Proceedings of the 19th ACM international conference on Information and knowledge management*, pages 1833–1836. ACM

Steven Bird, Ewan Klein, and Edward Loper, 2009. *Natural Language Processing with Python.* O'Reilly Media.

Delenn Chin, Anna Zappone, and Jessica Zhao. 2016. Analyzing twitter sentiment of the 2016 presidential candidates. *American Journal Of Science and Research.*

Yogesh Garg and Niladri Chatterjee. 2014. Sentiment analysis of twitter feeds. *In International Conference on Big Data Analytics,* pages 33–52. Springer.

Alec Go, Richa Bhayani, and Lei Huang. 2009. Twitter sentiment classification using distant supervision. *CS224N Project Report, Stanford*, 1(12).

Sepp Hochreiter and J¨ürgen Schmidhuber. 1997. Long short term memory. *Neural computation*, 9(8):1735–1780.

Diederik P Kingma and Jimmy Ba. 2014. Adam: Amethod for stochastic optimization. *arXiv preprint arXiv:1412.6980.*

Microsoft. 2015. Emotion detection and recognition from text using deep learning. www.microsoft.com/developerblog.

Petra Kralj Novak, Jasmina Smailovi´c, Borut Sluban, and Igor Mozetiˇc. 2015. Sentiment of emojis. *PloS one*, 10(12):e0144296.

Alexander Pak and Patrick Paroubek. 2010. Twitter as a corpus for sentiment analysis and opinion mining. In *LREc*, volume 10

Jeffrey Pennington, Richard Socher, and Christopher Manning. 2014. Glove: Global vectors for word representation. In *Proceedings of the 2014 conference on empirical methods in natural language processing (EMNLP),* pages 1532–1543.

R. Plutchik. 1989. *Emotion: Theory, Research, and Experience*. v. 4. Acad. Press.

Mohammed Abdel Razek and Claude Frasson. 2017. Text-based intelligent learning emotion system. *Journal of Intelligent Learning Systems and Applications*, 9(01):17.

Klaus R Scherer and Harald G Wallbott. 1994. Evidence for universality and cultural variation of differential emotion response patterning. *Journal of personality and social psychology*, 66(2):310.

Aliaksei Severyn and Alessandro Moschitti. 2015. Emotions from text: machine learning for text-based emotion prediction. In *Proceedings of the 38th International ACM SIGIR Conference on Research and Development in Information Retrieval*, pages 959–962, Santiago, Chile.

Statista. 2018. Twitter: Number of active users. www.statista.com/statistics/282087/number-of-monthlyactive-twitter-users.

Duyu Tang, Furu Wei, Bing Qin, Ting Liu, and Ming Zhou. 2014. Coooolll: A deep learning system for twitter sentiment classification. In *Proceedings of the 8th International Workshop on Semantic Evaluation*, pages 208–212, Dublin, Ireland.

Bincy Thomas, P Vinod, and KA Dhanya. 2014. Multiclass emotion extraction from sentences. *International Journal of Scientific & Engineering Research*, 5(2).

STRUM: A SEMANTIC TRUST-BASED MINER MODEL FOR DETECTING INFLUENTIAL SPREADERS IN SOCIAL NETWORKS

Heba M. Wagih[1], Hoda M. O. Mokhtar[2] and Samy S. Ghoniemy[1]
[1]*The British University in Egypt, Cairo, Egypt*
[2]*Cairo University, Cairo, Egypt*

ABSTRACT

Social Networks have become embedded in every aspect of today people's life. The success of online social networks has a significant role in shaping trust and influence among participants. They are continuing to gain ground every day, opening the opportunity for several research movements. Great attention is now given for identifying influential spreaders in many application domains as recommendation systems, viral marketing, epidemic control and others. Most of the recent research focused only on the network structure with its geospatial information disregarding the semantics underlying these networks. In this paper, we propose a semantic trust-based miner model (STRUM) that efficiently detects influential spreaders in social networks for enhancing recommendation services. STRUM considers both geospatial information and semantic information in defining each user in the social network. Different experiments have been conducted to verify and validate the proposed algorithm against the latest published using two real location based social networks namely; Brightkite and Weeplaces are used in the experiments.

KEYWORDS

Social Networks, Recommendation Systems, Influential Spreaders

1. INTRODUCTION

The proliferation of social network applications is significantly observable in today people's life. In social networks as Facebook, Twitter and others, people have large number of related connections with a varying number, type and strength from one person to another. The use of such applications leads to the generation of a colossal sum of data that opens new research opportunities and challenges to serve people and communities in many different domains. Among which is the epidemic control, recommendation systems, viral marketing and others.

Recommender systems have proven to be an important application that utilizes the current information diffusion in providing users with more customized information services. Location-based recommender applications are newly introduced applications where people can share information about their physical location as well as their common interests and activities. Rodríguez Hernández et al. (2005) presented an important survey that summarizes various location recommendation systems that were developed in different domains as tourism, news and shopping.

An important aspect that directs the recommendation process is trust. People are usually influenced by their trustworthy friends and are more likely to accept recommendations from their trusted friends rather than from random sources. Trust in social networks is a new topic with lots of unanswered questions. Jaouadi and Romdhane (2016) studied two types of social trusts namely; conversational and propagation trust. They develop statistical measures based on the timing and sequence of exchanged messages between users to quantify these trust types. Trust-aware recommender systems have recently gained a special attention in developing recommendation applications. Employing trust information has proven a noticeable enhancement in recommender systems where both the accuracy of recommendation as well as the users' experience are greatly improved.

Tremendous effort has been recently done to answer many research challenges that have been raised to understand and analyze the dynamics of social networks such influential spreaders which is part of our proposed research. Since detecting influential nodes has never been a minor errand and has an important role in the recommendation process. Thus, in recent years, many influential identification algorithms were introduced such as Degree Centrality (DCM), Betweenness Centrality (BCM), Closeness Centrality (CCM) as cited in Landherr et al. (2010), K-core decomposition as stated in Alvarez-Hamelin et al. (2005), and others. Bonchi (2011) presented an exhaustive survey on different algorithms introduced for detecting influential nodes and how information is propagated in social networks. Zhao et al. (2017) introduced another approach for influential detection known as the local centrality with a coefficient (CLC) algorithm.

Although this research problem has made noticeable strides in past few years, however most of the literature has been focusing only on the social network structure disregarding the importance of semantics aspects that describe these social networks.

Motivated by the strong impact of this research direction in different application domains, we follow the attempts introduced in previous works and present the following contributions:

1. Introduce a Semantic Trust-Based Miner Model (STRUM) for enhancing location recommendation services as well as detecting influential nodes. STRUM is an enhanced version of the proposed algorithm in Wagih et al. (2019) where both the network structure and the relevant semantic information associated are considered.
2. Investigate the role of influential nodes in the recommendation process and specifically in location recommendation.
3. Experimentally evaluate the proposed STRUM with other conventional algorithms on real social network dataset.

The rest of this paper is structured as follows: section 2 presents some related works to both the structural and semantical approaches for influential nodes detection, recommender systems and trusted social networks. In section 3, the semantic trust-based miner model is proposed. In section 4, we provide an experimental evaluation of the proposed algorithm. Finally, section 5 concludes and proposes directions for future work.

2. RELATED WORK

In recent years, several types of recommender systems have been proposed, among which are the location-based recommendation systems. Such systems deal with personalized and automatic data retrieved from different sources of information. Detecting trusted influential spreaders in these systems plays an important role in enhancing the quality of the provided recommendation services. Recently many researches have been focusing on discovering vital node as presented by Wei et al. (2018), Wang et al. (2017) and Kim et al. (2014).

Song et al. (2017) proposed a recommendation model named TrustTR based on trust relations and item ratings. The model counts trusted friends' recommendations, item reputation and user history ratings in providing recommendations. The authors experimentally proved that their model provides higher accuracy compared to other conventional recommendation models. Yang et al. (2017) proposed a TrustMF model which integrates both a truster model with a trustee model to address the cold start problem. They proved experimentally that their model outperforms other trust-based models. Recently Davoudi and Chatterjee (2018) introduced a new algorithm for modeling an accurate recommender system. The proposed algorithm considered both finding the relevant items for each user based on his/her interests as well as the social interactions between users. The authors used the probabilistic matrix factorization method to predict user rating for products and rating-based and connection-based similarity measurements for modeling similarity.

Few new researches started to consider the effect of utilizing the semantic information associated with each user in community detection as in Ben Amor (2016) as well as in discovering influential nodes as in Wagih et al. (2019), Hafiene and Karoui (2017), and Jaouadi and Romdhane (2016). Wagih et al. (2019) proposed a semantic based algorithm for detecting influential diffusion in social networks. The proposed algorithm is an extension to the work introduced by Wagih et al. (2019). The authors compared their algorithm with other prior models and the experiments showed a noticeable enhancement in detecting the influential nodes in the network. Jaouadi and Romdhane (2016) proposed a new algorithm called DIN which combines both the structure and the semantic aspects of the network to detect influential nodes. The authors validated their algorithm using artificial networks as datasets however the performance of their algorithm has not been experimented on real social networks.

3. SEMANTIC TRUST-BASED MINER MODEL

In this section, we propose a new model known as Semantic Trust-Based Miner Model (STRUM) for enhancing location recommendation services as well as discovering influential spreaders in social network. The proposed STRUM model is an extended version to the work proposed by Wagih et al. (2019). STRUM proposes solutions to some of the problems that were not addressed in Wagih et al. (2019) as creating a trusted social network and eliminating old visited locations that may affect the recommendation process. STRUM consists of three main Modules; trust calculation module, location mining module and semantic-based influence calculation module. Figure 1 shows the proposed framework. In the following subsections, we introduce each of these modules in details.

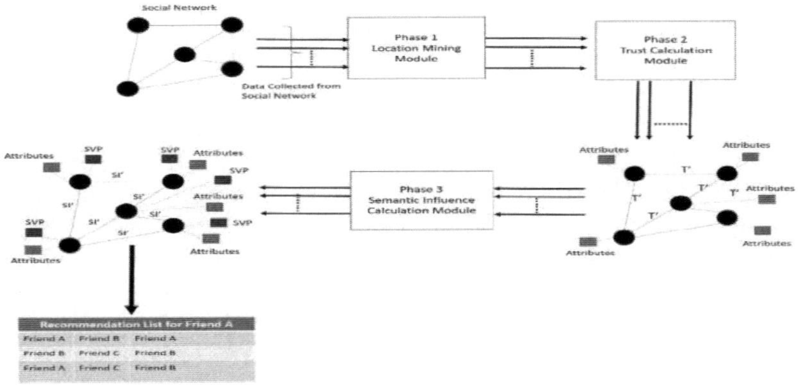

Figure 1. Proposed framework for semantic trust-based miner model

3.1 Location Mining Module

In this module, we extract all the visited locations for each user in the social network. For each visited location, we retrieve the visited frequency by each user and the check-in time. User's preferences and choices might change over time; therefore, it is important to eliminate all places that were checked-in before a certain time threshold as such places could falsely affect the recommendation process. Since the proposed model aims at enhancing location recommendation services, thus location filtering module is crucial to create a more trusted network. Figure 2 shows an example of visited locations log table after filtration from Brightkite dataset.

$$Imp(Loc) = \begin{cases} 1, & \text{VisitedTime} < \text{Threshold} \\ 0, & \text{VisitedTime} \geq \text{Threshold} \end{cases} \quad (5)$$

Location	User	Check-in Time	Frequency
Hotel	1	2009-05-15T14:29:15Z	1
School	1	2009-05-15T11:42:53Z	2
School	1	2009-09-20T18:07:01Z	2
Hospital	2	2009-09-08T06:16:10Z	1
Hotel	2	2010-08-23T18:25:44Z	3
Hotel	2	2009-08-23T18:25:13Z	3
Hotel	2	2008-07-29T20:50:54Z	3
Farm	3	2009-07-29T20:50:54Z	1

Location	User	Check-in Time	Frequency
Hotel	1	2009-05-15T14:29:15Z	1
School	1	2009-05-15T11:42:53Z	2
School	1	2009-09-20T18:07:01Z	2
Hospital	2	2009-09-08T06:16:10Z	1
Hotel	2	2010-08-23T18:25:44Z	3
Hotel	2	2009-08-23T18:25:13Z	3
Farm	3	2009-07-29T20:50:54Z	1

Figure 2. Visited locations log table

3.2 Trust Calculation Module

The interpersonal trust is the main factor that affects the influence diffusion in social networks. Forming trusted relationships in social networks is a new topic with lots of challenging questions. In the proposed model we employ the quantitative measurements introduce by Wagih et al. (2019).

Weight: for each pair of friends (f_i and f_j) in the social network, the weight of their relation is calculated as the correlation between their attributes using Pearson Correlation Coefficient, and is given by,

$$\text{Weight } (fi, fj) = PCC\ (fiattr, fjattr) \quad (1)$$

EdgeTrust: for each pair of friends (f_i and f_j) in the social network, there is an interpersonal trust, and this is known as the edge trust value. Having a dataset of *m* friends, we define the quantitative measure for edge trust as:

$$\text{EdgeTrust}(fi, fj) = \frac{Weight\ (fi,fj)}{\sum_{x=1}^{m} Weight\ (fi,fx)}, \quad \text{x= 1,2, 3, ... j, ..., m} \quad (2)$$

Where Weight (f_i and f_j) denotes the weight of the relation between friends (f_i and f_j) and Weight (f_i and fx) denotes the weight of all the relations between f_i and all directly connected friends in the network.

In social networks, some friends can have a degree of negative influence on other friends, especially if they do not trust. Since recommendation systems are based on trust among friends, thus we consider only the positive trust values among users. All relations with trust values less than an acceptable threshold are pruned creating a trusted web network.

$$Imp(\text{EdgeTrust}(fi, fj)) = \begin{cases} 1, & < \text{Threshold} \\ 0, & \geq \text{Threshold} \end{cases} \quad (3)$$

Consider a social network with relations between four friends A, B, C and D. Figure 3 shows an example of weighted relation social network.

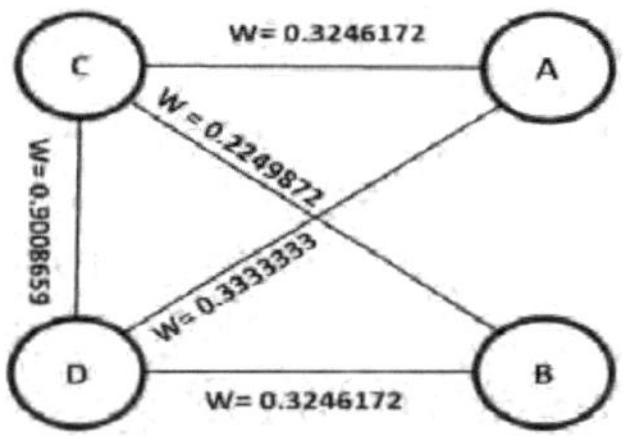

Figure 3. Weight values between friends in social network

Following the previous example, EdgeTrust between (Friend A, Friend C) is calculated as follows:

$$\text{EdgeTrust } (fA, fC) = \frac{0.3246172}{0.3246172 + 0.3333333}$$

NodeTrust: each friend in the social network has a trust value that he/she gains from other connected friends, this value is known as the node trust value. The higher the degree of trust value, the more trustworthy a friend is considered over the social network.

$$\text{NodeTrust}(fi) = \textstyle\sum_{x=1}^{m} \text{EdgeTrust}(fi, fj), \ \text{x} = \ 1,2,3, \ldots..\text{j}, \ldots\ldots, \text{m} \quad (4)$$

Having a social network with completed EdgeTrust calculation, NodeTrust for (Friend A) is calculated as follows:

$$\text{NodeTrust}(fA) = 0.565458095 + \ 0.414990168$$

3.3 Semantic-Based Influence Calculation Module

In this module, we extend the trust calculation module by introducing new metrics, namely, Semantic Visited Places Finding (SVP), Semantic Edge Influence (SEdgeInf) and Semantic Node Influence (SNodeInf).

SemanticVisitedPlaces (SVP): in most datasets, locations are presented with their longitude and latitude values. In order to get the semantic translation for these spatial coordinates, a set of functions which are available in the geonames package in R programming language are used. Function GNfindNearby is used to retrieve a structured list of coordinates, places, countries and other information related to each check-in value. Figure 4 shows an example of semantic representation for a place with longitude equals to 35.24012 and latitude equals to 24.80927.

$$\text{SVP}(\text{check\_in}_{\text{long,lat}}) = \text{List\$geonames\$fcodeName} \quad (6)$$

$$\text{List} = \text{GNfindNearby}(\text{lat}, \text{lng}, \text{radius}), \text{radius} = 0.01\text{km} \quad (7)$$

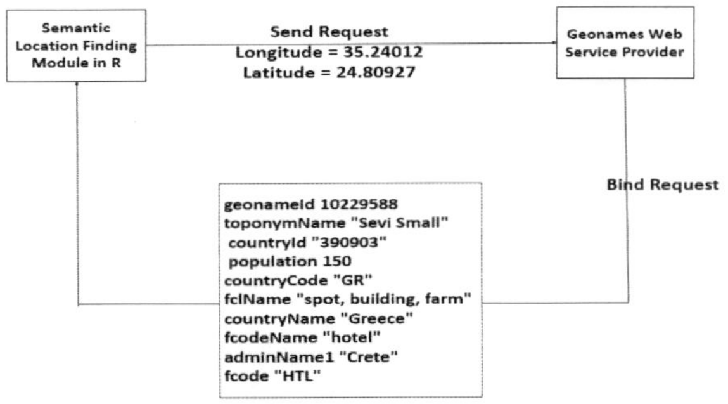

Figure 4. Semantic translation for geospatial coordinates

SemanticEdgeInfluence (SEdgeInf): each friend has a specific influence on each of his/her connected friends in the network which is known as the edge influence between every two friends. The influence f_i has on f_j is the product of the trust f_j has on f_i and the semantically based recommendation rate between f_i and f_j. The semantic recommendation rate (SRecRate) is the degree to which two friends might share common interests through analyzing the semantics of the check-in data for each user.

$$\text{SEdgeInf}(fi, fj) = \text{EdgeTrust}(fi, fj) * \text{SRecRate}(fi, fj) \quad (8)$$

$$\text{SRecRate}\,(fi, fj) = \frac{\text{SV P}(fi, fj)}{\text{TSV P}(fi)} \quad (9)$$

$$\text{TSVP}(fi) = \{|\text{SVP}(fi, \text{X})|\} \quad (10)$$

Following the previous example and having the SRecRate calculated between all friends, SEdgeInf between (Friend C, Friend A) is calculated as follows:

$$\text{SEdgeInf}\,(fC, fA) = 0.493376325 * 0.00003198874$$

SemanticNodeInfluence(SNodeInf): each friend in the social network has an influence degree on the whole network known as semantic node influence and is defined by the following equation.

$$\text{SNodeInf}(fi) = \textstyle\sum_{x=1}^{m} \text{SEdgeInf}(fi, fx) * \text{NodeTrust}(fi) \quad (11)$$

4. EVALUATION

In this research, the experiments are conducted on two real social networks, namely, Brightkite and Weeplaces which are available for public use. The Experiments are performed to evaluate the efficiency and accuracy of STRUM model against other conventional models. The Experiments highlighted the significance of adding semantic information in location recommendation services as well as in discovering the influential nodes in the network. Multiple layers of semantics are added to the dataset and after each layer, friends' influence is calculated and a list with the top influential friends is created for each friend in the network. Layers of semantics are added till we reach the highest abstract meaning for locations as shown in Figure 5.

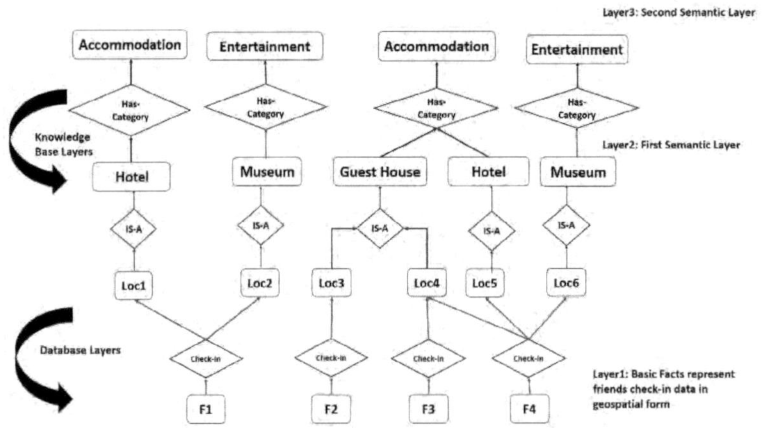

Figure 5. Semantic summary graph

The STRUM model is compared to the SIMBA algorithm proposed by Wagih et al. (2019), the influence-based algorithm proposed by Bagci et al. (2016) and weight-based algorithm proposed by Hangal et al. (2010) as shown in Figure 6. Remarkable enhancements are observed with each added layer of semantics. The proposed algorithm outperforms SIMBA by 15%, algorithm Bagci et al. (2016) by 30% and algorithm Hangal et al. (2010) by 40% in recommendation accuracy.

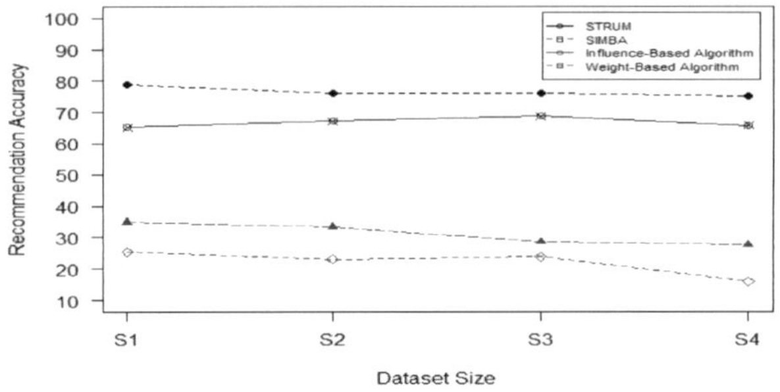

Figure 6. A recommendation accuracy comparison between STRUM, SIMBA, influence-based algorithm and weight-based algorithm.

We also compare the efficiency in detecting the influential nodes between STRUM, and other conventional algorithms as the degree centrality measure, betweenness centrality measure, closeness centrality measure, K-Core decomposition and CLC algorithm and the results are shown in Figure 7.

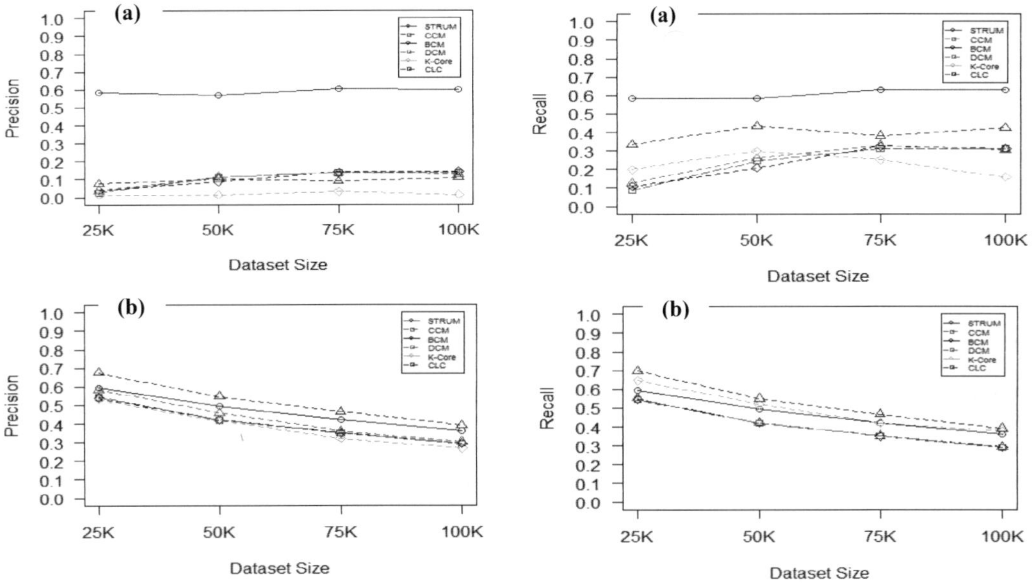

Figure 7. A Performance comparison between STRUM, DCM, BCM, CCM, K-core decomposition and CLC in terms of precision and recall for (a) Brightkite and (b) Weeplaces datasets

The experiments show that nodes with highest influence in the network might not have the highest power in recommendation (e.g. in STRUM, almost 35% of the recommendation comes from friends who have direct influence on their friends rather than having a significant influence on the network as shown in Figure 8.

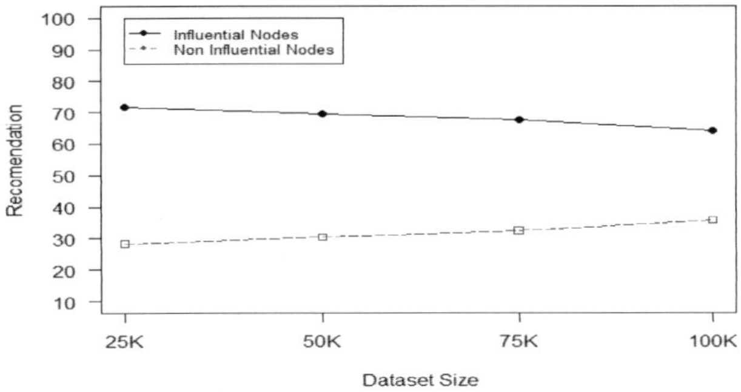

Figure 8. Recommendation percentage from influential and non-influential nodes

5. CONCLUSIONS AND FUTURE WORK

In this paper, we introduce a model for detecting influential nodes and enhancing the location recommendation process. The proposed model utilizes the trust concept between participants of social networks. It considers both the social and spatial information related to each friend in the network. We use two real datasets from different LBSNs for conducting our experiments; namely, Brightkite and Weeplaces. We proved experimentally that the proposed model outperforms relevant prior works for all datasets. Several future enhancements are to be considered related to the presented work. The proposed model can be extended to include more semantic information as well as indirect connections in social networks (friend of friend).

REFERENCES

Alvarez-Hamelin, J. I., Dall'Asta, L., Barrat, A. and Vespignani, A. (2005). *Large scale networks fingerprinting and visualization using the k-core decomposition.* In Proceedings of the 18th International Conference on Neural Information Processing Systems, NIPS'05, pp. 41–50, Cambridge, MA, USA, MIT Press.

Ben Amor, S., Ben Romdhane, L. and Harzallah, M. (2016). *Nouvelle approche sémantique pour la détection des communautés dans un réseau social.* In IC2016: Ingenierie des Connaissances, Montpellier, France.

Bonchi, F. (2011). *Influence propagation in social networks: A data mining perspective.* In 2011 IEEE/WIC/ACM International Conferences on Web Intelligence and Intelligent Agent Technology, volume 1, pages 2–2.

Davoudi, A. and Chatterjee, M. (2018). *Social trust model for rating prediction in recommender systems: Effects of similarity, centrality, and social ties*. Online Social Networks and Media, pp.1–11.

Hafiene, N. and Karoui, W. (2017). *A new structural and semantic approach for identifying influential nodes in social networks.* 2017 IEEE/ACS 14th International Conference on Computer Systems and Applications (AICCSA), pp, 1338–1345.

Bagci, H. and Karagoz, P. (2011). *Context-Aware Friend Recommendation for Location Based Social Networks Using RandomWalk*, Proceedings of the 25th International Conference Companion on World Wide Web, pp. 531–536,

978-1-4503-4144-8.

Hangal, S., MacLean, D., Lam, M. S. and Heer, J. (2010). *All friends are not equal: Using weights in social graphs to improve search.* In Workshop on Social Network Mining & Analysis, ACM KDD.

Jaouadi, M. and Ben Romdhane, L. (2016). *Din: An efficient algorithm for detecting influential nodes in social graphs using network structure and attributes.* In 2016 IEEE/ACS 13th International Conference of Computer Systems and Applications (AICCSA), pp. 1–8.

Kim, H., Beznosov, K. and Yoneki, E. (2014). *Finding influential neighbors to maximize information diffusion in twitter.* In Proceedings of the 23rd International Conference on World Wide Web, WWW '14 Companion, pp. 701–706, New York, NY, USA.

Landherr, A., Friedl, B. and Heidemann,J. (2010). *A critical review of centrality measures in social networks.* Business & Information Systems Engineering, pp. 371–385.

Martınez, D. C., Janowicz, K., and Hitzler, P. (2012). *A logical geo-ontology design pattern for quantifying over types.* in SIGSPATIAL 2012 International Conference on Advances in Geographic Information Systems (formerly known as GIS), SIGSPATIAL'12, Redondo Beach, CA, USA, pp. 239–248.

Rodríguez Hernández, M. C., Ilarri, S., Trillo, R., and Hermoso, R. (2015). *Location-aware recommendation systems: Where we are and where we recommend to go.* In CEUR Workshop Proceedings, pp. 1-8.

Song, H., Pei, Q., Xiao, Y., Li, Z. and Wang, Y. (2017). *A novel recommendation model based on trust relations and item ratings in social networks.* In 2017 International Conference on Networking and Network Applications (NaNA), pp. 17–23.

Wagih, H.M., Mokhtar, H.M.O. and Ghoniemy, S.S. (2019). *SIMBA: A Semantic-Influence Measurement Based Algorithm for Detecting Influential Diffusion in Social Networks.* The 13th IEEE International Conference on Semantic Computing, pp. 178-182.

Wei, H., Pan, Z., Hu, G., Zhang, L., Yang, H., Li, X. and Zhou, X. (2018). *Identifying influential nodes based on network representation learning in complex networks.* In PloS one, Public Library of Science.

Wang, J., Jiang, W., Li, K., and Li, K. (2017). *Detecting influential nodes incrementally and evolutionarily in online social networks.* In 2017 IEEE International Symposium on Parallel and Distributed Processing with Applications and 2017 IEEE International Conference on Ubiquitous Computing and Communications (ISPA/IUCC), pp. 182–189.

Yang, B., Lei, Y., Liu, J. and Li, W. (2017). *Social collaborative filtering by trust.* IEEE Transactions on Pattern Analysis and Machine Intelligence, 39(8), pp. 1633–1647.

Zhao. X., Liu. F., Wang, J., and Li, T. (2017). *Evaluating influential nodes in social networks by local centrality with a coefficient.* ISPRS International Journal of Geo-Information.

TOWARDS AUTOMATED COST ANALYSIS, BENCHMARKING AND ESTIMATING IN CONSTRUCTION: A MACHINE LEARNING APPROACH

Daqing Chen[1], Laureta Hajderanj[1] and James Fiske[2]
[1]*School of Engineering, London South Bank University, 103 Borough Road, London SE1 0AA, UK*
[2]*Royal Institution of Chartered Surveyors, 12 Great George Street, London SW1P 3AD, UK*

ABSTRACT

In this paper, a novel machine learning based approach is proposed for automated cost analysis on priced bill of quantities prepared by tenders in the construction industry. The proposed approach features: 1) An effective integration of structured project-specific information with surveyor's domain knowledge in order to model the complex interrelationships between the specifications and descriptions of an item and its trade category; 2) An effective transformation by supervised *t*-SNE to map the original data into a 2-dimensional space to tackle issues of high dimensionality in modelling and creating classifiers, and 3) Simple classifiers with a high classification accuracy and a good generalization capability. Relevant comparative experimental results have demonstrated the effectiveness of the proposed approach.

KEYWORDS

Construction Cost Benchmarking, Cost Analysis, Construction Data Analysis, Bill of Quantities, Dimensionality Reduction, Supervised *t*-SNE.

1. INTRODUCTION

The ability to extract information and analyze it into a consistent format is essential in the construction industry in order to be able to learn from and to benefit future projects. In particular, historical project cost data is essential for early stage estimating and to be able to benchmark projects against others to identify areas to investigate, improve to demonstrate that value for money is being achieved.

The challenge is that construction projects are all procured differently with inconsistent reporting data, so data analysis is becoming more time consuming, often error prone and inconsistent as it heavily depends on an individual doing the analysis. Due to the time-consuming nature of the activity, the process of analyzing projects is often left to more junior roles, if done at all. Therefore, the amount of data that the industry has to learn from is becoming less in terms of samples and of quality so anything that solves this challenge is of great importance to the construction industry.

In this paper, a novel machine learning based approach is proposed to address the problem. The focus is placed on developing a knowledge base to represent the interrelationships among specifications and descriptions of items and their analysis categories for analysis of bill of quantities (BQ) into trades. Due to the measurement rules adopted in the projects available, SMM7 (Standard Method of Measurement) is used as a basis to create the knowledge base, and domain knowledge of experienced surveyors has also been integrated into the knowledge representation effectively. As a result, a set of instances is generated. A supervised *t*-SNE algorithm (*t*-distributed stochastic neighbor embedding) based on dissimilarity measure (Hajderanj, L., *et al.*, 2019) is implemented to visualize the instances and map them into a 2-dimensional space. Consequently, a classifier can be trained to classify (assign) an identified item in a BQ into an appropriate trade category in this space, and the classifier itself effectively provides a form of knowledge representation. For comparison purposes, various classifiers have been created including multilayer perceptron (MP), *k*-nearest neighbors (*k*NN), decision tree, and Naïve Bayesian models, and all the models have demonstrated consistently a high classification accuracy and a good generalization capability.

Note that there are many different potential input data formats and structures from different procurement routes and measurement systems (e.g., NRM2, HMM, RMM, Uniclass, Uniformat, Masterformat etc.) and also many different analysis reporting formats (e.g. trade based, elemental based using the SFCA and international reporting standards such as ICMS etc.) (Gelder, J.E., 2015). This paper focuses on just one option in order to test the hypothesis and examines the analysis of SMM7 BQs into trades. In addition, how to identify items in different document formats, such as PDF, Excel, XML etc., is beyond the scope of this paper.

The remainder of the paper is organized as follows. Section 2 provides a brief critical review on the literature about machine learning based approaches to trade classification in priced BQ. Section 3 gives in detail the proposed methodology for effective trade classification. It also discusses how training samples can be created based on SMM7 and the domain knowledge of experienced surveyors. The training samples are visualized and mapped using supervised *t*-SNE, and classification in the low-dimensional space is carried out with a number of classifiers for comparison purpose. This is followed by a discussion on the experimental findings in Section 4. And finally, in Section 5 a conclusion is given along with suggested future work.

2. A BRIEF CRITICAL REVIEW ON RELATED WORK

The essence of a machine learning based approach to automate cost analysis lies in understanding and modelling the interrelationships among item specifications and the corresponding category of the item. On the one hand, item specifications and descriptions can be well-structured in a certain syntax, such as in SMM which specifies an item with respect to its category by using a set of codes structured hierarchically at several levels. On the other hand, uncertainties exist due to the fact that a same item could be described by different surveyors inconsistently with various wordings, particularly at a very low level of the description. Therefore, a good modelling of the relationships between an item's descriptions and its category should capture both structured and uncertain influential factors. In addition, a sufficient support of experienced surveyors is crucial in the modelling process.

Various machine algorithms have been considered in the literature for the modelling. In particular, case-based reasoning (CBR) was applied in several case studies (Kim, G.H., *et al.*, 2004, Ji, S.-H., *et al.*, 2011, Zima, K., 2015, Lésniak, A., and Ziam, K, 2018). CBR is based on a simple philosophy that a construction project or work of similar type is more likely to have a similar cost. The approach is easy to implement; however, it heavily depends on the similarity measure used and how many similar cases to be considered. Usually Euclidean distance is employed as similarity measure. This measure may not work well in a high dimensional space which is often the case for cost analysis since most of the variables involved are of categorical type.

Other algorithms explored include regression analysis, MP, and support vector machine (Arage, S.S., Dharwadkar, N.V., 2017, Petruseva, S., *et al.*, 2017). A comparison was made among CBR, MP, and regression algorithms by Kim, G.H., *et al.*, (2004). Although regression analysis is a typical technique, it may not be appropriate for cost analysis of BQs, since many regression variables are categorical type with each having many distinct values resulting in a very complex model. One of the main benefits of using an MP model is that it has a powerful mapping capability as a universal approximator.

Several non-machine learning approaches have been proposed, such as ontology-based approaches (Lee, S.-L., *et al.*, 2013, Ma, Z., *et al.*, 2013) and OLAP cubes enabled cost analysis (Martınez-Rojas, M., *et al.*, 2015, Martınez-Rojas, M., *et al.*, 2016).

As a summary, although a range of machine learning models have been applied in different scenarios for cost analysis and estimation, there is a clear lack of adopting a modelling strategy that integrates structured information on item specifications and its classification category with domain knowledge of experienced participating surveyors to tackle uncertainties in classifying items. As discussed in a survey by Elfaki, A.O., *et al.* (2014), there are two types of factors to be considered and incorporated in cost estimation: design-specific and estimator-specific, the former is well-defined and established, and the latter lacks standardization. In addition, the algorithms chosen should best fit the heterogeneous data sets associated.

3. METHODOLOGY

In the paper, the emphasis is placed on trade-based cost analysis on SMM7 BQs. An integrated modelling strategy has been adopted which incorporates SMM7-based structured information on an item's descriptions and its trade category with the domain knowledge of experienced surveyors to tackle uncertainties in BQs. A supervised *t*-SNE algorithm with dissimilarity measure (Hajderanj, L., *et al.*, 2019) has been chosen to transform the high dimensional BQ data into a 2-dimensional space, and further different classifiers can be built in this 2-dimensional space.

3.1 Data Capture and Understanding

Capturing the relevant data for the modelling has been conducted by extraction of regulations from SMM7 and interviews with expert surveyors in the industry. The data essentially contains a set of rules that define and describe an item and its corresponding trade group. In general, an item is specified by three levels of specifications hierarchically using certain codes or textual descriptions as shown in Table 1, where N/A indicates that the specifications at a certain level is not needed. The resultant data set has 1245 rules (instances), and the number of the unique values of the three levels 1, 2, and 3 are 7, 305, and 290, respectively. The total number of trades (classes) is 42. As all the variables in the data set are of categorical type, one-hot encoding transformation has been employed to transform the data, resulting in a target data set with 603 variables in total including the variable trade.

Table 1. Example of data descriptions

Trade	Item Code and Description at each Hierarchical level (Number of Unique Values)		
	Level 1 (7)	Level 2 (305)	Level 3 (290)
1and2Fix	Substructure	K10, K11-15, K20-21, K30-33, K41, L10, L20, L30, L42, N10, N15, N16, N20-23, P20, P22, P31	hardwood, softwood; floor, wall, ceiling/soffit/window board; partitions; cubicles; windows; doors; frames; stairs; fittings; cabinets; signs; fascia or gutter boards; skirting; architrave
Brickwork	N/A	F10, F11	brickwork; common bricks; facing bricks; engineering bricks; walls; piers; projections; arches; closing cavity/cavities; facework
Excavating	N/A	D11, D12, D20, D21, D40, D41	excavation, excavating, excavate; working space; earthwork support; reduce levels; disposal; surface treatments.
Miscellaneous	adaptation; alteration; builder's work; demolition	N/A	N/A
Paths	external	D20, E05, E20, E30, E40, Q10, Q20-26	excavation, excavating, excavate; working space; earthwork support; reduce levels; disposal; surface treatments; filling; filling to make-up levels; in-situ concrete, beds; reinforcement; formwork; paving.
Sheet roof	Substructure	G30, H30-32, H33, H43, H76	sheet roof, sheet roofing; decking; eaves; valleys; verges; ridges; hips; skirtings; kerbs; roof coverings; wall cladding; dormers; domes; spires.
Woodwool	Substructure	G32	decking; woodwool; roof coverings; wall cladding; cutting.

The number of samples for each trade group is shown in Figure 1. Note that although many of the trade groups have only a few samples, treating them as outliers may not be appropriate since they are all valid data from real BQs, and more importantly, in terms of cost, a small-sized trade group may attribute significantly.

3.2 Modelling

The target data set was mapped into a 2-dimensional space using the chosen supervised *t*-SNE based on dissimilarity measure. The transformation was considered necessary due to the high number of dimensions in the original space that could make classification difficult, and algorithms like *k*NN may not work appropriately because of the use of Euclidean distance for similarity measure. In addition, it provides an effective visualization of the data set. Figure 2 shows the mapped data instances with their trade labels using the original *t*-SNE (Maaten, L., Hinton, G., 2008) and the supervised *t*-SNE, respectively. Apparently, instances of the same trade group have been made much more compacted by the supervised *t*-SNE algorithm, and this could potentially facilitate the *k*NN algorithm. The settings of the supervised *t*-SNE were as follows: Perplexity 30, Number of iterations: 150, Learning rate: 100, and Momentum: 0.5.

The mapped data was used for modelling. The target data set was split randomly into three subsets of training, validation, and test, with each having 33.3% of the samples. Six models were built for the classification for comparison purposes as follows:

1) A multilayer perceptron model of single hidden layer with 2 input nodes, 20 hidden nodes, and 42 outputs nodes, respectively, and the inputs to the network was normalized using *z*-score standardization. The MP model was trained with 1000 iterations and a set of randomly-selected initial connection weights and biases from an even distribution;
2) A binary decision tree with 6 depths; A naïve Bayesian model, and *k*NNs with various number of nearest neighbors of 1, 5, and 10, respectively.

The experimental results are given in Table 2.

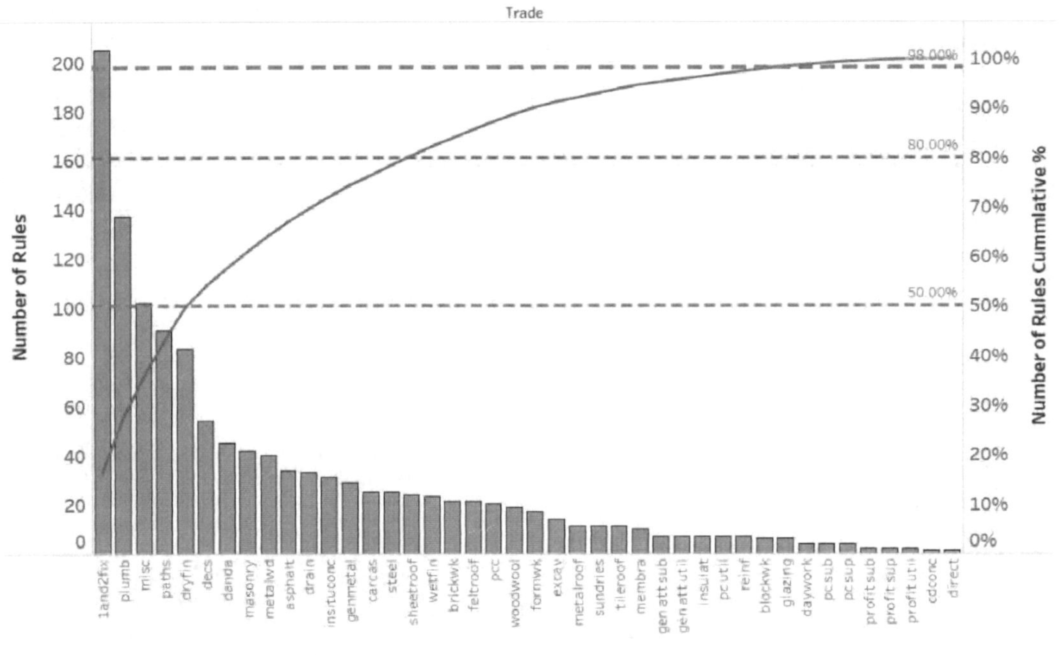

Figure 1. The absolute and percentage cumulative number of instances (rules) for each trade group

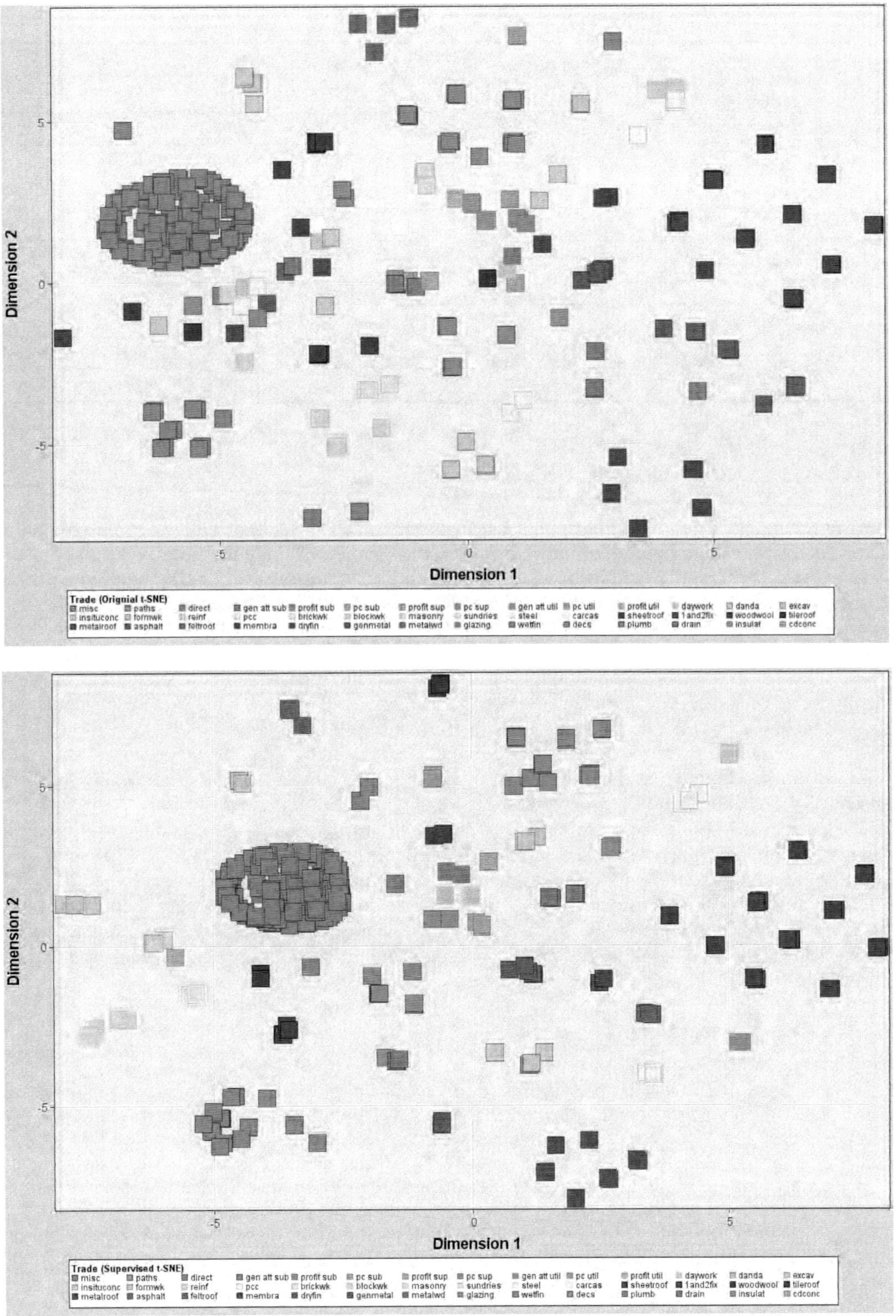

Figure 2. Mapping the data from the original 602-dimesional space to a 2-dimensional space using the original *t*-SNE (top) and the supervised *t*-SNE with dissimilarity measure (bottom). 42 trade groups considered

Table 2. Classification accuracy by % (Total number of trade groups: 42)

Dimensionality Reduction algorithm	Model	Multilayer Perception	Binary Decision Tree	Naïve Bayesian	*k*-Nearest Neighbors		
					k=1	*k=5*	*k=10*
None	Training	98.02	56.64	70.12	99.01	55.80	53.82
	Validation	48.52	45.30	56.69	43.07	46.34	43.87
	Test	45.62	44.50	54.36	41.97	41.28	43.17
Original *t*-SNE	Training	96.30	86.42	90.12	100	92.71	84.67
	Validation	91.83	58.17	86.14	97.78	89.11	82.18
	Test	91.06	54.13	84.40	97.48	89.91	82.11
Supervised *t*-SNE with Dissimilarity Measure	Training	97.28	97.28	95.80	100.00	96.23	92.96
	Validation	97.03	98.51	95.55	99.97	96.03	94.31
	Test	96.33	97.25	95.64	100.00	93.80	92.43

4. ANALYSIS AND DISCUSSION

From the simulation results a phenomenon has been observed: it is evident that all the models trained with the data mapped by the supervised *t*-SNE have achieved a consistently high classification accuracy with a good generalization capability. Contrastively, all the models trained by the original *t*-SNE have demonstrated a low generalization capability. In addition, all the models created in the original space (i.e., no dimensionality reduction) have performed poorly with the lowest classification accuracy across all the model groups. These findings suggest that the proposed transformation using the supervised *t*-SNE was effective and promising.

Transforming data into a 2-dimensional space has also made it possible that a simple model can be good enough for a classification problem. Note that in the experiments, the simplest model, i.e., the *1*-nearest-neighbor classifier has shown the best performance.

On the other hand, due to the dimensionality reduction, the number of parameters whose values need to be optimized through training can be reduced significantly, especially for models like multilayer perceptron. Consider, for example, a multilayer perceptron with a single hidden layer. The network has n input nodes, m hidden nodes, and l output nodes, respectively. Hence, the total number of the parameters that needs to be optimized is $m(n + l + 2)$. However, if the proposed transformation is used, the total number will be $m(4 + l)$ only. This will be beneficial for a modelling problem that lacks enough data.

From a modelling perspective, analyzing data into trades from BQ has posed a challenge about how to deal with a classification problem that involves a very high number of dimensions (over several hundred to several thousand) and a high number of classes coupled with imbalanced number of samples from each class.

5. CONCLUDING REMARKS

In this paper a novel approach has been proposed for cost analysis on BQs. The approach integrates structured information with surveyor's domain knowledge about the relationships between an item's descriptions and its trade membership. A supervised dimensionality reduction algorithm has been employed to transform the original data into a 2-dimensional space for classification. This has made a simple classification model work well with a high accuracy and a good generalization capability. The relevant experiments have demonstrated the effectiveness of the proposed approach.

This research has provided an alternative approach to deal with high dimensional classification problems with many classes. It is useful and applicable particularly to data that contains many categorical variables with a considerable number of distinct values.

The main limitation of the proposed approach is the interpretability of the mapped data using the original or the supervised *t*-SNE algorithms. From a business perspective, a model that can be easily and clearly interpreted would be more convinced and therefore useful. This limitation leads us into some further work in the future.

ACKNOWLEDGEMENT

The authors would like to thank Lindsay Pullen and Steve Pittard for their assistance.

REFERENCES

Arage, S.S., Dharwadkar, N.V., 2017, Cost Estimation of Civil Construction Projects using Machine Learning Paradigm. *International conference on I-SMAC (IoT in Social, Mobile, Analytics and Cloud)*, Palladam, India, pp. 594 – 599.

Elfaki, A.O., et al., 2014, Using Intelligent Techniques in Construction Project Cost Estimation: 10-Year Survey. *Advances in Civil Engineering*, Vol. 2014, pp. 8 – 19.

Gelder, J.E., 2015, The design and development of a classification system for BIM. *Building Information Modelling (BIM) in Design, Construction and Operations*, Vol. 149, pp. 477 - 491.

Hajderanj, L., et al., 2019, A New Supervised *t*-SNE with Dissimilarity Measure for Effective Data Visualization and Classification. *2019 8th International Conference on Software and Information Engineering (ICSIE 2019)*, Cairo, Egypt. In print.

Ji, S.-H., et al., 2011, Cost estimation model for building projects using case-based reasoning. *Canadian Journal of Civil Engineering*, Vol. 38, No. 5, pp.570 – 581.

Kim, G.H., et al., 2004, Comparison of construction cost estimating models based on regression analysis, neural networks, and case-based reasoning. *Building and Environment*, Vol. 39, pp. 1235 – 1242.

Lèsniak, A., and Ziam, K, 2018, Cost Calculation of Construction Projects Including Sustainability Factors Using the Case Based Reasoning (CBR) Method. Sustainability, Vol. 10, No. 5, p.1608.

Lee, S.-L., et al., 2013, BIM and ontology-based approach for building cost estimation. *Automation in Construction*, Vol. 41, pp. 96–105.Martınez-Rojas, M., et al., 2015, Cost Analysis in Construction Projects using Fuzzy OLAP Cubes. *2015 IEEE International Conference on Fuzzy Systems (FUZZ-IEEE)*, Istanbul, Turkey, pp. 96 – 105.

Ma, Z., et al., 2013, Ontology-Based Computerized Representation of Specifications for Construction Cost Estimation. The 30thCIB W78 International Conference, Beijing, China, pp.9 –12.

Maaten, L., Hinton, G., 2008, Visualizing Data using t-SNE. *Journal of Machine Learning Research*, Vol. 9, pp. 2579 – 2605.

Martínez-Rojasa, M., et al., 2016, An intelligent system for the acquisition and management of information from bill of quantities in building projects. *Expert Systems with Applications*, Vol. 63, pp. 284 – 294.

Petruseva, S., et al., 2017, Construction Costs Forecasting: Comparison of the Accuracy of Linear Regression and Support Vector Machine Models. *Technical Gazette*, Vol. 24, No. 5, pp. 1431 – 1438.

Zima, K., 2015, The Case-Based Reasoning Model of Cost Estimation at the Preliminary Stage of a Construction Project. *Procedia Engineering,* Vol. 122, pp. 57 – 64.

THE XML AND SEMANTIC WEB: A SYSTEMATIC REVIEW ON TECHNOLOGIES

Mohamed Alloghani[1,2], Dhiya Al-Jumeily[1], Abir Hussain[1], Ahmed J. Aljaaf[1,3], Jamila Mustafina[4], Mohammed Khalaf[5] and Sin Y. Tan[1]

[1]*Liverpool John Moores University, Liverpool L3 3AF, UK*

[2]*Abu Dhabi Health Services Company (SEHA), Abu Dhabi, UAE*

[3]*Centre of Computer, University of Anbar, Iraq*

[4]*Kazan Federal University, Kazan, Russia*

[5]*Almaaref University College, Anbar, Ramadi, Iraq*

ABSTRACT

The web and associated data have been around before the advent of big data and its related concepts. The semantic web refers to a Web of Data consisting of all sorts of data types and forms. In the context of Web of Data, many organizations prefer Linked Data formats for data publication, sharing and usage based on semantic web (SW) technologies. Conversely, the Extensible Markup Language (XML) is the commonly used data exchange format that the world wide web (WWW) uses today. Furthermore, innumerable international data exchange formats including Moving Picture Experts Group-7 (MPEG-7) and Institute of Electrical and Electronics Engineers Learning Object Metadata (IEEE LOM) rely on XML schema, and consequently, the web has a massive volume of XML format-based datasets. Of interest is the difference between SW and XML data models, frameworks as well as the language for implementing data queries. Hence, it is necessary to pursue interoperability and integration technologies for bridging the gap between SW and XML frameworks to ensure seamless data handling and retrieval in the web. The systematic survey used Preferred Reporting Items for Systematic Reviews and Meta-Analyses (PRISMA) methodology alongside DistillerSR to review articles addressing the interoperability and integration of XML and SW. The advanced search query focused on the article title, abstract, full text, and keywords that are related to the XML and SW technologies.

KEYWORDS

XML, WWW, XML Schema, Semantic Web (SW), SPARQL2XQuery, Xs2OWL

1. INTRODUCTION

One of the key features of data, especially those that are voluminous is the format and its compatibility with different analytical and information retrieval platforms. An exemplary example is the Web of Data, which unfortunately have several formats and standards depending on the industry, organization, and the purpose or strategic objective of the dataset. However, in the context of Web of Data, most organisations gravitate towards Linked Data because they rely on Semantic Web (SW) techniques for data publication with an expectation that target audience uses SPARQL to search, retrieve, and use the published data. It is imperative to note that SPARQL is a data query language without internal inferences and it retrieves data presented in a specific model or data format (Batra, Sachdeva, & Bhalla, 2018). However, Extensible Markup Language (XML) is the dominant data format used in the web, while most of the other international standards such as MPEG-7, IEEE LOM and MPEG-21 among others use XML schema making XML datasets the largest in the context of Web of Data.

Notably, semantic web (SW) is an extension of world wide web, and it qualifies as a Web of Data. Some of the semantic web technologies commonly used in data include but not limited to Resource Description Framework (RDF), Web Ontology Language (OWL), Simple Knowledge Organization System (SKOS), and SPARQL(Anonymous, 2014; Jing, Kay, Marley, & Hardiker, 2014; Scharffe, Zamazal, & Fensel, 2014). Despite the difference between SW and XML data format, applications and services must coexist within the web framework, and as such their interoperation is critical to the existence of applications with unfettered access to legacy systems (Zemmouchi-Ghomari, 2018). Both SW and XML schema and its related technologies will remain critical for the effectiveness of Web of Data, especially from the perspective of Linked Data.

Linked Data is the foundation of SW because it permits large scale integration of data on the web. The web contains all sorts and types of data including qualitative, quantitative, and visual data (Grossi, Romei, & Turini, 2017; Li, Martínez, & Rubio, 2017; Robson, 2016; Soylu et al., 2017). It is imperative to note that the format of these categories of data differs as well as the query language used to fetch them. It is important to note that platforms and retrieval forms are also different, but regardless of these differences, the categories and data types have a complex linkage that supports accessibility from single queries (Naumenko, Nikitin, Terziyan, & Zharko, 2005; Umar, 2005). That is, an implemented query returns search results that consist of images, videos, and texts concurrently, although most search engines present the results using relevant categories.

2. MOTIVATION AND SCOPE

The proliferation of technologies such as the Internet of Things, blogging, microblogging, and social media platforms have increased the volume of data on the web. Further, proliferation in digital entertainment platforms such as Netflix, Hulu, and website-based services providing video streaming services have also increased the amount of video-based data in the web. It is imperative to note that video streaming service providers such as Netflix and others tend to use different formats and compression technologies to improve the user experience. As such, Web of Data is becoming more diversified despite most of the data relying on XML schema and improvements are necessary to ensure synergy between XML formats and SW technologies.

The differences between SW technologies and XML schema data models require usage of different semantics and query languages that render data retrieval difficult. However, it is prudent to develop tools and algorithms that can bridge the gap between SW technologies and XML schemas, and notably, it is not plausible and practical to convert all the pertinent XML schema data and legacy data in general to SW data (Borkum & Frey, 2014; Chen, Chirkova, Sadri, & Salo, 2013; Ishaq et al., 2013). Such is the limitation encountered in bridging the gap, and it is essential to consider making SW and XML schema interoperable and integrable to ensure smoother data query services over the internet. The objective of pursuing interoperability and integration between the two models is to ensure that users can access heterogeneous external data without having to worrying about the sources of the data as well as the format of the data ("Conference Proceedings of the European Society for Computing and Technology in Anaesthesia and Intensive Care (ESCTAIC) 13th Annual Meeting in co-operation with Institut fur Anasthesiologie, UniversitatsSpital Zurich," 2002; Cordeiro & de Carvalho, 2002; Cristea, 2004; Mika & Akkermans, 2004; Payne & Tamma, 2005; Uschold, 2003). As such, it is increasingly becoming essential to provide universal search query endpoints as opposed to legacy data in the context of Linked Data and both SW and XML data formats.

As such, the systematic review explored the mechanisms for exploiting legacy data in the context of Web of Data while representing and discussing the disparate features of SW and XML. In specific, the review compares, and contrasts SW and XML technologies studied between 2010 and 2018 with the objective of identifying trends in those standards and technologies. Of importance is the focus of relevant developments that different groups have achieved on SW technologies as well as XML-based schema. Most importantly, the systematic review addresses some of the emerging techniques for dealing with interoperability and integration gap between SW and XML data models (Batet et al., 2012; El-Mekawy, Östman, & Hijazi, 2012; Tripathi, Gupta, & Bhattacharya, 2012; Valkenhoef, Tervonen, Brock, & Hillege, 2012). The exploration includes a detailed explanation of some of the emerging frameworks geared towards bridging the gap between the two data models.

3. NOVELTY AND CONTRIBUTION

The PRISMA methodology has a meta-analysis component that requires focus on epidemiological research design. However, given that the research focused on interoperability and integration of SW and XML data models, it became apparent that the meta-analysis component of the PRISMA systematic review model was invalid in this research. Consequently, the systemic review used aspects such as title, the structure of the abstract, rational and objective(s) clarification in the introduction, information sources presented in the methods sections, synthesis of results and discussion, and relevance of the conclusion as the basis for including articles in the review. It is the criteria considered for article qualification under the auspices of the PRISMA systematic review model that makes the difference in the used approach. As for the research contribution of the paper, Web of Data and the linkage between SW and XML requires real-time interoperation and integration of the two data models to improve the usability of the web data considering the differences in data formats. As such, the systematic review accounts for technological advancements that aim at improving interoperability and integration between SW and XML schema-based data models. Given the growth rate of data, whether Web of Data or Big Data, it is apparent that future systems must move towards collaborative and interaction when it comes to data handling and exchange. Regarding such issues, creating a scholarly profile that explains and documents some of the current technologies for bridging the gap between SW and XML data models. Against this backdrop, it is critical to note the role that such interoperability and integration will play in the sharing of big data in the context of Web of Data.

The systematic review approach adopted in the paper focused relied on modified PRISMA checklist and DistillerSR review tool parameters and protocols. DistillerSR is a systematic review literature review system that Evidence Partners administer and develop to conduct systematic reviews based on some of the standard review standards. Besides adherence to the standard PRISMA requirements, the researcher made several modifications in some of the PRISMA checklist sections to meet the review requirements for the papers published on XML and SW technologies. The review relied on specific words and phrases for the search and the filters used in the study included publication period, type of paper (full text and scholarly), and narrowed to peer-reviewed papers. Given that several journals publish papers on the subject, ProQuest Central was the ideal database to search because of the access it has to several journals. The diversity of the search results is essential for improving the quality of the review because the sampling is more compressive than using a database that tends to focus on fewer number of journals.

As for the search strategy, the keywords used in the database included XML Schema, SW Technologies, XML and SW data models, and interoperability and integration of XML and SW models were the critical search strategies. It is critical to note that the focus was on XML and SW data models alongside the technologies for bridging the gap between XML and SW data models. Moreover, these two areas appear to be obscure with most research focusing on individual subtopics and disregarding the intersection and interoperation of the two models.

4. RESULTS

A preliminary search based on *'(interoperability AND integration of XML AND SW models) AND (XML AND SW data models)'* search string return over 200 documents but based on the DistillerSR review research, a majority of the documents failed to directly address the address either the comparison between XML and SWL or the interoperability and integration between these two models of web data presentation. However, modifying the research string and using XML and SW as the lead search phrase, a total of 50 articles turned up as suiting the search criteria. However, even with the filters, some of the articles did not address some of the emerging technologies critical in bridging the gap between SW and XML data formats. Figure 1 shows PRISMA the flowchart illustrates the search results and filters including qualified papers. The search results also consider an additional query implemented on Web of Science although most of the papers retrieved from the database are from computer-related journals found in ProQuest Central.

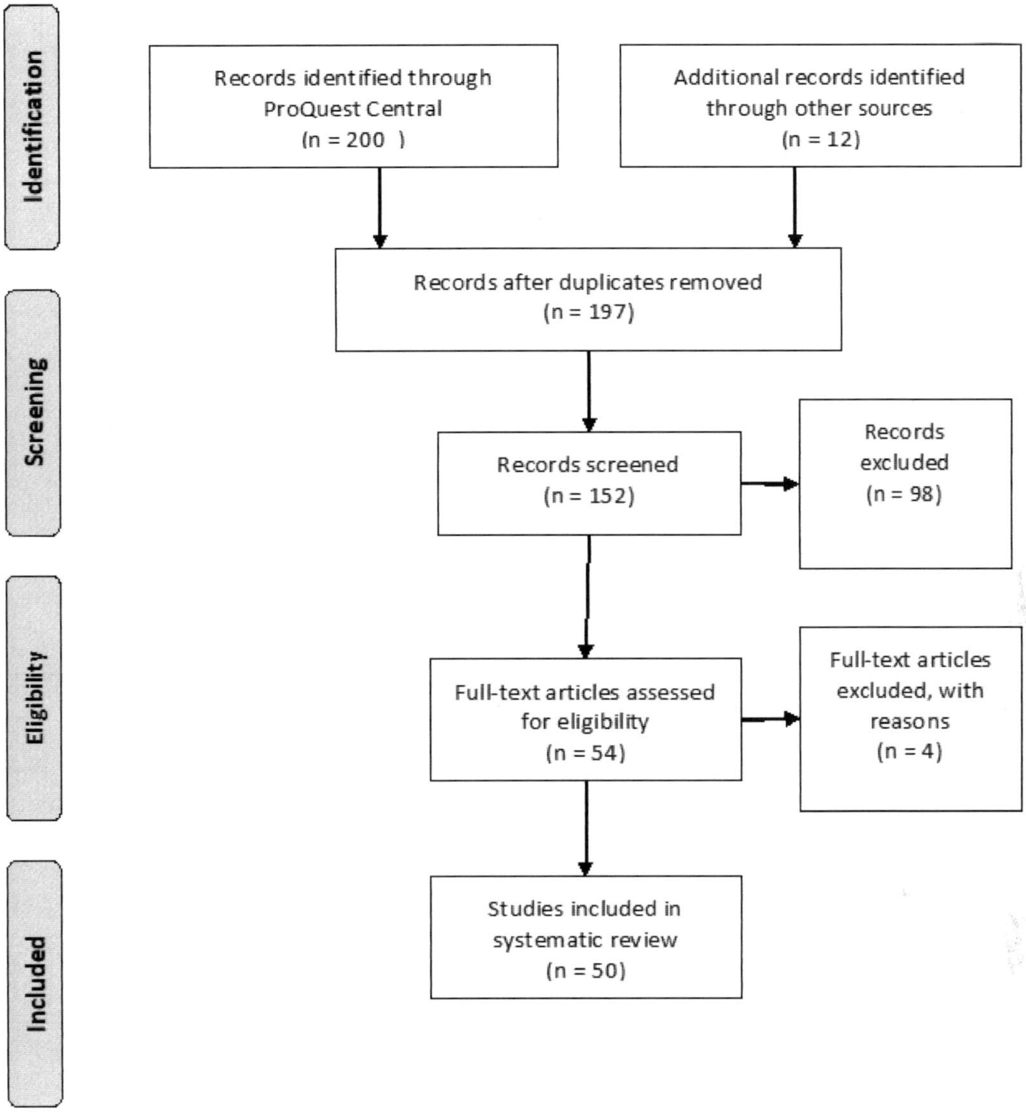

Figure 1. The PRISMA Framework and Article Analysis used in the Framework

5. HISTORICAL AND TECHNICAL DISCOURSE OF XML AND SEMANTIC WEB

Based on the previous discussion and results of the search strings, it is apparent that SW and XML models adopt and deploy different technologies. However, the differences observed and recorded between the two models are in three categories namely data, schema, and query levels. The standards that both XML and SW adopt at each of the three levels are different. For example, at the data level, XML models on XML data formats while SW uses RDF data format. At the schema level, XML model uses the XML schema while SW uses an RDF schema that leverages some of the features of OWL. Finally, at the query level, XML model uses XQuery while SW uses SPARQL. It suffices to note that XML is a data representation language in XML module while the RDF is a language for representing data in SW. The schema level describes the structure of the data both in XML and SW models with XML schema being the primary data model that the World Wide Web Consortium (W3C) recommends (Aleroud & Karabatis, 2017; Ameri & Patil, 2012; Kaur & Aggarwal, 2017). The number of articles published between 2010 and 2018 are distributed as follows.

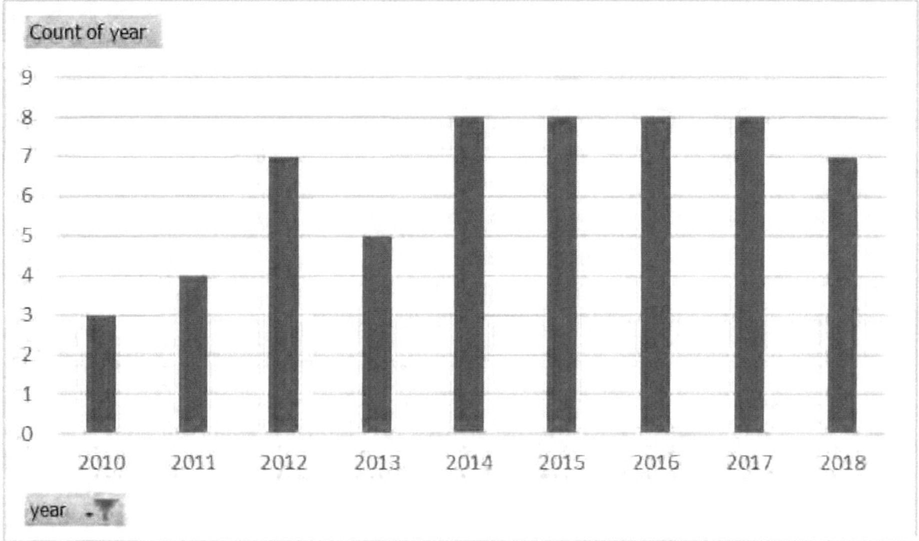

Figure 2. Distribution of the number of articles published on SW and XML between 2010 and 2018

As per Figure 2, the number of publications on SW and XML increased between 2010 and 2012, and after that between 2013 and 2014 before stagnating between 2014 and 2017. As per region distribution of the publications, the top three regions or more specifically cities leading in the publications include Heidelberg (13%), Dordrecht (11%), and Bradford (11%) refer to Figure 3.

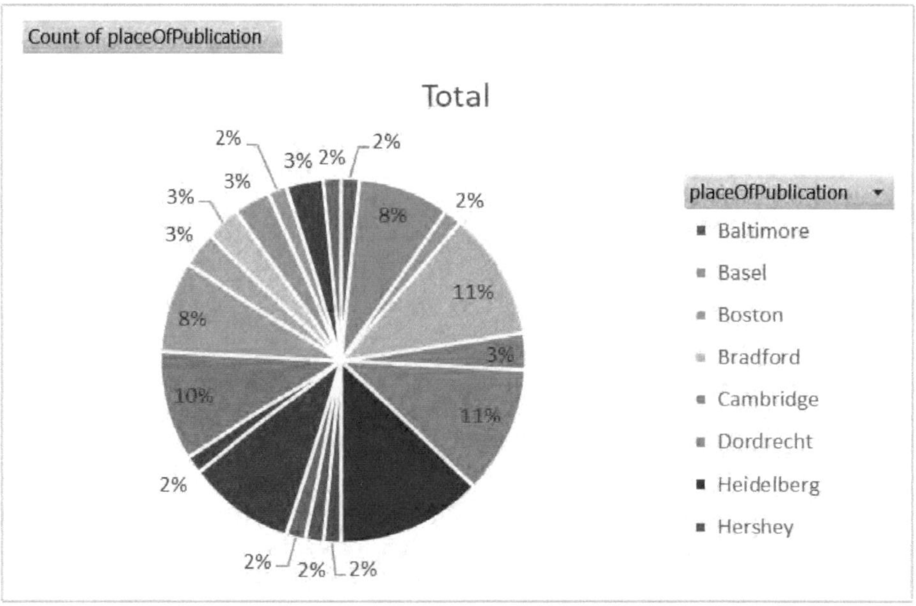

Figure 3. Distribution of Published Articles by Region

However, it is imperative to note that XML Schema 1.0 is under development and W3C has plans to launch the framework to boost data sharing within partner programs in future. As for SW, both RDF schema and OWL describe the semantics and structure of the RDF data used in SW data query and analysis. The OWL-based SW consists of OWL validator, pellet, protégé four alpha (Figure 3). TopBraid composer and Jena. Each of these components performs a specific and distinct function and role in SW data dispersion and sharing technologies. As for the nature of the query level technologies and mechanisms, XML uses XQuery (XML Query Language to conduct advanced searches on XML datasets. On the other hand, SW uses SPARQL language alongside RDF query protocols as the standard language for querying RDF data. The current version of SPARQL has debugging and additional amendments and services on protocols, service descriptions, hypertext transfer protocols for managing RDF graphics and other critical regimes and functionalities. It was paramount to explore the fundamental principles of XML and SW as documented in the reviewed research papers. The evolution of both SW and XML technologies are as shown in Figure 4.

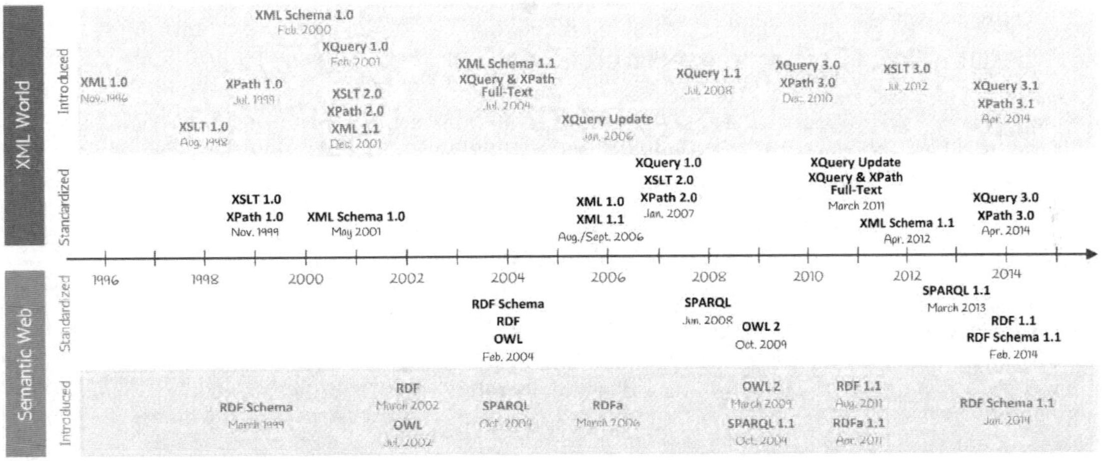

Figure 4. The Evolution of SW and XML Technologies between 2010 and 2018

5.1 Data Level Comparisons and Contrasts

As previously stated, the two data models exhibit obvious data level differences presented in the following discussions.

5.1.1 Extensible Markup Language

The is a representation of a document that in essence is a template or an outline for preparing documents based on the XML standard. It uses the same tags used in Hypertext Markup Language (HTML) although the XML tags lack restrictive tag and interpretive semantics. As such users can define and personalise tags to meet their document formatting and output needs. Hence, XML consists of a plain text that contains the content of the document and a markup that is an equivalence of a cascading styling sheet used in format and style HTML documents (Askarunisa, Punitha, & Ramaraj, 2011; Isern et al., 2011; Kovacevic, Ivanovic, Milosavljevic, Konjovic, & Surla, 2011; Nowling et al., 2011). The XML language uses tags that assume the tree-branch pattern. It is imperative to note that XML has distinct and standard elements including but not limited to nodes of the document, elements, comments, specs for namespaces, and instructions among others. The XML document structure has unique and standard features similar to those found in document processing languages such as Latex. A majority the data in the web are based on this data format, and due its importance and role in data available, several web data scrapping methods and tools have been devised to aid in the process of extracting, transforming and loading such data onto suitable analytical platforms.

5.1.2 Resource Description Framework

The RDF is also a general-purpose language that represents web information resources but on the semantic web side. In comparison to XML, the RDF is a lightweight language that models data using central RDF statements and concepts. It is flexible and simple to use because of its reliance on central RDF model concept that requires a subject, a predicate, and an object to create data nodes that users can query. In the context of RDF statement, the subject refers to the resources that the web data is describing while the predicate points towards a specific property of the object. The object in question must have a value, and it is imperative to note that the subject cannot be an Internationalized Resource Identifier (IRI) or a blank node. Conversely, it is mandatory for a predicate to an IRI while the object can either be a blank node, an IRI, or an RDF literal. Most importantly, graphically, RDF statements with clear labels are graphs with resources serving as the nodes and the statements forming the arcs in the resultant graphs(Dallas, 2016; Drewes, Kuglitsch, Adám, & Rózsa, 2016; Souag, Mazo, Salinesi, & Comyn-wattiau, 2016). Ideally, the arcs that the statements form connect subject and object nodes, and the graph in its entirety is the RDF Dataset.

5.2 Schema Level Comparisons and Contrasts

At the schema level, XML, RDF and OWL tend to exhibit distinct competitive features deduced from their functional differences. Some of the features and the differences observed from the systematic review are discussed in the following subtopic.

5.2.1 Extensible Markup Language Schema

The XML schema is a language schema that W3C developed using the XML syntax, and it describes the structure and format of all documents written in XML (Robson & Boray, 2015; Soylu, Giese, Jimenez-ruiz, Vega-gorgojo, & Horrocks, 2016). From a technical perspective, the XML syntax has rich capabilities that render one of the commonly used formats for web data. In practical applications, the XML schema specifies the specific element hierarchy including all data type constraints available as options within predefined options of the data. The optional constraints restrict the number of occurrences of the number as well as the nature of attributes.

A standard XML document consists of components that have root as the delimiting factor at the beginning and end of the said document. The delimiters are tags that specify the type of XML schema, and the tags are either simple or complex depending on the nature of the tags that the model uses. It is important to draw the similarities in syntax between XML schema and other programming languages regarding data types. That is, XML uses standard data syntax such as string, integer, and double among others. Furthermore, XML schema also has complex data types represented as classes and constructs that consist of features and attributes of desired elements of the resultant document.

As for the structure of the document, XL schema has rich structuring functionalities. In most cases, the schema document has a more or less or preprogrammed structure serving as a template based on specified sequences or unordered elements created using *choice* and all *tag* commands. Therefore, it is critical to understand that OWL has constructs assigned unique names and nested accordingly to manage and handle unnamed and unstructured data. However, it is imperative to note that unstructured and complex attributes may require referencing using appropriate attributes to avoid cyclic redundancies that would other derail the performance of the XML extraction process. Based on the information available on the OWL website in conjunction with the updates that W3C provides, OWL has two versions, and the second version has high in-memory efficiency for implemented complex references.

The XML schema 1.1 is compatible with Schema 1.0 although it introduced the alternative element that allows a user to have and specify a set of data types. The feature allows the schema to circumvent some of the dataset restriction it faces in the previous versions and the XML Schema 1.1 has a redefine function for recalibrating variables that do not conform to the limits predetermined in the options of the schema. Furthermore, XML Schema 1.1 has error management features, union capabilities for the value spaces of primitive attributes, and timestamp for tracing the time series associated with each of the attributes. Currently, XML Schema has reached its third version and an example of a document based on the XML Schema 3.0 and above id the Europass CV. The latest version the schema is XML Schema 3.2 that uses a top-down approach in handling its elements as well as additional elements such as key, imports, and attribute types (Burke, 2009; Torre, 2009). It is also imperative to note that the latest version of the schema has a wide variety of data types and the expansion accommodates some of the emerging complex data fields.

5.2.2 RDF Schema

The schema leverages the concept of RDF, and it builds vocabulary, and subsequent dictionary referred to as RDFS based on its relationship between the vocabulary library and the resources available within the referenced libraries and packages. As per fundamentals of RDF schema, such packages belong to instance class and the property value associated with confirms the relationship. It is pertinent to note that it is possible to rearrange XML data classes into based in hierarchical structures that are subparts of objects and properties. All the RDFs classes correspond to the concept type of categorisation of a given attribute. Of importance is to note that the function and characteristics of RDF stagnated regardless of the evolution in some aspects of the framework. Regardless of the similarities between the two languages, OWL is richer hence superior to RDF, and the basic difference is evident in the definition of OWL class construct as opposed to that of RDF.

5.2.3 Web Ontology Language

The OWL is the standard ontology for web data and content, and it is similar to the RDF. It has two versions with innumerable updates, but the latest introduction involved the inclusion of a temporal ontology element in an OWL. The latest edition focuses on the characteristics of temporal concepts that account and focus on the description of temporal properties of the resources used in WWW pages. It is also critical to recognise that OWL 2.0 and the latest versions (Löhe & Legner, 2010; Russomanno, Chari, & Halford, 2008; Sundberg, Sundberg, & Schofield, 2008). Despite the improvement between the versions of the frameworks, it is critical to note that most upgrades involved improvements that had little changes to do with the overall functionality of the framework. Besides modal differences, there is a difference observed based on concrete syntax, semantics, basic constructs, identity constraints, and user-defined data types and attributes.

5.3 Query Level Comparisons

The contrasts drawn at query level are the basis for exploring the differences between SW and XML data models.

5.3.1 XQuery and XPath

Given the differences between SW and XML data formats, it is prudent to explore query techniques that can address the gap between the two technologies. The current XML schema depends on XML Path Language to sect document nodes within the targeted XML dataset. The XPath query language is a component of the XQuery language and it has a tree-like structure for displaying the query results and all XML documents retrieved in the process(Fox & Kozyra, 2015; Ilie-Zudor et al., 2015; Kardan, Aziz, & Shahpasand, 2015; Ratnam et al., 2014; Robson, Caruso, & Balis, 2015). The XQuery has many features, but none of which addresses the gap between SW and XML and SPARQL has emerged as a technique of interest in bridging the gap.

Besides the security concern and mandate of W3C, one of the key concern areas is the advancement of and integration of crucial web data and communication technologies. SPARQL is the future solution to addressing this problem and future considerations ought to consider the influence and impact of SPARQL on the future of interoperability and integration of SW and XML data models(Hung et al., 2007; Paquette, 2007; Rasseneur-Coffinet, Smyrniou, & Tchounikine, 2007; Soroor & Tarokh, 2006). Regardless of the version of SPARQL, one of its major features is the support for data retrieval between these two data formats, and the key functionality and benefit of using SPARQL is the full range of query options including the options to select, construct, ask, and describe the construct of interest. As an operational principle, SPARQL executes a select query that returns an amalgamated sequence of output with restricted variable binding. Further, the results of the ask query is a Boolean response assuming either a value of yes or no. Most importantly, the most recent versions of SPARQL contains RDF modules with graphing and reporting capabilities for various solutions.

6. CONCLUSION

The opportunities for the application of SPARQL and other related interoperability and integration techniques are endless because Web of Data continues to grow, and the complexity of the wed data will require seamless integration between SW and XML data formats and related technology. The fact is that technologies such SPARQL are playing a crucial role in ensuring that SW and XML data are receivable with ease. However, it is pertinent to highlight that the search articles also captured and accounted for articles that are not necessarily addressing the area of interest and it would be prudent to conduct a survey target studies that have explored the interoperability and integration of SW and XML schemas and data formats.

REFERENCES

Aleroud, A., & Karabatis, G. (2017). Contextual information fusion for intrusion detection: a survey and taxonomy. *Knowledge and Information Systems*, *52*(3), 563–619. https://doi.org/http://dx.doi.org/10.1007/s10115-017-1027-3

Ameri, F., & Patil, L. (2012). Digital manufacturing market: a semantic web-based framework for agile supply chain deployment. *Journal of Intelligent Manufacturing*, *23*(5), 1817–1832. https://doi.org/http://dx.doi.org/10.1007/s10845-010-0495-z

Anonymous. (2014). Engineering & Physical Sciences in Medicine Conference 2013 Pan Pacific Hotel, Perth, Australia, 3-7 November 2013 Oral presentation abstracts. *Australasian Physical & Engineering Sciences in Medicine*, *37*(1), 153–269. https://doi.org/http://dx.doi.org/10.1007/s13246-014-0248-y

Askarunisa, A., Punitha, K. A. J., & Ramaraj, N. (2011). Test Case Generation and Prioritization for Composite Web Service Based on OWL-S. *Neural Network World*, *21*(6), 519–537. Retrieved from https://search.proquest.com/docview/1010622274?accountid=145382

Batet, M., Isern, D., Marin, L., Martínez, S., Moreno, A., Sánchez, D., … Gibert, K. (2012). Knowledge-driven delivery of home care services. *Journal of Intelligent Information Systems*, *38*(1), 95–130. https://doi.org/http://dx.doi.org/10.1007/s10844-010-0145-0

Batra, S., Sachdeva, S., & Bhalla, S. (2018). Entity Attribute Value Style Modeling Approach for Archetype Based Data. *Information*, *9*(1), 2. https://doi.org/http://dx.doi.org/10.3390/info9010002

Borkum, M. I., & Frey, J. G. (2014). Usage and applications of Semantic Web techniques and technologies to support chemistry research. *Journal of Cheminformatics*, *6*. https://doi.org/http://dx.doi.org/10.1186/1758-2946-6-18

Burke, M. (2009). The semantic web and the digital library. *Aslib Proceedings*, *61*(3), 316–322. https://doi.org/http://dx.doi.org/10.1108/00012530910959844

Chen, D., Chirkova, R., Sadri, F., & Salo, T. J. (2013). Query optimization in information integration. *Acta Informatica*, *50*(4), 257–287. https://doi.org/http://dx.doi.org/10.1007/s00236-013-0179-1

Conference Proceedings of the European Society for Computing and Technology in Anaesthesia and Intensive Care (ESCTAIC) 13th Annual Meeting in co-operation with Institut fur Anasthesiologie, UniversitatsSpital Zurich. (2002). *Journal of Clinical Monitoring and Computing*, *17*(7–8), 467. Retrieved from https://search.proquest.com/docview/217133632?accountid=145382

Cordeiro, M. I., & de Carvalho, J. (2002). Web services: What they are and their importance for libraries. *VINE*, *32*(4), 46–62. https://doi.org/http://dx.doi.org/10.1108/03055720210471148

Cristea, A. I. (2004). What can the Semantic Web do for Adaptive Educational Hypermedia? *Journal of Educational Technology & Society*, *7*(4), 40–58. Retrieved from https://search.proquest.com/docview/1287054280?accountid=145382

Dallas, C. (2016). Digital curation beyond the “wild frontier”: a pragmatic approach. *Archival Science*, *16*(4), 421–457. https://doi.org/http://dx.doi.org/10.1007/s10502-015-9252-6

Drewes, H., Kuglitsch, F., Adám, J., & Rózsa, S. (2016). The Geodesist’s Handbook 2016. *Journal of Geodesy*, *90*(10), 907–1205. https://doi.org/http://dx.doi.org/10.1007/s00190-016-0948-z

El-Mekawy, M., Östman, A., & Hijazi, I. (2012). A Unified Building Model for 3D Urban GIS. *ISPRS International Journal of Geo-Information*, *1*(2), 120–145. https://doi.org/http://dx.doi.org/10.3390/ijgi1020120

Fox, P., & Kozyra, J. (2015). eScience and Informatics for international science programs. *Progress in Earth and Planetary Science*, *2*(1), 1–9. https://doi.org/http://dx.doi.org/10.1186/s40645-015-0042-9

Grossi, V., Romei, A., & Turini, F. (2017). Survey on using constraints in data mining. *Data Mining and Knowledge Discovery*, *31*(2), 424–464. https://doi.org/http://dx.doi.org/10.1007/s10618-016-0480-z

Hung, P. C. K., Chiu, D. K. W., Fung, W. W., Cheung, W. K., Wong, R., Choi, S. P. M., … Cheng, V. S. Y. (2007). End-to-end privacy control in service outsourcing of human intensive processes: A multi-layered Web service integration approach. *Information Systems Frontiers*, *9*(1), 85–101. https://doi.org/http://dx.doi.org/10.1007/s10796-006-9019-y

Ilie-Zudor, E., Ekárt, A., Kemeny, Z., Buckingham, C., Welch, P., & Monostori, L. (2015). Advanced predictive-analysis-based decision support for collaborative logistics networks. *Supply Chain Management*, *20*(4), 369–388. Retrieved from https://search.proquest.com/docview/1691011014?accountid=145382

Isern, D., Moreno, A., Sánchez, D., Hajnal, Á., Pedone, G., & Varga, L. Z. (2011). Agent-based execution of personalised home care treatments. *Applied Intelligence*, *34*(2), 155–180. https://doi.org/http://dx.doi.org/10.1007/s10489-009-0187-6

Ishaq, I., Carels, D., Teklemariam, G. K., Hoebeke, J., Abeele, F. Vanden, Poorter, E. De, … Demeester, P. (2013). IETF Standardization in the Field of the Internet of Things (IoT): A Survey. *Journal of Sensor and Actuator Networks*, *2*(2), 235–287. https://doi.org/http://dx.doi.org/10.3390/jsan2020235

Jing, X., Kay, S., Marley, T., & Hardiker, N. R. (2014). Integration of an OWL-DL Knowledge Base with an EHR Prototype and Providing Customized Information. *Journal of Medical Systems*, *38*(9), 1–75. https://doi.org/http://dx.doi.org/10.1007/s10916-014-0075-4

Kardan, A. A., Aziz, M., & Shahpasand, M. (2015). Adaptive systems: a content analysis on technical side for e-learning environments. *The Artificial Intelligence Review*, *44*(3), 365–391. https://doi.org/http://dx.doi.org/10.1007/s10462-015-9430-1

Kaur, N., & Aggarwal, H. (2017). Evaluation of Information Retrieval Based Ontology Development Editors for Semantic Web. *International Journal of Modern Education and Computer Science*, *9*(7), 63. https://doi.org/http://dx.doi.org/10.5815/ijmecs.2017.07.07

Kovacevic, A., Ivanovic, D., Milosavljevic, B., Konjovic, Z., & Surla, D. (2011). Automatic extraction of metadata from scientific publications for CRIS systems. *Program*, *45*(4), 376–396. https://doi.org/http://dx.doi.org/10.1108/00330331111182094

Li, X., Martínez, J.-F., & Rubio, G. (2017). Towards a Hybrid Approach to Context Reasoning for Underwater Robots. *Applied Sciences*, *7*(2), 183. https://doi.org/http://dx.doi.org/10.3390/app7020183

Löhe, J., & Legner, C. (2010). SOA adoption in business networks: do service-oriented architectures really advance inter-organizational integration? *Electronic Markets*, *20*(3–4), 181–196. https://doi.org/http://dx.doi.org/10.1007/s12525-010-0046-7

MIKA, P., & AKKERMANS, H. (2004). Towards a new synthesis of ontology technology and knowledge management. *The Knowledge Engineering Review*, *19*(4), 317–345. Retrieved from https://search.proquest.com/docview/217528594?accountid=145382

Naumenko, A., Nikitin, S., Terziyan, V., & Zharko, A. (2005). Strategic industrial alliances in paper industry: XML- vs Ontology-based integration platforms. *The Learning Organization*, *12*(5), 492–514. https://doi.org/http://dx.doi.org/10.1108/09696470510611438

Nowling, R. J., Vyas, J., Weatherby, G., Fenwick, M. W., Ellis, H. J. C., & Gryk, M. R. (2011). CONNJUR spectrum translator: an open source application for reformatting NMR spectral data. *Journal of Biomolecular NMR*, *50*(1), 83–89. https://doi.org/http://dx.doi.org/10.1007/s10858-011-9497-1

Paquette, G. (2007). An Ontology and a Software Framework for Competency Modeling and Management. *Journal of Educational Technology & Society*, *10*(3), 1–21. Retrieved from https://search.proquest.com/docview/1287039622?accountid=145382

PAYNE, T., & TAMMA, V. (2005). Towards Semantic Web agents: Knowledge Web and AgentLink. *The Knowledge Engineering Review*, *20*(2), 191–196. Retrieved from https://search.proquest.com/docview/217507142?accountid=145382

Rasseneur-Coffinet, D., Smyrniou, G., & Tchounikine, P. (2007). Supporting Learners' Appropriation of a Web-Based Learning Curriculum. *International Journal of Distance Education Technologies*, *5*(4), 46–79. https://doi.org/http://dx.doi.org/10.4018/jdet.2007100104

Ratnam, J., Zdrazil, B., Digles, D., Cuadrado-Rodriguez, E., Neefs, J.-M., Tipney, H., … Chichester, C. (2014). The Application of the Open Pharmacological Concepts Triple Store (Open PHACTS) to Support Drug Discovery Research. *PLoS One*, *9*(12). https://doi.org/http://dx.doi.org/10.1371/journal.pone.0115460

Robson, B. (2016). Studies in using a universal exchange and inference language for evidence based medicine. Semi-automated learning and reasoning for PICO methodology, systematic review, and environmental epidemiology. *Computers in Biology and Medicine*, *79*, 299–323. https://doi.org/http://dx.doi.org/10.1016/j.compbiomed.2016.10.009

Robson, B., & Boray, S. (2015). Implementation of a web based universal exchange and inference language for medicine: Sparse data, probabilities and inference in data mining of clinical data repositories. *Computers in Biology and Medicine*, *66*, 82–102. https://doi.org/http://dx.doi.org/10.1016/j.compbiomed.2015.07.015

Robson, B., Caruso, T. P., & Balis, U. G. J. (2015). Suggestions for a web based universal exchange and inference language for medicine. Continuity of patient care with PCAST disaggregation. *Computers in Biology and Medicine*, *56*, 51–66. https://doi.org/http://dx.doi.org/10.1016/j.compbiomed.2014.10.022

Russomanno, D., Chari, S., & Halford, C. (2008). Sparse Detector Imaging Sensor with Two-Class Silhouette Classification. *Sensors*, *8*(12), 7996–8015. https://doi.org/http://dx.doi.org/10.3390/s8127996

Scharffe, F., Zamazal, O., & Fensel, D. (2014). Ontology alignment design patterns. *Knowledge and Information Systems*, *40*(1), 1–28. https://doi.org/http://dx.doi.org/10.1007/s10115-013-0633-y

Soroor, J., & Tarokh, M. J. (2006). Innovative SCM. *VINE*, *36*(3), 304–340. https://doi.org/http://dx.doi.org/10.1108/03055720610703597

Souag, A., Mazo, R., Salinesi, C., & Comyn-wattiau, I. (2016). Reusable knowledge in security requirements engineering: a systematic mapping study. *Requirements Engineering*, *21*(2), 251–283. https://doi.org/http://dx.doi.org/10.1007/s00766-015-0220-8

Soylu, A., Giese, M., Jimenez-ruiz, E., Kharlamov, E., Zheleznyakov, D., & Horrocks, I. (2017). Ontology-based end-user visual query formulation: Why, what, who, how, and which? *Universal Access in the Information Society*, *16*(2), 435–467. https://doi.org/http://dx.doi.org/10.1007/s10209-016-0465-0

Soylu, A., Giese, M., Jimenez-ruiz, E., Vega-gorgojo, G., & Horrocks, I. (2016). Experiencing OptiqueVQS: a multi-paradigm and ontology-based visual query system for end users. *Universal Access in the Information Society*, *15*(1), 129–152. https://doi.org/http://dx.doi.org/10.1007/s10209-015-0404-5

Sundberg, J. P., Sundberg, B. A., & Schofield, P. (2008). Integrating mouse anatomy and pathology ontologies into a phenotyping database: Tools for data capture and training. *Mammalian Genome*, *19*(6), 413–419. https://doi.org/http://dx.doi.org/10.1007/s00335-008-9123-z

Torre, I. (2009). Adaptive systems in the era of the semantic and social web, a survey. *User Modeling and User - Adapted Interaction*, *19*(5), 433–486. https://doi.org/http://dx.doi.org/10.1007/s11257-009-9067-3

Tripathi, R., Gupta, M. P., & Bhattacharya, J. (2012). Interoperability adoption among government and corporate portals in India: a study. *Journal of Enterprise Information Management*, *25*(2), 98–122. https://doi.org/http://dx.doi.org/10.1108/17410391211204374

Umar, A. (2005). IT Infrastructure to Enable Next Generation Enterprises. *Information Systems Frontiers*, *7*(3), 217. https://doi.org/http://dx.doi.org/10.1007/s10796-005-2768-1

Uschold, M. (2003). Where are the semantics in the semantic web? *AI Magazine*, *24*(3), 25–36. Retrieved from https://search.proquest.com/docview/208125637?accountid=145382

Valkenhoef, G. van, Tervonen, T., Brock, B. de, & Hillege, H. (2012). Deficiencies in the transfer and availability of clinical trials evidence: a review of existing systems and standards. *BMC Medical Informatics and Decision Making*, *12*, 95. https://doi.org/http://dx.doi.org/10.1186/1472-6947-12-95

Zemmouchi-Ghomari, L. (2018). Cohabitation of Relational Databases and Domain Ontologies in the Semantic Web Context. *Journal of Systems Integration*, *9*(1), 42–57. Retrieved from https://search.proquest.com/docview/2000969229?accountid=145382

USAGE OF PROCESS MINING IN THE 'OFFER TO PRODUCTION PROCESS' OF A CONTRACT MANUFACTURER FOR CAST COMPONENTS

Jens Kiefer and Melina Precht
University of Applied Sciences Ulm
Prittwitzstraße 10, 89075 Ulm, Germany

ABSTRACT

This paper presents potentials and current limits of the big data method process mining within the 'offer to production process' of a contract manufacturer for cast components. The considered process includes all essential activities from the offer inquiry to the production start of the ordered cast components. As a first step, the general goals and characteristics of the trendsetting method process mining are illustrated. After explaining the most important contents of the considered 'offer to production process', the usage of process mining within this topic field is demonstrated. Apart from methodical issues, information-technical and organizational aspects are discussed. In this context, one special focus is on the description of the required data preparation process, which forms one of the most significant fundamentals for an efficient and profitable execution of process mining. By means of a real existing practical example, the procedure, potentials and current limits of process mining using the software tools LANA and Celonis are critically evaluated. Finally, the paper ends with a conclusion and an outlook towards further research and development activities.

KEYWORDS

Process Mining, Data Management, Application

1. PROCESS MINING

According to van der Aalst (2016), process mining is an increasingly important and trendsetting method in the area of data science and big data approaches. In general, the goal of process mining is to gain information about real processes (e.g. production processes or administrative processes) based on real existing data stored in file- or database-based IT systems. Whereas classical data mining techniques are mostly data-centric, process mining is process-centric (Hand, 2001). The method process mining enables business processes to be reconstructed and analyzed based on 'digital traces' in IT systems. During process mining, specific data mining algorithms are applied to event log data in order to identify trends, patterns or details contained in event logs recorded by an information system (van der Aalst, 2011).

As illustrated in Figure 1, event logs can be used to conduct three types of process mining. The first type of process mining is *discovery*. The discovery technique aims to generate a process model based on log data without using any a-priori information. Currently, process discovery is the most popular process mining technique. The second type of process mining is *conformance*. The conformance technique compares an available process model with log data of the real process. As a result, the deviations between log data and process model are detected and visualized. Last and least, there is the *enhancement* technique. This approach enables the extension of an available process model by means of existing log data. Whereas the conformance technique measures the alignment between model and reality, this technique aims at extending or improving the a-priori model (e.g. addition of waiting times).

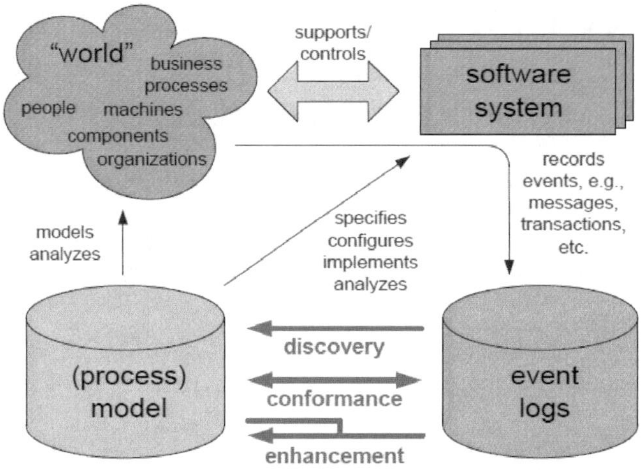

Figure 1. The three basic types of process mining: discovery, conformance and enhancement (van der Aalst, 2012)

According to van der Aalst (2016), process mining applications can be differentiated into three different ways: *continuously*, *repeated* and *ad-hoc*. The continuous application is appropriate for processes that shall be monitored on daily basis or in real time. Its implementation is quite expensive and only specific analyses can be executed because they must be implemented in the tool before. In contrast, the ad-hoc usage implies less effort during the implementation. This application is suitable for one-time analysis, which are never or seldom repeated. The ad-hoc usage is appropriate for unique optimizations and the detection of weaknesses in the process. The repeated application is located somewhere between the continuous and the ad-hoc solution. It is appropriate for analyzing processes e.g. on monthly basis or if the analysis only vary slightly.

This paper presents the usage of process mining focusing on process discovery and on ad-hoc analyses of the process data. Taking the real-existing application scenario 'offer to production process' of a contract manufacturer for cast components, potentials and current limits of process mining are portrayed and critically evaluated.

2. APPLICATION SCENARIO AND CHALLENGES

The process discussed in this contribution is located in the foundry sector. A contract manufacturer produces cast components – both ready-to-install parts and unfinished components – for various customers of different industries. Figure 2 illustrates the most important phases and their interrelations of the considered 'offer to production process'.

Before an offer inquiry of a customer is received, there is a series production of other products running. In parallel to this series production, the 'offer to production process' for new products is performed. This process starts with an incoming offer inquiry from a customer. After extensive planning steps such as the planning of the foundry process with the necessary production equipment as well as the corresponding logistics activities, an offer is presented to the customer. If the customer decides to accept this offer, the order allocation takes place. The incoming order represents the beginning of further activities: As a first step, the equipment for the casting process such as models or core boxes have to be planned in detail and manufactured. Afterwards, the production of the initial sample follows. If the customer accepts this sample, the Start of Production (SOP) enables the series production.

Due to recent developments the process of production planning is getting more and more complex. Customers tend to request ready-to-install components instead of unfinished parts. This development complicates the planning process significantly because there are only limited possibilities for further processing within the regarded company. The increasing customer expectations on the one hand and the rising number of requested products on the other hand lead to the necessity to gain more detailed knowledge about the actually lived processes as crucial basis to implement a KPI-driven continuous improvement process.

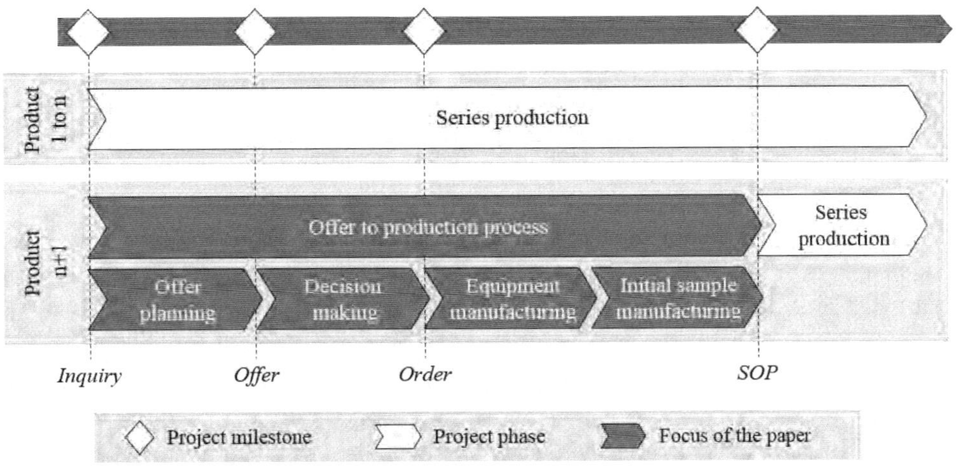

Figure 2. Simplified 'offer to production process' of a contract manufacturer

Within this application example, there are some specific challenges regarding the usage of process mining. At present, the most important challenges are:

- Process has a project character (e.g. different departments are involved in each offer planning process)
- Each subprocess (e.g. 'offer planning') contains several standard activities that are logically structured over a superior network (hereby, each standard activity can optionally be skipped)
- The 'offer planning' process consists of many activities that are conducted in parallel
- No concrete reference process due to high product and process variances
- Heterogeneous data sources (data are available in databases and file-based IT systems)
- Combination of automatically generated data and manual entered data
- About 30 % of the available data sets are incomplete
- Process model consists of different process sequences (e.g. not all offers result in an order)

3. METHODICAL IMPLEMENTATION

There are several preparation steps necessary before an analysis with process mining is possible. The most important steps are:

1. Selecting the right data – deep know-how about the available data is necessary
2. Rating the individual data sources maturity level according to the Process Mining Manifesto (van der Aalst et al, 2012) – shows the suitability of each source for the implementation of process mining
3. Generating a data model of the considered objects (e.g. an inquiry or a requested component) including their relations, the individual identification and attributes – the current connections and connection possibilities between objects and different data sources become clear
4. Merging the heterogeneous data sources – to form a unified data set

The maturity level rating in the Process Mining Manifesto (van der Aalst et al, 2012) rates the maturity level of '5' as the best case and the maturity level of '1' as the worst case in the light of applying process mining. In general, a maturity level of '5' should be aimed for using process mining but the usage of data sources with a maturity level of '4' or '3' can mostly also be used.

In the considered 'offer to production process', there are six different data sources (e.g. a CSV file or the SAP SP-module), which have to be rated first according to the defined maturity levels. Table 1 illustrates the result of this rating process. This analysis shows that most of the data sources are generally suitable for the implementation of process mining.

Table 1. Maturity levels of the used data sources

Maturity level	Number of sources
5	0
4	1
3	3
2	1
1	1

Due to the variety of the data sources that are used in the regarded process, the isolated rating of sources is not enough to specify the suitability for the process mining implementation. The combination of data sources must be considered additionally according to the specific process. In addition to that, the data quality must be rated in detail. Only if the data sources, the data relations and the data quality are known and good enough, so that a merging of the data sources is possible, an implementation of process mining is reasonable conceivable.

Figure 3 illustrates the developed data model regarding the merging process of the used heterogeneous data sources. When checking for connection possibilities, it is necessary that the individual object identifications can somehow be connected to the selected Case-ID. This connection can result from a third table, which owns both identifications (cp. Figure 3: 'Table'). A connection can also result from a data source that has one explicit identification and the identification of another data source as an extra attribute (cp. Figure 3: 'Data source 3'). If it is not possible to find a connection between all used data sources, the application of process mining is not possible for this case or another Case-ID must be considered.

In the considered 'offer to production process' a relation table is created as visualized in Figure 3. With this table it is possible to assign the Case-ID to each data set by using the possessed identification as a connecting element. After the heterogeneous data forms a unit, the following implementation of process mining is possible.

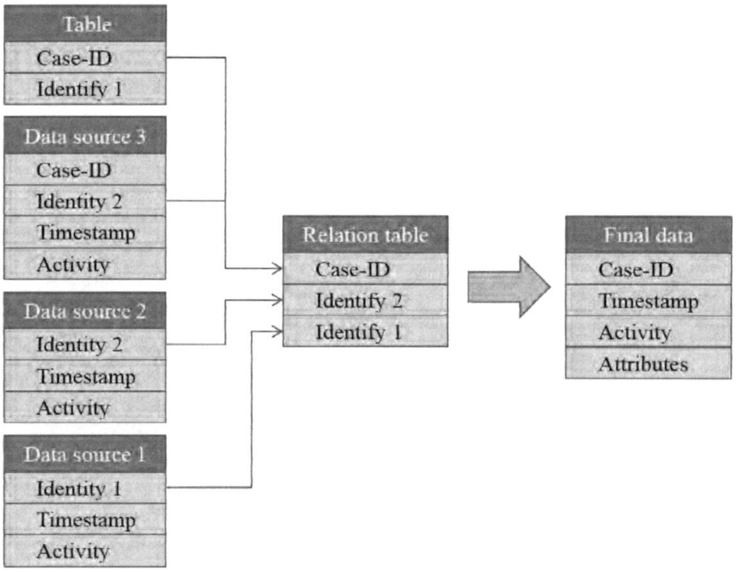

Figure 3. Data model of the merging process

The 'Final data' can now be played into the process mining tool. The tool arranges the activities according to the Case-ID and on basis of the timestamps. Thus, a process model is created, which displays how the single cases went through the process. First, the process model is chaotic and consists out of a wide range of activities (in this case up to 600 different activities are involved). If there are known filters to select the desired process, they are applied right away. Another possibility to gain model transparency is to reduce the visualized activities and paths between activities. However, this reduction would lead to information loss at the same time, because not all activities and paths that are executed are being displayed. To keep visualizing the complete process and still gaining clarity, several activities should be combined into one activity group. In order to carry this bundling process out as efficient as possible, this bundling should be based on logical aspects. Finally, the grouping of activities leads to a more transparent and clearer structured process model compared to the initial process model.

4. INFORMATION-TECHNICAL IMPLEMENTATION

4.1 Used Process Mining Tools

The information-technical implementation of the new developed process mining method was executed by using two different software tools: *LANA* and *Celonis*. LANA is a process mining tool from the Lana Labs GmbH, which was developed in 2016 as spin-off from the Hasso-Platter-Institute. Celonis was formed in 2011 and is currently the global leader of process mining tools (Peters and Nauroth, 2019). Both software products were used to analyze the considered 'offer to production process'. In this context, the focus was set on the process discovery, the conformance technique and the execution of ad-hoc analyses. Even though the method of process mining is the same, there are some differences in the application of these two software tools.

The process model generated with LANA is clear in the visualization. One branch in the model displays an exclusive gateway. However, in the current software version it is not possible to visualize parallel activities. The activity sequence is based on the start timestamps. LANA calculates the waiting time between activities by considering the start of the predecessor and the start of the successor activity. The run time of an activity is calculated by forming the difference between end and start timestamp. In case of parallel processes, this calculation procedure leads to misleading results.

For processes that do not consist out of parallel activities, the visualization in LANA is easy to understand and specific. If there are parallel activities involved in the process, the process model must be analyzed with caution. In the considered process it is known that there are no waiting times between the single activities for production planning because they are controlled over a workflow. In this case, the discovered bottlenecks in the waiting times can be ignored. The displayed follow-connections can't always be taken as the reflection of reality.

In contrast to LANA, Celonis chose a process visualization that is not specific. A branch in the process model can be an exclusive gateway and a parallel gateway at the same time. That's the reason why the frequencies on the paths don't always match up with the frequencies of the predecessors and the successors. However, in the considered process, the ability of the used process mining tool to visualize and analyze parallel paths is very important. That's why the usage of Celonis for process discovery fits better for the considered 'offer to production process' than the LANA solution. In this context it can be noted, that there are many processes that consist of parallel activities. E.g. the product creation process includes a high number of parallel planning steps, which is rising due to recent developments to reduce the time to market. The inability of a process mining tool to discover and display parallel processes presents an essential difficulty in these cases.

Apart from the differences in the ability to visualize parallel processes, these two software tools have similar properties. LANA tends to offer less options, e.g. when trimming the process to a specific extract or in terms of possible KPI monitoring. However, the usage is very intuitive and especially for 'process mining beginners' LANA is easy to use. Celonis offers a broad range of additional analysis possibilities, which make it possible to create individual dashboards to monitor KPIs or other evaluations. LANA provides a set kind of evaluations, which satisfied most expectations in the regarding process. In general, it can be set out that LANA offers less freedom in adjusting the analysis technique than Celonis does.

4.2 Analysis of the Considered Process using Celonis

In Figure 4, the discovered process model of the regarded process – with grouped activities – is visualized by using the process mining tool Celonis. The different shades in the background underline the former different data sets.

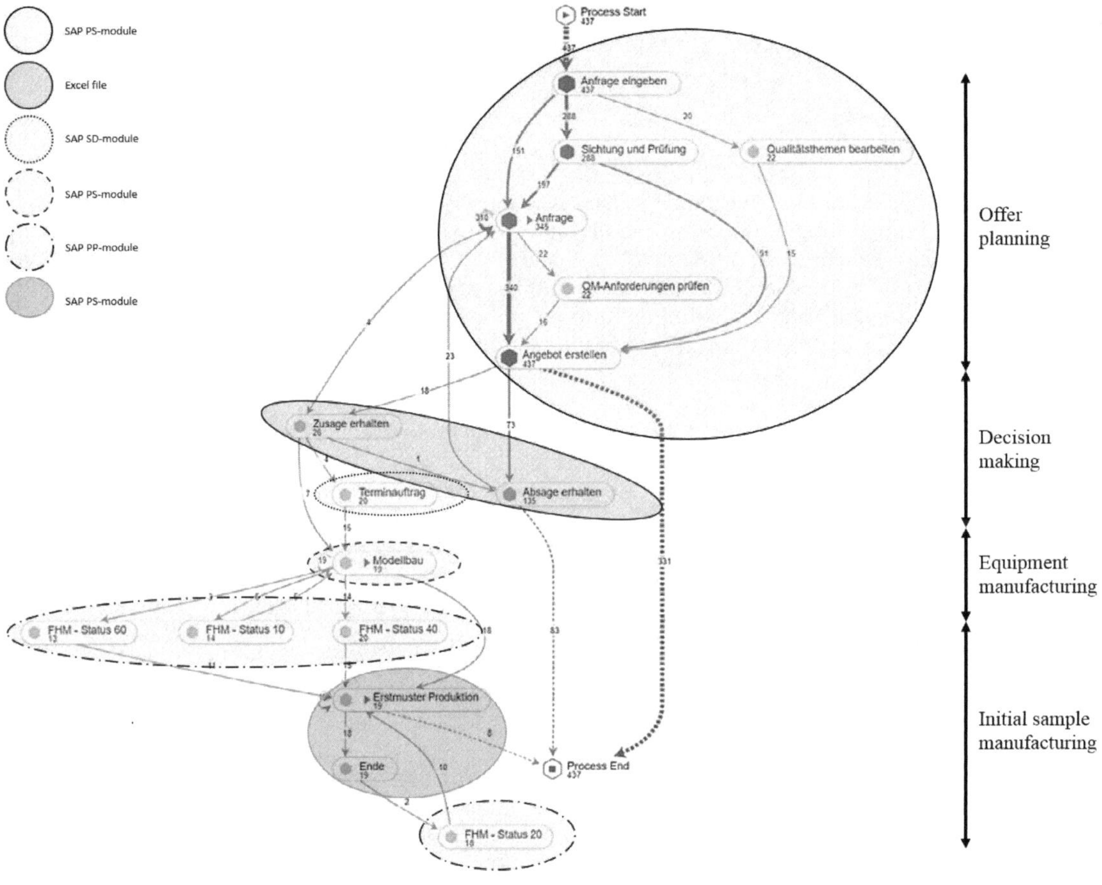

Figure 4. Process model (with logical groups) generated with Celonis

As shown in Figure 4, six data sources were used as basis for the analysis. The four subprocesses 'offer planning', 'decision making', 'equipment manufacturing' and 'initial sample manufacturing' (cp. Figure 2) are mapped in the used SAP PS-module with several activities. This module makes it possible to give a structure to a project by developing a project structure plan with several activities and to control the execution of these via a superior network. In addition to that, one data source origins from the SAP PP-module and another data source origins from the SAP SD-module. These data sources display the date of the query as well as some status changes of the casting equipment during the production of the initial sample. As part of an additional Excel file, the dates of the confirmation or rejection of the offer are documented, which were originally received via e-mail.

The process model in Figure 4 states a starting point for an analysis. The most common activities and paths are being displayed. As a next step, every process sequence can be analyzed in detail. Hereby, the focus is set on deviations from the expected behavior. For example, the rejection of an offer that is followed by further planning steps is an unwanted deviation from the process flow. Deep investigations about this sequence and the affected cases are necessary, which are supported by the process mining tool. In this context, diverse filter can be set to restrict the displayed model. Consequently, only the process cases are selected to form a model, that are relevant for the specific investigation. Furthermore, each particular case can be examined up to the single activities, their timestamps and attributes. This approach allows to find anomalies and to earn know-how about lead and waiting times of the process based on system data. This so called 'drill-down' is especially important because it starts by analyzing the big picture in which anomalies become clear that happen in a conspicuous frequency. As a next step, it is possible to look at explicit cases. In this context, it is possible to discuss the anomalies with the involved department, not only on KPIs or compromised data, but on real cases that are descriptive. This new possibility to state facts portrays the relevant characteristics of this new approach.

If there is a reference model that specifies the process sequence, this model can be imported into or created within the tool in form of a BPMN diagram. By using the conformance technique, the software tool compares the specified process model and the determined process model and visualizes the deviations between these two data models. However, this direct comparison between model and real data is only possible in parts of the regarded process, because many subprocesses have a project character and don't follow a certain target process.

5. CONCLUSION

This paper presents the usage of process mining within the 'offer to production process' of a contract manufacturer for cast components. By means of a real existing practical example, the application of this modern data mining technique – focusing on process discovery and on ad-hoc analyses – is illustrated. Apart from all the portrayed advantages and potentials of using process mining within this process, there are currently some limits and challenges, which have to be considered before introducing process mining into the operational practice.

The visualization of the process is only helpful, if it is possible to overlook the resulting process model. At first, this was not possible with up to 600 different activities displayed. The grouping of activities resolved this issue but also lead to an information loss because the connections between the grouped activities cannot be visualized and analyzed any more. If a process is supposed to be analyzed with process mining, it is recommended to choose either a shorter process or to reduce the activities' degree of detail.

The analysis of a process that has a project character and doesn't have to follow a certain target process is not ideal for the application of process mining. During the analysis some deviations can be worked out if the analyst has a deep process know-how or is even a process participant. Hence, it is certainly easier to be able to apply the conformance technique and visualize all deviations at once.

The variance in the process sequences is a further barrier. If the considered process shows a great variance in the length of the process sequence and amount of activities, a common analysis is difficult. Furthermore, the seldom occurrence of the desired path states a problem because process mining tends to hide seldom occurring paths and activities to keep the visualization simple and concisely. In this case, an alternative approach might be to separate the process sequences into two analyses. Hereby, the process sequences that stop after making an offer (no reply from the customer/ rejection of the offer) and the sequences that continue with further process steps (manufacturing of the casting equipment and initial samples) are displayed separately.

A further challenge refers to the presence of multiplex concurrent activities to be set out. Multiplex concurrencies occur especially in complex processes when several departments work on one product at the same time. According to Ly (2012), these concurrencies state a difficulty for any process discovery algorithms.

The listed challenges show what kind of process may have problems but at the same time gives an advice, which processes are ideal for being analyzed with process mining. Subsequently, general factors that have an impact on the application of process mining can be addressed. Hereby, the data analysis before the process mining implementation is essential. In this context, not only the data itself is relevant, but especially the analysis of the data quality.

In terms of data quality, it must be known if the data is complete, trustworthy and if the identification attributes have a reliable syntax. If the data that is going to be analyzed is incomplete, the evaluations are not reliable. If it is unknown that the data that is going to be analyzed is incomplete, conclusions might be drawn that are incorrect. Regardless of the type of analysis that is applied on data, the real population must be known so that the data input can be classified. The content of the data must also be investigated. If data is used, that is not trustful, it can't be expected to gain analysis results that are better than the input data. Since the method completely relies on the input data, the focus should be set on the data before doing an analysis. The goal of process mining to visualize the real process is only possible, if the data represents the reality. Therefore, the best data for process mining is produced by automated systems or machines instead of manual data input. The syntax of the data is another essential factor that must be considered. Especially if heterogeneous data sources are used for the analysis, the connecting elements for the allocation of the Case-ID must have an explicit syntax. If they don't, data loss is the consequence.

6. OUTLOOK

Dealing with data in general and the impact of process mining in particular largely depends on process and organizational aspects of a company. The economic impact of process mining rises and falls with the integration of process mining in a higher-level process management. Therefore, the aim of companies should be to integrate process mining as part of a seamless and consistent process management. This integration should be carried out in a holistic way taking into account the overall socio-technical system, which consists both of methodical, (information-)technical, organizational and human aspects (Netland et al, 2008). There are different approaches how to integrate process mining in an overall process management. One exemplary integration framework is described in Günther et al (2008). In addition to these technical integration challenges, the integration of process mining in the operational and organizational company and the associated organizational adaptations also play a significant role in the success of introducing process mining (Zhao and Zhao, 2014).

REFERENCES

Günther, C. et al, 2008. Using process mining to learn from process changes in evolutionary systems. *In Int. J. Business Process Integration and Management*, Vol. 3, No. 1.

Hand, D. et al, 2001. Principles of Data Mining. *In MIT press*, Cambridge, MA.

Ly, T. et al, 2012. Data Transformation and Semantic Log Purging for Process Mining. *In Advanced Information Systems Engineering. CAiSE 2012. Lecture Notes in Computer Science*, Vol. 7328, Springer, Berlin, Heidelberg.

Netland, T. et al, 2008. The new importance of socio-technical systems research on high-tech production systems. *In Proceedings of the HOPS Conference 2008*. Lausanne, Switzerland.

Peters, R. and Nauroth, M., 2019. *Process-Mining Geschäftsprozesse: smart, schnell und einfach*. Springer Gabler, Wiesbaden.

Van der Aalst, W., 2011. *Process Mining – Discovery, Conformance and Enhancement of Business Processes*. Springer-Verlag, Springer, Berlin, Heidelberg.

Van der Aalst, W., 2012. Process Mining: Overview and Opportunities. *In ACM Transactions on Management Information Systems*, Vol. 99, No. 99.

Van der Aalst, W. et al, 2012. Process Mining Manifesto. *In Business Process Management Workshops. BPM 2011. Lecture Notes in Business Information Processing*, Vol. 99, Springer Berlin, Heidelberg.

Van der Aalst, W., 2016. *Process Mining – Data Science in Action*. Springer-Verlag, Heidelberg.

Zhao, W. and Zhao, X., 2014. Process Mining from the Organizational Perspective. *In Foundations of Intelligent Systems. Advances in Intelligent Systems and Computing*, Vol. 277, Springer, Berlin, Heidelberg.

COMPLIANCE STUDY OF HAZARD ANALYSIS AND CRITICAL CONTROL POINT SYSTEM

Tatiana Sousa Pinto[1], Brigida Monica Faria[1,2], Luis Paulo Reis[2,3], Henrique Lopes Cardoso[2,3] and Tiago Santos[2,3]

[1]*Escola Superior de Saúde – Instituto Politécnico do Porto (ESS-P.Porto), Porto, Portugal*
[2]*Laboratory of Artificial Intelligence and Computer Science (LIACC), University of Porto, Porto, Portugal*
[3]*Faculty of Engineering, University of Porto (FEUP), Porto, Portugal*

ABSTRACT

Hazard Analysis and Critical Control Point (HACCP) system is based on a preventive methodology to avoid potential hazards that can cause harm and to ensure that unsafe food is not made available to consumers. This system is recognized by the Economic and Food Safety Authority, a criminal police responsible for food safety and economic inspection in Portugal. Every day, Economic and Food Safety Authority generates a large and complex volume of data from inspections and complaints, also in its classification, registration and in monitoring until the end of the process analysis. This study focuses on the reported entities that are related to non-compliance with HACCP, and tries to understand the most common infractions. Results show values between 30% and 37% related to non-compliance to HACCP. As main conclusions, from 2014 to 2018, the number of these infractions maintained the same level and it will be important to understand if the relationship between these problems are related to legislation understanding or application.

KEYWORDS

Public Health, Food Safety, Data Analysis Applications, HACCP

1. INTRODUCTION

Nowadays, modern society is more concerned and alert about the dangers, lack of security, hygiene, control of systems and services that can affect the consumer. Hazard Analysis and Critical Control Point (HACCP) system is based on a preventive methodology, in order to avoid potential hazards that can cause harm to consumers by eliminating or reducing problems, and to ensure that unsafe food is not made available to the consumer (Wallace and Mortimore, 2016). HACCP system is based on the application of technical and scientific principles in the production and handling of food aspects, from the beginning of their production to the final disposal to the consumer (Lawley, R. et al., 2013).

In order to prevent, eliminate or only reduce the hazards that may contaminate the food during its production process and subsequent distribution, requirements which, once contemplated, have led to the effective application of the HACCP system should be taken into account ('The food safety hazard guidebook', 2013).

The prerequisites control the hazards associated with the surrounding environment in the food production process, while the HACCP system controls the hazards associated with the production process(Stankovic, 2015): Structures and Equipment; Sanitation Plan; Pest Control; Water supply; Collection of waste; Materials in contact with food; Personal Hygiene; Training.

Economic and Food Safety Authority is a criminal police body specialized in the areas of food security and economic inspection in Portugal (ASAE, 2018b) (Mil-Homens, 2007). It is responsible for the evaluation and communication of risks in the food chain, as well as for legal compliance with economic activities in the food and non-food sectors (ASAE, 2018c). The Economic and Food Safety Authority 's mission is to supervise and prevent compliance with the regulatory legislation for the exercise of economic activities in the food and non-food sectors, as well as the evaluation and communication of risks in the food chain (ASAE, 2018c). Economic and Food Safety Authority has followed, with special attention, the growing of technological innovation and today is created the need to have capacity to control and store the data produced in the daily tasks of all its stakeholders, with the aim of improving public health and automation of inspector's tasks.

Economic and Food Safety Authority generates a large and complex volume of data in the various inspections it performs, in the reception of complaints, in its classification, in its registration and in the monitoring until the end of the process. This factor enhances the use of specialized storage tools capable of transforming data into information that positively influences decision making on inspection days (Lele, 2019). According to this expectation and with the predominant characteristic of the large volume of data, the techniques and tools for the analysis of these arise as a response, more concretely, through Data Analysis (Provost and Fawcett, 2013). To achieve formal declarations, the organization intends to use Data Analysis techniques, since it recognizes its capacity to respond to large amount of data (IRMA, 2016). Moreover, Economic and Food Safety Authority is the only organization in the world that brings economic security together with food security. Another aspect about Economic and Food Safety Authority it is the national connection body with its counterparts at European and international level (ASAE, 2018a). In fact, Economic and Food Safety Authority cooperates with other similar organizations around the world (ASAE, 2018a). As a criminal police body receives tens of thousands of complaints per year that convert into a lot of data. It is important to analyze the data available in the datasets and evaluate how can be an improvement in public health. Economic and Food Safety Authority generates a large and complex volume of data in the various inspections, in the reception of information requests and complaints, in its classification, in its registration and in the monitoring until the end of the process. This factor enhances the use of specialized storage tools capable of transforming data into information that positively influences decision making on inspection days (Regulamento (CE) n.º 852, 2004). According to this expectation and with the predominant characteristic of the large volume of data, the techniques and tools for the data analysis are related with Knowledge Discovery in Database and Data Analysis (Han, Kamber and Pei, 2012). To understand from the many data provided by Economic and Food Safety Authority those that are related to non-compliance with the HACCP system and to analyze its recurrence is the motivational factor of this study.

The remaining of the paper is structured as follows: section 2 presents the complaints flow, infractions classification and methodology used to understand and analyze data. Section 3 presents the results and discussion of the obtained result. The last part of this paper presents the major conclusions, and some directions for future work.

2. METHODOLOGY

This section presents the methods used to acquire more information about complaints that reach Economic and Food Safety Authority and which are related with non-compliance of HACCP system. First, a complaint is a formal complaint in order to expose an irregularity/non-compliance of economic group with the legislation (DL194/, 2012). All reports of the datasets were made online by filling in the form available on the Economic and Food Safety Authority website or sent by email. Then a decision circuit is made by inspectors to classify complaints in many aspects, such as competence (as can be seen in Figure 1) or type of complaints.

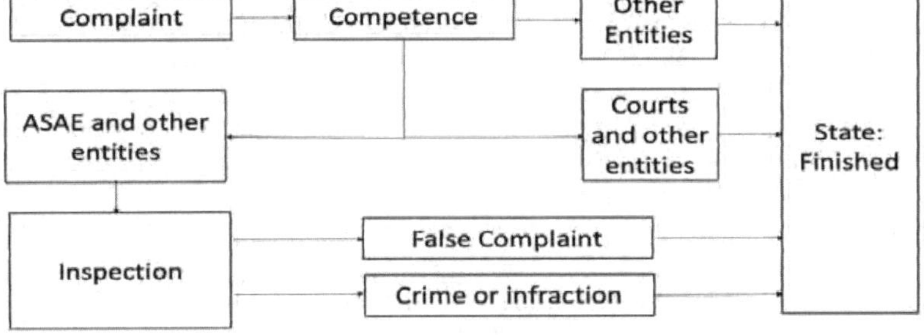

Figure 1. Complaint competence in decision circuit

In terms of competence, there are many complaints that should be treated by other entities such as courts or other institutional entities. In this work, only complaints that are from Economic and Food Safety Authority competence will be analyze. The competence complaints have code assigned in order to classify the kind of infraction is presented.

Figure 2 presents an example of classification codes and frequencies in the year 2014. In this example the code 1.C.31 has digits and letters that represent different information: 1 represents "Segal", an abbreviation for "Segurança Alimentar" that means food security; C represents hygiene and food safety; 31 represents "Failure to comply with general and specific hygiene requirements".

```
'2.R.19 ': 102,
' 1.B.00.9 ': 217,
'1.L.10 ': 238,
'1.C.31 ': 1577,
'1.B.00.8 ': 42,
'2.G.02.9 ': 211,
'3.ZA.04.1 ': 8,
' 1.C.31 ': 2109,
```

Figure 2. Frequencies and infractions codes

In this example, the most frequent infraction in 2014 was a HACCP compliance. Also, in this example there are different format related with the deep of detail in the code with two or three points dividing the fields of information.

2.1 Data and Ethical Issues

The available data range from 2014 until 2018 and is divided into two datasets: data on complaints and information requests and data related to type of complaints associated with infractions. Statistical analysis of the complaints file and information requests, a comparison was made between the number of complaints and information requests, including complaints and pending information requests per year. This statistical analysis was made using Python libraries, Pandas and NumPy (Mckinney, 2018). The first descriptive analysis was applied to five excel files related to the years of 2014 to 2018 with approximately 30MB each with a total of 120661 entries of complaints and information requests. This analysis was simple and with no setbacks because there was not missing values or incorrect data in any of the files. In 2018 the available data was only until October. Concerning the file related to denounced entities a 670mb file containing 2882629 reported entities was analyzed. The file's variables include:

- RNPC - National Registry of Legal Entities;
- Relation - If belongs to a head office or to an establishment;
- NIPC / NIF - Identification Number of Collective Person/ Tax Identification Number;
- Type - Type of Entity;
- Name - Entity Name;
- Postal Code;
- Community/Region;
- Address;
- District / County / Town;
- Legal Nature – RNPC;
- Main CAE – Main Code of Economic Activity;
- Secondary CAE – Secondary Code of Economic Activity.

The descriptive analysis about these variables focus on the type of entity most reported/denounced and in which districts most of the complaints were made. The Economic and Food Safety Authority has an epigraph file containing the meaning of each letter or code number associated with each infraction to make possible the analyses of the dataset related to type of complaints associated with infractions. Analyzing this file, it was verified that infractions beginning with the number "1" are related to HACCP. Each year between 2014 and 2018 corresponds an excel file with each report made, including the infringement code assigned to each report. After importing each excel file, per year, into the Jupyter Notebook (Mckinney, 2018) an initial observation was made to identify the columns of interest. Given the amendment to the General Data Protection Regulation, the directive and legislation on data protection have been replaced and all those involved in these works have signed terms in accordance with the new legislation to ensure the right of secrecy of both the complainant and of the complaint.

2.2 Data Analysis Methods

Descriptive data analysis was made using Pandas, a software library written for the Python programming language for manipulation and data analysis (DataCamp, 2001). It was also used NumPy that provides the data structures, algorithms, and it is needed for most scientific applications involving numerical data in Python(McKinney, 2018).

2.2.1 KDD Methodology

The data volume, generated and stored in the course of any activity, exceeds the capacity of human analysis and makes it impossible to extract knowledge from the same data, without resorting to a system that automates this process (Fayyad, Piatetsky-Shapiro and Smyth, 1996). This context justifies the existence of the research area of Knowledge Discovery in Databases (KDD), generally defined as "the non-trivial process of identifying valid and potentially useful patterns, perceptible from the data" (Fayyad, Piatetsky-Shapiro and Smyth, 1996), in which the principles associated to it are influenced by the areas of Artificial Intelligence, Automatic Learning, Pattern Recognition, Statistics, Database, Information Systems, among others(Maimon and Rokach, 2010). The method used to search the patterns in the data is called Data Mining and is considered the core step of the process of Knowledge Discovery in Databases, which is developed in several phases, such as: selection, preprocessing, transformation, data mining, interpretation and evaluation (Witten, Frank and Hall, 2005). These patterns may or may not represent useful knowledge, being one of the phases that normally requires the participation of the user (Fayyad, Piatetsky-Shapiro and Smyth, 1996). Data Analysis phase represents 20% in the KDD process and is better supported by software than the other phases. All other phases, from the selection of data to the interpretation of the patterns found, are more a matter of "art" than a routine that can be automated(Jothi, Rashid and Husain, 2015).

2.2.2 Data Pre-Processing

The data has some problems that were tackle using pre-processing. These problems were related with missing/incomplete values as can be analyzed in Table 1.

Table 1. Variables vs Percentage Invalid/Null data information

Variables	Invalid/Null (%)	Variables	Invalid/Null (%)
RNPC	< 0,01	Address	0,53
Relation	< 0,01	District	2,40
NIPC/NIF	< 0,01	County	6,05
Type	0,01	Town	90,74
Name	< 0,01	Legal Nature RNPC	0,60
Postal Code	73,23	Main CAE	41,20
Community/Region	0,43	Secondary CAE	89,73

In terms of missing values were identified the following problems:

- 3-digit suffix of the postal code missing;
- District / County / Town" field the information for "County" and "Town" to be filled.
- In terms of incorrect and/or outdated values:
- Town as region;
- Incomplete / ambiguous values;
- Data corruption;
- CAEs missing values.
- There were also inappropriate separators and delimiters:
- Mixture of separation by spaces, by "," and by ";".

The majority of data considered invalid or null is in the "CAEs", the "Postal Code" and the "Town". The missing data were filled matching it with online data bases with valid information. In case of unavailable information from online datasets, the lines with missing values were excluded from analysis.

From another dataset the column with the infractions codes is called "Infracções" as shown in Figure 3. In this column we have information about the infraction code, the type of infraction and a description that explains the meaning of the infraction code. All the following examples are from 2014 dataset.

Tipo	...	Ofícios para Denunciante	Produtos	Infracções	Fiscalizações Relacionadas	Processos Relacionados
E-MAIL	...	[S/290 /14/SC] Confirmação (competência da ASAE...	NaN	2.B.1 , CO, Exercício de actividades de anima...	NaN	NaN
E-MAIL	...	[S/303 /14/SC] Recepção - DIP	NaN	2.G.02.14 , CO, Violação das regras do contrat...	NaN	NUI/CO /001589 /15.5.EAPRT

Figure 3. Infractions column from 2014 dataset

2.2.3 Transformed Data

As the goal is to study the compliance analysis of Economic and Food Safety Authority's Hazard Analysis and Critical Control Point system the focus of study will be in the column selected in Figure 3.

Each complaint is associated with an NID, which is a code assigned to identify each complaint. In each complaint, more than one infraction can be identified, as demonstrated in Figure 4, and it is necessary to separate the different infractions within each complaint.

	NID	Infracções
0	E/8/14/SC	2.B.1 , CO, Exercício de actividades de animação turística sem registo\n 2.B.2 , CO, Exercício ...

Figure 4. NID and Infractions columns

As each infraction of the same complaint is separated by paragraph, the split is done by the paragraph as can be seen in Figure 5 the output.

	NID	Infracções
0	E/8/14/SC	2.B.1 , CO, Exercício de actividades de animação turística sem registo
1	E/8/14/SC	2.B.2 , CO, Exercício de actividades não reconhecidas como turismo de natureza na Rede Nacional ...

Figure 5. Output from split by paragraph

Since the infractions are separated it is necessary to split each code so that we can proceed to the count.

Since the infraction code, the type of infraction, and the description of the infraction are separated by commas in the column "Infracções", it is used the comma split. This split creates a new column (Figure 6) named 'Codes' that contains the infraction code that represents the infraction in each complaint. This column can be added to the original dataset for future studies in the database.

Using unique, one of the commands of the Pandas library, it turns out that split created a space at the end of each code. This space was removed so that it is possible to count the different infraction codes. In order to understand the meaning of each code it is necessary to analyze the file of epigraphs made available. By analyzing this file, it is verified that all the complaints started by the number '1' are related to the HACCP system. In order to know how many complaints are related to the HACCP system a new split was made. The output of this new split gives a 26083 total number of rows in the dataset for the year 2014. In order to know the number of 9726 complaints with the infringement code related to the HACCP system was applied a count of these entries. The same procedure described for the year 2014 was be applied for the years 2015, 2016 and 2018, trying to verify, through data analysis by descriptive statistics if there is any pattern over the years.

3. RESULTS

Data Analysis is a superset of Data Mining that involves extracting, cleaning, transforming, modeling and visualization of data with an intention to uncover meaningful and useful information that can help in deriving conclusion and take decisions (Abzalov, 2016). This Section presents the results obtained by analyzing the complaints and information requests and the complaints related to HACCP system from 2014 to 2018.

3.1 Descriptive Analysis about Infractions related to Complaints and Information Requests

From a total of 120661 entries between 2014 and 2018, 80358 of them are complaint and 40303 are information requests (see Figure 6).

"Complaints" represent the solved and archived complaints. "C_Hold" represent complaints on hold to be solved. "Information Requests" is related to information that the sender needs to be enlightened. "IR_Hold" represent information requests that have not yet been answered. The number of complaints has not decreased over the years. Complaints on hold (C_Hold) have not yet been solved. 2018 is the year with more "C_Hold" which is expected because there was no time for response yet. From a total of 120661 entries of denounced entities nearly 100% represent Economic Agents. To try to solve missing data related to entities addresses was used information in georeferenced websites. As a result of this cross-referencing of information 97,33% of data became complete.

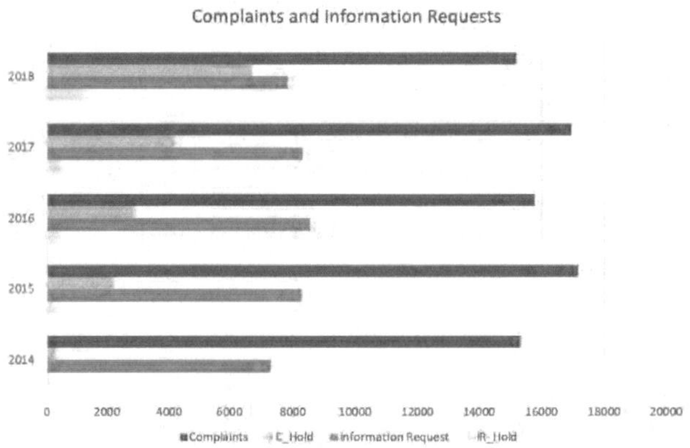

Figure 6. Complaints and Information Requests frequencies

3.2 Descriptive analysis about infractions related to HACCP system

The number of rows of all original datasets increased after the split (Fig. 6). Once each line represents a complaint and to each complaint is associated an infraction code, it means that there are complaints with more than one infraction code. In Figure 7 it is possible to compare the number of original rows with the number of rows created after the split from 2014 to 2018.

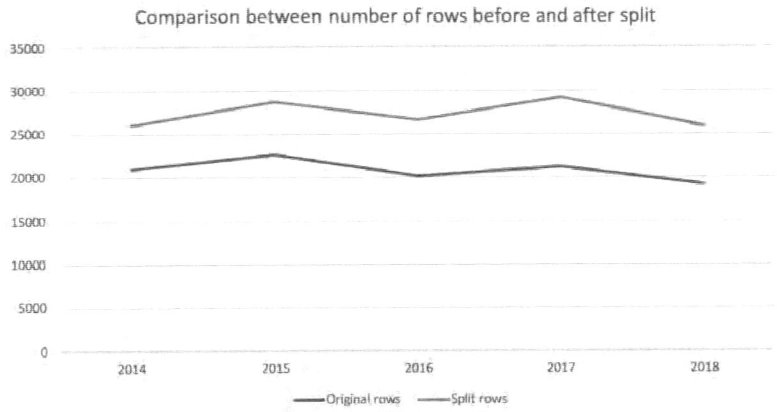

Figure 7. Comparison between the number of rows before and after split

As can be seen (Figure 7), in all datasets from 2014 to 2018 there are complaints with more than one infraction committed. As the objective is the analysis of compliance with the HACCP system, it is important to analyze the infractions committed related to this system in each year under study (Figure 8).

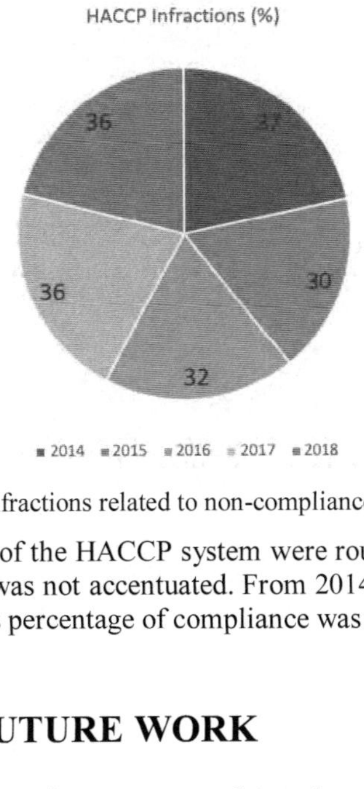

Figure 8. Percentage of infractions related to non-compliance with HACCP per year

The percentages of non-compliance of the HACCP system were rounded to the units. As can be seen, the variation between the interval of years was not accentuated. From 2014 to 2015 the compliance improved by 7%, however in the remaining years this percentage of compliance was disappearing.

4. CONCLUSIONS AND FUTURE WORK

Food and Economic Security Authority receives more complaints than information requests. It is important to try to understand where law enforcement is failing so that there is not a significant decrease in complaints over the years. Incomplete, incorrect and omitted data relating to the entities complained may be justified since the complainant does not always know the correct and complete data of the entity it intends to report. From the point of view of compliance with the HACCP system, values between 30% and 37% are relatively high since the Food and Economic Security Authority is responsible for food and economic security and not only for food security and hygiene. Although, as mentioned above, there was an improvement between the first two years under study, followed by worse results in the following years, the values related to the non-compliance rate did not have marked differences.

As future work, it would be interesting to evaluate the density of distribution of the complaints by regions. Once this has been done, and in an attempt to improve public health, it is necessary to associate them to the HACCP system related complain. Then try to understand what the most common complaint is and see if the problem is related to understanding the legislation or if it is related to the difficulty of complying with the legislation because it is too restrictive.

ACKNOWLEDGEMENT

The authors would like to thank the IA.SAE – "Inteligência Artificial na Segurança Alimentar e Económica" project, funded by the FCT/MCTES through national funds (PIDDAC), as part of the "Programa Iniciativa Nacional Competências Digitais" e.2030 – INCoDe.2030, enrolled in the National Reform Plan.

REFERENCES

Abzalov, M., 2016. *Exploratory data analysis*, in Modern Approaches in Solid Earth Sciences. doi: 10.1007/978-3-319-39264-6_15.

ASAE, 2018a. ASAE-Cooperação Internacional Bilateral, https://www.asae.gov.pt/cooperacao/internacional/bilateral/medio-oriente.aspx.

ASAE, 2018b. Como Actua a ASAE. Available at: https://www.asae.gov.pt/inspecao-fiscalizacao/como-atua-a-asae.aspx (Accessed: 30 May 2019).

ASAE, 2018c. Missão, Visão e Valores. Available at: https://www.asae.gov.pt/asae20/missao-visao-e-valores.aspx (Accessed: 30 May 2019).

DataCamp, 2001. *Python for Data Science*, Cheatsheet. doi: 10.1097/00007890-200105270-00005.

DL194/ (2012) 'Decreto-Lei no 194/2012 ASAE', Diário da República 1a série, pp. 4641 - 4646

Fayyad, U., Piatetsky-Shapiro, G. and Smyth, P., 1996. *The KDD process for extracting useful knowledge from volumes of data*. Communications of the ACM, 39(11), pp.27-34.

Han, J., Kamber, M. and Pei, J., 2012. *Data Mining: Concepts and Techniques*. doi: 10.1016/C2009-0-61819-5.

IRMA, I. R. M. A., 2016. *Big Data: Concepts, Methodologies, Tools, and Applications*. Information Resources Management Association ISBN-13: 978-1466698406

Jothi, N., Rashid, N. A. and Husain, W., 2015. *Data Mining in Healthcare - A Review*, in Procedia Computer Science. doi: 10.1016/j.procs.2015.12.145.

Lawley, R.; Curtis, L.; Davis, J., 2013. *The food safety hazard guidebook*, Choice Reviews Online. doi: 10.5860/choice. 46-3282.

Lele, A., 2019. *Big data*, in Smart Innovation, Systems and Technologies. doi: 10.1007/978-981-13-3384-2_9.

Maimon, O. and Rokach, L., 2010. *Introduction to Knowledge Discovery and Data Mining*, in Data Mining and Knowledge Discovery Handbook. doi: 10.1007/978-0-387-09823-4_1.

McKinney, W., 2018. *Python for Data Analysis Data Wrangling with Pandas, NumPy, and IPython*, Climate Change 2013 - The Physical Science Basis. doi: 10.1017/CBO9781107415324.004.

Mil-Homens, S., 2007. *ASAE - HACCP*. Available at: http://www.asae.gov.pt/pagina.aspx?back=1&codigono=54105579AAAAAAAAAAAAAAAA (Accessed: 19 January 2019).

Provost, F. and Fawcett, T., 2013. *Data Science and its Relationship to Big Data and Data-Driven Decision Making*. Big Data, 1(1), pp.51-59.

Regulamento (CE) n.o 852, 2004. Regulamento (UE) no 852/2004 do parlamento europeu e do conselho', *Jornal Oficial da União Europeia*, 139, pp. 54.

Stankovic, I., 2015. Codex Alimentarius, in *Encyclopedia of Food and Health*. doi: 10.1016/B978-0-12-384947-2.00180-X.

Wallace, C. A. and Mortimore, S. E. (2016) 'HACCP', in Handbook of Hygiene Control in the Food Industry: Second Edition. doi: 10.1016/B978-0-08-100155-4.00003-0.

Witten, I. H., Frank, E. and Hall, M. A., 2005. *Data Mining Practical Machine Learning Tools and Techniques*, Data Mining. doi: 0120884070, 9780120884070.

A BIG REMOTE SENSING DATA ANALYSIS USING DEEP LEARNING FRAMEWORK

Hanen Balti[1], Imen Chebbi[2], Nedra Mellouli[2], Imed Riadh Farah[1] and Myriam Lamolle[2]
[1]*RIADI Laboratory, University of Manouba, Manouba, Tunisia*
[2]*LIASD Laboratory, University of Paris 8 , Paris, France*

ABSTRACT

Spaceborne and airborne sensors deliver a huge number of Earth Observation Data every day. In this context, we can easily observe the whole earth from its different sides. Therefore, this big data is important in remote sensing and could be exploited in several domains requiring image classification, natural hazard monitoring, global climate change, agriculture, urban planning. Over the last five years, Convolutional Neural Networks (CNN) emerged as the most successful technique for the image classification task, as well as a number of other computer vision tasks. However, to train millions of parameters in CNN one requires a huge amount of annotated data. This requirement leads to a significant challenge if the available training data is limited for a target task at hand. To address this challenge, in the recent literature, researchers proposed various ways to apply a technique called Transfer Learning to transfer the knowledge gained by training CNNs parameters on some large annotated dataset to the target task with limited availability of training data. Most of our work in this paper was dedicated to proposing a hybrid classification of remote sensing images. This architecture combines Spark RDD image coding to consider image's local regions, pre-trained VGGNET-16 and UNET for image segmentation and SVM (Support Vector Machines) from spark Machine Learning to achieve labeling task.

KEYWORDS

Big Data, Remote Sensing, Deep Learning, Multi-label Classification, Feature extraction, Support Vector Machines

1. INTRODUCTION

Earth observation is a source of information in many fields of application such as remote sensing, cartography, aeronautics, etc. Over the years, the number of floating sensors in space is growing, hence the proliferation of captured images.

The various space borne and airborne sensors deliver a large number of earth observation data every day so that we can observe its different sides (Mingmin Ch et al., 2016). Indeed, these data are the main actor of big remote sensing data (BRSD) and has at least these classic 4Vs: the volume, the velocity, the veracity, and the variety.

Currently, the most active research area in machine learning (ML) is deep learning (DL). With its increased processing power and advances in processors and as the quantity of remote sensing data keeps rising, we are starting to talk about BRSD DL. It comes to play a major role in providing big remote sensing data analytic solutions for classification and clustering. Obviously, DL uses deep architectures in order to deal with complex relationships between the input data and the class label. In addition, DL and ensemble-based architectures are the most popular and efficient approaches for multi-source and multi-temporal land cover classification. They outperform traditional machine learning methods and cover both optical images and radar images. DL algorithms are showing better performance from hyper spectral and multispectral imagery such as extracting land cover types (Nataliia Kussu et al., 2017), pixel-based classification, semantic segmentation, or target recognition. They learn features from the data, where low-level features are extracted from texture and spectral information. The output features are represented at the highest level. In fact, DL has much well-established deep architecture like Deep Belief Network (DBN), Recurrent Neural Network (RNN), or Convolutional Neural Network (CNN). CNN is the most used architectures in image processing. This architecture is a multilayer network, composed of 2 stages: feature extractor and classifier. Many experiments have shown that the performance of remote sensing (RS) image scene classification has been significantly improved due to the powerful feature representation learned through different DL architectures (Xue-wen Chen, et al., 2014).

The most two devoted frameworks useful in deep learning are TensorFlow and Apache Spark. TensorFlow is an open source framework that is designated to ML and especially to DL. It has built-in support for DL and Neural Network (NN), so it makes easy to assemble a network, assign parameters and run the training process. Also, Tensorflow has a collection of samples trainable mathematic functions that are useful for NN. Due to the large collection of flexible tools, TensorFlow is compatible with many variants of ML. In addition, TensorFlow (Goldsborough, 2016) uses both CPUs and GPUs for computing hence it makes the compile time faster. Apache Spark is also an open source parallel computing framework, which has the advantage of MapReduce. It delivers flexibility, scalability, and speed to meet the challenges of Big Data. Spark integrates two main libraries SQL for querying large structured data and MLlib involving main learning algorithms with statistical methods (Anand Gupta et al., 2017).Obviously, MLlib is Spark's open-source ML library which includes several efficient training functionalities. It also supports different languages and provides a high-level API that rich Spark's ecosystem and facilitate the development of ML pipelines (Xiangrui Meng et al., 2017).

The purpose of our work is to analyze and classify heterogeneous multi-source remote sensing data in a parallel distributed architecture using two CNN models for feature extraction and SVM for the labeling. We used four different datasets according to image acquisition, image resolution, and image encoding in the perspective to evaluate the improvement of these two architectures.

The rest of this paper is organized as follows. In section II, we introduce the related work. In section III we present the proposed approach. Our results are detailed in section IV. A brief conclusion with perspectives for future studies is presented in Section V.

2. RELATED WORK

The most common challenge of RS applications is RS image classification. In fact, RS images can have a similar appearance but it belongs to different classes. Indeed, in a few recent years, the DL approaches come as a solution to this challenge. Deep Learning (DL) is proving that it has efficient results in hyperspectral and multispectral BRSD imagery in land cover types such as extracting forests, buildings, roads.

DL is taking off in remote sensing and many papers have been released talking about multiple applications of deep learning in remote sensing.

As DL is a deep feature learning architecture, it can learn semantic discriminative features and reach better classification compared with mid-level approaches.

In (Nataliia Kussul et al., 2017)a multilevel deep learning architecture is proposed using multi temporal images acquired by Landsat-8 and Sentinel-1A satellites. The proposed architecture is four-level architecture, including preprocessing (level 1), supervised classification (level 2), post-processing (level 3) and final geospatial analysis (level 4). 1-D and 2-D CNN architectures are proposed to explore spectral and spatial features. At the preprocessing level, Self-organizing Kohonen maps (SOMs) are chosen for optical image segmentation and restoration of missing data. SOMs are trained for each spectral band separately. The restoration of the missing values is done by substituting input sample missing components with neuron's weight coefficient. The restored pixels are lately masked. In the second level (Supervised Classification with CNN), two different CNN architectures are compared: 1-D CNN in which convolutions are in the spectral domain and 2-D CNN in which convolutions are in the spatial domain. These two architectures are composed of two convolutions layers, max pooling layer, and two fully connected layers. The two architectures use different train filters and a different number of neurons in the hidden layers. A combination of AdaGrad and RMSProp are used for moment estimation and it proved better performance in term of fast convergence comparing to gradient descent or stochastic gradient descent. In the last level, (Post processing and Geospatial Analysis) several filtering algorithms have been developed. They are based on the information quality of the input data and field boundaries providing a pixel-based classification map. Finally, data fusion allows interpretations of the classification methods. Another work was proposed by (Nguyen et al, 2013)in which CNN architecture is used for satellite image classification. They used three convolutional and two sampling layers on resized and transformed input images to gray. The detail is described in (Nguyen et al, 2013). In (Gong Cheng et al, 2018)features are used directly from the FCN (Fully Convolutional Network) as the classifier inputs. In contrast, (Yiping Duan et al, 2017)proposed an approach in which the CNN pooling layer is substituted with a wavelet constrained pooling layer. This layer is used in conjunction with Markov Random Field and super pixel in order to provide a segmentation map. In (Jie Geng et al, 2015)Used deep convolutional autoencoders (DCAE) for extracting features and automatic classification on high-resolution single polarization TerraSAR-X images. The architectures of the DCAE contain a convolutional hand-crafted first layer, and a scale transformation hand-crafted second layer using correlated neighbor pixel. The other layers are trained with a stacked autoencoder (SAE). In fact, (Ma, X et al , 2016)proposed a classification approach based on three decision levels: the first level is a local decision. A hyperspectral image will be sampled and the test sample is based on its neighborhood by calculating the Euclidean distance. The second level is a global decision based on supervised classification. It calculates a Euclidean distance between the sample and the classes. The third level is a self-decision. It is based on the label class involving spectral and spatial features. The first two decisions are applied to unlabeled samples in the training set. After that, the deep network is trained on the new training set to extract features and a classification map is generated from the self-decision.

In all the above-mentioned works, the heterogeneity of the images as well as their scaling, are considered separately. The aim of our work is to propose an adaptive framework to 1) solve the problem of scaling up and processing massive data using Spark RDD image coding to consider the image's local regions; 2) provide a semantic and generic classification tool processing multi-source and multi-resolution data using the best CNN models in the segmentation task and Spark Machine Learning in semantic labeling task.

3. PROPOSED APPROACH

Big Remote Sensing Data (BRSD) represents a challenge for the DL. In fact, BD involves a large number of samples as inputs, large varieties of classes as outputs and huge large dimensionality as attributes. This will lead to high running time and complex models. For all these reasons algorithms with a distributed framework and parallelized machines are required. In fact, we propose an approach based on a parallel architecture in order to classify BRSD. The approach is composed of three steps: data splitting, data processing and finally data reducing as following in figure (*cf.* Figure 1).

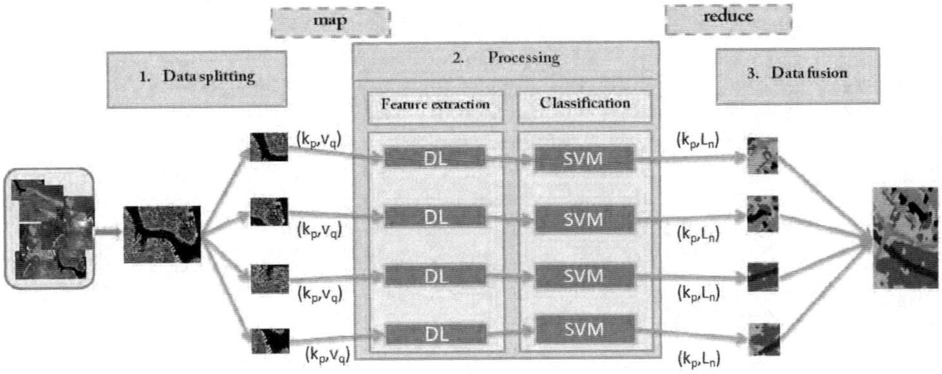

Figure 1. The proposed approach

First, we split the images into strips having the size of 144*144 and distribute the data over several Spark-consumer nodes. Therefore, consistency between the outputs of this first step and the inputs of the next step must be maintained, since we have heterogeneous remote sensing images captured from several sensors like SPOT, LANDSAT, Worldview, etc. the fact that the resolutions and the number of bands differ from one image to another, like RGB (3 bands) or multispectral (more than 3 bands).

In fact, after splitting the data we obtain a number of images having a homogeneous resolution. This data are going to be stored in Resilient Distributed Datasets (RDD) using MapReduce technique in order to perform distributed and parallel processing on large datasets in a distributed environment, i.e. write parallel computations, using a set of high-level operators. In these RDDs, each image is considered as a dataset element. Hence each image is represented by a vector of RDDs records reflecting a local region of the image source. When the RDDs vectors are established, they are forwarded to the deep neural network inputs wherein the number of networks is equal to each vector dimension. At the second step, we are looking for feature extraction using CNN models. At the third step, we pipeline outputs of the last step to an SVM machine learning with MLlib package to aggregate local labels into a final image label classes.

3.1 Remote Sensing Data Splitting and Storing in the RDDs

As we have heterogeneous RS data; multi-resolution i.e. the images have different resolutions, multi-spectral i.e. the images can contain several bands such as Red, Green, Blue, Coastal, NIR (Near-infrared), SWIR (Short wavelet infrared), etc. we divided these images into strips having the size of 144*144 i.e. we will deal with n image each image have the size of 144*144 and using the Map function each strip is processed to produce key-value pairs (k_p,v_q) as intermediate outputs (Figure 2). On the value of these pairs, we are going to apply the processing step which includes two stages: Feature extraction and classification.

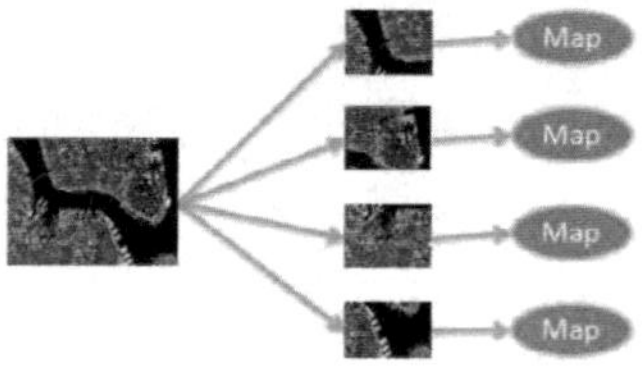

Figure 2. Image splitting task

The choice of the strip size was chosen by a heuristic approach taking into account the average size of an object to be detected based as well as all the resolutions of the original images. The detail of the splitting algorithm will be detailed in another paper.

For the storage and access of these strips, we decided to use RDDs because the only way to reuse our data between computations (Ex - between two "jobs" MapReduce) is to write them on an external stable storage system (Ex-HDFS). We used the concept of spark RDD to achieve faster and more efficient MapReduce operations. The RDDs are an immutable collection of distributed objects. Each set of data in RDD is divided into logical partitions, which are calculated on different nodes of the cluster. In addition, RDDs contain any type of Python object, Java or Scala, including the classes we have defined. The number of nodes that are in our cluster is the round of $(x * y/144 * 144)$ where x * y is the image size and 144*144 is the strip size.

The strips of images are stored as objects with their characteristics (origin, height, width, nChannels, mode, and data). After storing the images in these datasets we are going to apply the second step which is data processing.

3.2 Remote Sensing Data Processing

This step is composed of two sub-steps, as we mentioned above, feature extraction and classification.

3.2.1 Feature Extraction

Convolution is an efficient way to extract features (Han Liu, 2018), therefore, CNN architectures are suited for this task. In fact, we chose two CNN models, UNET and VGGNET, which are both of them, a stack of convolutional layers with pooling layers that are much like a filter to be applied to feature maps.

CNN architectures (but not limited to), UNET and VGGNET, to compare their added value in the face of image heterogeneity.

Feature extraction using UNET: A UNET is like a convolutional auto-encoder. It also has connections similar to the feature maps located before the bottleneck layer. It is generally used for semantic segmentation, in our case; UNET will be used as a feature extractor.

Firstly, we trained the model with 90 000 strips of multispectral images, then as the first part of the model is composed of a stack of traditional convolutional layers, we take the features extracted from the bottleneck layer, i.e. the feature map extracted from the bottleneck layer is considered our output.

Feature extraction using pre-trained VGGNET-16: The network is composed of 22 layers, 16 layers with learnable weights (13 convolutional layers, and 3 fully connected layers). For feature extraction, we neglected the last layer SOFTMAX layer, so the features are extracted from the last fully connected layer instead of the SOFTMAX layer.

Once the features are extracted, they will be stored locally in the RDDs in order to use them in the next task. Now, after getting the features extracted from the two models we are going to classify our images.

3.2.2 Classification

For this step, we used Linear Support Vector Machines (Linear SVM). Linear SVMs are supervised learning models with associated learning algorithms that analyze the data used for classification and regression analysis. The goal of the SVM algorithm is to find a hyperplane in N-dimensional space (N - the number of features) that distinctly ranks the data points. In our work, the purpose of using SVMs is to find a plan that has the maximum margin, that is, the maximum distance between the data points of the two classes. Maximizing margin distance provides reinforcement for classifying future data points with greater confidence.

In order to adapt SVM to our work, we used the one against one approach which is a series of classifiers applied on each pair of class. Thus, n(n-1)/2 machines are applied to each pair of classes. When all the classifiers have been attempted, a max-wins strategy has been used. The hyper-parameters that we used are the regularization parameter (or parameter C) and gamma. The Regularization parameter informs the SVM optimization how much we want to prevent misclassifying each training class and the gamma parameter describes how far the impact of a given example of training gets, with small values indicating "far" and elevated values indicating "near". In other words, with low gamma, points far from the plausible line of separation are regarded in the separation line calculation. Whereas in the calculation the points close to the plausible line are considered as high gamma. For the hyper-parameters selection, we used k-fold Cross Validation method.

The input of our algorithm is then the feature vectors of each strip of an image extracted with the UNET or VGGNET and stored locally in the RDDs. The output then is a 144*144 image segmented and classified. Now, as we have the strips of images classified we will combine it in order to reconstruct the images.

3.3 Remote Sensing Data Fusion

After extracting the characteristics and classifying the images, we will now reconstruct ~~it~~. To perform this step, we will use the Reduce function of MapReduce. The reducer receives the key-value pair of the last several tasks, and then it includes the intermediate data tuples in a set of tuples, which are the final result. More specifically, the key-value pairs that our reduce will receive are the pairs (k_p, L_n) with L_n are the outputs of the classification step, that is, the classified strips of images are going to be grouped in order to reconstruct our images.

4. EXPERIMENTAL RESULTS

In this section, we will present our experimental setup, a description of data and the main results.

4.1 Experimental Setup

For the validation of our work, we created a machine on Amazon AWS having the following characteristics: 16 GiB NVIDIA K80 GPUs, 64 vCPUs and 61 GiB of RAM, this machine is the master machine and the slaves have 8 GiB Nvidia 950m GTX GeForce GPUs, they have quad-core CPU and 16 GiB of RAM.

Data description: We have used four datasets to improve our approach: SIRI-WHU (Gong Cheng et al, 2017)which contains 12 classes each class contains 200 images measuring 200*200 pixels with 2-m spatial resolution, AID (Gui-Song Xia et al, 2016)which contains 10000 images having several resolutions within 30 classes, multispectral dataset, and we prepared a dataset which is composed of satellite images captured with different sensors like SPOT4, SPOT5, LANDSAT8 and so on. Our dataset has a number of 3,974 images within 10 classes. The images have a various resolution, and the multispectral dataset contains 1km x 1km satellite images in both 3-band and 16-band formats. The 3-band images are the traditional RGB natural color images. The 16-band images contain spectral information by capturing wider wavelength channels. This multi-band imagery is taken from the multispectral (400-1040nm) and short-wave infrared (SWIR) (1195-2365nm) range.

Evaluation metrics: The metrics that we used in order to evaluate the performance of our work are precision, recall, and F1-score.

$$\text{Accuracy}=\frac{TP}{TP+FP} \qquad \text{recall}=\frac{TP}{TP+Fn} \qquad \text{F1-score}=\frac{2*Accuracy*recall}{Accuracy+recall}$$

where TP (True Positives) denotes the number of correctly detected objects, FN (False Negatives) the number of non-detected objects and FP (False positives) the number of incorrectly detected objects.

4.2 Results

In this part, we are going to present the results that we obtained after applying our approach on the BRSD. The experiments have been performed over two types of images: 3 bands (RGB) and 16 bands. Firstly, we should mention that we used 80% of our data for the training and 20% of the data for the validation. For the CNN models i.e. VGGNET and UNET we had 15000 iterations, the batch size was 128 and the learning rate was 0.001.

In the following Table 1, we present the results obtained for each database using the 3 models; UNET, UNET-SVM and VGGNET-SVM.

Table 1. Comparison between the results obtained after testing our approach on 3 band databases and 16-band databases

	SIRI-WHU			AID			Our database			16- band database		
	Accuracy	Recall	F1-score	Accuracy	Recall	F1-score	Accuracy	Recall	F1-score	Accuracy	Rappel	F1-score
UNET	-	-	-	-	-	-	-	-	-	0.92	0.57	0.70
UNET-SVM	0.73	0.72	0.72	0.78	0.78	0.78	0.84	0.82	0.82	0.94	0.92	0.92
VGGNET-SVM	0.73	0.68	0.70	0.67	0.50	0.55	0.79	0.80	0.79	-	-	-

In the following Table 2, we present a comparison between the accuracy results obtained for our dataset per class using VGGNET-SVM and UNET-SVM.

Table 2. Comparison between the accuracy obtained for each class of our database using VGGNET-SVM and UNET-SVM

Classes	VGGNET-SVM	UNET-SVM
Buildings	0.33	0.62
Cars	0.61	0.69
Crops	0.62	0.84
FastH2O	0.55	1.00
Roads	0.71	0.93
SlowH2O	0.51	0.95
Structure	0.57	0.82
Tracks	0.42	0.75
Trees	0.12	0.75
Trucks	0.73	0.87

In the following Table 3, we present a comparison between the accuracy results obtained in the state of art over the 3 bands datasets and our results

Table 3. Comparison between our results and the state-of-art results

	Overall precision
(Gong Cheng et al, 2018)	81%
(Nataliia Kussu et al., 2017)	93.6%
(Nguyen et al, 2013)	80.83%
Our approach	**87.33%**

The execution time is very important since we deal with a huge and complex type of data and the fact of using a multi-node architecture helps us to gain in terms of time execution also. As a result, the mean execution time of our algorithm is 9.8 minutes.

4.3 Discussion

After presenting all the results in the previous section, we can say that using the encoder part of UNET as feature extractor is more efficient than VGGNET. In fact, the reshaping of pre-trained VGGNET can cause loss of image information. In contrast, the UNET model accepts any image with any size. Also, VGGNET is mainly used for RGB images contrariwise to UNET which don't impose RGB image as input, that's why we tested the UNET on the multispectral image (more than 3 spectral bands). We compared the results obtained with a simple UNET and the combination of UNET-SVM, the use of Linear SVM as classifier ameliorates the results. So the use of UNET allows us to gain in terms of precision also it allows us to manipulate data of different spectral resolution unlike the VGGNET with imposes the use of RGB images. In addition, the use of the distributed architecture allows us to manipulate images having different spatial resolutions i.e. to handle heterogeneous data. Our approach had slightly higher accuracy than (Gong Cheng et al, 2018) and (Nguyen et al, 2013) which used respectively FCN and a customized CNN architecture. In contrast, (Nataliia Kussu et al., 2017) with their multilevel deep learning architecture, outperform our approach results and this can be due to the first level in which they use SOMs for missing data restoration and optical image segmentation.

5. CONCLUSION

Big data and DL are both considered as a BIG deal for researchers. The concept of DL is to dig into a massive volume in order to identify patterns and extract features from complex unsupervised data without human intervention, which makes it an important tool for Big Data. In this paper, we proposed a DL algorithm for feature extraction and classifying satellite images based on two frameworks SPARK for storing, distributing and parallelizing Big Remote Data and Tensorflow for implementing and executing DL algorithms based on two CNN models (VGGNET16 and UNET). A benchmark dataset of remote sensing images was created for evaluation. For the future work, we are going to use hyperspectral Dataset for UNET results validation and we are going to develop other DL architectures in order to adapt our approach to different RS data types.

REFERENCES

Jie Geng et al. (2015). High-Resolution SAR Image Classification via Deep Convolutional Autoencoders. *IEEE Geosci. Remote Sensing Lett. 12(11)* , 2351-2355.

Gong Cheng et al. (2018). When Deep Learning Meets Metric Learning: Remote Sensing Image Scene Classification via Learning Discriminative CNNs. *IEEE Trans. Geoscience and Remote Sensing 56(5):* , 2811-2821.

Han Liu, Y. (2018, 09). Feature Extraction and Image Recognition with Convolutional Neural Networks. *Journal of Physics: Conference Series* , 062032.

Ma, X et al . (2016). Semisupervised classification for hyperspectral image based on multi-decision labeling and deep feature learning. *ISPRS Journal of Photogrammetry and Remote Sensing,* , 99-107.

Nataliia Kussul et al. (2017). Deep Learning Classification of Land Cover and Crop Types Using Remote Sensing Data. *IEEE Geosci. Remote Sensing Lett. 14(5)* , 778-782.

Xiangrui Meng et al. (2017). A Big Data Analysis Framework Using Apache Spark and Deep Learning. *Journal of Machine Learning Research 17* , 9-16.

Xue-wen Chen, et al. (2014). Big Data Deep Learning: Challenges and Perspectives. *IEEE Access 2* , 514-524.

Yiping Duan et al. (2017). SAR Image segmentation based on convolutional-wavelet neural network and markov random field. *Pattern Recognition* , 255-267.

Anand Gupta et al. (2017). A Big Data Analysis Framework Using Apache Spark and Deep Learning. *ICDM Workshop*, (pp. 9-16).

Goldsborough, P. (2016). A Tour of TensorFlow. *CoRR abs/1610.01178.*

Gong Cheng et al. (2017). Remote Sensing Image Scene Classification:Benchmark and State of the Art. *Proceedings of the IEEE 105(10):* , (pp. 1865-1883).

Gui-Song Xia et al. (2016). AID: A Benchmark Dataset for Performance Evaluation of Aerial Scene Classification. *Proceedings of the IEEE 105(10):* , 1865-1883.

Mingmin Ch et al. (2016). Big Data for Remote Sensing: Challenges and Opportunities. *Proceedings of the IEEE, 104(11), 2207-2219.*

Nguyen et al. (2013). Satellite image classification using convolutional learning. *AIP Conference Proceedings* (pp. 2237-2240). AIP.

VIABLE SYSTEM ARCHITECTURE APPLIED TO MAINTENANCE 4.0

Rafael Albuquerque Câmara[1], Henrique São Mamede[2] and Vitor Duarte dos Santos[3]
[1]*Universidade Aberta, 1269-001 Lisboa, Portugal*
[2]*Universidade Aberta, INESC TEC, 1269-001 Lisboa, Portugal*
[3]*Universidade Nova – IMS, 1070-312 Lisboa, Portugal*

ABSTRACT

Disruptive requirements that currently drive the so-called Industry 4.0 (I4.0) are increasingly present in today's industries, where factories are forced to innovate in search of improvement in the quality of manufacturing of products aligned with the reductions of: manufacturing time, environmental and cost impacts with the manufacturing process. For this, an Information Systems (IS) architecture is proposed to reduce the negative impacts on an industrial operation caused by manual configuration failures in manufacturing systems, machines that are worn out in the production process and unstable integrations between industrial subsystems. The suggested SI model uses the Viable Systems Model adapted to Maintenance 4.0 technologies (Cyber-physical Systems (CPS), Manufacturing Execution Systems (MES), Data Mining and Digital Manufacturing concepts/technologies) with the goal to create an automatic purchase flow to replace parts by mitigating impending failures in industrial equipment through data mining and predictive analysis.

KEYWORDS

Maintenance 4.0, Viable Systems Model, Cyber-Physical Systems, Manufacturing Execution Systems (MES), Digital Manufacturing, Data Mining

1. INTRODUCTION

The current industrial sector undergoes constant changes and process updates at a speed synchronized with business models never seen before, whose production process is sequential, fault-oriented and did not require changes to succeed in manufacturing. Currently, this monolithic model no longer supports dynamic markets in the face of the integration and speed necessary to the customer, supplier and production to stay competitive in the world market. In this scenario, industrial production needs to be continuously synchronized with the new technologies in order to remain flexible, efficient and integrated with partners, customers and suppliers. and all this in order to provide the industrial sector with greater profitability and quality at an acceptable and reduced cost, through the use of emerging technologies and concepts of Industry 4.0.

The Industry 4.0 consists of an "intelligence" where digital components are all interconnected with machines, tools, robots, men, finished and semi-finished products and raw materials in a single, fully integrated, flexible, independent and business-oriented network (Vuksanović, Ugarak, & Korčok, 2016). In this context of disruptive industrial maintenance called Maintenance 4.0, the manufacturing process in the industries requires a greater attention in the predictive maintenance of machines with the advance of the technology and complexity of the components, in line with the continuous use of properties of the computers to control and monitor the properties dynamics of a physical good inside the factory (Pires, 2018). In order to maintain this industrial automation stable and with minimum risks, the architecture must be implemented in a continuous and fully integrated way, that does not divide the systems in isolation and without many hierarchical layers to avoid gaps and communication failures in the existents IS platforms in the corporate environment, as it is in some cases of traditional architectures in today's organizations (Saturno, Moura Pertel, Deschamps, & De Freitas Rocha Loures, 2018).

Once this architecture is solved and the requirements necessary to implement new technologies related to Maintenance 4.0 are defined, several of these new technologies that can be implemented and adapted to the reality of the industry in order to obtain capital gains, better performance and quality in the manufacturing production process, in particular in the predictive analysis of machine failure (Scheer, 2015) (Algabroun, Iftikhar, Al-najjar, & Weyns, 2017). This results in a series of systems to be parametrized and constantly regulated and which requires constant manual intervention in some of them due to the absence of a system or set of systems that self-regulates and able to deal with the variables of the business processes in the environment corporate. There is a constant concern to regulate properly for the current industrial model or any new model that is coupled to the existing one, this if the traditional model allows, which usually does not occur in this way.

In order to solve this problem, a new model of intelligent and completely self-sustaining architecture is proposed, based on Stafford Beer's Model of Viable Systems (MVS) (Espejo, Gill, & Carvalho, 1997) that is flexible, adaptable and stable (Selin & Santos, 2018). In addition, the VSM model is adapted with new emerging technologies in Maintenance 4.0 such as: data collection through sensors, mining and predictive analysis of this data, resulting in accurate automatic suggestions for replacement of industrial parts imminent to failure (Pires, 2018).

It is an autonomous and self-regulating system in terms of business rules, information and flow of processes existing in the organization and that, many of these processes and information outputs, would not require human intervention due to the prediction of patterns and data behavior of a given automation system (Selin & Santos, 2018), thus allowing decision-making before failure in industrial machines for the context of Predictive Maintenance (Johnson, 2019).

For this automation process to be well defined, it is necessary first to classify and define a kind of taxonomy for each type of data and information generated in the business processes through the information flow of a factory. This process is achieved using injection techniques and data mining (using data obtained from the integration level of Information Systems to create plans and decision making (Crnjac, Veža, & Banduka, 2017)), classifying this analytical and relevant information into categories of information related to the metrics and industrial equipment information (Qin, Liu, & Grosvenor, 2016) (Chacada et al., 2018).

The present work proposes is a generic feasible system architecture for use in industry for M4.0 (Maintenance 4.0), where the implementation of this system (not covered by this work) will reduce the negative impacts on the industrial operation caused by manual configuration failures, machines (through predictive data analysis) and unstable integrations between subsystems, always synchronizing business flow with data flow more quickly and efficiently. Another motivating factor for this work was the search for a solution to the labor deficit in European industries in the face of the current situation of the population of European countries, where there is a high level of aging of the population and a significant technological competition of the industries with developing countries (Crnjac et al., 2017). With this, the proper use of the Cyber-Physical System, Internet of Things (IoT) and other disruptive technologies aimed at Maintenance 4.0 allows increasing the development of reducing the development time of products and the workforce needed for this production, optimizing manufacturing time, increasing production efficiency and providing cost reduction throughout the production process (Crnjac et al., 2017).

The result of the dissertation will be of great value for those who are interested in implementing autonomous solutions aimed at Maintenance 4.0, more precisely for those who want to obtain an architecture with visions of predictive data analysis in order to allow a preventive decision making in relation to the malfunction of industrial machines, if there is an imminence of failure.

2. INDUSTRY AND MAINTENANCE 4.0

2.1 Concepts, History and Principles

The core idea of Industry 4.0 is defined as a "smart" factory with all its networked components ranging from people to machines and products by flexible integration and integrate customers, partners, suppliers and products with efficiency. This model is always aimed at reducing costs, increasing performance and quality of production through automated processes (Vuksanović et al., 2016).

The history of the industrial revolution until the present times is subdivided in 4 stages (Vuksanović et al., 2016), as illustrated in figure 1.

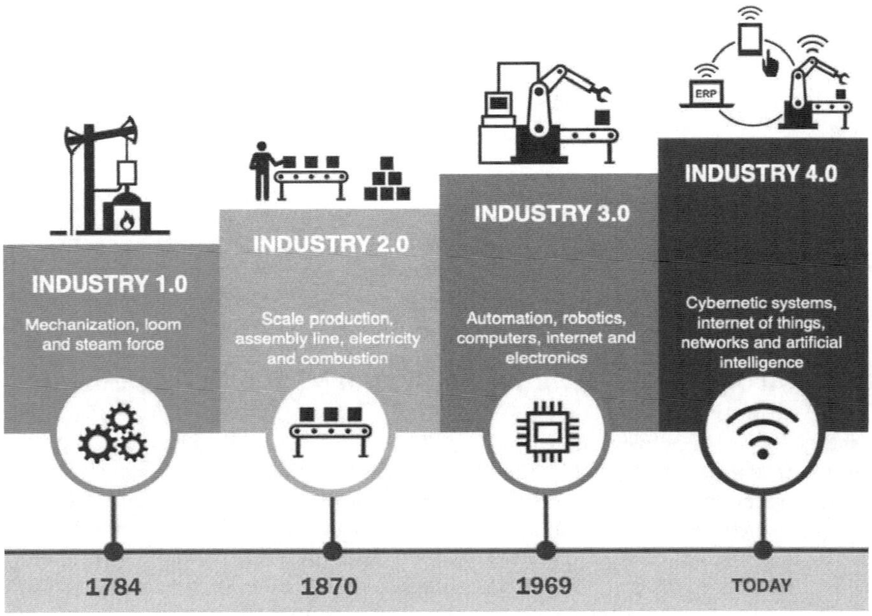

Figure 1. The 4 stages from the Industrial Revolution
(Adapted from: https://claudioperin.com.br/industria-4-0-qual-o-grau-de-maturidade-digital-da-sua-empresa/)

Still in the concept of interconnectivity, Table 1 illustrates the comparison of the use of Component, Machine and Production System in the current industries with technologies for Maintenance 4.0 with the concepts of I4.0, having as action the prevention and predictive analysis of these three elements mentioned.

Table 1. Comparison of today's factories with I4.0 factories
(Adapted from: https://www.researchgate.net/publication/303561107)

	Data Source	**Today´s industry**		**Industry 4.0**	
		Attributes	**Technologies**	**Attributes**	**Technologies**
Component	Sensor	Precision	Smart Sensors & Fault Detection	Self-aware Self-predict	Degradation Monitoring & Remaining Useful Life Prediction
Machine	Controller	Productivity and performance	Condition-based Monitoring & Diagnostics	Self-aware Self-predict Self-compare	Uptime with Predictive Health Monitoring
Production System	Networking	OEE Productivity	Lean Operations: Work and Waste Reduction	Self-configure Self-maintain Self-organize	Worry-free Productivity

Industry 4.0 is believed to be the new Industrial Revolution of the 21st century, as it allows for an autonomous vision and use of technology to produce services and products more intelligent, attractive, fast and flexible with the needs of today's market, always focusing on reduction of costs and increase in efficiency. On the other hand, there will be around 5 million types of jobs that could be extinguished due to this process of digitization in the main industrialized nations by 2020 (Vuksanović et al., 2016). Additionally, this is estimated to be a drastic reduction on demand for products where quality is doubtful and made by outdated technology, thus causing an outdated industry loss due to its inefficiency and high operating costs.

The design principles for Industry 4.0 are supported by 6 pillars that make up the technology for this new Era, which are (Horton, Prain, & Thiele, 2015) presented in Table 2.

Table 2. Design principles of each component from the Industry 4.0
(Adapted from:
https://www.researchgate.net/publication/307864150_Design_Principles_for_Industrie_40_Scenarios_A_Literature_Review) (Horton et al., 2015)

	Cyber-Physical	Internet of Things	Internet of Services	Smart Factory
Interoperability	X	X	X	X
Virtualization	X	-	-	X
Decentralization	X	-	-	X
Real-Time Capability	-	-	-	X
Service Orientation	-	-	X	-
Modularity	-	-	X	-

2.2 Architectures for Maintenance 4.0: From Vision to Implementation

Based on the concepts, principles and benefits of I4.0, we must think about the integration of all these components and information as a whole, thinking of an ideal architecture for a stable operation in a given IS, where its lack can lead to inconsistencies, risks of failures and, consequently, can lead to a total stop on an organization production day. In order to have a consistent and stable flow of information between different equipment and components in an automation solution, one must focus on new technologies focused on Maintenance 4.0 and forget the traditional models of automation that are based on the layered division, which can be a great bottleneck, as it creates isolated islands of Information Systems and obstacles that limit the access to some information of the system as a whole (Saturno et al., 2018).

To optimize industrial manufacturing processes through a new architecture that smartly uses the emerging new technologies in the market, a general analysis of the topology of the organization's current architecture is done, in order to identify the systems used, protocol types and the communication between them (Saturno et al., 2018). Then, it's verifies how adaptive the legacy systems are to receive the technologies offered and implemented in Maintenance 4.0, realizing their adherence and support with the new technologies.

Finally, the method called the Research Protocol Application (Saturno et al., 2018) is used, which consists of gathering information from the architecture across experts from each technological area, thus obtaining information from the current architecture topology in order to identify barriers, mitigate risks and impacts to receive the technologies coming from Maintenance 4.0.

Once identified the necessary requirements, solutions are researched to overcome these barriers and evolve to the implantation of these new technologies in the current platform of the organization.

Once the solution is designed to accept requirements of Maintenance 4.0, the organization analyzes the accepted components and selects the new technologies that would be of added value to the organization, with the aim of reducing costs, increasing performance and quality in production (Scheer, 2015).

One of the main components of a "Smart Factory" is the so-called Cyber-Physical Systems (commonly known as CPS), which consists of information systems for the intensive production chain, connected through the local network (or Internet) and capable of communicating with each other and also with other components equipped with the same "smart" communication technology through RFID or chip, where they carry their information of characteristics and qualities. Thus, the CPS allows the physical monitoring of objects and processes by creating a virtual simulation of the various elements of the physical world, thus decentralizing decision control with several autonomous devices (Pires, 2018).

It was also observed that the architectures of systems oriented to the industrial area should be focused on the product where, in addition, the logistics functions linked to the MES should have access to the characteristics and qualities of the product through the database (Scheer, 2015). This leads to another significant technology linked to Maintenance 4.0 for predictive analytics through a massive volume of data from the entire production process of the industry: the so-called Big Data (Scheer, 2015).

The implementation of such approaches requires a well-structured and driven architecture using the infrastructures of emerging Information and Communication Technologies (ICT) technologies and focused on the Maintenance 4.0. The ISO (International Standard Organization) defines a data communication standard for this type of systems architecture where the flow of this data begins at the top of the architecture where the monitoring configuration data is specified for the various sensors that monitor the equipment and, finally, result in actions to be taken by the maintenance and operations team. The figure 2 illustrates this data flow (Standard, Vibration, Standard, Cie, & Standard, 2004).

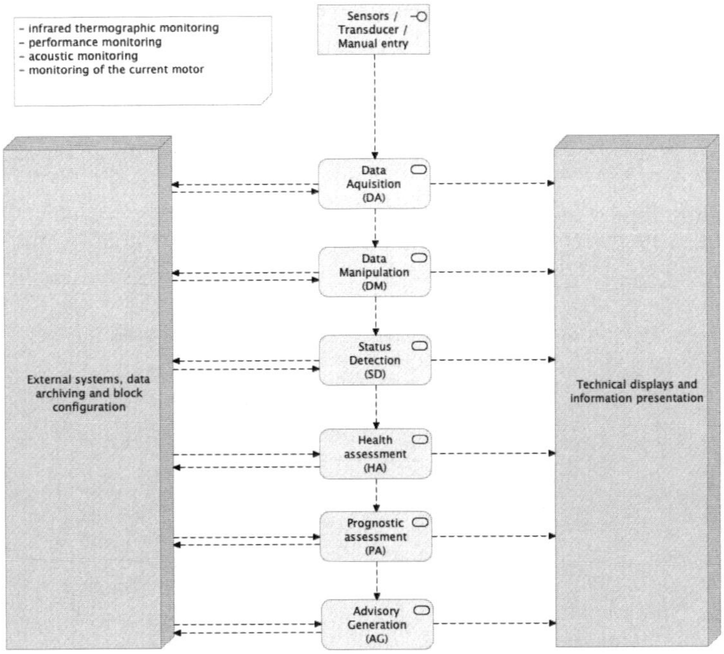

Figure 2. Data processing and information flow blocks
(Adapted from: https://www.sis.se/api/document/preview/903685/)

In model above, the "Open System Architecture for Condition-Based Maintenance" (OSA-CBM) standard (Lopes, 2012) is used, where data collection, extraction and use comprise seven generic layers to achieve a well-constructed system of layers, but currently considers six functional blocks that are:

- Data Acquisition: provides access to scanned data from sensors or transducers and records this data;
- Data Manipulation: performs single and / or multichannel signal transformations and application of specialized resource extraction algorithms to the collected data;
- State Detection: performs condition monitoring by comparing features with expected values or operational limits and returning the condition and / or alarms indicator;
- Health assessment: determines if the health of the system is suffering from degradation, considering the trend in health history, operational status and maintenance history;
- Prognostic assessment: projects the current state of asset integrity in the future, considering an estimate of future usage profiles;
- Advisory Generation: Provides recommendations related to maintenance and asset configuration modification actions, considering operating history, current and future mission profiles, and resource constraints.

2.3 Viable System Model adapted to Maintenance 4.0

Given the hard maintenance of large corporate monolithic systems, where their complex parametrizations are manually adjusted daily (even in organizations that already use emerging ICT technologies), this systemic set becomes an easy target for a possible general bottleneck in its integrations, subsystems and adjustments. In addition, this chaotic scenario may reflect directly on the business, forcing it to stop for example a factory production and causing a huge financial loss if the failure is not detected timely.

Thus, it is proposed in (Selin & Santos, 2018) a system model whose maintenance and adjustment is done automatically, by systems endowed with knowledge of the processes and information of an organization, through data mining and self-regulation of manufacturing systems configurations in accordance with the business model rules inserted (new or existing) in the context of the Corporate Information System in general or for part of a business process.

The proposed solution is to have an architecture adaptable to the reality of the factory production process, based on viable systems models (MSV) and using the new technologies related to Maintenance 4.0. The VSM (Viable System Model) acts in this context as an aid to the process of diagnosis and analysis of problems of the machines and/or equipment of the industry and to the process of organizational redesign in which the business models are aimed.

The model mentioned in (Selin & Santos, 2018) consists of five main components (subsystems) for its operation, plus 2 more components adapted (proposed solution) with new technologies from Maintenance 4.0. The illustration of figure 3 shows how these components are interconnected:

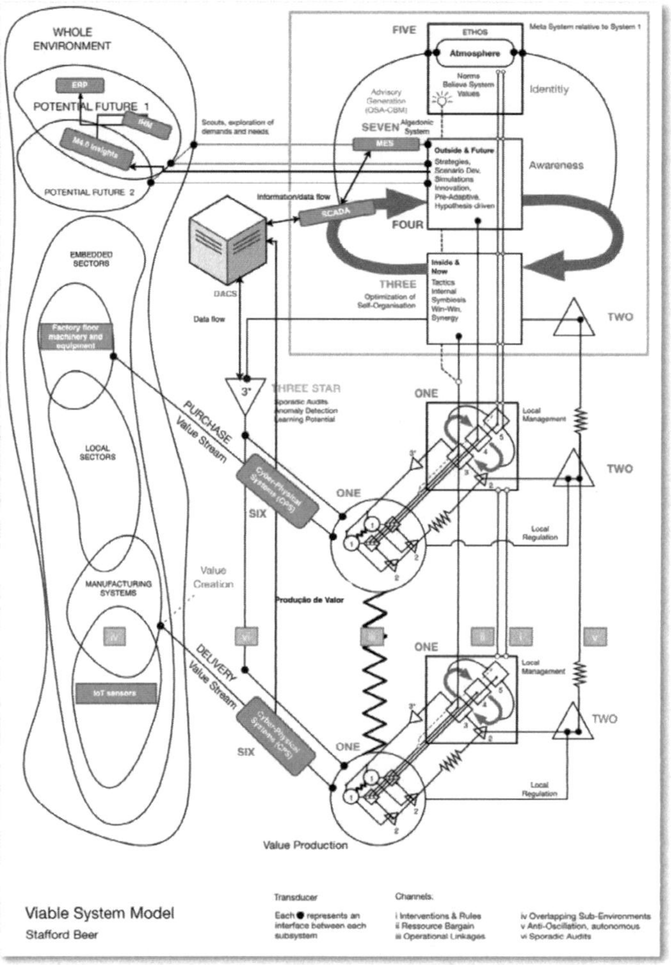

Figure 3. VSM architecture adapted for Maintenance 4.0
(Adapted from: http://www.ecotopia.com/images/vsmbig.gif)

As illustrated in the VSM model adapted in figure 3, the data flow to the generation of useful information for decision making follows:

a. The System 1 adapted to M4.0, different from the original VSM model that has just a operational systems collection, now receives (through the Cyber-Physical Systems - CPS) the data of operating machines, equipment and sensors that inform data about e.g. pressure, temperature, rotation and other data relevant for measuring the life of each essential equipment for a stable and optimized production;

b. System 2 performs according to the original VSM, collecting and analyzing the raw data collected from the CPS through Systems 6 (Schütze, Helwig, & Schneider, 2018) (Rossit, Tohmé, & Frutos, 2018), recursively;
c. System 3 controls and sends audited data from System 2 to the DACS (Data Acquisition and Control Servers), where it will be stored in databases and controlled through data mining mechanisms;
d. System 4, through SCADA and MES systems, receives the data already treated for simulations and predictive analysis of algorithms from segmentation and data mining;
e. System 5 continues to operate according to the original Viable System Model, in constant search of anomalies according to pre-defined variables for the correct functioning of each equipment, thereby assisting System 7 for analysis and predictive cues;
f. System 7 suggests in the HMI (Machine Interface) panels (Johnson, 2019) the equipment exchange improvements to be replaced, showing the probability of failure in a short time;
g. The manufacturing area manager automatically receives a notification for purchase approval in the system that controls the purchase of parts of the industry (ERP system or other), with the model and the correct amount of equipment in the imminence of failures, suggested by System 7 (Lu, Riddick, & Ivezic, 2016);
h. Once approved by the manufacturing manager, the purchase follows its internal flow normally for the replacement parts that have an almost exhausted useful life.

3. CONCLUSION

The main contribution of this work is the investigation of an ideal IS architecture for those industries that seek to innovate in the manufacturing sector of their organization, always having as information the ideal configurations (resilient to changes) and the monitoring of failures in the industrial environment by functions intelligent systems linked to autonomous systems through viable systems models.

In addition, the predictive analysis of the proposed model which is linked to the concepts and technologies offered in I4.0 through CPS and other emerging technologies, gives the manufacturing process more safety and fluidity without unexpected interruptions in the manufacturing of products by failure reasons of equipment or machine parts. This is thanks to this predictive and intelligent analysis carried out by the viable systems model adapted to the digital manufacturing (Cardoso & Coradine, 2016) with Maintenance 4.0, which identifies the imminence of the occurrence of failures and suggests a purchase requisition with the damaged part / machine information.

The fact that we are going through an industrial revolution today, which is the 4th revolution or Industry 4.0 (Souza, 2018), makes implementations in this field still in an early stage in much of the world. With this, the exploitation of production technologies with information technologies is still maturing, and it is difficult to find jobs that are more focused on this area. There are many others issues related Maintenance 4.0 technologies that impacts negatively to improve theses implementations, such as (Liao, Wang, & Lee, 2008):

- There is no variety of equipment level, and usually no infrastructure to cover these new technologies with a good performance;
- Doesn't exist a generic (and scalable) prognostic methodology, unless the companies use Cloud Computing for the entire productive process, but the trust on it is still rare;
- The degradation prediction tools and prognostics are poor and not trustable.

In summary, this suggested SI architecture will provide manufacturers with greater fluidity in the manufacturing process with the use of Maintenance 4.0 technologies discussed here (predictive and preventive analysis of machine data in imminent failures) and consequently a reduction of costs in the entire production system due to the constant automatic parametrization provided by the VSM.

REFERENCES

Algabroun, H., Iftikhar, M. U., Al-najjar, B., & Weyns, D. (2017). Maintenance 4 . 0 Framework Using Self- Adaptive Software Architecture. *Proceedings of 2nd International Conference on Maintenance Engineering, IncoME-II 2017 The University of Manchester, UK*, 1–11.

Cardoso, M., & Coradine, R. (2016). *Caminhos da Manufatura: Uma abordagem à Manufatura Digital* (1.ª ed.). São Paulo.

Chacada, A., Barbosa, J., Leitão, P., Geraldes, C. A. S., Deusado, L., Costa, J., … Romero, L. (2018). Maintenance 4.0 - Intelligent and Predictive Maintenance System Architecture. Italy. https://doi.org/10.1109/ETFA.2018.8502489

Crnjac, M., Veža, I., & Banduka, N. (2017). From concept to the introduction of industry 4.0. *International Journal of Industrial Engineering and Management*, *8*(1), 21–30.

Espejo, R., Gill, A., & Carvalho, J. Á. A. (1997). The viable system model as a framework for understanding organizations. *Malhotra, Y. (Eds.), Knowledge Management and Virtual Organizations, Idea Group Publishing, 2000.*, (October 2011), 350–364. Retrieved from http://www.moderntimesworkplace.com/good_reading/GRRespSelf/TheViableSystemModel.pdf

Horton, D., Prain, G., & Thiele, G. (2015). Design Principles for Industrie 4.0 Scenarios: A Literature Review. *Social Sciences*, (January). https://doi.org/10.13140/RG.2.2.29269.22248

Johnson, S. (2019). What Are the Advantages & Disadvantages of Hierarchical Structure? | Chron.com. Obtido 24 de Fevereiro de 2019, de https://smallbusiness.chron.com/advantages-disadvantages-hierarchical-structure-66002.html

Liao, L., Wang, H., & Lee, J. (2008). A reconfigurable watchdog Agent® for machine health prognostics. *International Journal of COMADEM*, *11*(3), 2–15. Retrieved from https://www.researchgate.net/publication/236891710

Lopes, Y. K. (2012). *Integração dos Níveis MES, SCADA e Controle da Planta de Manufatura com Base na Teoria de Linguagens e Autômatos*.

Lu, Y., Riddick, F., & Ivezic, N. (2016). *Advances in Production Management Systems. Initiatives for a Sustainable World* (Vol. 488). https://doi.org/10.1007/978-3-319-51133-7

Pires, L. M. (2018). *Manutenção na Indústria 4.0*. Retrieved from https://www.researchgate.net/publication/329240288

Qin, J., Liu, Y., & Grosvenor, R. (2016). A Categorical Framework of Manufacturing for Industry 4.0 and beyond. *Procedia CIRP*, *52*, 173–178. https://doi.org/10.1016/j.procir.2016.08.005

Rossit, D. A., Tohmé, F., & Frutos, M. (2018). Industry 4.0: Smart Scheduling. *International Journal of Production Research*, (November), 0–29. https://doi.org/10.1080/00207543.2018.1504248

Saturno, M., Moura Pertel, V., Deschamps, F., & De Freitas Rocha Loures, E. (2018). Proposal of an Automation Solutions Architecture for Industry 4.0. Em *DEStech Transactions on Engineering and Technology Research*. https://doi.org/10.12783/dtetr/icpr2017/17675

Scheer, A. (2015). Whitepaper - Industry 4 . 0 : From vision to implementation, (September).

Schütze, A., Helwig, N., & Schneider, T. (2018). Sensors 4.0 - Smart sensors and measurement technology enable Industry 4.0. *Journal of Sensors and Sensor Systems*, *7*(1), 359–371. https://doi.org/10.5194/jsss-7-359-2018

Selin, A., & Santos, V. (2018). *An architecture for a viable information system. Advances in Intelligent Systems and Computing*. https://doi.org/10.1007/978-3-319-77703-0_114

Souza, E. (2018). *Entenda Sobre Indústria 4.0: A Quarta Revolução Industrial que estamos vivendo Hoje!*

Standard, I., Vibration, M., Standard, I., Cie, S. E., & Standard, I. (2004). International Standard (Vol. 2004). Retrieved from https://www.sis.se/api/document/preview/903685/

Vuksanović, D., Ugarak, J., & Korčok, D. (2016). Industry 4.0: the Future Concepts and New Visions of Factory of the Future Development (pp. 293–298). https://doi.org/10.15308/sinteza-2016-293-298

EXPERIMENTAL ANALYSIS OF MPTCP CONGESTION CONTROL ALGORITHMS; LIA, OLIA AND BALIA

Toshihiko Kato[1, 2], Adhikari Diwakar[1], Ryo Yamamoto[1], Satoshi Ohzahata[1]
and Nobuo Suzuki[2, 3]
[1]*University of Electro-Communications*
1-5-1, Chofugaoka, Chofu, Tokyo 182-8585, Japan
[2]*Advanced Telecommunication Research Institute International*
2-2-2, Hikaridai, Seika-cho, Sorakugun, Kyoto 619-0288, Japan
[3]*Kindai University*
11-6, Kashiwa-no-mori, Iizuka, Fukuoka 820-0011, Japan

ABSTRACT

In Multipath TCP (MPTCP), the congestion control is realized by individual subflows (conventional TCP connections). However, there is some concern that the total data sending rate becomes too high compared with other single path TCPs if the associated subflows increase their own congestion windows independently. So, a coupled increase scheme of congestion windows, called Linked Increase Adaptation (LIA), is adopted as a standard congestion control algorithm for subflows comprising a MPTCP connection. But this algorithm supposes that TCP connections use Additive Increase and Multiplicative Decrease (AIMD) based congestion control, and if high speed algorithms such as CUBIC TCP are used, the throughput of MPTCP connections might be decreased. In order to increase the throughput of MPTCP connection, two modified congestion control algorithms, Opportunistic Linked-Increase Algorithm (OLIA) and Balanced Linked Adaptation (BALIA) are also introduced. However, they are still based on AIMD and there is some concern that they are weaker than high speed algorithms. This paper analyzes the performance of MPTCP congestion control algorithms through experiments. Specifically, this paper examines to compare LIA, OLIA or BALIA based MPTCP flow and a single TCP flow with TCP Reno or CUBIC TCP. These experiments show that LIA is weaker than both Reno and CUBIC, and OLIA and BALIA are weaker than CUBIC.

KEYWORDS

MPTCP, Congestion Control, LIA, OLIA, BALIA, TCP Reno, CUBIC TCP

1. INTRODUCTION

Recent mobile terminals are equipped with multiple interfaces. For example, most smart phones have interfaces for 4G Long Term Evolution (LTE) and Wireless LAN (WLAN). In the next generation (5G) mobile network, it is expected that mobile terminals will be equipped with more interfaces by using multiple communication paths provided multiple network operators [NGNM Alliance, 2015]. However, the conventional Transmission Control Protocol (TCP) establishes a connection between a single IP address at either end, and so it cannot handle multiple interfaces at the same time. In order to utilize the multiple interface configuration, Multipath TCP (MPTCP) [Paasch and Bonaventure, 2014], which is an extension of TCP, has been introduced in several operating systems, such as Linux, Apple OS/iOS [Apple Insider Staff, 2019] and Android [icteam, 2019]. Conventional TCP applications can use MPTCP as if they were working over conventional TCP and are provided with multiple byte streams through different interfaces.

MPTCP is defined in three Request for Comments (RFC) documents by the Internet Engineering Task Force. RFC 6182 [Ford et al., 2011] outlines architecture guidelines. RFC 6824 [Ford et al., 2013] presents the details of extensions to support multipath operation, including the maintenance of an MPTCP connection and subflows (TCP connections associated with an MPTCP connection), and the data transfer over an MPTCP connection. RFC 6356 [Raiciu et al., 2011] presents a congestion control algorithm that couples the congestion control algorithms running on different subflows.

One significant point on the MPTCP congestion control is that, even in MPTCP, individual subflows perform their own control. RFC 6356 requires that an MPTCP data stream do not provide too large throughput compared with other (single) TCP data streams sharing a congested link. For this purpose, RFC 6356 defines an algorithm called Linked Increase Adaptation (LIA), which couples and suppresses the congestion window size of individual subflows. Besides, more aggressive algorithms, such as Opportunistic Linked-Increases Algorithm (OLIA) [Kalili et al., 2013] and Balanced Linked Adaptation (BALIA) [Peng et al., 2016], are proposed. However, all of those algorithms are based on the Additive Increase and Multiplicative Decrease (AIMD) scheme like TCP Reno [Floyd et al., 2004]. That is, the increase of congestion window at receiving a new ACK segment is in the order of 1/(congestion window size). On the other hand, current modern operating systems uses high speed congestion control algorithms, such as CUBIC TCP [Ha et al., 2008] and Compound TCP [Tan et al., 2006]. These algorithms increase the congestion window more aggressively than TCP Reno. So, it is possible that the throughput of LIA and other MPTCP congestion control algorithms is suppressed when it coexists with them.

Based on these considerations, we presented the results of performance evaluation in our previous paper [Kato et al., 2019]. Specifically, we conducted two kinds of experiments. One is to replace the congestion control algorithm of MPTCP from LIA to TCP Reno or CUBIC TCP. The other is for evaluating the performance when a MPTCP connection with LIA and a single path TCP with TCP Reno / CUBIC TCP share a bottleneck link. The results of two experiments showed that the throughput of LIA is lower than that of TCP Reno and CUBIC TCP. But, the experiments have some issues that the number of experimental runs are limited and that the MPTCP used Ethernet and WLAN interfaces, the latter of which may decrease the MPTCP throughput. So, this paper presents more detailed and fair performance experiment and also gives the results for OLIA and BALIA. The rest of this paper is organized as follows. Section II explains the overview of MPTCP and the details of MPTCP congestion control algorithms. Section III describes the experimental setting for performance evaluation. Section IV shows the results of the performance evaluation where LIA, OLIA and BALIA coexist together with TCP Reno and CUBIC TCP over a bottleneck link. In the end, Section V concludes this paper.

2. BACKGROUNDS

2.1 Overview of MPTCP

As described in Figure 1, the MPTCP module is located on top of TCP. MPTCP is designed so that the conventional applications do not need to care about the existence of MPTCP. MPTCP establishes an MPTCP connection associated with two or more regular TCP connections called subflows. The management and data transfer over an MPTCP connection is done by newly introduced TCP options for the MPTCP operations.

When the first subflow is established, a TCP option called *MP_CAPABLE* is used within SYN, SYN+ACK, and the following ACK segments. When the following subflows are established, the *MP_JOIN* option is used so that the new TCP connections are associated with the existing MPTCP connection.

An MPTCP implementation will take one input data stream from an application, and split it into one or more subflows, with sufficient control information to allow it to be reassembled and delivered to the receiver side application reliably and in order. An MPTCP connection maintains the *data sequence number* independent of the subflow level sequence numbers. The data and ACK segments may contain a *Data Sequence Signal (DSS)* option depicted in Figure 2.

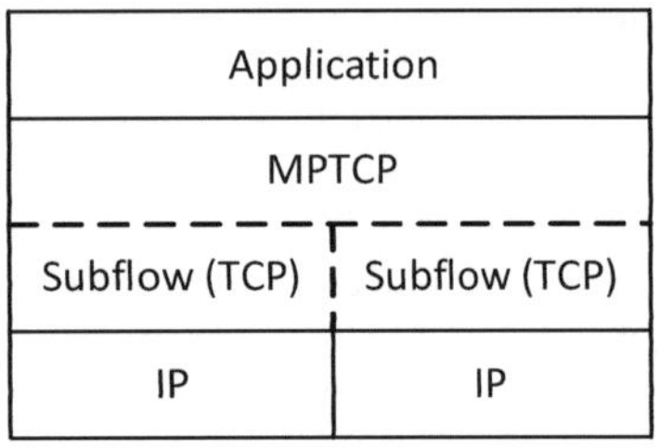

Figure 1. Layer structure of MPTCP

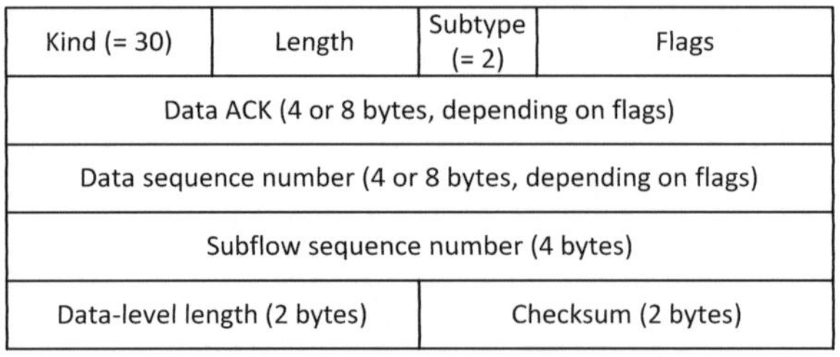

Figure 2. Data Sequence Signal option

The data sequence number and data ACK is 4 or 8 byte long, depending on the flags in the option. The number is assigned on a byte-by-byte basis similarly with the TCP sequence number. The value of data sequence number is the number assigned to the first byte conveyed in that TCP segment. The data sequence number, subflow sequence number (relative value) and data-level length define the mapping between the MPTCP connection level and the subflow level. The data ACK is analogous to the behavior of the standard TCP cumulative ACK. It specifies the next data sequence number a receiver expects to receive.

2.2 Overview of MPTCP Congestion Control

2.2.1 LIA

As described above, in MPTCP, only subflows manage their congestion windows, that is, an MPTCP connection does not have its congestion window size. Under this condition, if subflows perform their congestion control independently, the throughput of MPTCP connection will be larger than single TCP connections sharing a bottleneck link. RFC 6356 decides that such a method is unfair for conventional TCP. RFC 6356 introduces the following three requirements for the congestion control for MPTCP connection.

- Goal 1 (Improve throughput): An MPTCP flow should perform at least as well as a single TCP flow would on the best of the paths available to it.
- Goal 2 (Do no harm): All MPTCP subflows on one link should not take more capacity than a single TCP flow would get on this link.
- Goal 3 (Balance congestion): An MPTCP connection should use individual subflow dependent on the congestion on the path.

In order to satisfy these three goals, RC6356 proposes an algorithm that *couples* the additive increase function of the subflows, and uses unmodified decreasing behavior in case of a packet loss. This algorithm is called LIA and summarized in the following way.

Let $cwnd_i$ and $cwnd\_total$ be the congestion window size on subflow i, and the sum of the congestion window sizes of all subflows in an MPTCP connection, respectively. Here, we assume they are maintained in packets. Let rtt_i be the Round-Trip Time (RTT) on subflow i. For each ACK received on subflow i, $cwnd_i$ is increased by

$$min\left(\frac{\alpha}{cwnd\_total}, \frac{1}{cwnd_i}\right). \tag{1}$$

The first argument of min function is designed to satisfy Goal 2 requirement. Here, α is defined by

$$\alpha = cwnd\_total \cdot \frac{max_k\left(\frac{cwnd_k}{rtt_k{}^2}\right)}{\left(\sum_k \frac{cwnd_k}{rtt_k}\right)^2}. \tag{2}$$

By substituting (2) to (1), we obtain the following equation.

$$min\left(\frac{max_k\left(\frac{cwnd_k}{rtt_k{}^2}\right)}{\left(\sum_k \frac{cwnd_k}{rtt_k}\right)^2}, \frac{1}{cwnd_i}\right) \tag{3}$$

As we mentioned in our previous paper, equation (2) can be derived by the assumption that the increase and decrease of congestion window sizes are balanced and that the virtual single TCP connections corresponding the subflows have the same throughput as the MPTCP connection [Kato et al., 2019].

2.2.2 OLIA

Khalili et al. mentioned two problems of LIA in their paper [Khalili et al., 2013]. The first problem is that LIA is not Pareto-optimal, i.e., the use of MPTCP may reduce the throughput of other TCPs without any benefit to the MPTCP throughput. The second problem is that MPTCP may be excessively aggressive toward TCP. In order resolve these problems, they proposed a new congestion control algorithm for MPTCP called the opportunistic linked-increases algorithm (OLIA). OLIA is specified in the following way.

OLIA defines l_i for subflow i as the larger among the number of transmitted bits over subflow i between last two losses and the number of transmitted bits after the last loss. rtt_i is defined as RTT on subflow i. It defines two set of subflows M and B as follows.

$$M = \{k|k = arg\max_k cwnd_k\}. \tag{4}$$

$$B = \left\{k\middle|k = arg\max_k \frac{l_i}{{rtt_k}^2}\right\}. \tag{5}$$

Here M is the set of the subflows with largest congestion window, and B is the set of the subflows that are presumably the best at the time.

Using those concepts, OLIA is defined in the following way.

- For each ACK segment over subflow i, increase $cwnd_i$ by

$$\frac{\frac{cwnd_i}{{rtt_i}^2}}{\left(\sum_k \frac{cwnd_k}{rtt_k}\right)^2} + \frac{\alpha_i}{cwnd_i} \tag{6}$$

where α_i is calculated as follows:

$$\alpha_i = \begin{cases} \frac{1/number\ of\ subflows}{|B\backslash M|}, if\ i \in B\backslash M \neq \emptyset \\ -\frac{1/number\ of\ subflows}{|M|}, if\ i \in M\ and\ B\backslash M \neq \emptyset \\ 0, otherwise. \end{cases} \tag{7}$$

$B\backslash M$ is the set of elements in B but not in M, $\emptyset$ is the empty set, and $|B\backslash M|$ and $|M|$ are the number of elements of individual set.

- For each loss over subflow i, decrease $cwnd_i$ by $cwnd_i/2$.

By comparing equations (3) and (6), we can say that LIA and OLIA are quite similar. Difference is that OLIA introduces the second term in equation (6), and that OLIA uses the value for the current subflow instead of the maximum as the numerator of the first term. Therefore, OLIA is still considered that it is based on TCP Reno similarly with LIA.

2.2.3 BALIA

Peng et al. proposed another congestion control algorithm focusing on a good balance between friendliness and responsiveness. This algorithm is called the balanced linked adaptation (BALIA), which is applied to the AIMD of the congestion avoidance phase [Peng et al., 2016]. It should be noted that the minimum value of ssthresh is set to one packet instead of 2 packets when more than one subflows are available.

Similarly with the above, let $cwnd_i$ be the congestion window size of subflow i, and rtt_i be the RTT of subflow i. The window adaptation of BALIA

- For each ACK segment over subflow i, increase $cwnd_i$ by:

$$\frac{\frac{cwnd_i}{{rtt_i}^2}}{\left(\sum_k \frac{cwnd_k}{rtt_k}\right)^2} \times \frac{1+\alpha_i}{2} \times \frac{4+\alpha_i}{5}. \tag{8}$$

- For each loss over subflow i, decrease $cwnd_i$ by:

$$\frac{cwnd_i}{2} \times min(\alpha_i, 1.5). \tag{9}$$

Here, $\alpha_i = \frac{\max_k \frac{cwnd_k}{rtt_k}}{\frac{cwnd_i}{rtt_i}}$.

Similarly with OLIA, BALIA is also an extension of TCP Reno. Especially, when there is only one subflow, α_i is 1 and the increase and decrease of BALIA is identical to those of TCP Reno.

3. EXPERIMENTAL SETTINGS

Figure 3 shows the network configuration used in our experiment. An MPTCP data sender and a TCP (single path TCP) sender are connected to a 100 Mbps Ethernet hub. MPTCP sender has two Ethernet interfaces. A data receiver for MPTCP and TCP is connected to the hub through a bridge, which limits a data transmission rate to 25 Mbps. All nodes are running the Linux operating system, whose distribution is Ubuntu 16.04.

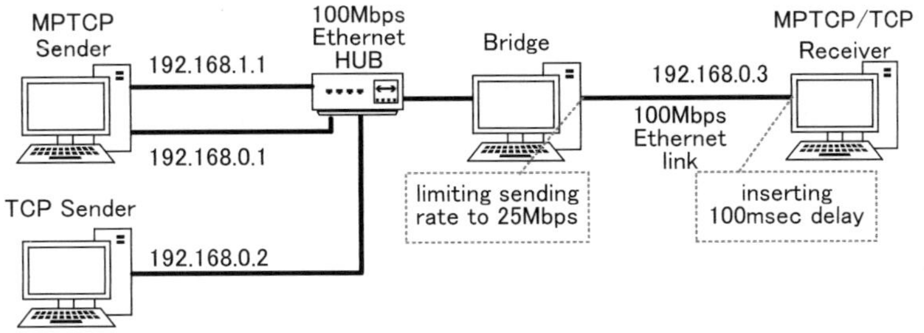

Figure 3. Network configuration used in experiment

Both MPTCP sender and receiver use an MPTCP software whose version is 0.94 stable, which is the newest version we can obtain [GitHub, 2019].

The IP addresses assigned to the network interfaces are shown in Figure 3. It should be noted that the LAN used in the experiment has subnet address 192.168.0.0/24, and the second Ethernet interface in the MPTCP sender another subnet 192.168.1.0/24. In the MPTCP sender side, the routing table needs to be specified for individual interfaces by using `ip` command. In the receiver side, a route entry to subnet 192.168.1.0/24 needs to be specified explicitly.

In the experiment, one MPTCP connection between the MPTCP sender and the receiver and one TCP connection between the TCP sender and the receiver are evaluated. In order to emulate a wide area Internet communication, 100 msec delay is inserted at the receiver. The bridge limits the data transmission rate from the senders to the receiver into 25 Mbps. Here, an actual congestion will occur. As for the congestion control algorithm, the MPTCP sender uses LIA, OLIA, or BALIA, and the TCP sender uses TCP Reno or CUBIC TCP. In actual measurement runs, iperf is used for data transfer whose communication duration is ten second in one measurement run.

4. RESULTS OF PERFORMANCE EVALUATION

4.1 Results of LIA for MPTCP Connection

First, we conducted a performance evaluation with LIA for an MPTCP flow and TCP Reno for a single path TCP (SPTCP) flow. We executed ten measurement runs and obtained the average and standard deviation for MPTCP and SPTCP, which are 1.56 Mbps and 0,02 Mbps, and 21.6 Mbps and 0 Mbps. These results means that MPTCP with LIA is weaker than SPTCP with TCP Reno.

Figure 4 shows the details of communication in one measurement run. Figure 4(a) gives the sequence number vs. time for two MPTCP subflows and an SPTCP. As this figure indicates, the increase of the sequence number of two subflows are very slow. Figure 4(b) gives the congestion window size vs. time for two subflows and one TCP. In this case, the congestion window size of two subflows keeps 10 packets, which is the initial value of congestion window size.

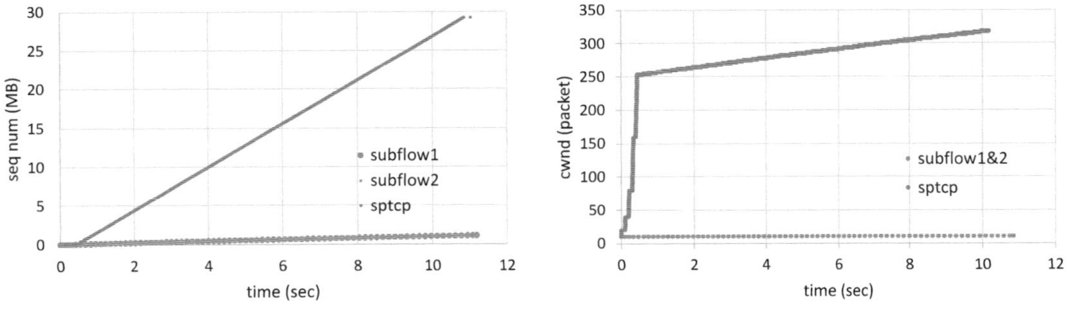

(a) Sequence number vs. time (b) Congestion window size vs. time

Figure 4. Result for LIA and TCP Reno

We also conducted a performance evaluation with LIA for MPTCP and CUBIC TCP for SPTCP. Similarly we executed ten measurement runs. The average and standard deviation are 3.66 Mbps and 2.82 Mbps for MPTCP, and 19.6 Mbps and 2.83 Mbps for SPTCP, respectively. In this case, MPTCP with LIA is also weaker than SPTCP with CUBIC TCP. The standard deviation is larger for LIA and CUBIC than for LIA and Reno.

Figures 5 and 6 show the details of one measurement run. Figure 5 gives the sequence number vs. time for two subflows and one SPTCP flow. Figure 5(a) shows that the sequence number of SPTCP increases rapidly compared with those of subflows. Figure 5(b) is a magnified graph for two subflows. The increase of two subflows is similar. Figure 6 give the congestion window size vs. time for two subflows and one SPTCP flow. From Figure 6(a), it is confirmed that the increase of congestion window size in SPTCP CUBIC TCP is very active, but on the other hand, those in two subflows are very slow. Figure 6(b) is a magnified graph for subflows. Three TCP connections suffer from packet losses around two second, when the congestion window size decreases. Before and after the packet losses, the increase of congestion window size is large for CUBIC TCP and low for LIA.

4.2 Results of OLIA for MPTCP Connection

Next evaluation is for OLIA and TCP Reno/CUBIC TCP. We conducted ten measurement runs. When OLIA and TCP Reno are used together, the throughput (average and standard deviation) is 15.8 Mbps/0.12 Mbps for OLIA and 7.51 Mbps/0.17 Mbps for TCP Reno. That means OLIA provides higher throughput than TCP Reno. Figure 7 shows the details of one measurement run. Figure 7(a) is the sequence number vs. time and Figure 7(b) is the congestion window size vs. time. The growth of sequence number and congestion window is large for one subflow, and small for the other subflow. The growth for the single path TCP is in between of them. As a result, the total throughput of MPTCP connection becomes higher than that of SPTCP connection.

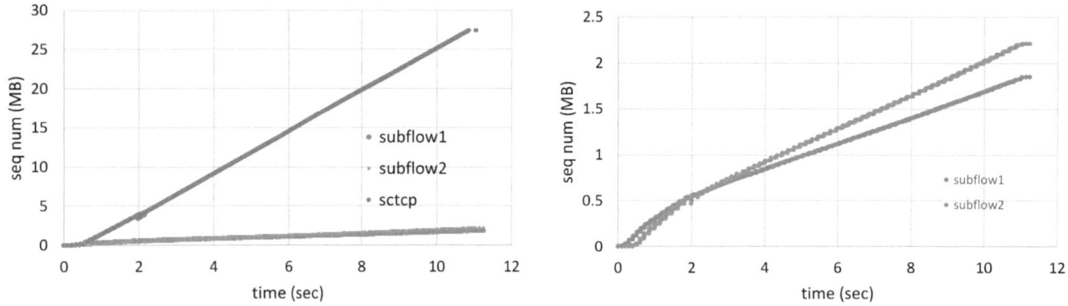

(a) for MPTCP and SPTCP (b) for two MPTCP subflows

Figure 5. Result of sequence number vs. time for LIA and CUBIC TCP

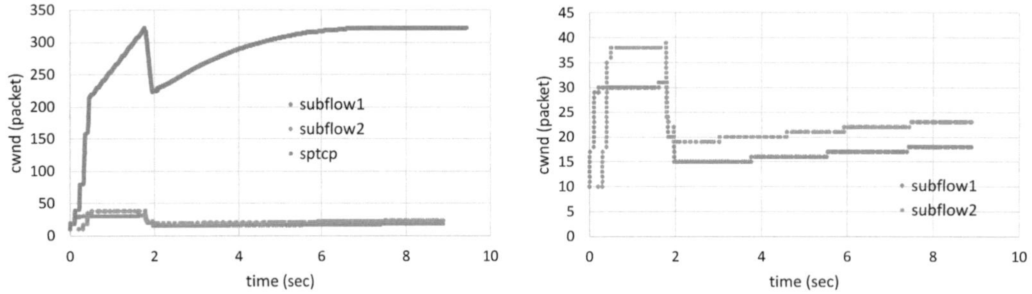

(a) for MPTCP and SPTCP (b) for two MPTCP subflows

Figure 6. Result of congestion window size vs. time for LIA and CUBIC TCP

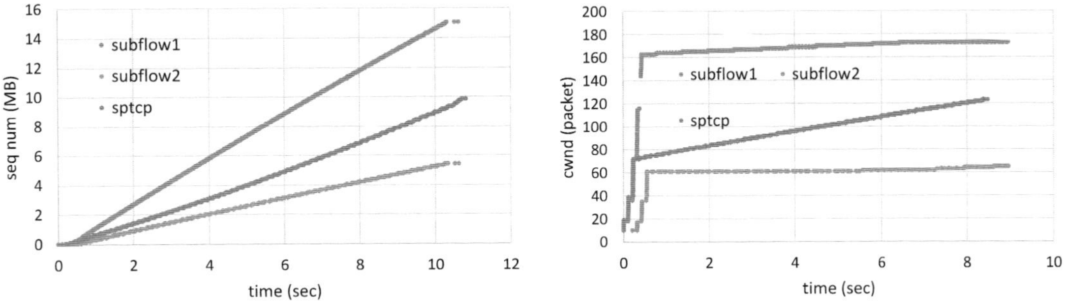

(a) Sequence number vs. time (b) Congestion window size vs. time

Figure 7. Result for OLIA and TCP Reno

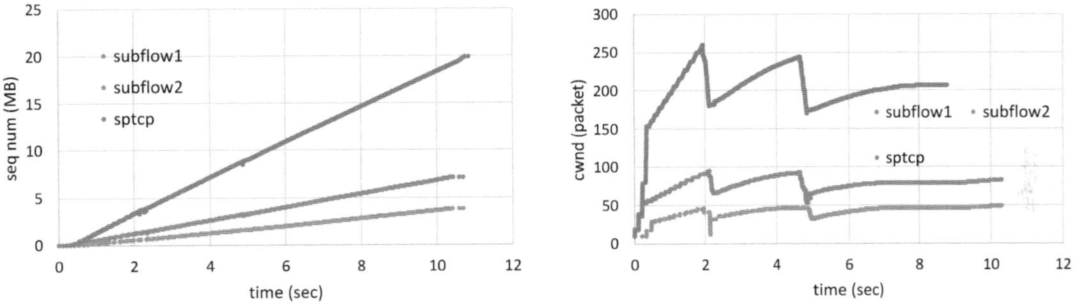

(a) Sequence number vs. time (b) Congestion window size vs. time

Figure 8. Result for OLIA and CUBIC TCP

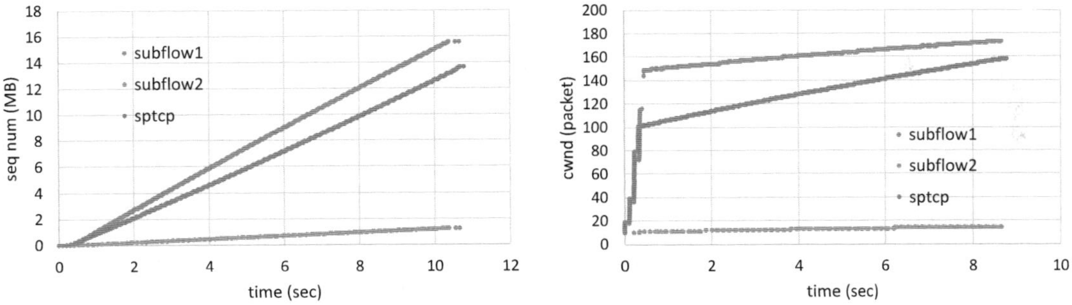

(a) Sequence number vs. time (b) Congestion window size vs. time

Figure 9. Result for BALIA and TCP Reno

When OLIA and CUBIC TCP are used together, the throughput (average and standard deviation) is 4.40 Mbps/2.83 Mbps and 18.8 Mbps/2.76 Mbps, respectively. In this case, SPTCP with CUBIC TCP provides higher throughput than OLIA MPTCP. Figure 8 shows the details of one measurement run. The growth of sequence number and congestion window size is larger than that of MPTCP subflows, and as a result the throughput is lower for OLIA than for CUBIC TCP.

4.3 Results of BALIA for MPTCP Connection

The last evaluation for BALIA and TCP Reno/CUBIC TCP. When BALIA and TCP Reno are used together, the throughput (average and standard deviation) is 12.9 Mbps/0.35 Mbps for OLIA and 10.4 Mbps/0.27 Mbps for TCP Reno. Similarly with OLIA, MPTCP provides higher throughput than Reno. Figure 9 shows the details of one measurement run, which indicates that both the sequence number and the congestion window size grow faster for BALIA, but the growth speed is similar in this case.

When BALIA and CUBIC TCP are used together, the throughput (average and standard deviation) is 4.43 Mbps/2.16 Mbps and 18.8 Mbps/2.16 Mbps, respectively. The result are very similar with the case of OLIA and CUBIC. The details of one measurement run shown in Figure 10 are similar with the case of OLIA.

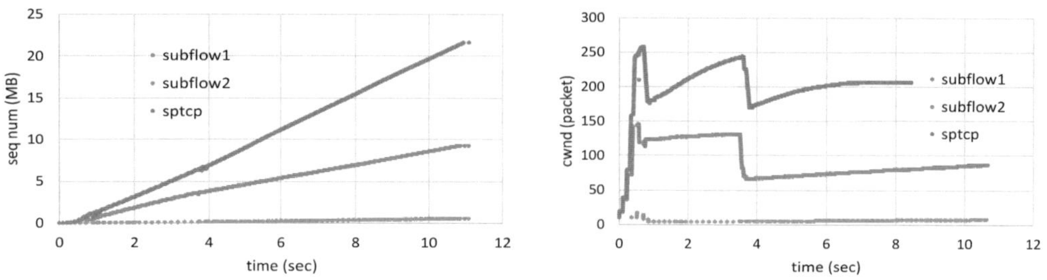

(a) Sequence number vs. time

(b) Congestion window size vs. time

Figure 10. Result for BALIA and CUBIC TCP

5. CONCLUSIONS

In this paper, we presented the results of performance evaluation for MPTCP congestion control algorithms, LIA, OLIA, and BALIA in the condition that a single path TCP flow with TCP Reno or CUBIC TCP is used over a congested link. LIA, which is the standard congestion control algorithm of MPTCP, provides poor throughput when it coexists with either TCP Reno or CUBIC TCP. On the other hand, OLIA and BALIA provide similar or higher throughput than TCP Reno, but their throughput is lower than that of CUBIC TCP.

REFERENCES

AppleInsider Staff, 2019. *Apple found to be using advanced Multipath TCP networking in iOS 7.* http://appleinsider.com/articles/13/09/20/apple-found-to-be-using-advanced-multipath-tcp-networking-in-ios-7.

Floyd, S., Henderson, T., and Gurtov, A., 2004. *The NewReno Modification to TCP's Fast Recovery Algorithm.* IETF RFC 3728.

Ford, A., Raiciu, C., Handley, M., and Bonaventure, O., 2013. *TCP Extensions for Multipath Operation with Multiple Addresses.* IETF RFC 6824.

Ford, A., Raiciu, C., Handley, M., Barre, S., and J. Iyengar, J., 2011. *Architectural Guidelines for Multipath TCP Development.* IETF RFC 6182.

GitHub, 2019. *Linux Kernel implementation of MultiPath TCP.* https://multipath-tcp.org.

Ha, S., Rhee, I., and Xu, L., 2008. CUBIC: A New TCP-Friendly High-Speed TCP Variant. *ACM SIGOPS Operating Systems Review*, vol. 42, no. 5, pp. 64-74.

icteam, 2019. *MultiPath TCP – Linux Kernel implementation, Users: Android.* https://multipath-tcp.org/pmwiki.php/Users/Android.

Kato, T., Diwakar, A., Yamamoto, R., Ohzahata, S., and Suzuki, N., 2019. Performance Evaluation of MaltiPath TCP Congestion Control. *ICN 2019: 18th International Conference on Networks*, pp. 19-24.

Khalili, R., Gast, N., Popovic, M., and Boudec, J., 2013. MPTCP Is Not Pareto-Optimal: Performance Issues and a Possible Solution. *IEEE/ACM Trans. Networking*, vol. 21, no. 5, pp. 1651-1665.

NGNM Alliance, 2015. *NGMN 5G White Paper.* https://www.ngmn.org/fileadmin/ngmn/content/images/news /ngmn_news/NGMN_5G_White_Paper_V1_0.pdf.

Paasch, C., and O. Bonaventure, O., 2014. Multipath TCP. *Communications of the ACM*, vol. 57, no. 4, pp. 51-57.

Peng, Q., Valid, A., Hwang, J., and Low, S., 2016. Multipath TCP: Analysis, Design and Implementation. *IEEE/ACM Trans. Networking*, vol. 24, no. 1, pp. 596-609.

Raiciu, C., Handley, M., and Wischik, D., 2011. *Coupled Congestion Control for Multipath Transport Protocols.* IETF RFC 6356.

Tan, K., Song, J., Zhang, Q., and Sridharan, M., 2006. A Compound TCP Approach for High-speed and Long Distance Networks. *IEEE INFOCOM 2006*, pp. 1-12.

IMPROVING EFFICIENCY OF A WEB-BASED DISTRIBUTED EVOLUTIONARY COMPUTING SYSTEM

Jerzy Duda and Wojciech Dłubacz
AGH University of Science and Technology, Faculty of Management
ul. Gramatyka 10, 30-067 Kraków, Poland

ABSTRACT

The paper presents a study on performance improvement of an evolutionary computing system built on the basis of JavaScript technology. The system consists of web browsers performing computational tasks and a web server based on Go programming language (Golang technology) that controls the computing environment. The newest web technologies such as HTML5 Web Workres and JavaScript WebAssembly are used to maximize the utilization of the resources provided by web clients. Computational experiments are performed on large instances of popular NP-hard problems: travelling salesman problem (TSP), flowshop scheduling problem (FSP) and recourse constrained project scheduling problem (RCPSP).

KEYWORDS

Distributed Computing, Evolutionary Computation, Social Computing, Grid Computing, Internet

1. INTRODUCTION

Since the launch of SETI@home project in 1999 and it successor BOINC (Berkeley Open Infrastructure for Network Computing (Anderson, 2004), grid computing basing on personal computers is becoming more and more popular and in many applications may be considered as viable alternative for very expensive super computers. On the other hand, growing interest in optimization of complex problems, as well as processing huge amount of data required for decision making in contemporary business and management steadily increase the demand for computing power not only from the side of research centers, government agencies or military organizations, but also from the side of large and medium-sized companies.

Despite their advantages, grid computer systems based on BOINC or similar platforms (e.g. Grid MP, distributed.net) have two major drawbacks. First of all a user participating in a computing project must download a special client application (agent) that communicates with the central server. Some users may not may not be willing to download software that regularly sends data from their computers. Moreover, such application is dedicated to a particular operating system and is device dependent (different versions must be installed for a computer, a mobile device, etc.), what further limits the number of potential participants in a computing grid. Another problem with such type of distributed systems can be caused by firewalls blocking communication between a client and the server as they usually use some non-standard TCP ports.

Introduction of Google's V8 JavaScript engine based on just-in-time compilation in 2008 started a new era for web browsers allowing a significant reduction of the execution speed gap between a JavaScript code and a machine code generated by such compiled languages as C or C++. This contributed to a growing interest in grid computing based entirely on web-browser clients.

Along with the introduction of HTML5 new APIs such as Web Workers have become available for JavaScript programmers. In the recent years web browser developers presented some new techniques which allow for further acceleration of the code written in JavaScript. The goal of this paper is the analysis of how those techniques may contribute to performance improvement of a web-based distributed computing.

2. WEB-BASED DISTRIBUTED COMPUTING SYSTEMS

First web browser based distributed computing systems emerged with the beginning of intensive development of JavaScript technology. Merelo et. al. presented a series of papers describing distributed evolutionary computing system. Their first system (Merelo et al., 2007) was based on a master-slave architecture. The server running on Ruby on Rails (RoR) technology maintained the population of solutions and sent the tasks consisting of fitness function calculation to the distributed clients (web browsers). The tasks were sent in the JavaScript Object Notation (JSON) format as an AJAX response to the request of awaiting clients. The system was difficult for scaling since only server performed the main routine of the evolutionary algorithm and due to poor distributing performance of RoR even small amount of clients have to wait for an answer form the server. An improved version of the system was described in (Merelo et al., 2008). It followed an island model of computations in which populations were run independently on clients' machines. The tasks for the server were only collecting the best individuals and sending them back in a response to clients' requests. An improved version of the system scaled much better and was able to serve more than 40 clients. In one of their latest papers the authors developed a simple NodEO server (Merelo et al., 2014) in order to show that a Node.js server with a master-slave architecture of parallel computing is more effective than peer to peer (P2P) computation.

Another group of web browser based computing systems consists of general purpose systems that may perform any kind of tasks provided in the form of a JS function that is run parallely on clients' machines. For example a system called WeevilScout was described in (Cushing et al., 2013). It is a master-slave distributed computing system in which the server uses REpresentational State Transfer (REST) service to queue awaiting computations. Web browsers pull packaged jobs from the server described in XML messages and send back the results to the REST service.

A separte group of systems are the systems in which the users' machines execute some unwilling computations. The system performing a parasitic JavaScript computations was proposed by Jenkin (2008). It utilized JSON and AJAX technologies and was able to limit the CPU load on the clients' machines by the application of timer based programming. The system was applied not only to solve an optimization problem (N-Queens) by a genetic algorithm, but also for ray tracing tasks and for perceptron learning in an artificial neural network. Another system that performed unwilling distributed computations was presented by Klein and Spector (2007). The system used PHP and Push technology on the server's side, whereas JavaScript and AJAX technologies were used on the clients' side to solve simple genetic programming problems.

Finally, MacWilliam and Cecka (2013) described a web-based volunteer computing system that used exclusively WebCL to solve Thomson nonlinear optimization problem.

3. WEB-BASED DISTRIBUTED COMPUTING SYSTEMS

Computational efficiency of an evolutionary distributed computing system is conditioned by two main factors:

1. Technological solutions used to code a server side, as well as the ones used to code a client's side.
2. Architecture of an evolutionary system itself.

The proposed evolutionary computing system uses Go programming language (Golang) on the server side, while Web Workers and WebAssembly technologies are used on the client's side. The architecture of the system is shown in Figure 1.

3.1 Server Implementation

In contrast to (Merelo et al., 2007) and our earlier system presented in (Duda, Dlubacz, 2013), the system supervisor - a WebSockets service that all clients connect to is implemented in Golang technology (Newmarch, 2017).

Research made at the initial stage of system development showed that the implementation of message exchange using Node.js have an additional overhead for handling each message reaching 40 ms, what after just-in-time-compilation (JIT) turns into an overhead of 15 ms, compared to the same implementation in Golang. JIT technique, which is built inside JavaScript, compiles frequently used functions preventing from their interpretation at each call (Martinsen et al., 2011). The Golang was developed by Google and it is a compiled language, with the ease of writing a scripting language, and in compare to naturally one-threaded JavaScript Node.js environment it has built-in multithreading support. Thanks to the use of this language, very high scalability of the system has been achieved, providing support for many simultaneous connections and dynamic communication between them.

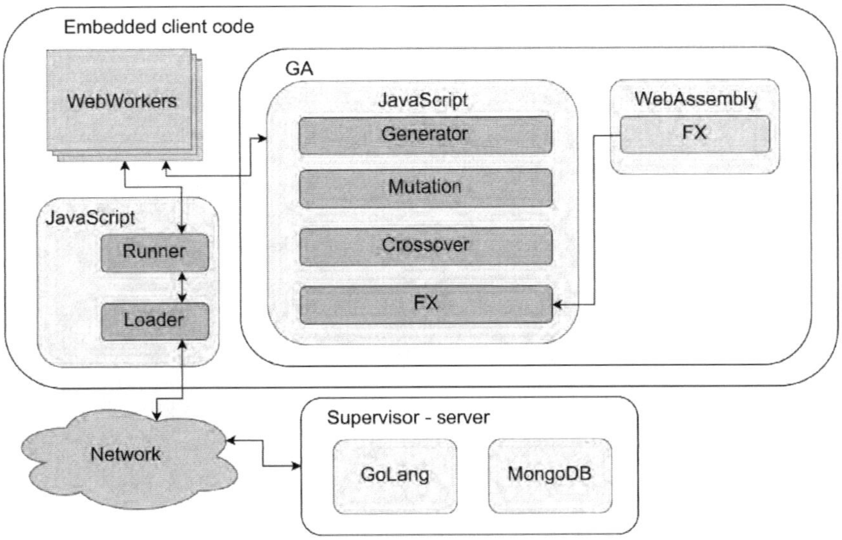

Figure 1. Platform workflow diagram

A non-relational database MongoDB (Plugge, 2010), which is also easily scalable and enables support of multiple simultaneous connections, was used to collect data obtained from the computing units.

Genetic algorithms can be easily run parallelly because by definition computations are made on the set of solutions (population of individuals). In general, three basic optimization models can be applied to a distributed system of genetic algorithms, as enumerated in (Talbi, 2006):

- global optimization model - calculations of the objective function for members of the population maintained on the server are executed in parallel on clients' computers; such approach was applied in (Merelo, 2017),
- master-slave model (synchronous island model) - the main population on the server communicates with subpopulations to collect the best solutions to obtain final solution,
- asynchronous island model - the central server is responsible only for collecting the best solutions from the population and sending them to clients.

In the presented platform the last of the above listed models has been implemented, as subpopulations can be potentially calculated on different heterogeneous machines with different computing power, including mobile devices. Additionally different versions of the genetic algorithm or some other algorithms (e.g. used for local search) may be delegated in the future to some clients, depending on their computing capabilities.

3.2 Client's Side Implementation

To make the whole evolutionary computing system flexible, its client's logic is built of interchangeable blocks of the algorithm codes:

- chromosome generators - create initial population, thus determine the representation of the solution (chromosome structure)
- fitness functions (FX) - represent objective function for a given optimization problem
- crossovers - create new solutions on the basis of two existing solutions
- mutations - alter some small portion of the solution (e.g. changes a gene value)

Those blocks are combined to form a calculation scheme. Parameters that can be additionally modified are:

- the probability of crossover,
- the probability of mutation,
- size of the population (number of members of a given population),
- calculation time limit for a single client.

The way in which a user can define the components of an evolutionary algorithm is shown on the example of the flowshop scheduling problem, which will be discussed in the following section.

Initially in the chromosome generation stage, a random permutation of jobs is generated. After a solution is created or altered by the means of genetic operators, its fitness value has to be evaluated. Listing 1 shows fitness evaluation for the flowshop scheduling problem.

```
return function fitness(c, p) {
    var m = 0, i = 0, t = {}, job = 0, n = p[0].length, mC = p.length;
    (function() {
        for (let j = 0; j < mC; j++) {
            t[j] = {};
            for (let k = 0; k < n; k++) {
                t[j][k] = 0;
            }
        }
    })();
    for (i in c) {
        i = parseInt(i, 10);
        job = c[i];
        if (typeof(job) !== 'number') { continue; }
        for (let m = 0; m < mC; m++) {
            if (m === 0) {
                t[m][i] = (p[m][job] + t[m][i - 1]) || p[m][job];
            } else if (typeof(t[m][i - 1]) === 'number') {
           t[m][i] = ((t[m][i - 1] > t[m - 1][i]) ? t[m][i - 1] : t[m - 1][i])
                   + p[m][job];
            } else {
                t[m][i] = t[m - 1][i] + p[m][job];
            }
        }
    }
    return t[mC - 1][n - 1];
};
```

Listing 1. Fitness function for the flowshop scheduling problem written in JS code

Next, the best fitted members in the population are selected to form a new generation basing on their fitness values. Selection algorithm (binary tournament) is currently embedded into the flow of the evolutionary algorithm and cannot be changed yet by the user. After selection stage, crossover (e.g. PBX) and mutation (e.g. swapping two jobs) operators are applied with the probability that can be set manually before running computations. The codes of the standard operators are already predefined in the system, but the user can define new operators.

4. EFFICIENCY IMPROVEMENTS

4.1 Test Problems

In order to test the performance of the system three different popular combinatorial optimization problems have been used:

- Symmetric Traveling Salesman Problem (TSP)
- Permutation Flowshop Scheduling Problem (FSP)

- Resource Constrained Project Scheduling Problem (RCPSP)

TSP is a classical problem in combinatorial optimization formulated first in 1930 and since then studied by many researchers. It can be formulated as follows: Given a list of cities and their pairwise distances, the goal is to find the shortest possible tour in which all cities are visited exactly once. Usually the position of the cities is provided as points' coordinates in 2D Euclidean space. Thus the length of the tour (fitness function) is a simple sum of distances between cities in the sequence (the last city becomes also the first city, as the salesman must return to the origin):

$$f(x) = \sum_{i=1}^{n} \sqrt{(q_{i,1} - q_{i+1,1})^2 + (q_{i,2} - q_{i+1,2})^2}$$

Such function is easy to compute regardless the language that is used.

Flowshop scheduling problem denotes the problem of determining the best sequence of jobs that have to be processed on each machine in the flow shop in exactly same order. The most frequently criterion of optimality for FSP is minimization of the total time necessary to compete all jobs on all machines (makespan). JavaScript code of such fitness function was presented in Listing 1. Solutions for FSP can have the same representation as for TSP, but its objective function is more complicated to compute.

The last problem that was tested - Resource Constrained Scheduling Problem - has even more complicated goal function. RCPSP considers resources of limited availability and activities of known durations, resource requests and precedence constraints. The goal is to find a schedule that minimizes total duration of activities by assigning a start time to each activity in the way that the precedence constraints and the resource availabilities are respected. Thus each time the fitness is calculated all the constraints have to be evaluated.

It is worth noting that for the computational experiments the test problems have been chosen in order to have different computational complexity of their objective functions.

4.2 Multithreading a JavaScript GA Algorithm

Due to the fact that nowadays even mobile phones have multi-core processors, one of the basic solution to speed up calculations is to use all CPU cores simultaneously. As it was mentioned earlier, in the case of GA, splitting calculations into more threads is relatively easy. In this approach the simplest solution is to let every computational thread manages its own population. These populations, after finding another better solution, communicates with the main thread of the computing procedure performed on the client's side and then the best one is sent to the server.

In JavaScript, currently the only API allowing to use more than one CPU core is called Web Worker. There is another JavaScript API named SharedWorkers but it also bases on the same mechanism of spawning new threads. JavaScript can spawn as many Web Workers as only are allowed by an operating system. To check for the amount of CPU cores JavaScript provides property called *navigator.hardwareConcurrency*. The main problem with Web Workers is that they communicate with the main thread by copying data rather than sharing them. To verify the efficiency of Web Workers technology, the tests shown in Table 1 were performed. For the code execution, a *setTimeout* method technique was used to prevent clients' web browsers from slowing down, analogously as in the system presented in (Duda, Dlubacz, 2013).

Amount of generated populations for Flowshop problem with 20 jobs and 10 machines for different Web Workers performed on Intel i5 4 core CPU processor was presented in Table 1. Data are presented as number of generations performed per second.

Table 1. Generations per sec. for different WebWorkers amount

Main	1	2	3	4	5	6
88.62	99.93	199.76	297.37	398.84	472.43	542.43

The results show almost linear increase of the system performance until the number of used Web Workers equals to the number of CPU physical cores. After exceeding this limit, due to the use of the processor unloading technique, the increase in the number of computed generations still occurs, but no longer in a linear way. This experiment shows also that calculations run on a separate Web Worker are more efficient than these run in the main thread which is also responsible for rendering web page.

4.3 Analysis of the Algorithm's Components

To further increase GA performance on the client's side some studies have been performed to identify its bottlenecks. For this purpose, code profiling for different sizes of the FSP and RCPSP problem was performed.

The results showing the impact of the particular stage of the evolutionary algorithm performed by a client are gathered in Table 2 and Table 3.

Table 2. Running time for JavaScript implemented objective function, crossover and mutation for FSP problem

EA stages	20x10	50x10	100x10	200x10
Fitness calculation	87.91%	85.90%	80.70%	71.45%
Crossover calculation	11.96%	14.06%	19.27%	28.53%
Mutation calculation	0.12%	0.05%	0.03%	0.02%

Table 3. Running time for JavaScript implemented objective function, crossover and mutation for RCPSP problem

EA stages	30	60	120
Fitness calculation	94.52%	96.51%	97.90%
Crossover calculation	5.44%	3.48%	2.10%
Mutation calculation	0.05%	0.01%	0.01%

Analyzing the above results it can be clearly seen that the most time consuming stage of the evolutionary algorithm is the calculation of the fitness function. To compare the time spending on the particular stages of GA both crossover and mutation probability were set to 1.0 (100%). In real cases probability of crossover is usually set between 0.5 and 0.9, while mutation probability usually does not exceed 0.05. This means that in real cases the fitness calculation will be using even more computational power relatively to the calculation of the crossover stage, while the computing power spent on the mutation stage is virtually meaningless.

4.4 Using of WebAssembly

In February 2017, four major browser manufacturers: Chrome, Edge, Firefox, and WebKit, came to an consensus on the technology for linking compiled high-level language code into JavaScript. That consensus included a JavaScript API and binary code format. This technology is currently named WebAssembly (WASM). It is a binary instruction format for a virtual machine and is designed as a portable target for compilation of high-level languages.

Developers of the WebAssembly believe that this technology is extremely fast – application can run almost with the speed of a native binary code execution. It should be emphasized that rewriting JavaScript fitness function into WebAssembly code was not obvious due to frequent changes in its specification and small community. Listing 2 presents C++ code for counting flowshop fitness function that was compiled with Emscripten - recommended tool to compile C/C++ code into WebAssembly binary.

```
int EMSCRIPTEN_KEEPALIVE fitness(int n, int m, int *t, int *o) {
    int w;
    int *C = new int[m + 1];
    C[0] = t[o[0] * m + 0];
    for (int j = 1; j < m; j++)
      C[j] = C[j - 1] + t[o[0] * m + j];
    for (inti = 1; i < n; i++) {
        C[0] += t[o[i] * m + 0];
        for (intj = 1; j < m; j++)
          C[j] = (C[j - 1] > C[j] ? C[j - 1] +
t[o[i] * m + j] : C[j] + t[o[i] * m + j]);
    }
    w = C[m - 1];
    delete[] C;
    return w;
}
```

Listing 2. WebAssembly fitness function written in C++

The compiled binary file with the .wasm extension was then added as a dependency for the evolutionary algorithm. The results presenting calculation time measured for the fitness function for different problems and different size are presented in Table 4.

Table 4. Running time comparison for JS, WASM and C/C++

Problem/size	JavaScript	WebAssembly	Visual C++
TSP 100	0.100	0.099	0.000
TSP 1000	0.799	0.099	0.001
TSP 10000	7.100	0.100	0.006
TSP 100000	18.399	0.900	0.062
FSP 50x5	0.100	0.099	0.000
FSP 200x20	0.800	0.099	0.001
FSP 800x60	11.000	0.299	0.019
FSP 2000x120	15.000	1.399	0.081
RCPSP 30	1.499	0.099	0.000
RCPSP 60	3.099	0.099	0.000
RCPSP 120	28.699	0.200	0.009
RCPSP 240	55.299	2.699	0.086

The results of experiments discloses that the usage of WebAssembly technology can enable to perform complex calculations in a significantly shorter time than standard JavaScript execution. It is also visible that WebAssembly is still not as fast as native binary code due to necessary data transfer to WASM module form JavaScript script.

In Table 5 the savings in execution time for the fitness evaluation function and for the whole genetic algorithm procedure are shown for different optimization problems and their sizes.

Table 5. Time reduction for fitness function and the whole GA execution resulting from applying WASM module

Problem/size	Fitness time reduction	GA time reduction
TSP 1000	87.63%	71.19%
TSP 10000	98.59%	80.10%
TSP 100000	95.11%	77.27%
FSP 200x20	87.63%	71.19%
FSP 800x60	97.28%	79.03%
FSP 2000x120	90.67%	73.66%
RCPSP 30	93.40%	88.27%
RCPSP 60	96.81%	93.43%
RCPSP 120	99.30%	96.87%

Since objective function in the resource constrained project scheduling problem (RCPSP) is more complicated and time consuming than makespan calculation for the flowshop scheduling problem, applying WASM module in a distributed system brings significant reduction in computational time for the whole genetic algorithm even for small size of problem instances. Time reduction varies from 88.3% to almost 97%, which means that the distributed system can process from 9 to 33 times more tasks (e.g. generations) than the system without the WASM module. For the FSP problem a significant gain from applying WASM can be observed for the instances with 100 jobs and more. In such cases time reduction varies from 71.2% to 79.0%, which means that the distributed system with WASM module can perform about 3 times more tasks.

5. CONCLUSIONS

The presented distributed evolutionary computing system thanks to its independent component structure pointed the weaknesses of a typical way in which genetic algorithm is implemented. The conducted research showed that the main factor influencing the number of evolutionary algorithm generations that can be computed in a single second on a client's machine was the calculation of the fitness function.

The technologies examined in this article, such as Web Workers and WebAssembly allowed for a significant performance increase of the evolutionary distributed computing system.

Web Workers technology seems to linearly increase system speed to the limit of the amount of physical CPU cores installed on the client's machine. This technology have its main bottleneck in the data transfer mechanism that is making a serialized copy between host thread and Web Worker instead of sharing a reference.

The obtained results indicate that in many cases WebAssembly technology can significantly speed up the function execution. However, due to constantly changing specification and difficulties related to transferring complex JavaScript structures to the function module, it can be assumed that this technology should be only used to implement functions that have the greatest impact on the performance of the evolutionary algorithm.

In the future the application of GPGPU will be considered, however, contrary to WebAssembly, the WebCL standard allowing for easy integration of OpenCL expressions with a JavaScript code is currently not implemented in any web browser.

ACKNOWLEDGEMENT

This work is financed by grants for the maintenance and development of research capacities.

REFERENCES

Anderson, D. P., 2004. Boinc: A system for public-resource computing and storage. *Proceedings of the 5th IEEE/ACM International Workshop on Grid Computing GRID'04*, IEEE Computer Society, pp. 4–10.

Cushing, R. et al., 2013. Distributed computing on an ensemble of browsers. *Internet Computing*. IEEE, Vol. 17, No. 5, pp. 54–61.

Duda, J., Dlubacz, W., 2013. Distributed evolutionary computing system based on web browsers with Javascript. *11th International Conference, Applied Parallel and Scientific Computing PARA 2012*, Springer Berlin Heidelberg, pp. 183–191.

Jenkin, N., 2008, COMP520-08 Report: Parasitic JavaScript.

Klein, J., Spector, L., 2007. Unwitting Distributed Genetic Programming via Asynchronous JavaScript and XML. *Proceedings of the 9th Annual Conference on Genetic and Evolutionary Computation GECCO'07*, ACM, pp. 1628–1635.

MacWilliam, T., Cecka, C., 2013. CrowdCL: Web-based volunteer computing with WebCL. *High Performance Extreme Computing Conference (HPEC)*, IEEE, 2013, pp. 1–6.

Martinsen, J. K., Grahn, H., Isberg A., 2011. A Comparative Evaluation of JavaScript Execution Behavior. *Web Engineering. ICWE 2011*. Lecture Notes in Computer Science, vol 6757. Springer, Berlin, Heidelberg.

Merelo, J. J. et al., 2007. Browser-based Distributed Evolutionary Computation: Performance and Scaling Behavior. *Proceedings of the 9th Annual Conference Companion on Genetic and Evolutionary Computation GECCO'07*, ACM, pp. 2851–2858.

Merelo, J. J. et al., 2014, NodEO, a Multi-paradigm Distributed Evolutionary Algorithm Platform in JavaScript. *Proceedings of the 2014 ConferenceCompanion on Genetic and Evolutionary Computation Companion*. GECCO Comp'14, ACM, pp. 1155–1162.

Merelo-Guervos, J. J. et al., 2008. Asynchronous distributed genetic algorithms with Javascript and JSON. *Evolutionary Computation*, pp. 1372–1379.

Newmarch, J., 2017, *Network Programming with Go: Essential Skills for Using and Securing Networks*. Apress, Berkely, CA, USA.

Plugge, E., 2010. *The Definitive Guide to MongoDB: The NoSQL Database for Cloud and Desktop Computing,* Apress, Berkely, CA, USA.

Syswerda, G., 1991. *Schedule optimization using genetic algorithms*, Handbook of Genetic Algorithms, New York, USA.

Talbi, E.-G., 2006. *Parallel Combinatorial Optimization (Wiley Series on Parallel and Distributed Computing)*, Wiley-Interscience, New York, USA.

METHOD OF CHEMICAL FORMULAS COMPARISON

Nataliya A. Vayngolts, Dmitriy M. Korobkin, Sergey A. Fomenkov, Sergey G. Kolesnikov
and Alla G. Kravets
Volgograd State Technical University
Russia, Volgograd, Lenin av., 28

ABSTRACT

To establish the uniqueness of patented technology a patent examiner needs to compare the patent application with the existing patent array documents and make sure there are no present analogs of the suggested invention. Analyzing chemical classes patents requires to compare chemical formulas which can be represented in various formats including MDL, InChI, SMILES, structural formulas, molecular fingerprints. This paper describes the development of a software module that automates the procedures for converting various methods of chemical formulas formalization, chemical formulas contained in a patent application and patent array documents comparison, similar patents revealing based on the results of the comparison of chemical compounds taken from patents. The implemented software module has shown high efficiency (high values of completeness and accuracy for searching patent analogs based on chemical formulas, low values of information loss and information noise) during control check on a test patent array.

KEYWORDS

Chemical Formula, SMILES, InChi, MDL Molfile, Molecular Fingerprint, Patent Database Analysis

1. INTRODUCTION

With the increase in the number of patents (more than 20 million patents are registered in the world currently), the time to consider a patent application increases. To establish the uniqueness of patented technology a patent examiner needs to compare it with similar patents (sometimes it's necessary to analyze over a thousand documents) and make sure there are no existing analogs of the invention.

Present automated expert patent examination assistance systems (Korobkin, 2018a) do not provide complete automation of the process (Korobkin, 2018b, p. 48). The expert examines the application and performs a patent search based on the keywords he manually selected from the patent application.

Analyzing chemical classes patents requires to compare chemical formulas (Encyclopedia Britannica, n.d.), i.e. formalized chemical compounds representations that contain information about the atomic composition of a single chemical compound molecule. Chemical formulas can be given in various formats: MDL (MDL Information Systems Inc., 2003), InChI (Heller, 2009), SMILES ("D*aylight Theory: SMILES*", n.d.), structural formula (Encyclopedia Britannica, n.d.), molecular fingerprint (Dalke, 2008).

The US Patent Office (USPTO) (United States Patent and Trademark Office, n.d.) provides free access to the file storage of patents that contains zip archives with XML files (patent text) and related documents. These documents also include files of the MDL Molfile format which contain a list of chemical compounds.

The MDL Molfile (MDL Information Systems Inc., 2003) chemical table files provide information about atoms, bonds, valences, and coordinates contained in a compound. MDL files consist of a header block, counts line, atom block, bond block, properties block.

The structural formula (Encyclopedia Britannica, n.d.) represents the molecular structure of a chemical compound that shows atomic bonds and how atoms are located in space relative to each other.

The InChI (IUPAC International Chemical Identifier) (Heller, 2009) is an international chemical compounds text identifier that provides a way to encode information on the structure and composition of the molecules. InChI uses many levels to describe a compound: formula, bonds, isotopes, stereochemistry.

The SMILES (Simplified molecular-input line-entry system) specification ("D*aylight Theory: SMILES*", n.d.) is a system of rules for the unambiguous description of the structure of chemical compounds by ASCII character strings.

Molecular fingerprinting (Dalke, 2008) is a way to encode the molecule structure. It is a bit string with each bit corresponding to a chemical property, mainly substructures. Molecular fingerprints are commonly used to search for similar chemical compounds.

Thus, the actual problem is to automate the assistance to an expert while considering a chemical class patent application. Since the chemical formulas included in a patent application can be represented in all possible ways (MDL, InChI, SMILES, structural formula, molecular fingerprint, etc.), there is a need to develop automated procedures to convert various methods of chemical formula formalization and compare chemical compound formulas contained in a patent application and patent array documents.

There are four existing analogs for the developed software module: Chemical compounds database "ChemSpider" ("ChemSpider reaches 50 million compound", n.d.); Chemical compounds database "PubChem" ("About PubChem", n.d.); Chemical compounds database "ChemSynthesis" ("Chemical Database – ChemSynthesis", n.d.); Chemical recognition system "NCI/CADD Chemical Identifier Resolver" ("NCI/CADD Chemical Identifier Resolver", n.d.).

As a result of the analysis of the presented analogs, it was decided to develop a software module which performs the following functions: (a) Patent array processing aimed to extract elements of patents descriptions and chemical formulas represented in MDL, SMILES, InChI, structural formulas, molecular fingerprints; (b) Chemical formulas conversion to all representations listed above; (c) Chemical compounds comparison based on molecular fingerprints; (d) Similar patents search based on the results of the chemical compounds comparison contained in the patents.

2. CHEMICAL CLASSES PATENTS DATABASE FORMING METHODS

The general algorithm for chemical classes patents database forming that contains information on patents, chemical compounds representations, data on similar chemical compounds and similar patents revealed, is shown in Figure 1.

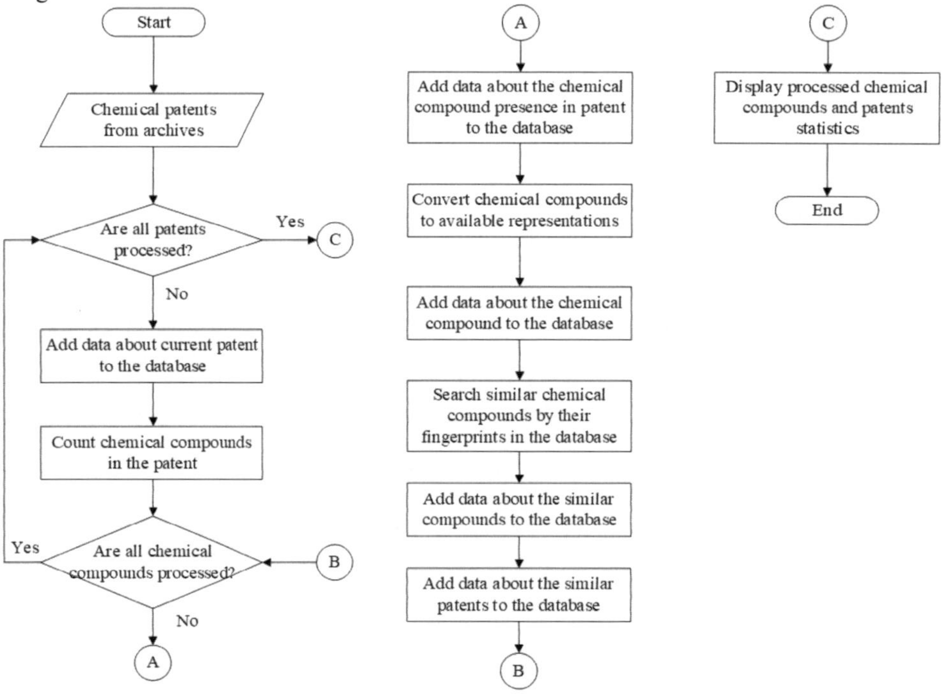

Figure 1. Extracting and writing patent information to the database algorithm

At the initial stage, the information revealing on chemical classes patents (Korobkin, 2018c) and chemical formulas which are contained in the patents is carried out (Korobkin, 2016).

Then the patent array processing runs chemical patents parsing and writes certain patent characteristics to the database. Chemical compounds contained in the patent are also extracted as their representations and stored in the database.

Before comparison of chemical compounds described in various representations, chemical formulas are converted from MDL Molfile format in SMILES, InChI, structural formulas, molecular fingerprints. The converting chemical formulas in various representations algorithm is shown in Figure 2.

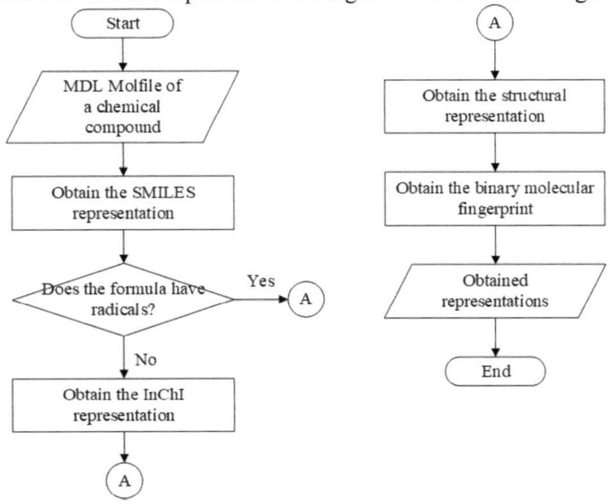

Figure 2. The chemical compounds representations conversion algorithm

2.1 The Chemical Compounds Comparison Algorithm

Chemical formulas comparison is based on molecular fingerprints applying. The Tanimoto coefficient ("Tanimoto (cdk 2.1-SNAPSHOT API)", n.d.) is used to calculate their similarity. The Tanimoto coefficient is calculated with the following formula:

$$T_S = \frac{\sum_i (X_i \cap Y_i)}{\sum_i (X_i \cup Y_i)}, \qquad (1)$$

where X_i stands for the ith bit from the first molecule fingerprint; Y_i stands for the ith bit from the second molecule; $\cap$ stands for bitwise AND; $\cup$ stands for bitwise OR; T_S stands for the Tanimoto coefficient for X and Y fingerprints. The resulting value is in [0; 1] range.

Chemical formulas comparison algorithm using molecular fingerprints is shown in Figure 3.

The input of the algorithm serves two binary molecular fingerprints. Chemical formula #1 has the following SMILES representation: C1=CC(OC1=O)=O. Chemical formula #2 has the following SMILES representation: C1=CC(=C(C(=C1*)*)*)O.

The chemical formula's #1 binary molecular fingerprint consists of 48675 characters (0 or 1), 15010 of them are set. The chemical formula's #2 binary molecular fingerprint consists of 57960 characters (0 or 1), 20440 of them are set. The fingerprints are aligned: zeroes are added to the smaller print until both fingerprints are equal in length.

Then the bitwise "AND" and "OR" are applied to both fingerprints separately; the number of bits set with "AND" and "OR" is calculated. In case molecular fingerprints are identical, the number of set bits after the bitwise "AND" and bitwise "OR" applied will be the same. For the example considered, the number of bits set after operation "AND" applied is 3800, the number of bits set after operation "OR" applied is 5985. Their ratio gives a similarity coefficient of 0.634921. It is considered if the chemical formulas have structural similarity or they do not, depending on the adjusted threshold value for the similarity coefficient.

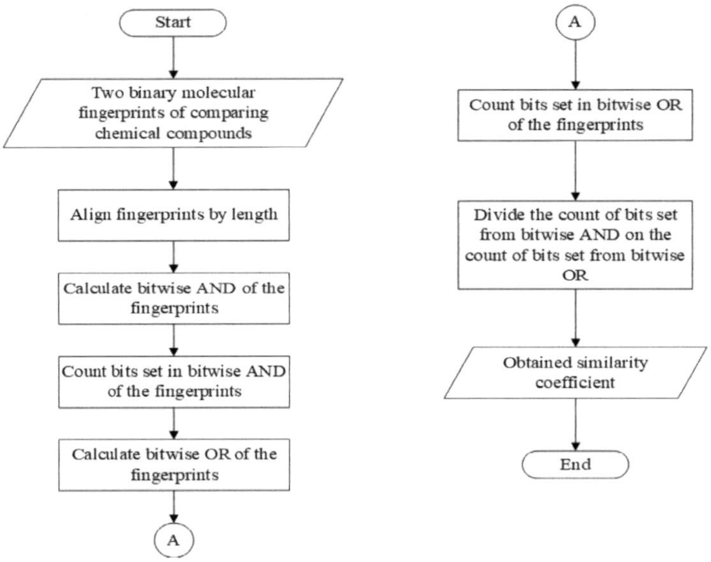

Figure 3. The chemical compounds comparison algorithm

2.2 The Patents Comparison Algorithm

Similar patents revealing is made on the basis of the chemical formulas molecular fingerprints comparison performed for the compared patents. The patents comparison algorithm is shown in Figure 4.

Consider the operation of the algorithm presented in Figure 4, step by step. The input of the algorithm serves two patents. Their information cards are presented in Table 1 and Table 2.

Table 1. The patent #1 description

Field	Value
Name	Moldable compositions containing carbinol functional silicone resins or anhydride functional silicone resins
Publication number	US07807012
Publication date	2010-10-05
Applicant	Dow Corning Corporation
IPC classification	B29C 67/00; C09J 5/06; C04B 37/00; C08F 283/12; C08G 77/00; C08G 77/38; C08L 83/00

Table 2. The patent #2 description

Field	Value
Name	Isolated aqueous enzymatic preparation and the use thereof for the functionalization of the surface of paper or cellulosic substrates
Publication number	US09702087
Publication date	2017-07-11
Applicant	UNIVERSITAT POLITECNICA DE CATALUNYA; RatnerPrestia; Universitat Politecnica de Catalunya; Nopco Paper Technology Holding AS
IPC classification	A61K 38/43; D21H 19/12; D21H 25/02; D21H 17/00; D21H 17/06; D21H 21/14; D21H 21/16; B05D 1/02; B05D 1/18; D21H 17/14; C12N 9/02; D21H 19/12; B05D 1/02; B05D 1/18; C12N 9/0061; C12Y 110/03002; D21H 17/005; D21H 17/06; D21H 17/14; D21H 21/14; D21H 21/16; D21H 25/02

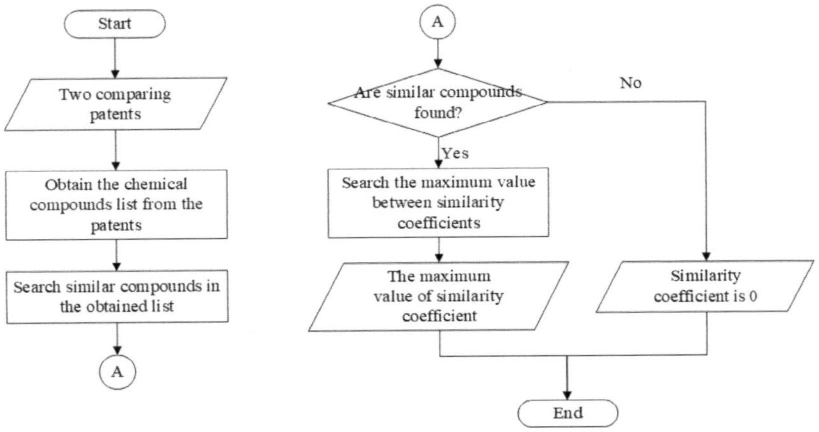

Figure 4. The patents comparison algorithm

Chemical compounds from compared USPTO patents are contained in MDL Molfile files.

The patent #1 has the following chemical formulas:

1. C1(=CC(C2C(C1)C(OC2=O)=O)[Si](C)(C)OC)C;
2. C1(=CC(C2C(C1)C(OC2=O)=O)C)C;
3. C1=CC(OC1=O)=O.

The patent #2 has the following chemical formulas:

1. C1=CC(=C(C(=C1*)*)*)O;
2. C1=C(C(=C(C=C1C(=O)O*)O*)O)*;
3. C1(=C(C(=C2C(=C1*)CCC(O2)(CCC=C(C)CCC=C(C)CCC=C(C)C)C)*)*)O;
4. C1=C(C(=C(C=C1C(=O)O*)O*)O)*;
5. C1(=C(C(=C2C(=C1*)CCC(O2)(CCCC(C)CCCC(C)CCCC(C)C)C)*)*O;
6. C1=C(C(=C(C=C1C(=O)O*)O*)O)*;
7. C1=C(C=CC=C1)C(C=2C(=C(C=C(C2)C(C=3C=CC=CC3)C)C(C=4C=CC=CC4)C)O[H])C;
8. C1(=CC=C(C=C1)OC=2C=CC(=CC2)O)C(F)(F)F.

A molecular fingerprint is calculated for each chemical compound file related to a patent. Then a pairwise comparison for the molecular fingerprints from patents #1 and #2 between each other runs (Table 3).

Table 3. Comparison of chemical compounds contained in the patents

Chemical formula of patent #1	Chemical formula of patent #2	Tanimoto coefficient
C1(=CC(C2C(C1)C(OC2=O)=O)[Si](C)(C)OC)C	C1=CC(=C(C(=C1*)*)*)O	0.564756
C1(=CC(C2C(C1)C(OC2=O)=O)[Si](C)(C)OC)C	C1=C(C(=C(C=C1C(=O)O*)O*)O)*	0.487217
C1(=CC(C2C(C1)C(OC2=O)=O)[Si](C)(C)OC)C	C1(=C(C(=C2C(=C1*)CCC(O2)(CCC= C(C)CCC=C(C)CCC=C(C)C)C)*)*)O	0.455891
C1(=CC(C2C(C1)C(OC2=O)=O)[Si](C)(C)OC)C	C1=C(C(=C(C=C1C(=O)O*)O*)O)*	0.458193
C1(=CC(C2C(C1)C(OC2=O)=O)[Si](C)(C)OC)C	C1(=C(C(=C2C(=C1*)CCC(O2)(CCCC (C)CCCC(C)CCCC(C)C)C)*)*)O	0.634921
C1(=CC(C2C(C1)C(OC2=O)=O)[Si](C)(C)OC)C	C1=C(C(=C(C=C1C(=O)O*)O*)O)*	0.612731
C1(=CC(C2C(C1)C(OC2=O)=O)[Si](C)(C)OC)C	C1=C(C=CC=C1)C(C=2C(=C(C= C(C2)C(C=3C=CC=CC3)C)C(C=4C=CC=CC4)C)O[H])C	0.598742
C1(=CC(C2C(C1)C(OC2=O)=O)[Si](C)(C)OC)C	C1(=CC=C(C=C1)OC=2C=CC(=CC2)O)C(F)(F)F	0.473124

For the first chemical formula of patent #1, the fifth chemical formula of patent #2 (the Tanimoto coefficient is 0.634921) is the most similar.

The ratio of the sum of the Tanimoto coefficient maximum values for compared chemical compounds from a smaller set with chemical compounds from another patent to the size of the least set is taken as the patents similarity coefficient resulting value.

$$K_T = \frac{\sum_i \max_j T_S}{\min(|C_1|,|C_2|)}, \quad (2)$$

where C1, C2 stand for chemical compounds plurality for patent #1 and #2 respectively; min(|C1|,|C2|) stands for the minimal size of chemical pluralities for two patents; i stands for enumerating index of the minimum chemical compounds plurality; $\max T_S$ stands for the Tanimoto coefficient maximum value for the ith chemical compound.

3. THE SOFTWARE MODULE DESIGN

The software module (architecture in Figure 5) is implemented in Java with Spring Framework 5.0.1 ("Spring Framework Overview", n.d.) technology. H2 ("Spring Boot and H2 in memory database - Why, What and How?", n.d.) is used as a DBMS for the module due to high-quality integration with the Spring Framework. The Chemistry Development Kit (CDK) ("Chemistry Development Kit", n.d.) library is selected as a collection of processing chemical information tools.

The developed module shows:

- information on patents and chemical compounds contained in patents (Figure 6);

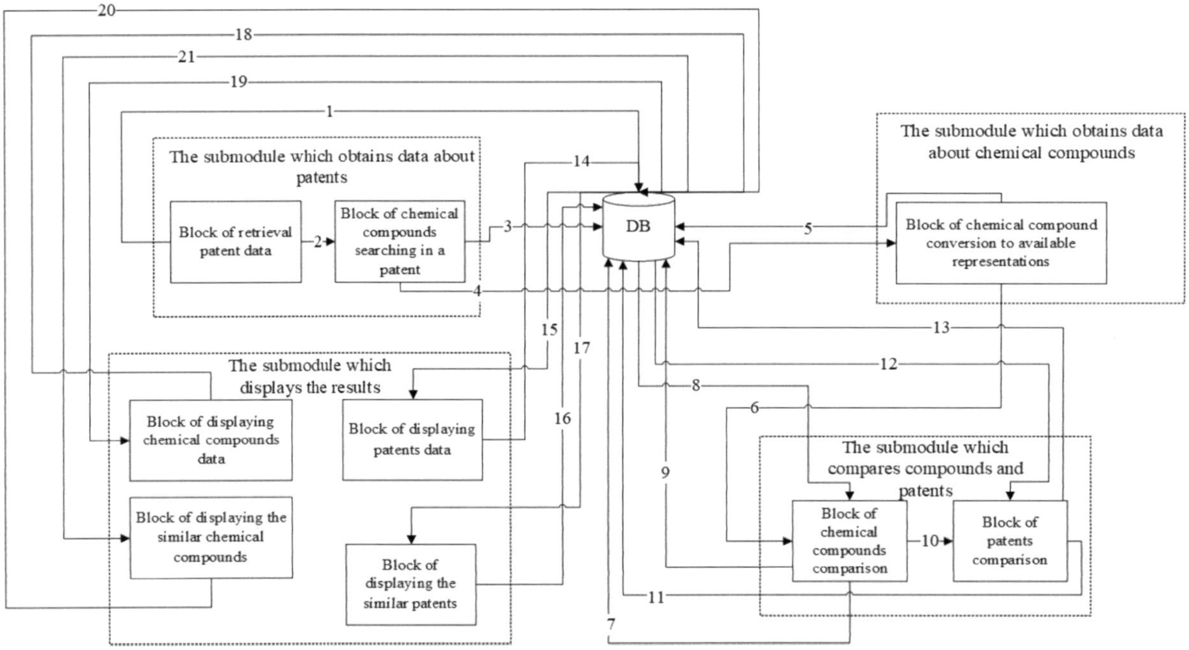

1 – save a record with information about a patent in the database;
2 – call the block of chemical compounds searching in a patent;
3 – save a record with information about chemical compounds present in a patent;
4 – call the block of chemical compound conversion to available representations;
5 – save a chemical compound record in the database;
6 – call the block of chemical compounds comparison;
7 – query to the database to retrieve chemical compounds records;
8 – retrieve chemical compounds records from the database;
9 – save chemical compounds comparison results in the database;
10 – call the block of patents comparison;
11 – query to the database to retrieve patents records;
12 – retrieve patents records from the database;
13 – save patents comparison results in the database;
14 – query to the database to retrieve patents records;
15 – retrieve patents records from the database;
16 – query to the database to retrieve patents similarities records;
17 – retrieve patents similarities records from the database;
18 – query to the database to retrieve chemical compounds records;
19 – retrieve chemical compounds records from the database;
20 – query to the database to retrieve chemical compounds similarities records;
21 – retrieve chemical compounds similarities records from the database.

Figure 5. Architecture of the module

- chemical compound characteristics and the list of patents that contain the compound;
- list of chemical compounds similar to the selected compound;
- list of patents similar to the selected patent.

To test the efficiency of the developed module, a sample comprising 53 patents from the list of citations of another 15 patents was compiled.

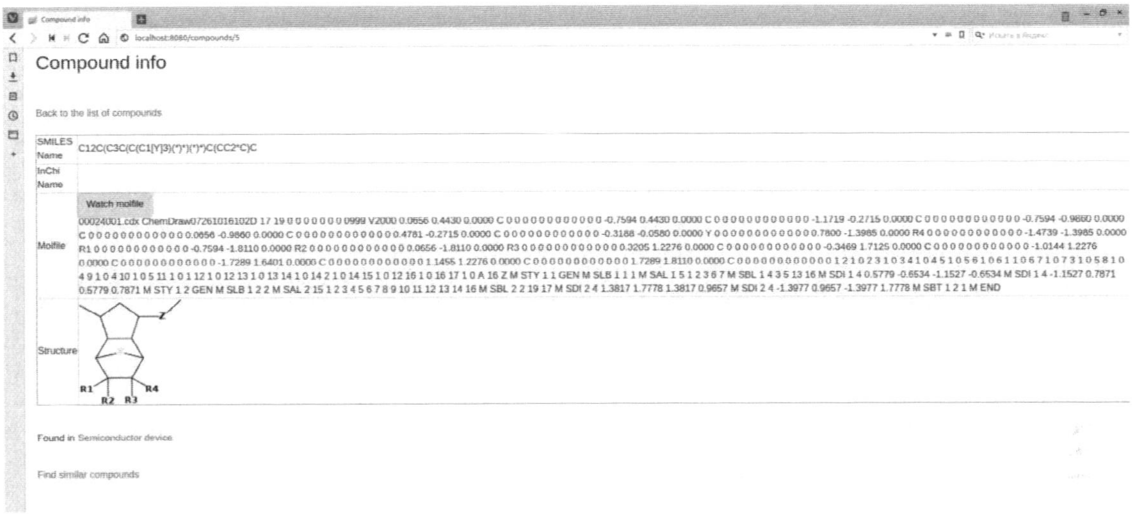

Figure 6. A web page with information about the selected chemical compound

As a result, information on 53 patents and 187 chemical compounds was extracted. 41 pairs of similar patents and 120 pairs of similar chemical compounds were found. Based on the data obtained, the following search performance indicators were calculated (Vayngolts, 2017):

$$R = \frac{a}{a+c} \times 100\%, \quad (3) \qquad P = \frac{a}{a+b} \times 100\%, \quad (4)$$

$$L = \frac{c}{a+c} \times 100\%, \quad (5) \qquad N = \frac{b}{a+b} \times 100\%, \quad (6)$$

where R stands for the patents recall; P stands for the patents precision; L stands for the losses coefficient; N stands for the noise coefficient; a stands for the number of relevant patents which were detected; b stands for the number of irrelevant patents which were detected; c stands for the number of relevant patents which were not detected; a = 41, b = 0, c = 12.

The recall is 77.3%; the precision is 100%; the losses coefficient is 22.6%; the noise coefficient is 0%.

4. CONCLUSION

As a result of the automating chemical formulas comparison module development, the following goals were achieved:

- chemical classes patents database forming methods have been developed;
- converting chemical compounds in various representations, chemical compounds comparison, similar patents search based on the chemical compounds comparison results algorithms have been developed;
- the chemical formulas analysis module has been designed, implemented and tested.
- The next steps to improve the software module:
- development of patents and chemical compounds search by a given key;
- development of a patent search algorithm regarding the list of citations;
- expanding the list of available chemical compounds representations, extracting IUPAC names from patents text;
- chemical classes patents clustering on various features and patents trends prediction.

ACKNOWLEDGEMENT

The reported study was funded by RFBR (research projects 18-07-01086, 19-07-01200) RFBR and Administration of the Volgograd region (research projects 19-47-340007, 19-41-340016).

REFERENCES

About PubChem. [online] Available at: https://pubchemdocs.ncbi.nlm.nih.gov/about [Accessed 18 May 2019].

Chemical Database - ChemSynthesis. [online] Available at: http://www.chemsynthesis.com/ [Accessed 18 May 2019].

Chemistry Development Kit. [online] Available at: https://cdk.github.io/ [Accessed 19 May 2019].

ChemSpider reaches 50 million compounds. [online] Available at: http://www.rsc.org/journals-books-databases/librarians-information/librarians-notes/all-articles/2016/jun/chemspider-reaches-50-million-compounds/ [Accessed 18 May 2019].

Dalke, A., 2008. Molecular fingerprints, background. [online] Dalkescientific.com. Available at: http://www.dalkescientific.com/writings/diary/archive/2008/06/26/fingerprint_background.html [Accessed 15 May 2019].

Daylight Theory: SMILES. [online] Available at: http://www.daylight.com/dayhtml/doc/theory/theory.smiles.html [Accessed 15 May 2019].

Encyclopedia Britannica. (n.d.). Chemical formula. [online] Available at: https://www.britannica.com/science/chemical-formula [Accessed 15 May 2019].

Heller, R. and McNaught, A., 2009. The IUPAC International Chemical Identifier (InChI). Chemistry International -- Newsmagazine for IUPAC, 31(1).

Korobkin, D., Fomenkov, S., 2018. Method of detection of technical functions performed by physical effects IOP Conference Series: Earth and Environmental Science. Vol. 194 – URL: http://iopscience.iop.org/article/10.1088/1755-1315/194/2/022014/pdf.

Korobkin, D., Fomenkov, S., Golovanchikov, A., 2018. Method of identification of patent trends based on descriptions of technical functions Journal of Physics: Conference Series. - 2018. - Vol. 1015. – 7 p.

Korobkin, D., Fomenkov, S., Kolesnikov, S., Golovanchikov, A., 2016. Technical Function Discovery in Patent Databases for Generating Innovative Solutions In Proceedings of the MCCSIS 2016 ed. by Piet Kommers [etc.], pp. 241-245.

Korobkin, D., Fomenkov, S., Kravets, A., Kolesnikov S., 2018. Methods of Statistical and Semantic Patent Analysis In Proceedings of the CIT&DS 2017 (Ser. Communications in Computer and Information Science; Vol. 754), pp. 48-61.

MDL Information Systems, Inc., 2003. MDL Information Systems, Inc. CTFile Formats. MDL Information Systems, San Leandro, USA.

NCI/CADD Chemical Identifier Resolver. [online] Cactus.nci.nih.gov. Available at: https://cactus.nci.nih.gov/chemical/structure_documentation [Accessed 18 May 2019].

Spring Boot and H2 in memory database - Why, What and How?. [online] Spring Boot Tutorial. Available at: http://www.springboottutorial.com/spring-boot-and-h2-in-memory-database [Accessed 19 May 2019].

Spring Framework Overview. [online] Available at: https://www.tutorialspoint.com/spring/spring_overview.htm [Accessed 18 May 2019].

Tanimoto (cdk 2.1-SNAPSHOT API) Available at: http://cdk.github.io/cdk/2.1/docs/api/org/openscience/cdk/similarity/Tanimoto.html [Accessed 18 May 2019].

United States Patent and Trademark Office. [online] Available at: https://bulkdata.uspto.gov/ [Accessed 25 May 2019].

Vayngolts, I., Korobkin, D., Fomenkov, S., Golovanchikov, A., 2017. Synthesis of the Physical Operation Principles of Technical System. In Proceedings of the CIT&DS 2017 (Ser. Communications in Computer and Information Science; Vol. 754), pp. 575-588.

EXTRACTION OF STRUCTURAL ELEMENTS OF INVENTIONS FROM RUSSIAN-LANGUAGE PATENTS

Dmitriy M. Korobkin, Sergey S. Vasiliev, Sergey A. Fomenkov and Vladimir I. Lobeyko
Volgograd State Technical University, Russia, Volgograd, Lenin av., 28

ABSTRACT

The paper investigates the issue of extracting structured data from Russian-language patents in the field of new technical solution synthesis. The predicate-argument constructions that characterize the composition of the structural elements of the inventions and the relations between them are the extracted entities. The paper also analyses existing natural language processing tools as applied to patent processing. The authors have offered a new method for extracting predicate-argument constructs taking into account the specificity of the text of patents based on shallow parsing and segmentation of sentences. The value of the F1 metric with a rigorous and lax evaluation of data extraction is 63% and 79%, respectively, which suggests that the proposed approach is promising. The extracted structures are used to construct the graph of the structural elements of the invention.

KEYWORDS

Patents, Information Extraction, SAO, Claims, CAI-Systems, Shallow Parsing

1. INTRODUCTION

In recent years, automation development of inventions has been gaining momentum, and automated support systems are used to search for new technical solutions (Korobkin, 2018a) - CAI systems (Computer-Aided Invention - the search for innovative solutions using a computer). The success of such systems largely depends on the completeness of the ontologies of the subject areas and the fullness of the various knowledge bases that allow generating new technical solutions. However, data enrichment is often a very laborious process. Therefore, an active search continues for effective means of extracting structured data for this purpose. The sources of technical information may be a patent array. However, current approaches to extracting structured data and natural language processing (NLP) tools are poorly oriented to work on an array of patents. In this regard, it is necessary to develop new efficient methods for extracting data from patents.

The task of information support for new technical solution synthesis (Korobkin, 2018b) can be seen as the task of extracting the SAO (Subject - Action - Object) semantic structures. In particular, elements of the design of a technical object (TO) and the relationship between them are considered as the source of information support. Claims are considered to be a direct source of data for retrieval. They express the essence of the invention and are based on a description; therefore it is of the greatest interest for the extraction of technical information. In this case, the object of analysis is an array of Russian-language patents.

2. RESEARCH BACKGROUND

Various systems (Choi, 2011, Guo, 2016, Wang, 2015, Yang, 2017) are known for processing English-language patents, including the use of the SAO formalism to extract various concepts. In (Yang, 2017), a tree syntax analysis was applied with a separate identification of the subject, the action and the object to improve the quality of parsing. The authors state the following averaged values of precision and recall: 0.8058 and 0.8446, respectively. At the same time, the project was implemented in the GATE system, which is poorly suitable for the Russian language. In (Wang, 2015), the SAO structures are extracted based on the rules using the Stanford parser software, but there are no ready-made models for the Russian language. Papers (Guo, 2016, Souili, 2015) process patents using linguistic markers (specific verbs and nouns) and lexical-syntactic patterns, while (Souili, 2015) notes the need to study the structure of patent documents to improve the quality of data extraction. The emphasis is mainly on rule-based systems, since for statistical analysis systems a lot of marked-up data is obviously needed. This causes additional development difficulties.

The specific style of writing a patent claims complicates the work of existing parsers. Highlight the problems: (a) the length of the sentences of the claims is excessively long; (b) the claims are described predominantly with noun-phrases, often with a chain of definitions and participial constructions; (c) the availability of specific words and constructions can affect the correct operation of NLP tools.

Considering the system for extracting structured data from Russian-language texts, the development of Yandex Tomita-parser is most often distinguished. Extraction takes place according to the rules, written in an extended context-free grammar. Despite the expressive power of context-free grammars and the Tomita-parser tool, the question of organizing the effective extraction of SAO structures from the claims remains open.

Of the available systems of syntactic and semantic-syntactic analysis, for which there is an opportunity to work with the Russian language, we can distinguish Link Grammar Parser, MaltParser and UDPipe (UFAL, 2019).

Among the available Russian language analyzers can be identified: TreeTagger, MyStem, TnT, pymorphy2, FreeLing. A number of works (Asiryan, 2017, Blazhievskaya, 2016, Dereza, 2016) are devoted to the comparison of morphological analyzers of the Russian language. In the works (Blazhievskaya, 2016, Dereza, 2016) on the quality of determining the parts of speech (POS), TreeTagger is best distinguished, but they do not take into account the work of the Yandex MyStem tool. In (Asiryan, 2917), already taking into account MyStem, the latter was chosen as the best tool with the F1 metric value of 94%. At the same time, an experiment is being conducted to improve the quality of parsing by combining tools (correcting MyStem with pymorphy2 with an increase in F1 to 95%). However, the full use of the analyzer MyStem is difficult due to the issuance of grammatical signs in the form of an unordered list of alternatives. At the same time, there are no attributes for the correct choice of a single grammatical form, the alternatives simply follow in alphabetical order. The TreeTagger morphoanalyzer is devoid of such a feature - the grammar is issued without alternatives. The disadvantage of TreeTagger is that its speed is somewhat lower than the speed of processing MyStem on large texts.

Having considered certain aspects of the processing of Russian-language texts, we summarize the problems that arise when extracting structured data (SAO structures) from texts of Russian-language patents when solving the problem of information support for automated invention: (a) the claims are written in a specific sublanguage of patents that impede text analysis (specific terminology); (b) the structure of the claims is poorly suited for parsing by ready-made syntactic analyzers (given the prevalence of sentences and the presence of multiple participle clauses); (c) the structure of the claims is not fully decomposed by simple heuristics; (d) the available NLP tools will certainly be mistaken in the analysis, so relying on one tool in the processing of complex structures is not always rational.

The presented limitations make it difficult to create an efficient data extraction system from patent claims using publicly available NLP tools (without considering complex commercial or closed systems).

However, given that the texts of patents are written in a template (not only in the structure of sections, but also in the structure of phrases), and it is possible to combine NLP tools for mutual correction of analysis errors; the authors suggest the following approach to processing the text of the claims, including the steps:

- segmentation of the patent claims based on shallow parsing;
- organization of the extraction of SAO structures based on the valence bond theory;
- post-processing of SAO structures with linking concepts to a common repository.

3. APPROACH DESCRIPTION

As the source of data for the extraction of technical descriptions, the main clause of the multi-tier claim of the invention on the device in the patent text is selected. The unit of extraction is the predicate-argument construction in the form of the SAO structure, which semantically describes the structural elements of the device and the connections between them.

As instruments of NLP in the experimental mode are used: (a) UDPipe (tokenization, tagging, lemmatization and syntactic analysis); (b) MyStem (lemmatization, correction of morphology); (c) pymorphy2 (Korobov, 2015) (declination of word forms); (d) Chanker of noun phrases of Russian (to define the boundaries of actants).

The ultimate goal of extracting data is to build a related graph of structural elements of the invention, reflecting the structure of the invention itself. Let us consider in more detail each of the stages.

3.1 Segmentation of Patent Claims

On the basis of a well-established patents language, the authors made the assumption that it is possible to identify certain patterns of segments in a patent claims, and that shallow parsing with a number of heuristics will be enough to successfully extract the necessary structures.

The segment of the independent claim will be called the element of the sentence, which is indicated by punctuation (comma, and/or semicolon). In the Russian language, such segments can act as simple-main sentences, be subordinate clauses, participal and verbal adverb phrases, isolated definitions, etc. In addition, one should take into account the logical division of the claim into the restrictive and distinctive parts (if such separation exists), usually demarcated by the construction of "characterized in that".

The purpose of segmentation is to identify the linear structure of the proposal of the claims for the subsequent extraction of SAO-objects based on the analysis of the morphological and linear-combinatorial characteristics of the text. Let us explain it with the example of the text of the patent "Pressure sensor", the syntactic analysis of which is presented in Figure 1.

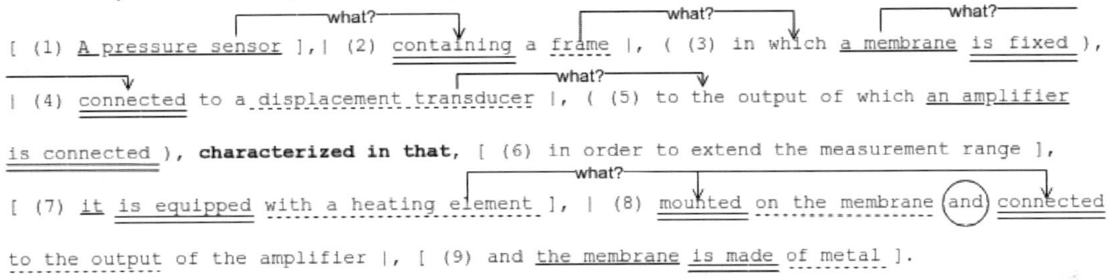

Figure 1. Parsing sentence

In parentheses are marked linear numbers of segments without taking into account the demarcation design "characterized in that". At the same time, the verb forms without specifying the role in the sentence are highlighted with a double line.

The sentence includes: generic term (1); participle clause (2, 4, 8); subordinate-attributive (3, 5); simple two-part (7, 9). The tasks of segmentation include the identification of segments by composition and the definition of the relationship between the main and dependent words. In the future, this information is necessary for the direct extraction of SAO-objects.

To identify the nature of writing segments and formalize the definition of their types, a set of fourteen main claims was taken, mainly from different sections of the international patent classification (IPC). The total number of segments in the sample was 187 elements.

After a detailed manual analysis, the following conditional segment types were derived (see Table 1).

At the same time, the symbol for the segment was formed from acronyms, taking into account the basic structure of the segment, i.e., the POS and / or elements that characterize it: Noun (N); Verb (V); Adjective (A); "which" is a demonstrative pronoun in subordinate clauses; Adverb (AV); and others. The legend of the segments in the future act as markers in the system.

Apparently from results of the analysis, all the segments met a finite number of fairly typical sentence constructions. Of course, it is not possible to thoroughly analyze the entire array of patents manually. Therefore, the authors made the assumption that the number of types of segments (in terms of the overall structure of writing) of a larger mass of the claims is also limited.

Table 1. Types of segments of the test sample claims

Type of segment	Symbol	Example of a segment
Noun phrase	N	'contact electric current modulator'
Participle clause	V_N	'containing vibration transducer'
Independent segment	N_V_N	'it is equipped with an additional vibration converter'
Isolated attribute	A0	'identical to the main'
Rather independent segment	(N_) which_V_N	'which input is the input of the device'
Dash instead of a predicate	N_-_N	'and the cathode through resistance - with the anode'
Comparative turns	AV	'less'
Subordinate clauses	SC	'that they have sufficient fatigue strength'
Verbal adverb phrase	V<C>	'preventing the deformation of the first destructive elements'
Service segments	SEPARATOR	besides; and; and also; at the same time;
	NAMED	'called decaying elements'
	PURPOSE	'for the purpose of range extension of measurements'

Since the segmentation is carried out in the context of the task of extracting predicate-argument structures, the elements of this extraction are partially embedded in the process in the form of highlighting non-significant (service) segments and the target semantic classes of verbs.

Semantic classes of verbs are needed to find to SAO target ligaments, potentially describing constructive elements and the connections between them. A samples of such verbs is presented in Table 2.

Table 2. Semantic classes of verbs

Semantic class	Verbs
Existence of a structural element	contain (on); equip; include (between; in; with; in;); have; supply; enter (into); consist (from);
Inter-element couplings	set (on; as); connect (to); fasten (in; on); place (in; on);

The overall sequence of operations for the segmentation of the claims:

1) Text pre-processing.

2) The process of obtaining initial segments is associated with sequential fragmentation of the text by punctuation marks with auxiliary treatments. A specific feature of the stage is the final fragmentation based on the results of the syntactic analysis obtained after using the UDPipe tool. Tokenization is also performed by this tool. This decision is justified by the need to take into account the context for better analysis: submitting partially fragmented text to the analyzer input (based on strong signs of separation - for example, different parts of the claims or a semicolon), but without carrying out fragmentation on commas, it is possible to receive more adequate syntactic marking; analysis of segments completely isolated from each other potentially also leads to errors.

3) The next step is the process of correcting morphology. If a segment token refers to parts of a verb, adjective, or adverb speech, then a part of speech is checked using MyStem. Moreover, if the result does not coincide with the initial one, then the morphological information of the token is updated taking into account the conversion of tags from MyStem into UDPipe format (CoNLL-U).

4) One of the fundamental stages of segmentation is the determination of the type of segment (see Table 1). The type of segment allows you to introduce certainty in the use of certain heuristics processing in the future. This problem is solved in two steps: the determining of a segment pattern and the determining the type of segment by pattern using a finite state machine (FSM).

The definition of a segment pattern is based on finding out its main composition; what is based on the priority of the presence of POS. Example of the dictionary of symbols in the template is presented in Table 3.

Table 3. Template dictionary

Symbol	Part of speech	Note
N	noun	Index 0 means accusative or a nominative case
V	verb	Possible litters: <P> - participle; <F> - finite verb; <C> - adverbial participle; <I> - infinitive; <U> - undefined.
A	adjective	Index 0 means the top of the sentence (indirect attribute)
PR	pronoun	Index 0 means the nominative case Direct replacement of the word «which» is possible.
X	formula	For the case of explanation of the formulas

5) Binding of segments. The main binding mechanism in the Russian language is coordination according to gender, number, and case. Therefore, the segmentation is carried out on the data of the extracted morphology, and the task is reduced to finding this agreement between the words in the sentence. At the same time, segment types limit the set of binding rules.

Proceeding from a linear logic of the description of the formula, it is possible to connection of segments in one straight pass (from left to right). An exception is the case of a rupture of the sentence by an enclosed turnover. As a rule, the second part of a broken sentence begins with finite verb. When finding such a segment, it is necessary to find the closest missing segment of the noun group to the left. The assembly of such segments precedes the main straight passage.

The result of segment linking for an example (Figure 1) is shown in Figure 2.

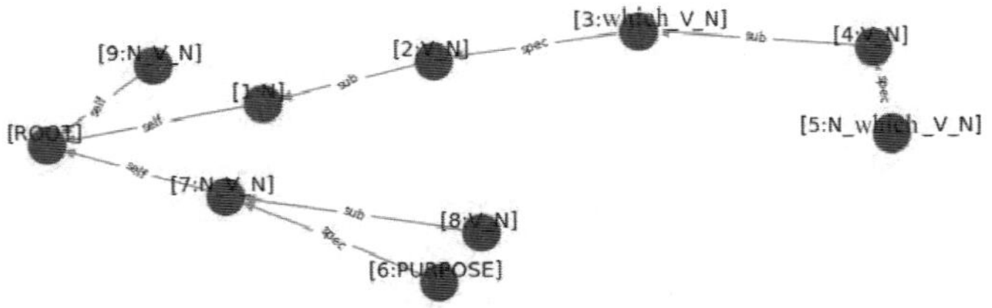

Figure 2. The graph of segments for an example

3.2 Extracting SAO Primary Structures

The extraction of predicate-argument constructions is based on the results of segmentation and valency of the target verbs (see Table 2). The valence of the verb determines the number of possible arguments. It is enough to define the "subject" and "object" of the structure being extracted.

The subject can be determined by the following cases (see Example 1): by the nominative case (1), by the word of the participle being defined (2) or it can be completely absent (3), implying a generic term.

Example 1. The definition of the subject in the segments.

(1) The magnetic gearbox is equipped with a rotor ...

(2) ... magnetic gearbox, equipped with a rotor ...

(3) ... characterized in that ..., a rotor is introduced, ...

The definition of the object is somewhat complicated due to the lack of explicit universal expression in the predicate arguments. The role of an object in a predicate corresponds to a specific case, which can be formed using prepositions.

Consider the cases of determining the object from Example 2: accusative case without preposition (1), dative case formed with the preposition "to" (2), several actants with prepositions (3); in the latter case, the preposition "through" generates an adverb (connected as? - "through a non-magnetic ring"), the target actant is a combination with the preposition "with" (connected with what? - "with the body").

Example 2. The definition of the object in the structure,

(1) including shaper

(2) connected respectively *to* the output of the amplifier

(3) connected *with* the body *through* a non-magnetic ring

It should also be taken into account that the predicate can be expressed by a verb with a compound preposition (for example, "made in the form of"). In addition, information on binding to the predicate can already be partially determined at the end of the segmentation.

When detected in the segment of the target verbs (see Table 2), the sequence of currents to the right and left of the verb extends to the left and right parts, respectively. For full-length segments (types "N_V_N", "N_which_V_N", "which_V_N" and "N _-_ N" from Table 1), the right and left parts are formed in the same segments, and for subordinates (type "V_N") the left part is replaced and forms the found subject connecting.

Next comes the key stage of extraction: the search for the structures of the object and subject in the selected parts of the segment according to the predicate valencies. The order of searching for a subject and an object is determined by the possible position of actants indicated in valency (the “entry” field).

The search for valencies in the definition of a subject and an object in parts of a segment is carried out using the token-marking mechanism. The following label sets are used:

- for the subject (P-SBJ, N-SBJ, I-SBJ and A-SBJ);
- for an object (P-OBJ, N-OBJ and I-OBJ)
- for auxiliary valencies (P-ON, P-VIA, N-ON, N-VIA, N-BY, N-WHOM).

The label prefix corresponds to the functional purpose of the token: P- (Preposition); N- (Noun), A- (Adjective) - the top of the noun group; I- (Inside) - the entry of a token into a noun group.

Marks in parts of the segment are placed for the object according to the predicate valences, and for the subject - for the nominal case of a noun (or less often an adjective).

If there is a mandatory preposition in valency, the occurrences of the specified preposition are first sought, in case of failure, the search is interrupted. The search for additional valences for an object is more priority than the search for the valence of the object itself, i.e. starts first.

3.3 Creation a Tree of Relations of Elements of Structures

Creation a tree of relationships requires determining the final vertices of the graph, taking into account the presence of identical concepts, as well as identifying implicit relations of generic terms between elements.

For further binding of the primary SAO objects, preprocessing is necessary:

- the separation of homogeneous members in the description of structural elements along the border of the composing union "and" provided it is located between the labels of the vertices of the noun group (ie, "N-SBJ" or "N-OBJ").
- generation of the normal form of the actants (in the nominative case) and the genitive case (further as the Gent-form).
- after preprocessing, the primary SAO object is considered prepared.

Actants are declined using the pymorphy2 tool. This is followed by linking the prepared SAO objects into a single graph. The mechanism consists in the sequential transformation of actants of subjects and objects into a set of anchor points from a common glossary of terms, followed by memorization of the relation (predicate) for the identified points of the subject and object.

The general graph of relations is stored in the form of a dictionary of terms, a dictionary of relations and a map of relations containing the parental relations between the actants through predicates (from the dictionary of relations).

Anchor points are formed when analyzing the subject and object of the prepared SAO objects. When terms are added (the normal form of an actant's sentence), the parent relationship with another term is searched. The operation is carried out under the condition that the normal form of the actant has a sequence of tokens in the genitive case (marked with an "I-GEN" label in the analysis). An example of a parent relationship search is shown schematically in Figure 3.

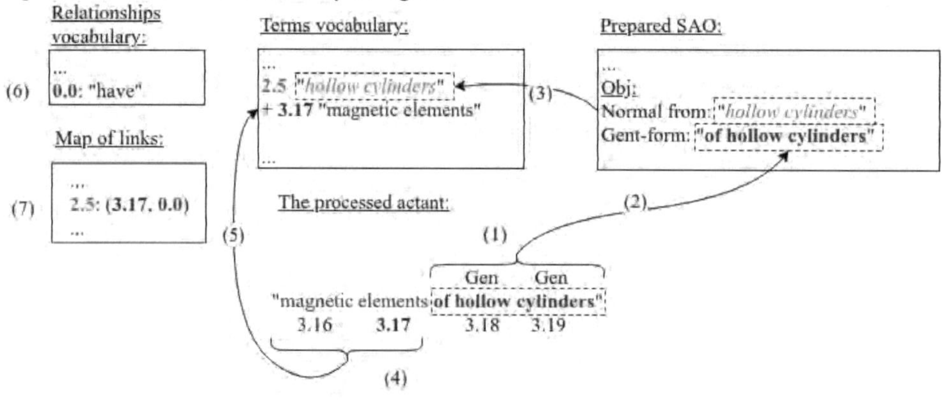

Figure 3. The search logic of the parent relationship

If the final sequence of tokens in the processed actant is in the genitive case (1), then the word forms in the array of prepared SAO objects (2) are checked for coincidence. The parent actant index in the terms vocabulary (3) is restored by the bundle identifier or normal form. The processed actant is cleared from the gent-ending and a new actant is added to the terms vocabulary (5). The "have" parent relationship is already included by default in the relationships vocabulary (6). Next, the map of links is updated to reflect the new ratio of anchor points (7).

In this case, the indices in the vocabularies are the coordinates of the vertex of the noun group (including the segment number and the token number in the segment).

After receiving the anchor points, consisting of the coordinates and the normal form of the structural elements, the map of connections is filled: the actants of the subject act as parent concepts for the actants of the object connected through the predicate. The results of processing the prepared SAO objects are buffered, and after checking the semantic classes of actants, the graphs of the entire device are updated.

4. SOFTWARE EVALUATION METHODOLOGY

The quality of data extraction was assessed for primary SAO objects (i.e., excluding post-processing with the separation of homogeneous members and taking into account the semantic classes of actants). For this purpose, a manual marking of an independent test set was carried out, including the main points of the claims 30 patents. The markup was made taking into account the semantic classes of verbs introduced into the system, which characterize the target relations between the components of the technical object. In this case, it was allowed to add into the system descriptions (valencies) of previously not encountered target verbs.

The following metrics were used as evaluation metrics: precision, recall and F1-measure. A test data set of 30 documents on the basis of manual marking included 318 SAO objects. The results of counting the number of extracted test data set objects are presented in Table 4 (first row). The design data set of 14 documents contained 136 recoverable structures. The results of counting the number of extracted SAO objects of the design data set are presented in Table 4 (second row).

Table 4. Extracted test data set objects

Parameter	Rf (all SAO structures extracted by the system)	Rrel_1 (relevant SAO structures with a rigorous entry of the entire noun group in the argument	Rrel_2 (relevant SAO structures taking into account that the vertex of the noun group are in the argument)	Srel (manually selected SAO structures)
Amount	305	198	248	318
Amount	142	118	129	136

The result of the counting of the extraction quality metrics (according to formulas 1–3) for the test and design data set is presented in Table 6.

Table 6. Metric counting results

Metrics	Test data set		Design data set	
	Lax evaluation	Rigorous evaluation	Lax evaluation	Rigorous evaluation
Precision	0,81	0,65	0,91	0,83
Recall	0,78	0,62	0,95	0,87
F1-measure	0,79	0,63	0,93	0,85

5. CONCLUSION

Extracting structured data from patents depends on the specifics of the writing of documents. The peculiarities of writing claims of the invention include excessive length of sentences, complication of the participle clauses, characteristic terminology. Practical experience has shown that NLP tools do not always produce a stable result on the domain of patents. Thus, they are ineffective in building high-quality data extraction systems with direct application. Therefore, special approach to the pre-processing of patent texts seems necessary. It is worth noting that in practice they often use a combination of tools to improve the quality of processing.

Due to the sublanguage of patents and the availability of common templates for the formation of documents, the author made an assumption about the sufficiency of morphological and shallow parsing analysis with a number of heuristics to effectively extract structural elements from the description of the claims.

The developed method of extracting SAO structures involves two main stages: segmentation of the sentences of the claims and the extraction of technical implementations in the form of predicate-argument structures. Segmentation is based on the derivation of typical structures in the sentence and coordination of dependent words on cases. The extraction of structural elements of technical objects is based on a verbs set corresponding to certain semantic classes. After that, the extracted structural elements are linked into a graph, taking into account homogeneous members and parental relations.

ACKNOWLEDGEMENT

The reported study was funded by RFBR (research project 18-07-01086), RFBR and Administration of the Volgograd region (research projects 19-47-340007, 19-41-340016).

REFERENCES

Asiryan, A.K., 2017. Morphological tagging tools comparison. Paper presented at the INTELLECTUAL POTENTIAL OF THE XXI CENTURY '2017, November, <https://www.sworld.com.ua/konferu7-317/27.pdf>.

Blazhievskaya, A. et al, 2016. Morphological Analysis for Russian: Integration and Comparison of Taggers. Analysis of Images, Social Networks and Texts. Springer, Vol. 661, pp. 162-171.

Choi, S. et al, 2011. SAO network analysis of patents for technology trends identification: A case study of polymer electrolyte membrane technology in proton exchange membrane fuel cells. Scientometrics, pp. 863-883. doi: 10.1007/s11192-011-0420-z

Dereza, O.V. et al, 2016. Automatic Morphological Analysis for Russian: a Comparative Study. Computational Linguistics and Intellectual Technologies: Proceedings of the International Conference «Dialogue».

Guo, J. et al, 2016. Subject–action–object-based morphology analysis for determining the direction of technological change. Technological Forecasting and Social Change, No. 105, pp. 27-40.

Korobkin D., Fomenkov, S., Golovanchikov, A., 2018. Method of identification of patent trends based on descriptions of technical functions Journal of Physics: Conference Series. - 2018. - Vol. 1015. – 7 p.

Korobkin, D., Fomenkov, S., Kolesnikov, S., 2018. The method for detecting the dependencies between technical functions and physical effects Proceedings of theMCCSIS 2018. – [Madrid], 2018. – pp. 225-228.

Korobov, M., 2015. Morphological Analyzer and Generator for Russian and Ukrainian Languages. Analysis of Images, Social Networks and Texts, pp. 320-332, arXiv:1503.07283v1

Souili, A. et al, 2015. Starting from Patents to Find Inputs to the Problem Graph Model of IDM-TRIZ. Procedia Engineering, Vol. 131, pp. 150-161. doi: 10.1016/j.proeng.2015.12.365

UFAL UDPipe, 2019, <http://ufal.mff.cuni.cz/udpipe>.

Wang, X. et al, 2015. Identification of technology development trends based on subject–action–object analysis: The case of dye-sensitized solar cells. Technological Forecasting and Social Change. No. 98, pp. 24-46.

Yang, C. et al, 2017. SAO Semantic Information Identification for Text Mining. International Journal of Computational Intelligence Systems, Vol. 10., pp. 593–604. doi: 10.2991/ijcis.2017.10.1.40

AN EXAMINATION OF STUDENT LEARNING OF SCIENCE CONCEPTS USING INTERACTIVE INSTRUCTIONAL MULTIMEDIA TECHNOLOGY

Maria Georgiou
School of Education, Northcentral University, 85255 Arizona, 92106 San Diego, California, United States of America
Cyprus Ministry of Education and Culture, 1434 Nicosia, Cyprus

ABSTRACT

This study examined if there were any significant differences in students' achievement scores in science for three units that were taught using traditional methods of instruction and a unit that was taught using a multimedia-based instruction. A one-way repeated measures ANOVA was carried out to assess if the differences between the test means were significantly different. Findings showed that students' scores for the four units were significantly different, $F(3, 219) = 22.702$, $p < 0.0005$. Students scored higher on the posttest after the use of interactive multimedia technology in instruction. The results of the current study indicate the need to change educational anticipations, as teaching methods become more active, student-centered and constructivist. Multimedia has attributes that can help students improve their learning and motivation while being engaged in active and constructivist learning environments. The use of instructional interactive multimedia provides more than one learning modality that can be more effective in meeting students' learning needs.

KEYWORDS

Constructivist Learning Environment, Multimedia

1. INTRODUCTION

Science teaching has changed in the last years to include a more constructivist approach to teaching that is more student-centered and allows students to explore ideas and experience real life situations that promote problem-solving and higher order thinking skills (Birgan, 2010; Dalal, 2014; Hunter & Krantz, 2010). This student-centered approach promotes also creativity, critical thinking and communication skills that are lacking in today's science students (So & Kong, 2007; Ulusoy, 2011). Researchers have found that teaching science with a constructivist approach provides active, student-centered learning environments that can improve student interaction and allow knowledge construction (Adegoke, 2011, Butts, 2008).

Research has shown that students receiving computer-based instruction learn 40% faster than students receiving traditional-based instruction (Dalal, 2014; Stokes, 2011). Traditional-based instruction refers to an instructional communication where the instructor has the overall control in the classroom and sends the educational material to the students who mostly learn at the same pace (Delgado, 2007). Traditional methods of instruction mainly focus on memorization of educational information by the students who passively receive information (Malik, 2010). This method of instruction includes lectures only and lacks of the use of technology tools (Yamauchi, 2008).

Multimedia tools that combine text, audio, video, animation and images have been found to be progressive instructional tools when used in the learning environment (Adegoke, 2011; Singleton, 2009). For instance, multimedia technology can help difficult concepts in science to be visually presented (Birgan, 2010). The use of multimedia in science can help students increase their emotional involvement because multimedia connects students with inaccessible places (Ulusoy, 2011). The use of multimedia technology in science instruction can improve student learning and allow students to be actively engaged in the learning process (Malik, 2010; Morano, 2014). Multimedia can appeal to more than one sense and increase students' success and motivation (Weiss, Kramarski, & Talis, 2006). Motivation is directly related to metacognition and when students feel excited about learning with multimedia then their metacognitive thinking process may be stimulated (Cottrell, 2014; Dalal, 2014). Multimedia can motivate students because it can stimulate curiosity and make students wonder about the world around them (Mazzotti, 2010; Ulusoy, 2011).

Constructivist learning environments include active learning and help promote critical thinking and problem-solving skills that can be enhanced through the use of multimedia (Butts, 2008; Du, 2013). A multimedia-based instruction that applies the constructivist principles is more authentic and promotes collaboration among the students (Birgan, 2010). The use of multimedia can be a factor that can affect student learning and achievement because multimedia learning supports the idea that learning is not a process of knowledge absorption but rather a process of knowledge construction that promotes critical thinking (Dalal, 2014; Singleton, 2009). A multimedia-based learning environment in which constructivist principles are applied can motivate students to want to learn because the constructivist theory is based on the idea of discovery learning that supports that students are motivated towards the lesson (Johnson, 2009; Rhodes, 2013). With multimedia instruction students learn faster because the educational material is processed through various presentations that can improve student understanding (Dalal, 2014; Rhodes, 2013; Zheng, Yangt, Garcia, & McCadden, 2008). In contrast to traditional methods of instruction, a multimedia-based instruction allows students to create their own learning sequence and this helps them develop and promote important skills that are necessary in order to become independent learners (Adegoke, 2011; Cottrell, 2014; Kingsley & Boone, 2008).

Students' achievement in science is low because of incompetent methods of instruction and passive learning (Adegoke, 2011; Malik, 2010). The purpose of this quantitative study was to examine if there were any significant differences in students' achievement in science for three units that were taught using traditional methods of instruction and a unit that was taught using interactive multimedia technology in instruction. The study focused on the following research question: Is there a significant difference between the four units and students' scores? The hypotheses were as follows: H10. There is no significant difference between the four units and students' scores. H1a. There is a significant difference between the four units and students' scores.

2. METHODOLOGY

The study used a quasi-experimental with a one group pre-posttest research design. A total of 320 third grade students constituted the population group because of low achievement scores (Papanastasiou & Zembylas, 2004). The sample for this study was selected using a convenience sampling method and included a total of 74 students. A Power analysis was conducted that showed that a total of 74 students were sufficient for a sample at the 95% confidence level, with a confidence interval of 5%. Participants attended five 80 minute science lessons in which interactive multimedia technology was used. All of the instructional material was entered into the multimedia program HyperStudio that was used in the multimedia-based instruction. This multimedia software is a creativity tool that can be used for project-based learning and creating stacks of cards that may include text, images, animations, sounds, and video (Garthwait, 2004).

Data were collected from pretest and posttest scores as well as from archival data that included students' tests scores for three past science units that were taught using traditional methods of instruction. Statistical analyses were conducted using SPSS, version 20. Descriptive statistics such as means and standard deviations were used to describe the general tendencies in the data (Trochim & Donnelly, 2008). Also, measures of central tendency, the median and mode, were used to describe the average scores of the participants. One-way repeated measures ANOVA was conducted in order to compare students' scores on tests for the four units and to determine whether the differences, between the score means, were significantly different. Assumptions of the one-way repeated measures ANOVA were also tested.

3. RESULTS AND DISCUSSION

For the results to be valid, the normality assumption for the one-way repeated measures ANOVA should hold. Science achievement (dependent variable) should be approximately normally distributed for the four science units (independent variable). A Shapiro-Wilk's test and a visual review of the histograms, normal Q-Q plots and box plots showed that science achievement was approximately normally distributed for the four science units, with a skewness of -0.116 and a kurtosis of -0.942 for unit 1; a skewness of -0.079 and a kurtosis of -0.738 for unit 2; a skewness of -0.157 and a kurtosis of -0.781 for unit 3; and a skewness of -0.589 and a kurtosis of 0.218 for unit 4 (posttest). All z-values of skewness and kurtosis for the four units were within +/- 1.96. We can assume that the data are approximately normally distributed in terms of skewness and kurtosis.

The null hypothesis for the Shapiro-Wilk's test is that the data are normally distributed. The null hypothesis is rejected if the p-value is below 0.05. As shown in Table 1, all p-values are above 0.05 (0.214, 0.214, 0.301, 0.096), so the alternative hypothesis is rejected. In terms of the Shapiro-Wilk test, we can assume that the data are approximately normally distributed. Additionally, the histograms, normal Q-Q plots and box plots were examined for the four units. All histograms had the approximate shape of a normal curve. The data are approximately normally distributed and approximately symmetrical.

Table 1. Tests of Normality

	Kolmogorov-Smirnov[a]			Shapiro-Wilk		
	Statistic	df	Sig.	Statistic	df	Sig.
u1	.109	74	.083	.952	74	.214
u2	.101	74	.201	.952	74	.214
u3	.115	74	.052	.958	74	.301
u4	.121	74	.041	.967	74	.096

Mauchly's Test of Sphericity was carried out in order to test the sphericity assumption. As shown in Table 2, the assumption of sphericity has been met, x^2 (5) = 10.478, p = .063. If the data are perfectly spherical in the population, there is a 6, 3% chance of finding the deviation from sphericity that is observed in this sample. It is therefore assumed that the sphericity assumption has been met. The data seem spherical.

Table 2. Mauchly's Test of Sphericity

Measure: MEASURE_1							
Within Subjects Effect	Mauchly's W	Approx. Chi-Square	df	Sig.	Epsilon[b]		
					Greenhouse-Geisser	Huynh-Feldt	Lower-bound
unit	.812	10.478	5	.063	.867	.916	.333

The means and standard deviations are shown in Table 3. On average, the highest scores were gained on the posttest for science unit 4 (M=88.46).

Table 3. Descriptive Statistics

	Mean	Std. Deviation	N
u1	86.4930	5.74581	74
u2	87.1375	5.23560	74
u3	88.1754	5.32678	74
u4	88.4657	3.56718	74

As shown in Table 4, there was a significant effect for the science units, Wilks's Lambda = .52, F (3, 71) = 12.659, p< .0005, multivariate partial squared = .438 (large effect size). The results indicate that students' scores increased significantly over time and over the units. The p< .05 and therefore there is a statistically significant effect for the units. There was a change in students' scores throughout the units. The significant p-values show an effect of the independent variable on the dependent variable as revealed by the repeated measures. All the multivariate tests show a significant interaction between the units and students' scores, indicating that the science units had a significant effect on students' scores over time.

Table 4. Multivariate Tests

Effect		Value	F	Hypothesis df	Error df	Sig.
unit	Pillai's Trace	.427	12.659^b	3.000	71.000	.000
	Wilks' Lambda	.526	12.659^b	3.000	71.000	.000
	Hotelling's Trace	.812	12.659^b	3.000	71.000	.000
	Roy's Largest Root	.812	12.659^b	3.000	71.000	.000

The results of the Tests of Within-Subjects Effects are presented in Table 5. There was a significant effect of science unit on students' scores, F (3, 219) = 22.702, p = .000. Specifically, there is a significant difference between the four unit tests in terms of the average score gained. The p-value is .000, which means that if the means are perfectly equal in the population, there is a 0% chance of finding the differences between the means that were observed in this sample. Consequently, the null hypothesis of equal means is rejected. The significance of F is .000 which is less than the criterion value of .05. Hence, there was a significant difference between the students' scores for the four units.

Table 5. Tests of Within-Subjects Effects

Measure: MEASURE_1							
Source		Type III Sum of Squares	df	Mean Square	F	Sig.	Partial Eta Squared
unit	Sphericity Assumed	152.764	3	50.921	22.702	.000	.217
	Greenhouse-Geisser	152.764	2.608	58.575	22.702	.000	.217
	Huynh-Feldt	152.764	2.697	56.642	22.702	.000	.217
	Lower-bound	152.764	1.040	146.888	22.702	.000	.217
Error(unit)	Sphericity Assumed	491.213	219	2.243			
	Greenhouse-Geisser	491.213	129.275	3.799			
	Huynh-Feldt	491.213	143.192	3.430			
	Lower-bound	491.213	52.986	9.271			

The pairwise comparisons are presented in Table 6 that show whether the difference between each pair of units is significant. The only significant differences between group means were between units 1 and 3, units 1 and 4, units 2 and 3, and units 2 and 4. No other differences were significant.

Table 6. Pairwise Comparisons

(I) unit	(J) unit	Mean Difference (I-J)	Std. Error	Sig.[b]	95% Confidence Interval for Difference[b]	
					Lower Bound	Upper Bound
1	2	-.623	.298	.258	-1.412	.190
	3	-1.785*	.315	.000	-2.589	-.938
	4	-2.104*	.402	.000	-3.162	-.945
2	1	.623	.298	.258	-.190	1.412
	3	-1.176*	.287	.002	-1.948	-.419
	4	-1.523*	.358	.001	-2.396	-.426
3	1	1.785*	.315	.000	.938	2.589
	2	1.176*	.287	.002	.419	1.948
	4	-.247	.354	1.000	-1.176	.703
4 (posttest)	1	2.104*	.402	.000	.945	3.162
	2	1.523*	.358	.001	.426	2.396
	3	.247	.354	1.000	-.703	1.176

Based on estimated marginal means

*. The mean difference is significant at the .05 level.

b. Adjustment for multiple comparisons: Bonferroni.

The mean science achievement score was 86.49 on unit 1; 87.13 on unit 2, 88.17 on unit 3, and 88.46 on unit 4. ANOVA shows that students' scores on the four units are significantly different, $F(3, 219) = 22.702$, $p < 0.0005$. The null hypothesis that the means of the scores on the four unit tests are the same is rejected, so at least one unit has a different mean. There is strong evidence to support the assertion that there is a difference in the mean scores of the four units. It seems that the use of interactive multimedia technology in instruction causes an initial improvement in students' achievement in science.

4. CONCLUSIONS

Interactive multimedia technology has the potential to improve student learning, achievement and motivation (Butts, 2008; Cottrell, 2014). The use of multimedia in instruction allows the combination of educational material that can provide more than one learning modality (Morano, 2014). Including more than one learning modality can be more effective in meeting students' various learning needs (Malik, 2010). Results from one-way repeated measures ANOVA revealed that there was a change in students' scores across the four units. There was a statistically significant effect for the science units $F(3, 219) = 22.702$, $p < 0.0005$. Students had a higher score on the posttest for unit 4 that was taught using interactive multimedia technology in instruction while they obtained lower mean scores on the tests for units 1, 2 and 3 that were taught using traditional methods of instruction. It is assumed that the difference in mean scores is the result of the use of interactive multimedia in instruction. The current study attempted to present an instructional method that was based on the use of multimedia technology that can be used as an advancing learning tool in order to help students promote and develop problem-solving and higher order thinking skills, while being engaged in active, experiential and constructivist learning. The results of the study depict the need for a change in student expectations as the methods of instruction develop into more active and constructivist (Butts, 2008). The results of the current study illustrate that the use of multimedia technology in science instruction can provide benefits to the students and help them increase their achievement. In accordance with the theory of multimodal learning, the results of the study showed that students' achievement in science could be improved with the use of interactive multimedia technology in instruction. This finding extends results from previous studies that showed that the use of multimedia technology improved student learning and achievement (Adegoke, 2011; Dalal, 2014; So & Kong, 2007). Multimedia offers students access to images, animations, sound, and video and creates a multi-modal learning environment that allows teachers to address students' needs individually, which is necessary in education (Malik, 2010).

The current study tried to make a contribution to research on the use of interactive multimedia technology in elementary education. Additional research is still needed on this research area. Generalization of the results of this study was limited. It is therefore suggested that future research should include a population with different conditions with regards to sample size, student age, geography and subject matter. Multimedia present educational material in a multi-modal format and move the focus of instruction from instructors to the students (Chapman, 2013; Morano, 2014). The individualized nature of multimedia can challenge more students and increase their motivation in the classroom (Rhodes, 2013). The use of multimedia technology in a constructivist learning environment is more likely to result in continuous improvements in student learning, achievement and motivation (Dalal, 2014; Ramos & De La Paz, 2010).

REFERENCES

Adegoke, B.A. (2011). Effect of multimedia instruction on senior secondary school students' achievement in physics. European journal of Educational Studies, 3(3), 537-550.

Birgan, L.J. (2010). The effects of multimedia technology on students' perceptions and retention rates in mathematics at a community college (Ed.D., Northcentral University)., 109. In ProQuest Dissertations and Theses, (275867748).

Butts, L.J. (2008). Exploring constructivist learning environments: a case study (Ed.D., University of Houston). In ProQuest Dissertations and Theses, (304604619).

Chapman, D.L. (2013). Multimedia instructional tools and student learning in computer application courses. (Ph.D., The University of Southern Mississippi)., 154. ProQuest Dissertations and Theses. (1461743173).

Cottrell,T.L. (2014). An assessment of the effect of multimedia on critical thinking outcomes. (Northern Illinois University). , 202. In ProQuest Dissertations and Theses, (1554012341).

Dalal, M. (2014). Impact of multi-media tutorials in a computer science laboratory course-an empirical study. The Electronic Journal of e-Learning, 12(4), 366-374.

Delgado, A. (2007). The effects of multimedia technology on the learning of math story problems of elementary and middle school deaf students. (M.S., Lamar University - Beaumont). 57. In ProQuest Dissertations and Theses, (1452086).

Du, X. (2013). An empirical study on multimedia-based social constructivist model in english vocabulary acquisition. Journal of Language Teaching and Research, 4(5), 1036-1043.

Garthwait, A. (2004). Use of hypermedia in one middle school: a qualitative field study. Journal of Educational Multimedia and Hypermedia, 13(3), 219-243.

Hunter, J. L., & Krantz, S. (2010). Constructivism in cultural competence education. Journal of Nursing Education, 49(4), 207-14.

Johnson, T. (2009). The effect of closed interactive multimedia learning environments on student memory retention: A linear versus non-linear approach. (Ed.D., University of North Florida). , 120. In ProQuest Dissertations and Theses, (3354374).

Kingsley, K., & Boone, R. (2008). Effects of multimedia software on achievement of middle school students in an american history class. Journal of Research on Technology in Education, 41(2), 203.

Malik, I.Z. (2010). Effects of multimedia-based instructional technology on African American ninth grade students' mastery of Algebra concepts. (Ed.D., University of Phoenix). In ProQuest Dissertations and Theses, (3452767).

Mazzotti, V.L. (2010). Effects of a multimedia goal-setting intervention on students' knowledge of the self-determined learning model of instruction and disruptive behavior. (Ph.D., The University of North Carolina at Charlotte). In ProQuest Dissertations and Theses, (3404854).

Morano, J.A. (2014). An exploration of multimedia reading instruction and its impact on students' online/offline reading comprehension. (Ph.D., Fordham University). , 219. In ProQuest Dissertations and Theses. (1561350869)

Neo, M., & Neo, T.K. (2010). Students' perceptions in developing a multimedia project within a constructivist learning environment: a Malaysian experience. The Turkish Online Journal of Educational Technology, 9(1), 176-184.

Papanastasiou, E.C., & Zembylas, M. (2004). Differential effects of science attitudes and science achievement in Australia, Cyprus, and the USA. International Journal of Science Education, 26(3), 259-280.

Ramos, P.H., & De La Paz, S. (2010). Learning history in middle school by designing multimedia in a project-based learning experience. Journal of Research on Technology in Education, 42(2), 151-173.

Rhodes, A.E. (2013). The effect of teacher designed multimedia on student comprehension and retention rates within introductory college science courses. (Ph.D., Kansas State University)., 178. In ProQuest Dissertations and Theses. (1417767259).

Singleton, C.M. (2009). An examination of student attitudes and understanding of exponential functions using interactive instructional multimedia. (Ph.D., Southern University and Agricultural and Mechanical College)., 88. In ProQuest Dissertations and Theses, (3465446).

So, W.W., & Kong, S. (2007). Approaches of inquiry learning with multimedia resources in primary classrooms. Journal of Computers in Mathematics and Science Teaching, 26(4), 329-354.

Stokes, S.D. (2011). A multi-metric assessment on the impact of I Can LearnRTM (ICL) multimedia on actual and perceived student achievement in developmental mathematics. (Ph.D., Southern University and Agricultural and Mechanical College)., 91. In ProQuest Dissertations and Theses, (3454223).

Trochim, W., & Donnelly, J. (2008). The research methods knowledge base (3rd ed.). Mason, OH: Cengage Learning.

Ulusoy, K. (2011). Effects of multimedia usage in students' attitude towards Turkish Republic Revolution History and Kemalism Lesson. Educational Research and Reviews, 6(4), 358-366.

Weiss, I., Kramarski, B., & Talis, S. (2006). Effects of multimedia environments on kindergarten children's mathematical achievements and style of learning. Educational Media International, 43(1), 3-17.

Yamauchi, L. (2008). Effects of multimedia instructional material on students' learning and their perceptions of the instruction. (M.S., Iowa State University). , 61. In ProQuest Dissertations and Theses, (1453140).

Zheng, R. Z., Yangt, W., Garcia, D., & McCadden, E. P. (2008). Effects of multimedia and schema induced analogical reasoning on science learning. Journal of Computer Assisted Learning, 24(6), 474-482.

A CLUSTERING-BASED JUDGMENT METHOD OF FALSE POSITIVE ALERTS

Shinya Iwasaki[1], Tomo Kakuta[1], Yoshihiro Sekiguchi[1], Yukihiro Konishi[1], Tomoya Ohtori[1] and Norihisa Komoda[2]
[1]*Hitachi Systems, Ltd., 1-2-1, Osaki, Shinagawa-ku, Tokyo 141-8672, Japan*
[2]*Code Solutions Co., Ltd., 1-2-11, Edobori, Nishi-ku, Osaka 550-0002, Japan*

ABSTRACT

This paper proposes a clustering-based judgment method for false positive alerts generated by security devices. In the proposed method, firstly, alerts with the same attack source IP address over a certain period of time in the past are extracted. After the extraction, using the accumulated signature amount from extracted alerts, the alerts with similar patterns are classified into several clusters using a method combining DBSCAN and K-means++. Then, the judgment of false positive alerts is done based on the number of alerts in each cluster. From a trial usage of the proposed method on two 7-day alert sets from two different networks, it was found that the recall rate was 100%, the precision rate was 34%, and the F-measure was 50%. The precision rate was improved by more than ten times compared to K-means++ alone, and about 2.4 times compared to DBSCAN alone.

KEYWORDS

Cyber Security, Incident Response, Clustering, DBSCAN, K-means++, Anomaly Detection

1. INTRODUCTION

In recent years, since the cyber security of companies and public organizations has become increasingly important, it has become necessary to speed up responses to incidents. Here, an incident refers to "a security problem in the operation of the information system." Examples include information leakage, unauthorized access, and falsification of websites. The first action in incident response is to investigate the alerts generated by security devices such as IDS (Intrusion Detection System) and UTM (Unified Threat Management). However, the majority of the massive amount of generated alerts are erroneously detected (Mukherjee, Heberlein and Levitt, 1994). Therefore, since a massive amount of effort is wasted on false positive alerts, these false positive alerts hinder the incident response by cyber security analysts. For this reason, it is necessary to judge and to eliminate these false positive alerts. There are two approaches to judge false positive alerts: use information of alerts only, and use logs of applications layer other than alerts(Munoz, Mana and Javier, 2013). However, since the latter approach requires another sensor and is difficult to implement, the former approach is mainstream. This paper aims to improve the judgment accuracy of false positive alerts by the former approach.

This paper proposes a clustering-based judgment method for false positive alerts. In the proposed method, firstly, alerts with the same attack source IP address over a certain period in the past are extracted. After the extraction, using the accumulated signature amount from extracted alerts, the alerts with similar patterns are classified into several clusters using a method combining DBSCAN (Density-based spatial clustering of applications with noise) (Ester *et al.*, 1996) and K-means++ (Arthur and Vassilvitskii, 2007). Then, the judgment of false positive alerts is done based on the number of alerts in each cluster.

2. A JUDGMENT METHOD OF FALSE POSITIVE ALERTS

Security devices generate security alerts when they detect events that may be attacks. Figure 1 shows an example of an alert generated by a security device. The alert contains a detected time, an attack source IP address, a used communication protocol, and a signature. The signature indicates what type of attack it may have been. This example shows an alert generated by a UTM manufactured by Palo Alto Networks, Inc. This alert indicates that the attacker (source IP address 203.0.113.3) attacked with an attempt at malware infection on June 29, 2017. Alerts occur when the UTM has a pattern of attack traffic defined, called "signature rules." Basic signature rules are defined by UTM vendors. The security administrators can add, delete, and modify the signature rules.

```
0123456,THREAT,wildfire-virus,1,2017/06/29 21:13:11, 203.0.113.3,192.168.12.201,
                                time               attack source IP address

0.0.0.0,0.0.0.0,From_Internet_To_MTA_SMTP,,,smtp,vsys1,Untrust,

DMZ,ethernet1/1,ethernet1/2,MSS,2017/06/29 21:13:11,347809,1,28943,

25,0,0,0x2000,tcp,drop,"a.xls",Virus/Win32.WGeneric,any,medium,
                               signature

client-to-server,2289,0x0,PA,192.168.0.0-

192.168.255.255,0,,0,,,0,,,,,,,0,0,0,0,0,InternetFW,i000PAL01
```

Figure 1. An example of an alert from a security device

The majority of alerts generated by the security devices are not attacks. These alerts are generated because the security device erroneously assesses normal traffic as attack traffic. In this paper, this alert is called an "false positive alert." Normally, the cyber security analysts judge and remove the false positive alerts. However, this operation requires a massive amount of time. Therefore, to shorten the time required for incident response including this, it is necessary to reduce the false positive alerts judged by the cyber security analysts.

Traditional approaches for reducing the time required to judge the false positive alerts are classified into the following three types:

(1) Adjustment of the signature rules of the security devices

The generation of false positive alerts often depends on the characteristics of the network monitored by the security devices. Therefore, the signature rules of the security devices may be added, deleted, and/or modified to match the network characteristics by the security administrator. By adjusting the signature rules, the occurrence of false positive alerts by UTM can be reduced (Juniper Networks, 2016). For example, when the false positive alerts of a specific signature occur frequently, the signature rule generating the false positive alerts should be invalidated. Fujita proposed a new description method for increasing the flexibility of the signature rules (Fujita, 2005). Using this, since the improper rules can be easily modified, the number of false positive alerts may be reduced, and the total time required for the judgment can be shortened. However, since the attack types and vulnerabilities frequently change, this approach is difficult to operate because signature rules must be fine-tuned frequently. On the other hand, outsourced security services are becoming popular in companies and public organizations. Such services often use unified signature rules, because it is very costly to change the signatures for each network.

(2) Visualization of the alerts

Alerts generated by security devices are difficult for security analysts to understand intuitively. Therefore, methods of visualizing alerts to make them easier to understand for security analysts are proposed. Abdullah reported a study to visualize the occurrence flow of the alerts on a two-dimensional map in association with the local network IP address (Abdullah *et al.*, 2005). Inoue reported on visualization of the communication between the monitoring sensor and the dark net and visualization of the propagation of malware (Inoue *et al.*, 2012). Livnat reported a study on visualization of the correlation by grouping alerts (Livnat *et al.*, 2005). Their studies are aimed at reducing the time required for the false positive alert judgment by security analysts. However, it is difficult for security analysts to judge all of the generated alerts. Therefore, this method alone is insufficient to shorten the time required for the false positive alert judgments.

(3) Judgment alerts by using a mechanical method

A typical mechanical method is the "unsupervised anomaly detection method" (Eskin *et al.*, 2002). In the security field, studies using an unsupervised anomaly detection method are popular because the tendencies of attacks change in a relatively short period of time due to the growing sophistication of attacks, discovery of vulnerabilities, changes in trends, and the like (Portnoy, Eleazar and Stolfo, 2001) (Muda *et al.*, 2011) (Depren *et al.*, 2005) (Liang Hu *et al.*, 2015). The unsupervised anomaly detection method is a method of classifying alerts with similar tendencies. Because the set of the alerts consists of many false positive alerts and a few true attack alerts, the false positive alerts and the attack alerts can be classified by the unsupervised anomaly detection method. This method can classify input alerts only, and it is not necessary to study in advance with teacher data. However, the unsupervised detection method is inferior in accuracy to other anomaly detection methods such as the supervised abnormality detection method. Yin proposed a judgment method using RNN and reported that it is more accurate than the existing judgment method using random forest and support vector machine(Yin *et al.*, 2017). However, to use the supervised detection method in the security field, it is necessary to regularly learn and update the judgment method.

3. A CLUSTERING-BASED JUDGMENT METHOD

3.1 Process of the Proposed Judgment Method

Since recent cyber-attacks are often the combination of the multiple attack methods, this type of attack causes alerts with various signatures in a single attack. On the other hand, the false positive alerts are characterized by a large amount of alerts with specific signatures. Therefore, the alerts that detect attacks correctly are considered to have different tendencies in signatures compared to the false positive alerts. Considering this characteristic, it is possible to classify the alerts into several groups by using the clustering method based on the signatures in the alerts. The alerts in the large groups are judged as the false positive alerts, because the false positive alerts consist of alerts with many similar signatures. By using clustering, the judgment of the false positive alerts can be done only from alert information without depending on the network.

The proposed method is composed of the following three steps:

(1) Extraction of alerts with the same attacker IP address

For each alert generated by the security device, the alerts having the same attacker IP address are extracted from the alerts over a certain period of time in the past.

(2) Calculation of generated alerts with same signature name from the extracted alerts.

Section 4.2 explains this step in detail.

(3) Judgment of false positive alerts by using clustering.

Section 4.3 explains this step in detail.

3.2 Calculation of Generated Alerts

In this step, signature trends are extracted from alerts for cluster classification.

Firstly, the generated amount by the signature name is aggregated from the alerts extracted in the previous step. For example, in Figure 2, let us use "Alert 4" as an evaluated alert. "Alert 1" and "Alert 2," which have the same attacker IP address (203.0.113.3) as "Alert 4" within a certain period in the past, are extracted. By aggregating the signature names of the extracted "Alert 1" and "Alert 2," the signature A is one time and the signature B is two times. By executing this operation for all alerts, the generation amount by signature name is aggregated.

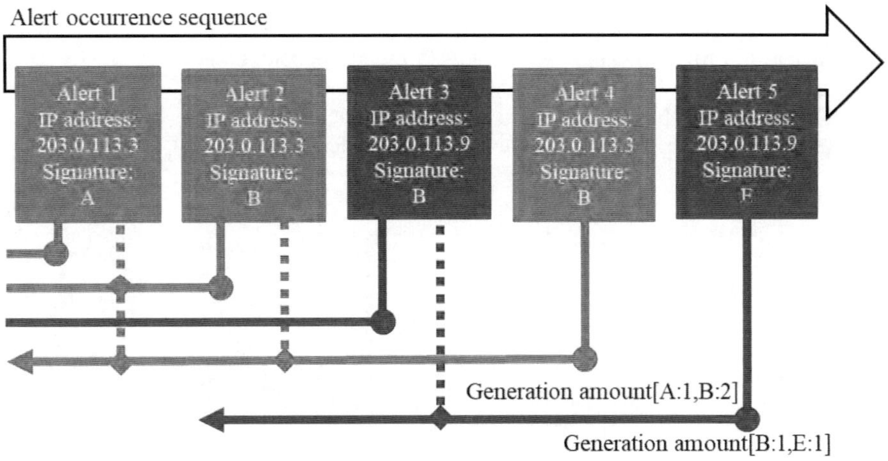

Figure 2. Aggregation of generated amount by signature in alert

Next, the result of counting all alerts is converted to a matrix form. A signature which has not occurred is filled with 0. For example, in the case of the previous example, the result of aggregating "alerts 1-5" is Table 1.

Table 1. Matrix example of aggregated result

	Signature A	Signature B	Signature E
Alert 1	1	0	0
Alert 2	1	1	0
Alert 3	0	1	0
Alert 4	1	2	0
Alert 5	0	1	1

The generation amount by signature name of one alert is called a "signature pattern." The signature pattern represents the trend of the event that generated the targeted alert.

3.3 Judgment by Clustering

If the learning models such as SVM (support vector machine) are used for classification, before learning, it is necessary to preliminarily assign the false positive alert flag to the alerts. On the other hand, in the clustering method, as shown in the right side of Figure 3, the classification can be done only from the alert information. Since there is no need to assign a flag, the clustering method is suitable for the judgment of the false positive alerts.

In the proposed method, the alerts are classified together into several clusters having the same pattern by using clustering based on aggregation results. The clustering methods DBSCAN and K-means++ are combined. By combining the clustering methods, the false positive alerts are judged as much as possible while correctly judging the attack alerts.

Figure 4 shows the flow of judgment of alerts. Most false positive alerts of similar signature patterns are judged by classification of DBSCAN. After that, false positive alerts among the remaining alerts are judged by classification using K-means++. DBSCAN is an algorithm that constitutes a cluster according to the density of input data. In this method, mechanically optimal clusters are determined with the distance threshold (eps) and the minimum inclusion count (minPts). For this reason, since DBSCAN can classify outliers not belonging to any cluster, DBSCAN can separately classify the alerts into large clusters of the false positive alerts and the isolated attack alerts from the clusters.

Therefore, at first, based on the aggregation result in the previous step, the alerts are classified by DBSCAN. As a result of classification by DBSCAN, the alerts belonging to the cluster are judged as "false positive alerts." Then, the alerts belonging to outliers are classified by K-means++. In the K-means++ classification, input data can be classified into clusters of a specified number. As a result, the alerts belonging to outliers can be classified as false positive alerts or attack alerts.

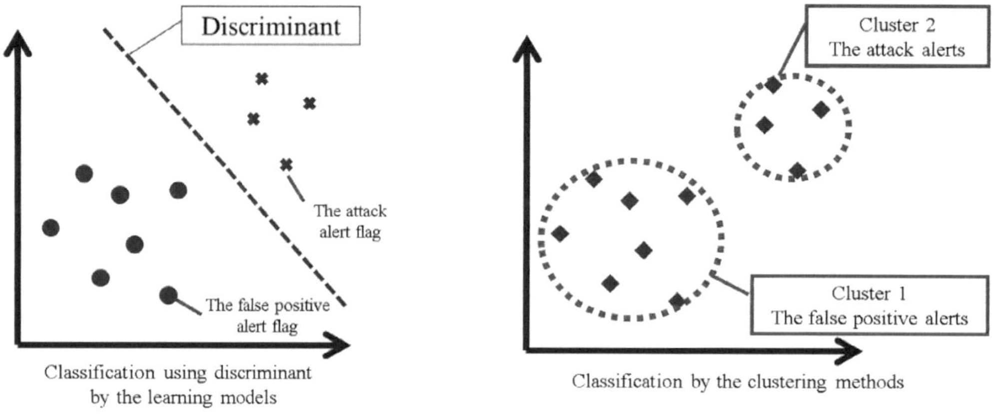

Figure 3. A model of the difference between learning models and clustering methods

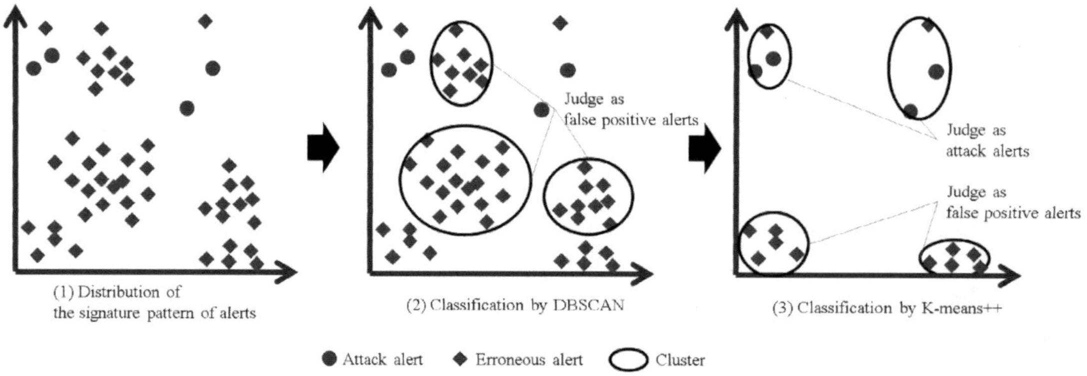

Figure 4. Flow of judgment of alerts using clustering by the proposed method

4. EXPERIMENT

The proposed method was applied to two data sets. Table 2 shows the characteristics of the alert set used for evaluation. Datasets A and B are 7 days of alerts from different security devices monitoring different networks. "Attack alert" and "False positive alert" are judged by cyber security analysts. For comparison, in addition to the proposed method, K-means++ only and DBSCAN only were also evaluated. The "certain period of time in the past" was 30 minutes based on the opinion of cyber security analysts.

The result is shown in Table 3 and 4. As a result of classification by DBSCAN, Dataset A was classified into 10 clusters, and Dataset B was classified into 3 clusters.

Table 2. Data set and judgment result by the cyber security analysts

Dataset	Attack alerts	False positive alerts
A	7	7023
B	9	13223

Table 3. The evaluation result by three methods

		Dataset A		Dataset B	
		Attack alerts	False positive alerts	Attack alerts	False positive alerts
K-means++ alone	Attack alerts	7	364	9	174
	False positive alerts	0	6659	0	13049
DBSCAN alone	Attack alerts	7	96	9	32
	False positive alerts	0	6927	0	13191
Proposed method (DBSCAN & K-means++)	Attack alerts	7	22	9	11
	False positive alerts	0	7001	0	13203

Table 4. The accuracy of three methods

	Recall rate	Precision rate	F-measure
K-means++ alone	1.00	0.03	0.14
DBSCAN alone	1.00	0.14	0.24
Proposed method (DBSCAN & K-means++)	1.00	0.34	0.50

16 attack alerts in total of datasets A and B were properly judged as attacks by all methods, and the recall rate for attacks was 100%. The 100% recall rate is important for cyber security because attacks cannot be overlooked. However, there are differences in false positives in 538 cases for "K-means++ only," 128 cases for "DBSCAN only," and 33 cases for the proposed method. As a result, the precision rate of the proposed method is 34% and the F-measure is 50%, which is the best when compared to other methods. The reason is that as a result of classification by DBSCAN, attack alerts of unique signature patterns were classified as outliers. Furthermore, by classifying the alerts of outliers using K-means++, it is possible to appropriately judge false positive alerts rarely occurring.

5. CONCLUSION

This paper proposed a clustering-based judgment method for false positive alerts generated by security devices. In the proposed method, firstly, alerts with the same attack source IP address over a period of time in the past are extracted. After the extraction, using the accumulated signature amount from extracted alerts, alerts with similar patterns are classified into several clusters using a method combining DBSCAN and K-means++. Then, the judgment of false positive alerts is done based on the number of alerts in each cluster. From a trial usage of the proposed method on two 7-day alert sets from two different networks, it was found that the recall rate was 100%, the precision rate was 34%, and the F-measure was 50%. The precision rate was improved by more than ten times compared to K-means++ alone, and about by 2.4 times compared to DBSCAN alone. The reason is that as a result of classification by DBSCAN, attack alerts of unique signature patterns were classified as outliers. Furthermore, by classifying the alerts of outliers using K-means++, it is possible to appropriately judge false positive alerts rarely occurring.

REFERENCES

Abdullah, K. et al., 2005. IDS RainStorm: Visualizing IDS Alarms. *Proceedings of IEEE Workshop on Visualization for Computer Security*. pp. 1-10.

Arthur, D. and Vassilvitskii, S., 2007. k-means++: the advantages of careful seeding. *Proceedings of the eighteenth annual ACM-SIAM symposium on Discrete algorithms*. pp. 1027-1035.

Depren, O. et al., 2005. An Intelligent intrusion detection system (IDS) for anomaly and misuse detection in computer networks. *Expert Systems with Applications*. 29(4), pp. 713–722.

Eskin, E. et al., 2002. A Geometric Framework for Unsupervised Anomaly Detection. *Proceedings of Applications of Data Mining in Computer Security*. Springer, Boston, pp. 77–101.

Ester, M. et al., 1996. A density-based algorithm for discovering clusters in large spatial databases with noise. *Proceedings of Second International Conference on Knowledge Discovery and Data Mining*. pp. 226–231.

Fujita, N., 2005. Development of Injustice Access Processing System That Reduces Log Output Using a Flexible Description for the Intrusion Detection Policy. *The transactions of the Institute of Electronics, Information and Communication Engineers*, 88(2), pp. 391–400 (in Japanese).

Inoue, D. et al., 2008. nicter: An Incident Analysis System Toward Binding Network Monitoring with Malware Analysis. *Proceedings of WOMBAT Workshop on Information Security Threats Data Collection and Sharing*. pp. 58–66.

Juniper Networks, 2016. Understanding IPS Signatures - TechLibrary. Juniper. Available at: https://www.juniper.net/documentation/en_US/junos-space15.2/topics/concept/junos-space-ips-policy-signature-understanding.html (Accessed: 31 March 2019).

Liang Hu et al., 2015. False positive elimination in intrusion detection based on clustering. *12th International Conference on Fuzzy Systems and Knowledge Discovery (FSKD)*. pp. 519–523.

Livnat, Y. et al., 2005. A visualization paradigm for network intrusion detection. *Proceedings of the Sixth Annual IEEE Systems, Man and Cybernetics (SMC) Information Assurance Workshop*. pp. 92–99.

Muda, Z. et al., 2011. Intrusion Detection based on K-Means Clustering and Naïve Bayes Classification. *Proceedings of the 7th International Conference on IT in Asia (CITA'11)*. pp. 1-6.

Mukherjee, B., Heberlein, L. T. and Levitt, K. N., 1994. Network intrusion detection. *IEEE Network. 8(3)*, pp. 26–41.

Munoz, A., Mana, A. and Javier, G., 2013. Dynamic Security Properties Monitoring Architecture for Cloud Computing, *Security Engineering for Cloud Computing: Approaches and Tools*. IGI Publishing Hershey, pp. 1–18.

Portnoy, L., Eleazar, E. and Stolfo, S., 2001. Intrusion detection with unlabeled data using clustering. *Proceedings of ACM CSS Workshop on Data Mining Applied to Security*. pp. 5-8.

Yin, C. et al., 2017. A Deep Learning Approach for Intrusion Detection Using Recurrent Neural Networks. *IEEE Access*. 5, pp. 21954–21961.

AN ENERGY-EFFICIENT RANDOM FINGERPRINT AND VERIFICATION FOR WIRELESS SENSOR NETWORKS AUTHENTICATION PROTOCOLS

Youssou Faye[1], Hervé Guyennet[2] and Pierre Cyrille Héam[2]
[1]*Department of Computer Sciences, University Assane Seck of Ziguinchor, Senegal*
[2]*Department of Computer Sciences, University of Franche Comte, France*

ABSTRACT

Sensor devices are limited resources (memory storage, energy, power computation and transmission), thus providing security mechanisms with lightweight resources is a very challenge in Wireless Sensors Network (WSNs). Recently, we show that, Vaidya and al.'s Improved Robust scheme for Dynamic User Authentication in WSNs is vulnerable to the risk of forgery attacks and Denial-of-Service (DoS) and we have proposed a lightweight solution which is adequate for resource constrained sensor networks. In this paper, we derive from password a much shorter string that could serve as random fingerprint to improve Login and Authentication phase. After having taken note that the security analysis of authentication protocols has already demonstrated through hash function properties and computational complexity, we propose an evaluation by experimenting firstly on the real sensor platform SensLab to measure energy consumption. After, we verify secrecy and authentication properties by the widely accepted AVISPA (Automated Validation of Internet Security Protocols and Applications) tool and validate protocols through simulation based on attacks.

KEYWORDS

Wireless Sensor Networks, Authentication, Password, Verification of Authentication Protocols

1. INTRODUCTION

Wireless Sensors Network are often deployed in hostile environments which make them more vulnerable to various attacks. In this context access control become necessary (Faye, 2011). In WSNs critical applications, network should be protected by preventing unauthorized users from gaining the information. User Authentication is the most basic used solution in traditional networks. Nowadays in WSNs, it has been adequately addressed with sensors limited resources. Many researchers have proposed a number of WSN authentication schemes (Vaidya, 2009), (Faye, 2012), (Wong, 2006), (Das, 2016), (Zhang, 2018), (Li, 2018). Recently, Vaidya and al. proposed an Improved Robust Dynamic User Authentication Scheme for WSNs (Vaidya, 2009). Only four phases are used in this scheme, namely, Registration Phase (RP), Login Phase (LP), Authentication Phase (AP), and Password−changing Phase (PP). In (Faye, 2012), authors shown that Vaidya and al.'s scheme is insecure and cannot prevent from DoS attacks. Hash function properties and computational complexity are generally used in password-based authentication schemes for performance evaluation and security (Kumari, 2015).

In this paper, to overcome the challenge of optimizing energy consumption in (Faye, 2012) and all schemes using the same approach during the Login Phase and the Authentication Phase which are the most time-consuming part of transmission, we reduce the bits transmitted by deriving from password a much shorter string that could serve as randomized fingerprinting function to improve LP and AP phases.

In the rest of the paper, Section 2 presents related works. The lack of energy reduction in (Faye, 2012). The proposed randomized fingerprinting technique is described in Section 4 and its security is discussed in Section 5. The implementation on SensLAB is done in section 6, and after, a security check and validation with AVISPA are made in section 7. Finally, we conclude the paper in section 8.

2. RELATED WORKS

For monitoring access control in many existing applications and computer systems, User Authentication (UA) has been the most widely used basic solution. Initially, traditional UA schemes (Awasthi, 2003), (Hwuang,2002), (Lee, 2002), (Shen, 2003),(Sun, 2000) based on (Lamport, 1981) scheme are quite interesting to examine various works on smart cards, they are based on static login ID and use the techniques of Password-based authentication for remote UA, on which a verification table is no longer required in the remote system. For existing Password-based authentication solutions, some schemes use the technique of a weak password, which facilitates the memorization of the password. However, they are very difficult to apply in WSN because it is based on public-key cryptographic techniques. The others (Awasthi, 2003), (Das, 2004) use strong-password and lead lighter computational because of using only one-way hash function and exclusive-OR operation (XOR). That's made it feasible to be adapted into the WSN environment. Their disadvantage lies in the difficulty of memorizing the password. (Lee, 2005) have shown that solutions like (Das, 2004) based on a dynamic login are vulnerable to reply attacks and modified login message attacks. They also proposed an improved UA scheme, which offers a low computation cost based on one-way hash functions. For better adaptation in WSN environment, (Wong, 2006) improves Lee's framework to provide the dynamic UA. (Vaidya, 2009), propose a variation of strong-password based solution proposed by (Wong, 2006). This scheme claimed to provide protection against the replay attacks of login message and forgery attacks. In (Faye, 2012) , authors have shown that (Vaidya, 2009) is vulnerable to DoS attack and forgery attacks, and have proposed a solution. Using the same approach, (Xue, 2013) proposed mutual authentication based on the same technique of hash functions and XOR operations. (Jiang, 2015) points out vulnerabilities in Xue et al.'s scheme and proposed a two-factor authentication solution. (Das, 2016) showed that Jiang et al. does not produce proper authentication during the login and authentication phases and proposes a solution based on three authentication factors. Recently, some works in WSN and IoT field, such as (Zhang, 2018), (Ling, 2017), (Li, 2018) are also use technique of one-way hash function and exclusive-OR operation and the handshake structure of Registration Phase (RP), Login Phase (LP) and Authentication Phase (AP) on multi-hop communication. For an evaluation of the energy cost, all solutions use almost the same comparative approach based on analytical computational and communication complexity (Kumari, 2015).

3. LACK OF ENERGY REDUCTION

In order to better express the lack of energy reduction on schemes (Vaidya, 2009),(Wong, 2006), (Faye, 2012), (Xue, 2013), (Zhang, 2018), (Li, 2018), we will review the protocol in (Faye, 2012) as an example..

3.1 Review of Protocol in (Faye, 2012)

We briefly describe schemes in Vaidya et al, and Faye et al. The notations involved are listed in Table 1.

Table 1. Notations

Symbols	Description
UD	Users Device such PDA, PC
GW **and** LN	Respectively Registration Sensor Gateway **and** Sensor login Node
H() **and** $H_p()$	Respectively One-way hash function **and** H()mod (p)
$\oplus$ **and** $\|\|$	Respectively Exclusive-or (XOR) operation **and** Concatenation
Succ_Reg	Successful Registration message
Acc_login	Accept login message
Succ_Chenge	Successful Changes message
X	Secret key known to the GW
UID **and** PW	Respectively Users identity and Password chosen by user
TS	Registration time
t, T_0, T_1, T_2, T_3	Current time recorded by one of the nodes
ΔT	Allowed time interval for transmission delay
$\rightarrow$	transmission of message
P	a prime number

3.1.1 Registration Phase

It is important to note that, there is one-hop communication between user's mobile device and the LN during the login phase, and a multiple hops communication between the LN and the gateway node.

RP1 - In (Vaidya, 2009), it is not necessary to compute vpw=H(PW), because it is as vulnerable as the PW. Thus, in (Faye, Niang, & Guyennet, 2012), user UD can only choose a PW.

RP2 - At a time TS, the UD submits its identity UID and the password PW to the GW in secure mode.

RP3 - The GW computes X=H(UID||x) and replies to UD for successful registration, stores (UID, H(PW), X, TS), and distributes (UID, X, H(PW),TS) to sensor nodes, which can provide a login interface to users.

3.1.2 The Login Phase

LP1 - The user computes A= H(H(PW)||t) and submits (UID, A, t) to a login node

LP2 - After receive the login request at time T0, the LN checks its lookup table to verify if UID is a valid. The login request is rejected if it is not.

LP3 - The login node computes A'= H(H(PW)||t), checks if A=A' and T_0 - t $\geq \Delta T$ (the password is valide if A=A'). The login request is rejected if it is not. Otherwise, the login node retrieves the corresponding A, computes $C_K = (X \oplus A \oplus T_0)$ and computes $t' = H^2(PW) \oplus t$. The expression $H^n(PW)$ denotes the application of *n-times* hash operations on PW. That is, $H^n(PW)=H(H^{n-1}(PW))$.

3.1.3 Authentication Phase

AP1 -The gateway checks the validity of UID and t. The login request is rejected if they are not valid. Otherwise, the GW Computes $t=t' \oplus H^2(PW)$, checks if $T_1 - T_0 \geq \Delta T$; $T_0 - t \geq \Delta T$. If the condition is satisfied, then the login request is a replay message and is rejected. The gateway retrieves the corresponding H(PW) and A, computes A' = H(H(PW)||t) and $C_K' = (X \oplus A' \oplus T_0)$. The login request is rejected if $C_K \neq C_K'$. Otherwise, the GW computes $V_M = H(X||A'||T_1)$.

AP2 -GW validates the login request, sends accept message (Access_login, V_M, T_1) to the LN; and stores t.

AP3 -The LN computes V_M', and after checking of $V_M = V_M'$, it calculates $Y_K = H(V_M'||T_2)$

AP4 - The LN sends (Access_login, Y_K ,T_1, T_2) to the user UD

AP5 - Upon receiving the message at time T_3, the UD checks if $T_1 - T_0 \geq \Delta T$; $T_0 - t \geq \Delta T$. If the conditions are true, then the Access login message is rejected, else, the LN retrieves A, performs $V_M'' = H(X||A||T_1)$ and $Y_K' = H(V_M''||T_2)$, and checks if $Y_K = Y_K'$. If the condition holds, then the UD starts getting data, else, the accept Access login message is rejected.

3.2 Costly communication: similar approaches to Vaidya et al. and Faye et al.

Similar solutions Wong et al., Xue et al., Zhang et al., Li et al., to Vaidya et al. and Faye et al. use the technique of hash functions and XOR operations and are based on the handshake structure of Registration Phase (RP), Login Phase (LP) and Authentication Phase (AP) on multi-hop communication. During the login phase PL3, the LN after verification, calculates $CK = (X \oplus A \oplus T_0)$ and $t' = H^2(PW) \oplus t$ and sends them to the GW through a multi-hop communication provided by the sensors. Since the transmission is the most energy consuming operation in wireless communication, the long string of bit C_K is equal to the maximum number of bits between X and A. Therefore, a long string of bit login or password can lead to a high energy consumption in the network. Thus finding ways to minimize the number of bits transmitted during this multi-hop communication between LN and GW without compromising security becomes necessary for energy saving. Since the length bit of timestamps is very small compared to X and A, we applying some standard hashing or check technique to derive from X and A a much shorter string that could serve as a fingerprint of X and A.

4. REDUCTION OF THE BITS TRANSMITTED BY FINGERPRINT

In order to avoid the propagation of a large number of bits through a multi-hop communication provide by sensors, we propose a technique based on the modulo operator on prime numbers. To do this, in the same way as the hash function H(), a random prime number p is generated by the LN and the GW in login phase RP1. To produce much shorter string, we use reduction modulo p as the fingerprinting function $H_p()$ such as $H_p(x) = H(x)(\text{mod}_p)$ and where H(x) is the integer represented by the bit string x. If p is not too large, then the fingerprint function Hp() can be transmitted as a short string of bits. The property $H_p(x) = H(x)(\text{mod } p)$ is checked if $x = y$ and checked with some probability if $x \neq y$. When p becoming increasingly smaller, $Hp(x)$ becomes a more short binary sequence. Thus registration phase (RP1, RP2, RP3) and the two first steps of login phase (LP1, LP2) are not changed. However the third phase LP3 which induces a multi-hop communication through the sensors may be proceed according to the following algorithm.

```
Begin
  LP1—UD: A = H(H(PW) ∥ t);
  LP2—UD → LN : UID, A, t;
  LP3—LN:
  if (UID is not valid) then
    |Reject login request;
  else
    |A' = H(H(PW) ∥ t);
    if( A ≠ A') then
      |Reject login request;
    if( T0 − t ≥ ΔT) then
      |Reject login request;
    else
      |Ck = X⊕A⊕T0;
      |t' = H²(PW)⊕t
  LP4—LN → GW: UID, CK, T0, t';
end
```

Algorithm 1. Protocol in (Faye, Niang, & Guyennet, 2012): LP

```
Begin
  LP1—UD: A = H(H(PW) ∥ t);
  LP2—UD → LN : UID, A, t;
  LP3—LN:
  if (UID is not valid) then
    |Reject login request;
  else
    |A' = H(H(PW) ∥ t);
    if( A ≠ A') then
      |Reject login request;
    if( T0 − t ≥ ΔT) then
      |Reject login request;
    else
      |Ck = Hp(X)⊕Hp(A)⊕T0;
      |t' = H²(PW)⊕t
  LP4—LN → GW: UID, CK, T0, t';
end
```

Algorithm 2. Proposed solution: LP

5. SECURITY ANALYSIS

This technique reduces the number of bits transmitted between the LN and the GW. The value of the prime number p is one of the main keys for efficiency. When p is small, the number of transmitted bit length becomes more shortly but allows the possibility of a false match, in which x and y have the same fingerprint even though they are different. The weakness of this technique is that, if p is held fixed, then there are certain pairs of strings x and y on which the method will always fail. A more advantageous method, which avoids such bad pairs x and y, is to determine randomly the prime p on every time the equality of two strings is to be checked, rather than to agree on p in advance. This solution does not compromise security, because registration phase is not change. According to the size of prime number p the hash function $H_p()$ can have all properties of the hash function $H()$ with a very low probability (even zero) to permit the possibility of a false match in which x and y have the same fingerprint $(H_p(x) = H_p(y))$ even though they are different ($x \neq y$). In other words $H_p(x) \equiv H_p(y)$ mod p. Clearly, if $x = y$ then this algorithm gives the correct answer (*since* $H_p(x) = H_p(y)$). However, if $x \neq y$, there is a chance that this algorithm gives a wrong answer. But the probability that the algorithm will fail is extremely small. We upper bound this probability. If n is the number of bits to transmit without use reduction modulo p as the fingerprinting function, failure can occur only if p divides $|H(x) - H(y)|$. It is well known that for any prime number $p > 2$, if $|H_p(x) - H_p(y)| \leq 2^n$, there are at most n primes that divide $|H(x) - H(y)|$ (Karp, 1991). Therefore, n is an upper bound on the number of primes, i.e. those that if we select the algorithm will fail. It is well known and well-studied in number theory that the number of minimum password length of 8 or more characters is equivalent to a minimum of 64 bits in 8-bit ASCII. Figure1 shows, for 104 bits (a password length of 12 characters) to be transmitted, the probability of failure Pr depending on the number of bits effectively transmitted based on fingerprinting function. We can notice that from a transmission of a fingerprint $\geq$ 24 bits, we have a very good probability

$\leq$ 0,000000292. For a minimum password length of 8 characters (64 bits to be transmitted), a transmission of a fingerprint = 24 bits have a very good probability of 0,000000318. Table 2 shows the probability of failure P r for a password length of 64 bits and 104 bits based on fingerprinting length for a set of values between 1 and 40.

```
Begin
  AP1—GW
   if (UID and t are valid) then
     |Retrieves dataset (UID, X, TS, H(PW));
     |t = t' ⊕ H²(PW);
   else
     |Rejects login request;
   if( T₁ − T₀ ≥ ΔT and T₀ − t ≥ ΔT)
     |Reject login request;
   else
     |A' = H(H(PW) ‖ t;
     |C'ₖ = (X⊕A'⊕T₀);
   if (C'ₖ ≠ Cₖ) then
     |Reject login request;
   else
     |V_M = H(X ‖ A' ‖ T₁)
     |stores t;
  AP2—GW → LN: Access_login, V_M, T₁;
  AP3—LN:
  if (T₂ − T₁ ≥ ΔT) then
    |Reject login request
  else
    |V'_M = H(X ‖ A ‖ T₁)
   if (V'_M ≠ V_M) then
    |Reject login request
  else
    |Yₖ = H(V'_M ‖ T₂)
  AP4—LN → UD: Access_login, Yₖ, T₁T₂;
  AP5—UD:
   if( T₁ − T₀ ≥ ΔT and T₀ − t ≥ ΔT) then
    |Rejects Access_login message;
   else
    |V''_M = H(X ‖ A ‖ T₁);
    |Y'_K = (V''_M ‖ T₂)
   if (Y_K ≠ Y'_K) then
    |Rejects Access_login message;
   else
    |starts to obtain data
end
```

Algorithm 3. Protocol in (Faye, Niang, Guyennet, 2012): AP

```
Begin
  AP1—GW
   if (UID and t are valid) then
     |Retrieves dataset (UID, X, TS, H(PW));
     |t = t' ⊕ H²(PW);
   else
     |Rejects login request;
   if( T₁ − T₀ ≥ ΔT and T₀ − t ≥ ΔT)
     |Reject login request;
   else
     |A' = H(H(PW) ‖ t;
     |C'ₖ = H_p(X)⊕H_p(A')⊕T₀);
   if (C'ₖ ≠ Cₖ) then
     |Reject login request;
   else
     |V_M = H_p(X ‖ A' ‖ T₁)
     |stores t;
  AP2—GW → LN: Access_login, V_M, T₁;
  AP3—LN:
  if (T₂ − T₁ ≥ ΔT) then
    |Reject login request
  else
    |V'_M = H_p(X ‖ A ‖ T₁)
   if (V'_M ≠ V_M) then
    |Reject login request
  else
    |Yₖ = H(V'_M ‖ T₂)
  AP4—LN → UD: Access_login, Yₖ, T₁T₂;
  AP5—UD:
   if( T₁ − T₀ ≥ ΔT and T₀ − t ≥ ΔT) then
    |Rejects Access_login message;
   else
    |V''_M = H(X ‖ A ‖ T₁);
    |Y'_K = (V''_M ‖ T₂)
   if (Y_K ≠ Y'_K) then
    |Rejects Access_login message;
   else
    |starts to obtain data
end
```

Algorithm 4. Proposed solution AP

Algorithm 3: Protocol in (Faye, Niang, Guyennet, 2012): AP **Algorithm 4**: Algorithm 4: Proposed solution APprimes less than *z* is asymptotic to $\frac{z}{\ln(z)}$, i.e. the number of primes up to z is about (Karp, 1991). Then we can deduce that the probability of failure (false match i.e. x≠y, while $H_p(x) = H_p(y)$) is equal to *Pr[failure]= Pr[H(x)mod p = H(y)mod p]* is $Pr = \frac{n}{\frac{2^n}{\ln(2^n)}}$. This probability varies depending on the number of reduced bits according to the size of the prime p. if the prime p is becoming increasingly smaller, the transmitted bits are reduced and the probability of failure *Pr* increases. Thus, there is a need to find a compromise between the number of transmitted bits and the probability Pr. It is important to estimate the length of hash values for applications. In variety of tools and security templates, the password must be at least 8 characters. If we take account human memory limitations, we shall assume a secure password can be composed by a minimum of 8 characters, where each character can be any of the 95 characters readily represented with keyboard.

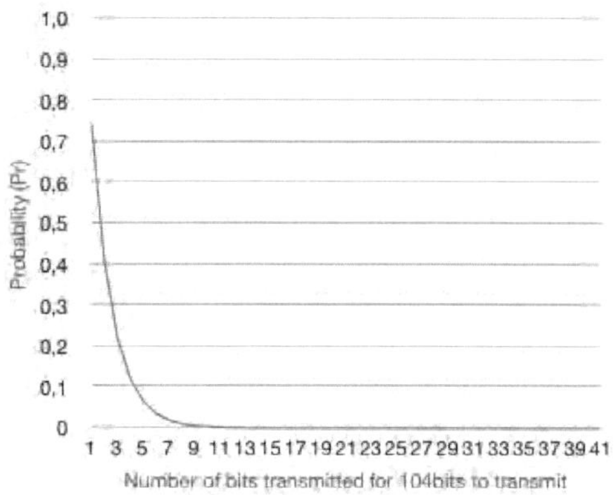

Figure 1. Probability of failure depending on the number of bits transmitted / 104bits to transmit

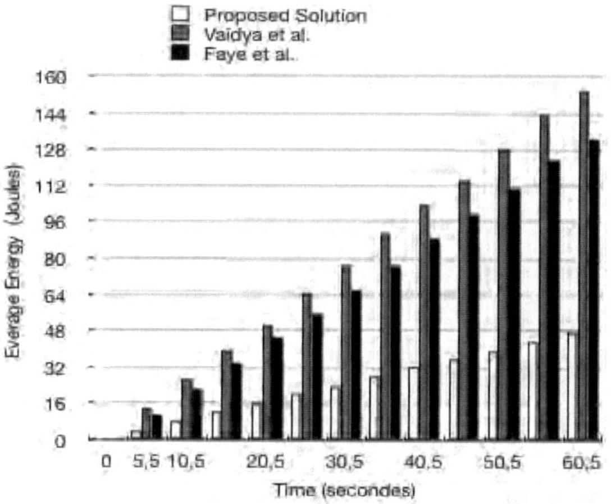

Figure 2. Energy consumption

Table 2. Pr for a set of values of fingerprint length

Fingerprint	1	4	10	19	32
Pr for 104 bits	**0,739**	**0,120**	**0,00275**	**794.10^{-8}**	142. 10^{-11}
Pr for 64 bits	**0,754**	**0,126**	**0,00293**	**860. 10^{-8}**	155. 10^{-11}

In this case, random prime p can be generated by LN and GW from the forty least significant bits of the password, and where the twentieth bit is set to 1. The random prime is the nearest prime value got from the resulting binary suite.

6. IMPLEMENTATION

We have implemented the proposed solution on real sensor platform SensLAB. The SensLAB testbed is composed of 1024 nodes over 4 sites. In this paper we present only results on the 3-dimensional grid composed of sensor node with wsn430 (cc1101) (Texas, 2011), (Chipcon, 2007). The electrical energy consumption is calculated through the linear energy model defined by the following equation:

$E = P_1t_1 + P_2t_2 + P_3t_3 + ... + P_{n-1}t_{n-1} + P_nt_n$; With P_i : the average power consumption of node i at the time t_i. For a five-hop communication model, Figure 2 shows the average energy evolution of 6 sensor nodes involved in the process. We found out that our proposed scheme has better energy consumption and does bring significant improvements.

7. VERIFICATION AND VALIDATION

We use the standard AVISPA (Armando, 2005) to validate our solution. Its ability to process protocols has been demonstrated through IETF (internet engineering task force) library protocol specified in High Level Protocol Specification (HLPSL) (Tseng, 2007). We checked secret property of the stored password, and strong authentication of LNs by the GW.

7.1 Validation of Solution

We check now the secrecy property of stored password and the strong authentication of the LNs by the GW.

- **Secrecy property of the stored password**: we must ensure that the stored password is kept confidential between the user, the LNs and the GW. This part involves in two different sessions the user, the GW, the LN and the intruder. The first session called here normal session consists of the legitimate user, the LN and the

GW. The second session or intruder session involves the intruder playing the role of a user in order to attack the protocol.

```
- Normal session: User (u) - LN (l) - GW (g)
- Intruder session: Intruder (i) - LN (l) - GW (g)
```

Figure 3 presents results achieved by AVISPA. We can see in the results that the protocol is declared **SAFE**, i.e no attacks returned.

- Secrecy and strong authentication: this must guarantee that the stored password is confidential and at the same time a strong authentication between the LNs and the GW. There are three different sessions. A normal session, a second session in which the intruder claims to be the user, and in the third session in which the intruder plays the role of the LN.

```
-Normal session : User (u) - LN (l) - GW (g)
-Intruder session 1 : Intruder (i) - LN (l) - GW (g)
-Intruder session 2 : User (u) - Intrus (i) - GW (g)
```

```
MacBook-Pro-de-YFAYE:Simulations$ avispa secret.hlpsl --cl-atse
SUMMARY
 SAFE
DETAILS
 BOUNDED_NUMBER_OF_SESSIONS
 TYPED_MODEL
PROTOCOL
 /Applications/avispa-1.1/testsuite/results/secret.if
GOAL
 As Specified
BACKEND
 CL-AtSe
STATISTICS
 Analysed  : 9 states
 Reachable : 9 states
 Translation: 0.07 seconds
 Computation: 0.00 seconds
```

Figure 3. Verification of security properties of secret

```
MacBook-Pro-de-YFAYE:Simulations$ avispa SecAuth.hlpsl --cl-atse
SUMMARY
 UNSAFE
DETAILS
 ATTACK_FOUND
 TYPED_MODEL
PROTOCOL
 /Applications/avispa-1.1/testsuite/results/SecAuth.if
GOAL
 Secrecy attack on (n25(PW))
BACKEND
 CL-AtSe
STATISTICS
 Analysed  : 0 states
 Reachable : 0 states
 Translation: 0.09 seconds
 Computation: 0.00 seconds
ATTACK TRACE
 i -> (u,11): starter
 (u,11) -> i: {u.n25(PW)}_ki
          & Secret(n25(PW),set_122); Add u to set_122; Add g to
set_122;
```

Figure 4. Verification of security properties of secret and authentication

7.2 Discussion and Analysis of Results

On Figure 4, the protocol is declared **UNSAFE**, i.e. not secure, and an attack is returned. An attack can take place without compromising security. After analyzing attack's traces, we see that the intruder claims to be a LN to the user according to the following events:

```
i → (u, 11): start.
```

The intruder i initializes a session with the identifier (11) by sending a signal "start" composed of the identity of the user u, and the session (11) to the user so that the last one sends back to him an encrypted message with ki (key made by i and sent to u).

```
(u,11)→{u.n25(PW)}_ki & Secret(u.n25(PW), set_122), Add u to set_122,
Add g to set_122;
```

In the same session (11), the event (u, 11) → {u.n25(PW)} ki indicates that the user u sends back to the intruder his identity concatenated with the password n25 encrypted with the key ki. The fragment & Secret(u.n25(PW), set 122) indicates that the PW identified by n25 is secret and is stored in variable set 122 which is generated automatically. Finally, the two events Add u to set 127 and Add g to set 122 indicate that only u (user) and g (gateway) are allowed to know the variable. In conclusion, an attack is conducted without success, the intruder i, does not have the secret after this attempt.

8. CONCLUSION

In this paper, we have proposed a scheme to improve energy consumption by reducing the number of bits transmitted in Vaidya and al. (Vaidya, 2009), and in (Faye, 2012). The proposed technique is applicable to all solutions using the same approach with a very low probability of compromising security for a significant reduction of transmitted bits. Also, this technique can be easily applied to almost many existing user authentication schemes. The implementation on the SensLab plate shows that our scheme has better energy consumption. A verification and validation of the security properties with AVISPA justifies its resistance to the attack.

REFERENCES

Armando A. et al, 2005. *The AVISPA tool for the automated validation of internet security protocols and applications",* Computer Aided Verification, Springer, Berlin, pp 281-285.

Awasthi A. K. et al, 2003. *A remote user authentication scheme using smart cards with Forward Secrecy*. IEEE Transactions on Consumer Electronics, vol. 49, 4 pp.1246-1248.

Chevalier Y. et al, 2004. *A high level protocol specification language for industrial security-sensitive protocols*, Proc. SAPS, vol. 4, p. 193–205.

Chipcon , 2007, *CC2420 2.4GHz IEEE 802.15.4 RF transceiver.* http://www.ti.com/lit/gpn/ cc2420.

Das M. et al, 2004, *A Dynamic ID-based Remote User Authentication Scheme*, IEEE Transactions on Consumer Electronics, vol.50, 2. pp 629-631

Das K. et al, 2016, *A secure and robust temporal credential-based three-factor user authentication scheme for wireless sensor networks*. Peer-to-peer Networking and Applications, vol. 9, p. 223-244.

Faye Y. et al, 2011. *A Survey of Access Control Schemes in Wireless Sensor Networks,* World. Academy of Science, Engineering and Technology. Issue 59: 2011, Paris, France, pp 814-823,

Faye Y. et al, 2012. *A user authentication-based prob- abilistic risk approach for Wireless Sensor Networks*. In: Mobile and Wireless Networking (iCOST), International Conference on Selected Topics in. IEEE, 2012. p. 124-129.

Hwang M. et al, 2002. *An ElGamal-like cryptosystem for enciphering large messages*, IEEE Trans .on Knowledge and Data Engineering, vol. 14, 2, pp.445-446.

Jiang Q. et al, 2015. *An efficient two-factor user authentication scheme with unlinkability for wireless sensor networks*. Peer-to-peer Networking and Applications, 6, vol. 8, p. 1070-1081.

Karp M. 1991. *An introduction to randomized algorithms.* DiscreteApplied Mathematics, 34(1-3), 165-201.

Kumari S. et al, 2015. *User authentication schemes for wireless sensor networks: A review*. Ad Hoc Networks,vol. 27, p. 159-194.

Krovetz T. et al, 2001. *Fast Universal Hashing with Small Keys and No Preprocessing: The PolyR Construction.* D. Won (Ed.): ICISC 2000, LNCS, Springer-Verlag Berlin Heidelberg, pp. 73-89

Lamport L., 1981. *Password authentication with insecure communication*, Communications of the ACM, 1981.Commun ACM, vol.24, no.11, pp.770-772

Lee C. et al, 2002. *A remote user authentication scheme using hash functions*, ACM Operating Systems Review, vol. 36, n4, pp.23-29.

Lee C. et al, 2005. *An Improved Low Communication Cost User Authentication Scheme for Mobile Communication*, Proceedings of the IEEE 19th International Conference on Advanced Information Networking and Applications, Taiwan.

Li X. et al, 2018. *A three-factor anonymous authentication scheme for wireless sensor networks in internet of things environments.* Journal of Network and Computer Applications, pp 194-204.

Ling C. et al, 2017. *A Secure and Efficient One-time Password Authentication Scheme for WSN*. IJ Network Security, 19(2), pp 177-181

Shen J. J. et al, 2003. *A modified remote user authentication scheme using smart cards,* IEEE Trans. on Consumer Electron. vol. 49, 2, pp.414-416.

Sun H., 2000. *An Efficient remote user authentication scheme using smart cards*, IEEE Trans. on Consumer Electron. vol. 46, 4, pp. 958-961.

TexasInstruments, 2011, *CC1101 Low-Power Sub-1GHz RF Transceiver,* .http://www.ti.com/lit/gpn/cc1101.

Tseng H. et al, 2007. *An improved dynamic user authentication scheme for wireless sensor networks*. In Proceedings of the IEEE Global Communications Conference (GLOBECOM07), pp 986-990.

Vaidya B. et al, 2009. *Improved Robust User Authenti- cation Scheme for Wireless Sensor Networks.* Wireless Communication and Sensor Networks (WCSN), Fifth IEEE Conference

Wong K. et al, 2006, *A dynamic user authentication scheme for wireless sensor networks*, In Proceedings of the IEEE International Conference on Sensor Networks, Ubiquitous, and Trustworthy Computing, vol. 1, pp. 244-251

Xue X. et al, 2013, *A temporal-credential-basedmutual authentication and key agreement scheme for wireless sensor networks,* Journal of Network and Computer Applications, 1, vol. 36, p. 316-323.

Zhang X. et al, 2018. , Xin, *An novel anonymous user WSN authentication for Internet of Things."Soft Computing* : 1-9.

VIEW: A CONCEPT FOR AN IMMERSIVE VIRTUAL REALITY IMAGE INTERPRETATION WORKBENCH

Alexander Streicher, Julien Hoffmann and Wolfgang Roller
Fraunhofer IOSB, Karlsruhe, Germany

ABSTRACT

Virtual Reality (VR) and serious gaming can increase the learning motivation and outcome in image interpretation. This paper presents the concept of an VR game-like assistance system called Virtual Reality Image Exploitation Workspace (VIEW). It can be used to evaluate the learning-supporting immersion or presence level of image interpreters while solving typical interpretation tasks. The problem statement is centered on the realization aspects of a VR assistance system for image interpretation which provides a high level of immersion. This work combines the setting of a real serious game for formal image interpretation training with virtual reality to increase the immersion level of the users. Enhanced image quality and organizational requirements from professional image interpretation impose additional complexity on VR for image interpretation. The presented VIEW concept deals with multiple aspects in respect to e-learning, professional training and virtual reality for image interpretation. Preliminary evaluation results from a realized prototype show the feasibility and user acceptance of the VIEW concept.

KEYWORDS

Virtual Reality, Immersion, Image Interpretation, Serious Games, Assistance Systems

1. INTRODUCTION

Serious Gaming and Virtual Reality (VR) have long since been an active topic in professional training (Freina and Ott, 2015; Mazuryk and Gervautz, 1996). With the currently available commercial off-the-shelf hardware these training applications and the research therein have seen a staggering increase (Ganbatte DevBlog, 2018). VR is especially well suited for immersive experiences. In combination with gaming, virtual worlds provide users with rich playable environments, welcoming playing, testing and learning.

The application area of our work is aerial and satellite image interpretation. The interpretation of aerial and satellite images poses a wide range of challenges because of different imagery sensor types, difficult image material or unknown objects. Professional image interpretation is done in various fields, ranging from the microscopic level in medicine, e.g., diagnostics in histopathology, to the macroscopic level of aerial or satellite images, e.g., civilian applications like search-and-rescue, agriculture, oceanography, or military intelligence acquisition (Roller et al., 2013). Image interpretation requires the detection, recognition, identification and analysis of structures and objects, according to a given task based on optical, infrared and radar imagery. Besides highly developed assets, sensors and image exploitation systems, the success of a reconnaissance mission depends on the interpreter's analysis performance. Special face-to-face training courses blended with technology-enhanced learning tools, such as e-Learning courses, simulations and serious games, ensure that image analysts are qualified to a high standard. Our application scenarios focus on intelligent assistance and e-learning systems that help users to perform their work effectively and efficiently.

An immersive virtual environment can promote the motivation for continuous usage and therefore it can ultimately promote learning. A VR system with a high immersion capacity facilitates the sensation of presence, i.e., the sensation of "being there" (Riva et al., 2003). The notion of immersion and presence often go hand in hand and several terms have been coined with subtle differences, e.g., immersion, presence, involvement, emotional response or degree of interest. In this paper, we use immersion as the technical form factor that features presence. Besides the motivational aspects of immersion or presence, there are further technical benefits for image interpretation, such as the efficient display of 3D data or spatial objects, ease of spatial cognition (Hubona and Shirah, 2005), virtually infinite space, or dislocated collaboration.

In the past huge efforts were needed to make spatial data tangible, e.g., by producing statuary, or by using 3D glasses for anaglyphic stereoscopic printing (red-green) or for 3D monitors. With VR one can immerse in a virtual environment and directly experience 3D.

In aerial image interpretation, the cognitive experience of the spatial data can have a considerable impact on the quality of the interpretation reports, e.g., when spatial relations could be experienced in more detail and with a natural access to reference scales. For example, VR can easily mediate topographic map data.

To achieve immersion we follow gamification and digital game based learning paths (Prensky, 2001). The combination of gamification and VR is obvious - as the entertainment industry proves with VR games numbered in the millions (Ganbatte DevBlog, 2018). In a professional (or serious) context, VR can be combined with aspects of serious gaming. A serious game is a digital game not just for entertainment but with at least one characterizing goal (Dörner et al., 2016), e.g., learning or training. In digital game based learning (Prensky, 2001) the game design is highly oriented at the target group and the learning objectives. A high acceptance for the game's assets and game mechanics promote the acceptance by the users which enables immersion, which in turn promotes the intrinsic motivation for playing or training, which positively influences flow and ultimately could increase the learning efficacy (Connolly et al., 2012).

The superordinate research question (and application scenario) of our work is how to optimally train and support professional image interpreters. This paper specifically addresses how to increase the immersion level in assistance systems for image interpretation using VR. The adjacent subquestion is how to design VR systems for image interpretation that fulfill the quality requirements regarding image fidelity, high resolution and optimal usability in a professional working context.

This paper presents the concept study and prototype realization of the *Virtual Reality Image Exploitation Workspace* (VIEW), a VR assistance as well as a training system for image interpreters. The realization targets commercial VR hardware and implementation in a VR capable game engine. The concept offers answers to some challenges that are specific for VR for image interpretations, e.g., image fidelity, interaction paradigms or display of high-resolution imagery.

2. RELATED WORK

VR itself has long been an active research topic with multiple industrial appliances (Nomura and Sawada, 2001). The dome-like display for urban planning by Nomura et al. influenced our concept (Nomura and Sawada, 2001). Of further inspiration has been the work of (Streitz et al., 2001); they analyzed how to build interactive office environments by integrating various display types. In some parts, this has influenced our concept, e.g., the design and placement of our virtual displays and interaction elements. Other driving work has been from the hierarchy of needs in VR development by Cronin (Cronin, 2015), with special focus on the factors interpretability (sense) and usefulness (value).

For image interpretation VR has been used for visualization geoscience data, e.g, by Lin et al. with a VR geoscience image interpretation workplace (Lin and Loftin, 1998). We followed also their Closed World Interaction (CWI) concept that influences the complexity – or rather simplicity – of intuitive VR interface design with low affordance. Such interaction concepts should be followed to benefit from VR visualization advantages (Loftin and Nelson, 2000), although no VR interaction standards exist yet (Malaika, 2015).

The advantages of using VR for visualizing high resolution image data in an immersive virtual environment has been presented by (Billen et al., 2008; Loftin and Nelson, 2000). This is in line with other work which show that geoscience can benefit from VR interaction possibilities (Furumura and Chen, 2004; Ohno and Kageyama, 2007). A Study by Lackey et al. (Lackey et al., 2016) show how positive VR experiences can reduce stress and workload. Such kind of immersive environments can optimally utilize the brain's cognitive capacity to process visual information (Hubona and Shirah, 2005).

3. VIRTUAL IMAGE EXPLOITATION WORKSPACE (VIEW)

VIEW is a concept for a VR assistance system for image interpreters which incorporates immersive elements suitable[1] for professional image interpretation. In this context an operational image interpretation assistance system, ViLand (Figure 1}, has been used as a base model for VIEW. Such systems offer tools for image navigation, manipulation and annotation as well as specific reporting functionalities, e.g., standardized reporting processes and formats.

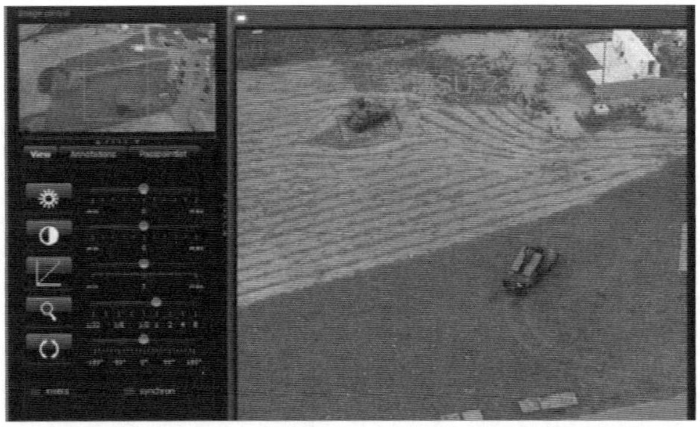

Figure 1. Assistance system ViLand for image interpretation and reporting

3.1 Virtual Image Display (VID)

For *image* interpretation, the Virtual Image Display (VID) is apparently the most important aspect. Based on requirements analysis with experts on aerial and satellite image interpretation the demands for a VR display comprise: high resolution, image fidelity, multi-channel imagery and image manipulation.

The VID is a virtual monitor where the imagery data is displayed, navigated or modified; it is VIEW's primary user interface (UI) component. In the game engine this is technically a dynamic texture. Various manifestations of the texture's underlying model have been discussed and evaluated (Figure 2): flat or curved plane, quarter-, half- or full dome, or 360 degree panorama. The objective is to maximize the visible display for quick and sound recognition. Although this leads to a half- or full dome or a 360 degree panorama, it is not the typical type of content in image interpretation. Also it necessitates ample head movements which hinders quick recognition and has the risk of fatigue (Hoppe, 2016). Dome-like approaches (Figure 2) inherently impose too much unacceptable vertical and horizontal distortions on the image data. Image interpreters require a reliable and undistorted display. Although a flat plane does not impose distortions effects on the texture (no curvature), it proved difficult for the users to view content in the corners for a big VID. This leads to a compromise: a curved VID (Figure 2). The curved model requires less head movements and can cover the peripheral vision.

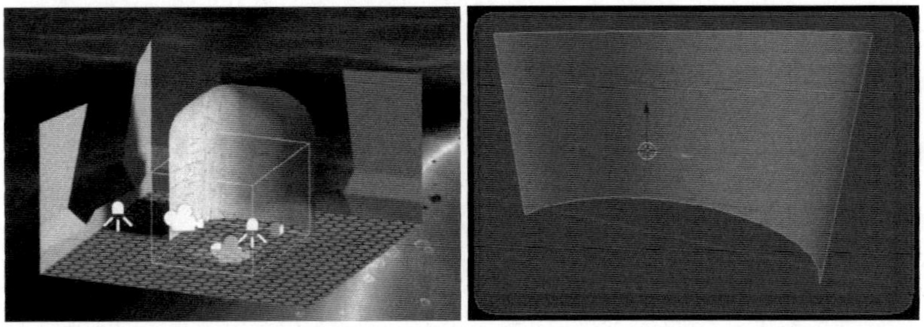

Figure 2. Tested display concepts; (left) dome-like display with avatar in the center; (right) curved display

[1] Suitable in this context means that the professional or serious context is being considered, i.e., less entertainment in favor of productivity.

3.1.1 High Resolution

The "virtual resolution" should be as high as possible to display as much content as possible. Professional image interpreters often use multi-monitor workstations for maximum display of image data as well as instant access to tools. Especially in aerial or satellite image interpretation with huge images or maps one monitor is used for maps, one for the tools (e.g., reporting tool), and the remaining monitors for displaying and working with one or multiple images, e.g., navigating, annotating, modifying, etc.

The challenge is to display huge image data that does not fit into the GPU memory. A typical aerial image easily exceeds 50 megapixels and 1500 MB. Today's game engines and GPU allow a maximum size of 8192x8192 pixels for a texture. Therefore, the image has either to be scaled (loosing details) or split up.

The solution approach is to use tiled rendering. We propose to use a software architecture (Figure 3) with a mapserver, e.g., GeoServer[2], and a slippy map framework, e.g., UnitySlippyMap[3] for Unity3D. This enables the integration of various sources, e.g., vector maps, (geo-referenced) images, markers, etc.

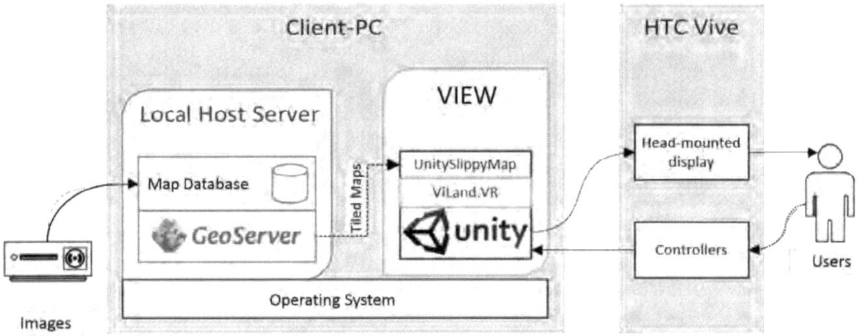

Figure 3. VIEW software architecture using Unity3D game engine and GeoServer for image or map tiling

3.1.2 Image Fidelity

The correct and sound image rendering and display is essential; the user acceptance towards the interpretation system highly correlates with the subjectively recognizable display quality. Professional image interpretation implements technical measures to ensure image fidelity, e.g., special hardware with higher color range (i.e., 10 bit per color channel instead of consumer 8 bit) or calibrated displays. Software measures include lossless compression or accountable metadata management, e.g., for validated documentation processes. The geospatial server approach solves this for our VIEW concept. In the rendering engine, image modifications (e.g., compression) must be disabled, and textures must have uniform, neutral-colored lighting.

Critical and not yet solved issues concerns the VR hardware, in particular the head-mounted display (HMD). Whereas continuous development shows an increase in the HMD display resolutions, some negative effects can still be seen (Anthes et al., 2016), like the latency, screen-door effect, lens distortions, ring effects or light rays. We propose to lay the focus on the usability and the subjective acceptance level for the target group, e.g., by a pre-study and requirement analysis.

3.1.3 Multi Channel Imagery Display

A further requirement is the possibility to display various types of imagery data, i.e., electro-optical (EO), infrared, radar and hyperspectral. Ideally, video streams should be supported as well. Important is the overlay aspect and geo-referencing. It must be possible to display the very same object or area in different visual channels but with identical alignment. For an area this means that the location of the overlaid images must be identical. The mapserver approach solves this by providing access to different map or image sources which can be combined with overlay layers. In VR/VIEW the VID is just the window to the mapserver and the layer switching is propagated to the server by means of standard protocols (e.g., web map service, WMS).

---

[2] www.geoserver.org, open source mapserver server for geospatial data sharing.

[3] https://github.com/jderrough/UnitySlippyMap

3.2 Interaction Concepts

Especially in a professional working context the interaction paradigms must be swift and without risk of fatigue, and, of course, the typical usability requirements must be met. In VR no commonly accepted interaction standards have been defined yet (Hoppe, 2016; Malaika, 2015). Analogous to smartphone gestures development the ongoing VR development will show which emerging interaction paradigms will succeed (Malaika, 2015). Table 1 summarizes some common interaction paradigms.

In general, commonly accepted usability principles like Fitt's Law provide helpful design guidelines. Fitt's Law states user interface requirements for fast and purposeful movements. A study by (Hoppe, 2016) shows that the UI must be quick, intuitive and easy to work with. We adopted the study's strategies in our concept. A special focus is on the workplace suitability, i.e., wearisome sweeping gestures risk fatigue, or the UI must be easy to find and use.

In our concept we focus on the HTC Vive hardware with two controllers. For the interaction with the VID the principles from gesture and smartphone interaction are followed. Display translation can be done via pointing a virtual "laser pointer" and using a controller button dedicated for "left-click" and moving the controller in the designated direction. This is similar to smartphone interaction for moving the display content with one finger. The operations for zooming/scaling and rotating are analogous, i.e., moving controllers apart for zooming, and rotating one controller around a fixed controller for rotation.

The tools must always be ready and easy to use. We propose to adopt the interaction-cube idea from Google Tilt Brush[4]. It should provide easy access to the most common operations, like layer selection, image or scenario reset, contextual assistance.

Table 1. Overview of some common interaction concepts from arbitrarily selected example VR applications

Concept	Manifestation	Example
Locomotion		
With teleportation	Point-to-teleport	Vivecraft
	Teleportation with sphere	The Lab
Without teleportation	No teleportation	Keep Talking
	Float using touchpad	Google Earth VR
	Walk using touchpad or controller	Subnautica
	Walk (room-scale)	The Lab
Interaction With Images		
Zoom	Head movements	Keep Talking
	Stepwise by area selection	World of Comenius
	Dragging finger on touchpad	Batman VR
Pan / move	Press and drag	Google Earth VR
	Head movements	VR Cross View
Manipulations		
Extended functionality	One hand activates functions for other hand	Tilt Brush
	Separate console	Subnautica
Text input	Speech recognition	Starship Cmd. VR
	Large virtual keyboard	Onward
Object manipulation	Controller grip and movement	Nvidia Funhouse

4. APPLICATION

We have verified our concept in a prototype which we implemented using the Unity Game Engine (Figure 4). For the VR integration with the HTC Vive hardware we used *Steam VR* and the feature rich *Virtual Reality Toolkit*[5] (VRTK). To increase the immersion level we implemented the elements of the VIEW concept. This includes scenery, display and interaction paradigms. Gamification aspects involve the integration of assets

[4] www.tiltbrush.com, 3D painting VR application useable with motion controllers.
[5] https://vrtoolkit.readme.io, a collection of scripts for Unity3D for VR development.

from a serious game for image interpretation (Atorf et al., 2019). We adopted the original game's science fiction setting which plays in space in a far future. The virtual image interpretation display is placed on the game's spaceship bridge, but whilst the original game itself has a fixed camera position, in VIEW the player is able to move around and play with various elements of the virtual bridge. Lighting and arrangement of the assets are congruent to the original game that has been developed in close cooperation with the target group of image interpreters. To further increase immersion, we added ambient "sci-fi bridge" background sounds. The virtual image display is curved to completely match the field of vision of the players - if they stay directly in front of it. To fulfill fidelity requirements the virtual display lighting is uniform in neutral white, i.e., no spots, no colored light, no shadows. Especially for radar images this is of high importance because of the black-white nature of the image material.

As explained in the VIEW concept we decided against a 360 degree virtual display because of the increased movements efforts and risk of fatigue. This also holds true for a virtual dome. The virtual display is a curved texture with a slippy map image tiling approach. When the user interacts with the texture, it is modified accordingly, e.g., translation, rotation or scaling. The use can select the type of image on the interaction cube, i.e., switch between the various layers of the underlying mapserver to display different image channels for the displayed map location. In the VIEW prototype users can compare three different image channels, i.e., select between a vector map from OpenStreetMap.org, a high-resolution optical satellite image, and a radar image (Figure 5). In our example setting each image channel displays the same location, the Aswan High Dam in South Egypt (Figure 5). One of the challenges for realizing the prototype was to find usable image material from the same location that met the quality requirements (e.g., up-to date or almost identical recording time, high resolution, integrity, etc.). For gamification, the image interpretation tasks are aligned to a storyline which deals with the Aswan High Dam and sabotage actions of fictional rebels. Users must solve image interpretation tasks, e.g., locate rebel camps or analyze road networks, to help the local authorities capture the rebels. In the training scenario additional challenges have been introduced to adjust the difficulty and cover all learning objectives, e.g., clouded high-resolution optical images which prompt the users to switch to radar imagery which is not affected by atmospheric conditions.

Figure 4. (left) VIEW prototype with bridge scene, teleportation interaction, and curved display for maps and images. (right) 3D model interaction mode

Figure 5. Same location, Aswan High Dam, different image channels: (left) vector map, (center) clouded optical image, (right) radar image

5. DISCUSSION

A preliminary evaluation of the VIEW prototype with n=16 users (average age 35, 14 male) showed an overall positive acceptance rate and good presence level. The game elements have been evaluated positively and as beneficial for immersion. Also positively evaluated were the 3D modes (Figure 4, right), the different image layers and that the user always is in control. Of negative impact was the grip interaction; the location of the button on the HTC Vive controller was unclear to the participants. Table 2 shows positive and negative statements (translated from German). The results indicate that image interpretations can benefit from VR by increased immersion (e.g., by gamification or spatial presence) and by experiencing spatial content or 3D objects in a more natural way.

Table 2. Positive and negative responses to VIEW

Positive	Negative
I felt comfortable on the bridge. I'd very much wanted to continue walking there all the time.	*My hands are not to be seen, that would be cool - I do not know if that's possible.*
The game elements were fun and motivated to carry on with the task.	*The sound does create a higher immersion, but I'd like to have my rest at work.*
Interaction with map was super! Scaling as intuitive as expected. It was super that the map got caught exactly on the [pointing] ray.	*Grip is difficult because the button on the controller is placed oddly.*

A systematic evaluation is going to study the VIEW concept along the dimensions user acceptance, immersion, image quality recognition, and image interpretation effectivity and efficiency (including usability). The hypothesis is that VIEW offers effective and immersive support for image interpretation tasks and helps in training image interpreters. The questionnaires of interest for us are the Igroup Presence Questionnaire (IPQ), the System Usability Scale (SUS) score (Brooke, 1996), and RawTLX to measure workload. A Web-browser 2D replica is going to serve as a reference model. The replica will mimic most of the features of the VR prototype but obviously address presence and immersion at a different level.

6. CONCLUSION

This paper presents the concept study for a VR assistance system for image interpretation, the *Virtual Reality Image Exploitation Workspace* (VIEW). The application field is aerial image interpretation, i.e., detection, recognition, identification and analysis of structures and objects, according to a given task based on optical, infrared or radar imagery. The concept study explored various approaches for virtual displays as well as interaction paradigms matching the demands for professional image interpretations. Our concept proposes a virtual environment enriched with game elements to increase the immersion level. To display high-resolution imagery data a software architecture for tiled rendering is proposed. Gamification elements like real assets from a congruent serious game, an instruction story, or the possibility to explore the environment promote playability and immersion. The architecture includes a slippy map module and a server for geospatial data, e.g., the open source mapserver software. This approach allows including interoperable image data, labels, annotations, etc. from various sources.

ACKNOWLEDGEMENT

The underlying project to this article is funded by the Federal Office of Bundeswehr Equipment, Information Technology and In-Service Support under promotional references. The authors are responsible for the content of this article.

REFERENCES

Anthes, C., Garcia-Hernández, R.J., Wiedemann, M., Kranzlmüller, D., 2016. State of the art of virtual reality technology. *Aerospace Conference*. pp. 1–19.

Atorf, D., Kannegieser, E., Roller, W., 2019. Balancing Realism and Engagement for a Serious Game in the Domain of Remote Sensing. In: Söbke H. Gentile M., A.M. (Ed.), *Games and Learning Alliance*. Springer International Publishing, Cham, pp. 146–156.

Billen, M.I., Kreylos, O., Hamann, B., Jadamec, M.A., Kellogg, L.H., Staadt, O., Sumner, D.Y., 2008. A geoscience perspective on immersive 3D gridded data visualization. *Computers and Geoscience*. 1056–1072.

Brooke, J., 1996. SUS - A quick and dirty usability scale. *Usability Evaluation in Industry*. 189, 4–7.

Connolly, T.M., Boyle, E.A., MacArthur, E., Hainey, T., Boyle, J.M., 2012. A systematic literature review of empirical evidence on computer games and serious games. *Computers & Education*.

Cronin, B., 2015. The hierarchy of needs in virtual reality development. *Medium.com*, URL https://medium.com/@beaucronin/the-hierarchy-of-needs-in-virtual-reality-development-4333a4833acc.

Dörner, R., Göbel, S., Effelsberg, W., Wiemeyer, J., 2016. *Serious Games - Foundations, Concepts and Practice*. Springer International Publishing, Cham.

Freina, L., Ott, M., 2015. A literature review on immersive virtual reality in education: State of the art and perspectives. *Proceedings of eLearning and Software for Education (eLSE)(Bucharest, Romania, April 23--24, 2015)*.

Furumura, T., Chen, L., 2004. Large scale parallel simulation and visualization of 3D seismic wavefield using the earth simulator. *CMES - Computer Modeling In Engineering And Sciences* 6, 153–168.

Ganbatte DevBlog, 2018. Analysing the VR market based on 2017 Steam data. *ganbattegame.com*. URL https://ganbattegame.com/blog/2018/01/14/analysing-the-vr-market-based-on-2017-steam-data/.

Hoppe, A.H., 2016. *Interaktionskonzepte für WIMP-Applikationen in Virtual Reality*. KIT.

Hubona, G.S., Shirah, G.W., 2005. Spatial Cues in 3D Visualization. In: *Ambient Intelligence for Scientific Discovery*. Springer Berlin Heidelberg, pp. 104–128.

Lackey, S.J., Salcedo, J.N., Szalma, J.L., Hancock, P.A., 2016. The stress and workload of virtual reality training: the effects of presence, immersion and flow. *Ergonomics 0139*, 1–13.

Lin, C.-R., Loftin, R.B., 1998. Application of Virtual Reality in the Interpretation of Geoscience Data. In: *VRST '98 Proceedings of the ACM Symposium on Virtual Reality Software and Technology*. ACM Press, New York, New York, USA, pp. 187–194.

Loftin, R.B., Nelson, H.R., 2000. Interaction with geoscience data in an immersive environment. In: *Proceedings IEEE Virtual Reality 2000 (Cat. No.00CB37048)*. IEEE Comput. Soc, pp. 55–62.

Malaika, Y., 2015. GDC Vault - Interaction Design in VR: The Rules Have Changed (Again). *GDC Europe 2015*.

Mazuryk, T., Gervautz, M., 1996. Virtual reality-history, applications, technology and future. *Virtual Reality*.

Nomura, J., Sawada, K., 2001. Virtual reality technology and its industrial applications. *Annual Reviews in Control* 25, pp 99–109.

Ohno, N., Kageyama, A., 2007. Scientific visualization of geophysical simulation data by the CAVE VR system with volume rendering. *Physics of the Earth and Planetary Interiors* 163, 305–311.

Prensky, M., 2001. True Believers: Digital Game-Based Learning in The Military. *Digital Game-based Learning*. 1–18.

Riva, G., Davide, F., IJsselsteijn, W.A., 2003. Being there: Concepts, effects and measurements of user presence in synthetic environments. Ios Press.

Roller, W., Berger, A., Szentes, D., 2013. Technology based training for radar image interpreters. *6th International Conference on Recent Advances in Space Technologies (RAST)*. IEEE, pp. 1173–1177.

Streitz, N.A., Tandler, P., Müller-Tomfelde, C., Konomi, S., 2001. Roomware - Towards the Next Generation of Human-Computer Interaction Based on an Integrated Design of Real and Virtual Worlds. *Human-Computer Interaction in the New Millennium*. Pp. 553–578.

Short Papers

TEXT MINING APPLICATIONS TO FACILITATE ECONOMIC AND FOOD SAFETY LAW ENFORCEMENT

Gustavo Magalhães[1], Brigida Monica Faria[1,2], Luis Paulo Reis[2,3] and Henrique Lopes Cardoso[2,3]
[1]*Escola Superior de Saúde – Instituto Politécnico do Porto (ESS-P.Porto), Porto, Portugal*
[2]*Laboratory of Artificial Intelligence and Computer Science (LIACC), University of Porto, Porto, Portugal*
[3]*Faculty of Engineering, University of Porto (FEUP), Porto, Portugal*

ABSTRACT

Economic and Food Safety Authority receives on a daily basis reports and complaints regarding infractions, delicts and possible food and economic crimes. These reports and complaints can be in different forms, such as e-mails, online forms, letters, phone calls and complaint books present in every establishment. This paper aims to apply text mining and classification algorithms to textual data extracted from these reports and complains in order to help identify if the responsible entity to analyze the content is, in fact, the Economic and Food Safety Authority. The paper describes text preprocessing and feature extraction procedures applied to Portuguese text data. Supervised multi-class classification methods such as Naïve Bayes and Support Vector Machine Classifiers are employed in the task. We show that a non-semantical text mining approach can achieve good results, scoring around 70% of accuracy.

KEYWORDS

Text Mining, Economic and Food Safety, Natural Language Processing, Text Classification, Multi-class Classification

1. INTRODUCTION

Natural Language Processing (NLP) is a discipline between Computer Science and Linguistics (Kurdi, 2016). The extraction of features and patterns present on text can be of great value to data analysis and prediction. Natural language understanding systems allow the conversion of human text samples into a representation that a computer can read and understand (Thanaki, 2017). Therefore, text mining is of paramount importance to NLP research as it is defined as the process of extracting explicit knowledge from unstructured data, i.e., text (Jo, 2019). Text mining encompasses processes such as information retrieval, text classification and clustering, in turn allowing for better natural language perceiving and knowledge extraction (Kao and Poteet, 2007). Economic and Food Safety Authority is Portugal's national criminal police body responsible for supervising and preventing criminal delicts in the food and other economic sectors (*Missão, Visão e Valores*, 2019). Several reports and complaints are directed to Economic and Food Safety Authority regarding infractions, delicts and possible food and economic crimes. These reports and complaints can be submitted in several ways, such as via e-mails, online forms, letters, phone calls or complaint books present in every establishment. The main objective of this paper is to classify entries of text related to reports and complaints, present in Economic and Food Safety Authority's databases, concerning their respective competent institution. This is accomplished using data mining techniques (more specifically, text mining) such as text processing and supervised machine learning. Using text mining and machine learning techniques can help immensely Economic and Food Safety Authority's supervision and prevention mission by speeding up reports and complaints follow-up processes. In turn, this allows for faster response mechanisms and better law enforcing. This classification process is, at the time of writing, completely human-based.

2. RELATED WORK

Text mining is an area with several applications and generally refers to the process of extracting information from text. This process involves several phases such as structuring the input text like addition of linguistic features, removal of words, stemming and conversion to lower case letters, deriving patterns within the structured data and finally the evaluation and interpretation of the results (Feinerer, Hornik and Meyer, 2008).Text classification, text clustering, ontology and taxonomy creation, document summarization and latent corpus analysis are standard techniques in this area. Classical applications in text mining come from the data mining such as document clustering and document classification (Faria, Pimenta and Moreira, 2009).

Chaovalit and Zhou (Chaovalit and Zhou, 2005) establishe comparisons between machine learning approaches (corpus based) to semantic orientation. Machine learning approaches are largely dependent on preprocessing and feature selection and wield more accurate results. Semantic analysis, while more resource friendly and efficient, isn't as accurate and can be skewed due to how human speech is constructed and interpreted (Chaovalit and Zhou, 2005). Joachims (Joachims, 1998) uses Support Vector Machines (SVM) for text categorization. Stemming words is suggested, as well as reducing the number of features from the text by computing the number of times these words occur in any given document and excluding those that are considered stop-words. Inversed document frequency (IDF) is also suggested to improve performance. The paper also establishes comparisons between SVMs and other classifiers such as Naïve Bayes and K-Nearest Neighbors (k-NN) and, concludes that SVMs are well suited for text categorization. A study conducted at the School of Economic and Business, Telkom University (Arusada, Putri and Alamsyah, 2017), investigates how training data optimization can improve a multiclass text classification problem. The case study uses human-defined set of categories (supervised learning) and tries to fit sentences to their respective category. The preprocessing steps applied to the text are tokenization (separating words), stop-word removal, stemming and inverse document frequency weighting. The training data is separated into three conditions: each complaint is directly labeled in its category; a label is given for each sentence manually (built upon its keyword) and a sentence with more than one complaint will be separated into suitable categories for each. Both Naïve Bayes and the SVM classifier were observed to shown similar results across the three categories although a bigger discrepancy is shown when using the first condition (each complaint is directly labeled).

3. METHODOLOGY

This chapter presents the main phases following the Knowledge Discovery in Databases (KDD) methodology. KDD methodology divides in 9 phases from business understanding (application domain), data set selection, data cleaning and preprocessing, feature selection, model creation, model selection, data mining (pattern recognition), results interpretation and applying the knowledge acquired to the business model (Fayyad, Piatetsky-Shapiro and Smyth, 1996). Knowledge discovery should be efficient and able to extract valuable information from the data. It should also be efficient in space and in time to coupe with large data sets (Feldman and Dagan, 1995). Each of the KDD phases are described below along with their respective procedures.

3.1 Data Preparation and Text Preprocessing

The dataset used totaled 120193 entries ranging from the years 2014 to 2018, each having 49 attributes. While there are many attributes in the dataset, most are directly or indirectly related to the content of the complaint or report. The targeted attribute of this article is the "competence" as it is one of the first steps in automating the complaints and reports process. This attribute is divided into 7 categories: ASAE, ASAE and courts, ASAE and another Entity, another Entity, another Entity and Courts, and Courts. From these entries, 5000 samples were selected for further analysis and classification due to computational requirements. Of these, train and test samples were selected with the test size being 30% of the train size.

Preprocessing encompasses several steps such as tokenization, standardization, cleansing of the text data, removal of stop words and stemming or lemmatization (Murugan, Hill and Nolan, 2019). The objective of text processing is returning cleansed tokens from raw text. Tokens are single words or groups of words that can be fed to machine learning algorithms to be able to understand how the data is structured and how it can help predict attributes related to it (Murugan, Hill and Nolan, 2019). As a first step, the text data was tokenized using the NLTK (Natural Language Toolkit) package. NLTK allows the building of Python programs to work with human language data (Bird, Klein and Loper, 2009). This package uses regular expressions (context-independent syntax that represent a variety of character sets that define a search pattern) to tokenize the text (IEEE, 2016). This package also splits standard contractions, treats most punctuation characters as separate tokens, splits of commas and single quotes when these are followed by whitespaces and separates periods that appear at the end of line (*nltk.tokenize.treebank — NLTK 3.4.1 documentation*, no date). The tokens retrieved were evaluated against a set of Portuguese stop words and removed if present. The same was done regarding punctuation and special characters as well as any single character. Furthermore, stemming was applied on the tokens. Stemming is the process in which a word is reduced to its stem, base or root. This stem is shared between words from the same etymological family (Viera and Virgil, 2007). It works by cutting of the end or the beginning of the word, sometimes making the word unreadable or lose its context. Snowball stemmer was chosen due to its support for the Portuguese language, unlike its previous iteration Porter stemmer (Porter, 1980). The Snowball stemmer is faster and is an improvement over the original Porter stemmer (Porter, 2019).

One popular method of feature weighting is term frequency-inverse document frequency (Tf-idf). "Tf-idf" values terms proportionally to their frequency but reduces their weight based on the frequency they appear on the corpus (inverse document frequency). This is illustrated on equation 1 where "n" stands for the total number of documents in the document set and df(t) the document frequency of t (number of documents in the document collection that contain the term t).

$$idf(t) = log\frac{1+n}{1+df(t)} + 1 \qquad \text{(Eq.1)}$$

Term frequency-inverse document frequency weighting was chosen due to its ability to inherently give less importance to terms that appear frequently in most documents and a higher weight to those that appear often in a small collection of documents (Jones, 1973). The vocabulary extracted was based on the length of the features extracted.

3.2 Multinomial Class Prediction

Several multi-class prediction algorithms were employed: Multinomial Naïve Bayes (NB), Support Vector Machines (SVM), Decision Trees (DT), Random Forest (RF), K-Nearest Neighbors (k-NN) and Logistic Regression (LR). The results were then compared. A grid search was conducted which featured options varying from 1-gram (unigrams) to 2-grams (bigrams) and 3-grams (trigrams) with N-gram being a sequence of "N" words. This was done to select the best n-gram range for each classifier. Table 1 shows these results.

Table 1. Best N-grams found for each classifier

Classifier	N-grams
Linear Support Vector	Unigrams and Bigrams
Random Forest	Unigrams
Decision Tree	Unigrams
Logistic Regression	Unigrams and Bigrams
Multinomial Naïve Baye	Trigrams
K-Neighbors Classifier	Unigrams

The selected algorithms were all implemented from the Scikit-learn packages and their default values were not altered to provide a baseline evaluation. To evaluate the models, several scoring measures were calculated: Accuracy, precision, recall and F1. Accuracy is a ratio of correctly predicted observations to the total observations. It is a simple scoring measure and usable in cases where there is similar ratio of false positives and false negatives. Precision measures how precise the model is according to how many of the positive samples are correctly labeled as positive. Recall represents the ratio of correctly predicted positive observations (True Positives) to the total positive observations. It should be used when there is a high False Negative cost. F1 Score is the weighted average of precision and recall. It takes in consideration False Negatives and False Positives and should be used in cases where there is uneven class distribution. Precision, recall and averaged F1 were all calculated with the class weight "macro" setting which takes label imbalance in consideration, as is our case. Central Processing Unit time (CPU time) stands for the amount of time that a central processing unit (CPU) was used since instructions were given. It is measured in clock ticks and is more accurate than the measurement of real time elapsed (Gnu, 2019).

4. RESULTS

Out of the six evaluated classifiers, the most accurate was the support vector machine with linear kernel (70.2%), followed by Logistic Regression Classifier (66.3%) and the Random Forest Classifier (60.5%). Regarding precision, the most precise model was the K-Neighbors Classifier with results of approximately 70% (69.9%), followed by the SVM with 61.9%, and closely followed by the RF with 58.2%.

The Recall scoring measure was observed to have similar results at the lower end of the spectrum between Multinomial NB and K-Neighbors Classifier (23.8% and 20.3% respectively). The SVM reached predictions of 50% (49.9) with the second best being the Decision Tree (39.2%) which had a slightly higher percentage than the LR with 38.2%. The weighted average between precision and recall (F1 score) calculated for the SVM was 53.1%, the best result of all the classifiers, followed by the RF classifier (40.5%) and DT (40.2%).
All the results outlined above can be seen in Table 2.

Table 2. Scoring for each model fitted.

Model	Accuracy	Precision	Recall	F1
Linear Support Vector	0.702	0.619787	0.499354	0.531114
Random Forest	0.604667	0.582377	0.362279	0.405056
Decision Tree	0.561333	0.415173	0.391984	0.401897
Logistic Regression	0.662667	0.44028	0.38222	0.396264
Multinomial Naive Bayes	0.538667	0.565695	0.237704	0.233666
K-Neighbors Classifier	0.484	0.699205	0.202965	0.175576

It was observed that some of the predicted labels had individual F1 scores of 0, which meant that a prediction was not established. This, in turn lowers the weighted F1 score. On one hand, the Support Vector Machine model was able to achieve high F1 scoring, approximately 53%, and high accuracy (70.2%). It was also observed that it had the highest scores for each measure but precision, achieving the second best result with approximately 62%. On the other hand, the SVM model was the second slowest model to train with 2.2 Central Processing Unit time while the fastest model trained was the Random Forest (0.82). The central processing unit time (CPU time) for each model trained was also calculated, as seen in Figure 1.

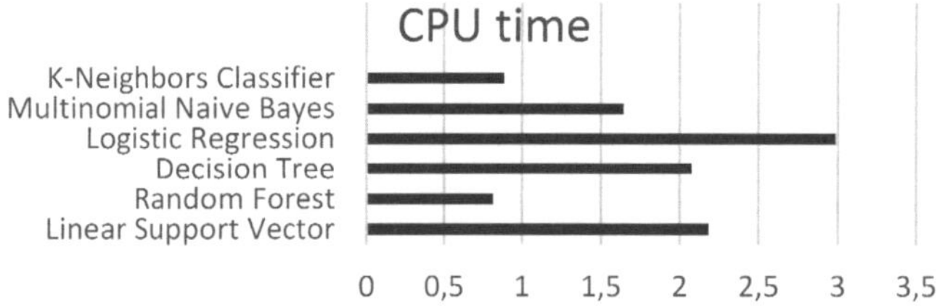

Figure 1. Central Processing Units Time (CPU Time) for each model fitted

Multinomial Naïve Bayes, although expected to be faster than the Random Forest Classifier, had mixed results regarding CPU time (1.64). Inconsistent results were also observed regarding prediction scoring with low recall and F1-score which can be explained by labels with no predictions. Although baseline results demonstrated high accuracy (~70%) regarding the Linear Support Vector model, F1 scoring was observed to be average (~53%). The LSVC was the second slowest model to train despite achieving the best results. However, CPU time is a measure that can be influenced by several factors external to the models and was only calculated to establish comparisons between the models and how each model fared regarding their computational performance.

5. CONCLUSION AND FUTURE WORK

This paper provides a comparison between established methods of text classification using supervised machine learning regarding their ability to predict categories in a multi-class example and their computational performance. There are many different algorithms that can be used to classify textual data, with varying degrees of success and speed. The algorithms chosen here were selected due to their established capabilities and lower processing requirements. It was concluded that the support vector machine classifier outperformed the others by a significant margin regarding every measure. Since the macro setting was considered when calculating the F1 score, the metric was biased towards the least populated classes. In turn, this can mean that the smaller labels were misclassified. In addition, the SVM classifier was shown to have higher precision than recall which means that the classifier predicts many actual true positive labels as true positives (high precision) but fails to predict a lot of the relevant items from the total amount of relevant items (low recall). Even though the number of tools available to conduct text mining procedures in the Portuguese language is expanding, these are still lacking when comparing to the English language. This, in turn, makes it harder to conduct text mining procedures on Portuguese unstructured data and even more so when conducting lexical analysis due to the lack of Portuguese lemmatizers. Furthermore, grammatical errors are prone to increase the number of features of the data and, because of this, spelling correction applied on the input data can help reduce dimensionality and increase the classifiers' performance but at the cost of preprocessing run times. The process described in this article can be helpful to automate classification tasks. One such case is the attribution of "competence" to each complaint and report directed to Economic and Food Safety Authority. This application has a positive impact on the speed which complaints and reports are analyzed and processed, meaning faster responses, swifter inspections and law enforcing.

ACKNOWLEDGEMENT

The authors would like to thank the IA.SAE – "Inteligência Artificial na Segurança Alimentar e Económica" project, funded by the FCT/MCTES through national funds (PIDDAC), as part of the "Programa Iniciativa Nacional Competências Digitais" e.2030 – INCoDe.2030, enrolled in the National Reform Plan.

REFERENCES

Arusada, M. D. N., Putri, N. A. S. and Alamsyah, A., 2017. *Training data optimization strategy for multiclass text classification, 5th International Conference on Information and Communication Technology, ICoIC7 2017*, 0(c). doi: 10.1109/ICoICT.2017.8074652.

Bird, S., Klein, E. and Loper, E., 2009. *Natural Language Processing with Python - Analyzing Text with the Natural Language Toolkit*.

Chaovalit, P. and Zhou, L., 2005. *Movie Review Mining: a Comparison between Supervised and Unsupervised Classification Approaches*, 00(C), pp. 112c-112c. doi: 10.1109/hicss.2005.445.

Faria, B. M., Pimenta, R. and Moreira, J., 2009. *Projects of Fisioterapia and Terapia Ocupacional: A Classification Approach using Text Mining in R*, in Rocha, Á. et al. (eds) *Sistemas e Tecnologias de Informação*. APPACDM. Póvoa de Varzim, Portugal: 4ª Conf. Ibérica de Sistemas e T. de Informação, Sistemas e Tecnologias de Informação, pp. 367–372.

Fayyad, U., Piatetsky-Shapiro, G. and Smyth, P., 1996. *From Data Mining to Knowledge Discovery in Databases, Al Magazine*.

Feinerer, I., Hornik, K. and Meyer, D., 2008. *Text Mining Infrastructure in R*, Journal of Statistical Software, 25(5).

Feldman, R. and Dagan, I., 1995. *Knowledge Discovery in Textual Databases (KDT)*, The First International Conference on Knowledge Discovery and Data Mining (KDD), pp. 112–117. doi: 10.1.1.47.7462.

IEEE, 2016. *Standard for Inf. Technology — Portable Operating System Interface (POSIX ®) Technical, IEEE Xplore*.

Jo, T., 2019. *Text Mining Concepts, Imp., Big Data Challenge*, in Springer, pp. 3–6. doi: 10.1007/978-3-319-91815-0.

Joachims, T. (no date) 'Text Categorization with SVM: Learning with Many Relevant Features', pp. 2–7.

Jones, K. S. (1973) 'Index term weighting', *Inf. Storage and Retrieval*, 9(11), pp. 619–633. doi: 10.1016/0020-0271(73)90043-0.

Kao, A. and Poteet, S. R., 2007. *Natural language processing and text mining*. doi: 10.1007/978-1-84628-754-1.

Kurdi, M. Z., 2016. *Natural Language Processing and Computational Linguistics*.

Missão, Visão e Valores, 2019. Available at: https://www.asae.gov.pt/asae20/missao-visao-e-valores.aspx (Accessed: 29 April 2019).

Murugan, A., Hill, C. and Nolan, T., 2018. *Practical Text Analytics: Maximizing the Value of Text Data*.

nltk.tokenize.treebank — NLTK 3.4.1 documentation, 2019. Available at: https://www.nltk.org/_modules/nltk/tokenize/treebank.html#TreebankWordTokenizer (Accessed: 24 April 2019).

Porter, M. F., 1980. *An algorithm for suffix stripping*, Program. doi: 10.1108/eb046814.

Thanaki, J., 2017. *Python Natural Language Processing,* Packt Publishing Ltd, ISBN: 978-1-78712-142-3.

Viera, A. F. G. and Virgil, J., 2007. *Uma revisão dos algoritmos de radicalização em língua portuguesa*, Inf. Research.

REDDIT SENTIMENT ANALYSIS TO IMPROVE ELECTION PREDICTIONS

Bryant Hwang
Korea International School, South Korea

ABSTRACT

Despite high rates of past success, the majority of polling agencies were unable to predict the outcome of the 2016 United States presidential election between Hillary Clinton and Donald Trump. Further research has hypothesized that these agencies underestimated the amount of support for Trump and overestimated the representation of recent college graduates. Sentiment analysis of posts on popular social media sites presents promising possibilities for better gauging public opinion. In our research, we analyze positive and negative sentiment in Reddit posts from key dates during the 2016 election that mention either candidate. The results of our study match the results of a poll conducted by the New York Times, which showed that public opinion for Trump tended to stay consistent while Clintons positive sentiment decreased over time. Our study also shows that public opinion expressed on Reddit changed drastically in accordance to major events, like debates and email controversies. Alone, our work in sentiment analysis does not produce statistically significant enough results to predict the final outcome of an election, but having the ability to gauge public opinion through social networks is a powerful way that polling agencies and researchers can strengthen their predictions in real time.

KEYWORDS

Sentiment Analysis, Election Prediction, Social Media, Reddit, Aylien

1. INTRODUCTION

Despite prior consistent success in predicting the outcomes of presidential elections, only fifteen out of 150 polls predicted Donald Trumps victory in the 2016 race (RealClearPolitics, 2019). This is a remarkable decrease from the 80% of pollsters that accurately predicted Barack Obamas victory against Mitt Romney in 2012 (RealClearPolitics, 2019). The American Association of Public Opinion Research conducted a study on this seemingly irrational result that narrowed down the the cause to three main reasons: the nonresponse bias, Shy Trumper hypothesis, and social desirability bias ("Election Polls in the U.S.").

The nonresponse bias is the idea that people continually refuse to respond to surveys, which caused pollsters to over- estimate the number of college graduate voters ("Election Polls in the U.S."). The Shy Trumper hypothesis states that Trump advocates hide their preference for Trump and is closely related to the social desirability bias, which is the idea that people vote for the candidate that is more favorably viewed by society ("Election Polls in the U.S."). Combined, the Shy Trumper hypothesis and the social desirability bias caused pollsters to underestimate the number of Trump supporters.

The presence of social media is quickly becoming influential in major elections. Both Barack Obama and Mitt Romney used social media sites like YouTube, Instagram, Facebook, Twitter, Tumblr, Pinterest, and Spotify to reach their younger constituents, but Obama had a much higher follower count: compare 18.5 million to 850 thousand followers (Pardee, 2019). More recently, Donald Trump used his Twitter feed to reach his 15.4 million followers.

In this study, we aim to evaluate the use of social media to predict the outcome of presidential elections. We use Google BigQuery and SQL to analyze sentiment on Reddit, a popular online forum. Reddit contains threads with diverse topics and is a far-reaching social media site, which gives us a variety and abundance of natural language data.

2. RELATED WORKS

The relationship between the sentiment analysis of social media posts and the offline political landscape has been a controversial matter. A few political analysts claim that the Twittersphere shows political opinion to a certain extent, but others fear that the majority of comments on social media compose a pointless bubble. Tumasjan et al., however, have found that the frequency a political party is mentioned online has high correlation with the actual offline political landscape; most of the time, these numbers were found to be similar to the traditional election poll results and were sometimes found to have a higher correspondence to the true results than the traditional election polls.

Previous research done by Tumasjan et al. involved acquiring Tweets and checking if online Tweets mirrored offline political sentiment (2019). They used the Linguistic Inquiry and Word Count text analysis to determine if the sentiment of each message was positive, negative, or neutral towards a certain political party or politician. They concluded that Twitter was indeed used for political deliberation and reflected the offline political landscape.

We combine these two methods to analyze Reddit data: the volume of data and a sentiment analysis algorithm used by Gayo-Avello et al (2019).

3. METHODOLOGY

We analyze the frequency of certain occurrences and the sentiment of politically-related posts on Reddit, a popular internet forum. We use Reddit because it has high traffic and organizes its conversations by topic, which would give us a large amount of data about public opinion.

3.1 Dataset

We gather original posts (OPs) and responses to OPs that contain any combination of Donald, Trump, Hillary, or Clinton (case insensitive). We also restrict our data to a few key dates from the 2016 presidential election, presented in Table 1.

Table 1. Key Dates from The Presidential Election

Date	Event
July 18-21, 2016	Republican National Convention
July 25-28, 2016	Democratic National Convention
September 9, 2016	Clinton calls Trump voters ignorant deplorables
September 26, 2016	First presidential debate
October 7, 2016	Trumps grab her by the pussy remarks surface
October 9, 2016	Second presidential debate
October 28, 2016	FBI reviewed new evidence Clinton emails
November 7, 2016	Day before the election

3.2 Volume Analysis

We first analyzed the Reddit traffic each candidate received and then compared it to the actual election. In a simple meta- analysis, we check if the number of times a candidate is mentioned online, without analyzing for sentiment, can predict the outcome of an election.

3.3 Sentiment Analysis

We use Aylien to classify each post as containing positive, negative, or neutral sentiment towards Clinton or Trump. We discard the neutral posts. The probability of candidate c1 winning the election is proposed to be where the positive/negative value of a candidate is the percent- age of data for that candidate with that sentiment multiplied by the number of Reddit posts that candidate has.

$$p(c1) = \frac{pos(c1) + neg(c1)}{pos(c1) + neg(c1) + pos(c2) + neg(c2)}$$

4. RESULTS AND DISCUSSION

4.1 Volume Analysis

In the entire dataset we collected, Clinton and Trump were mentioned approximately equally as many times, with Trumps name being more frequent on July 18th-21st and October 7th and Clintons name being more frequent on September 9th and October 28th. These results, however, had a mean absolute error (MAE) of 18.5%. With such a high MAE, we conclude that volume analysis alone is not enough to predict who will win the election and move on to sentiment analysis.

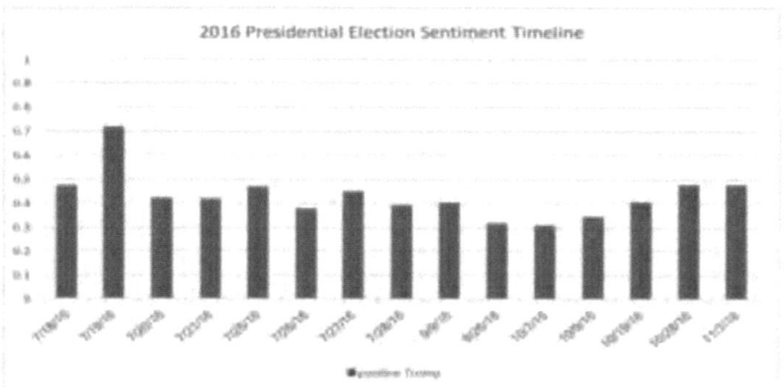

Figure 1. Positive Sentiment for Donald Trump

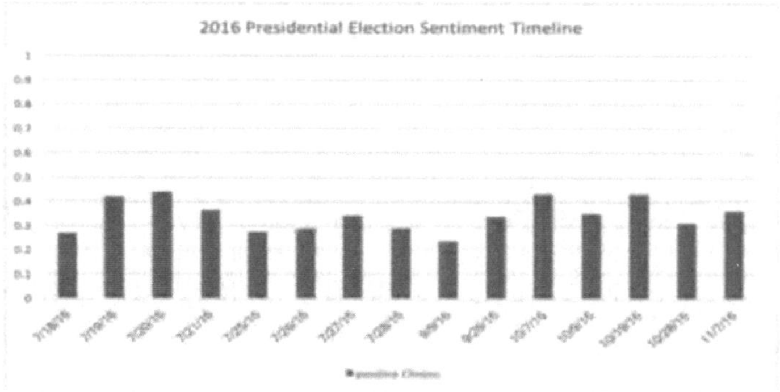

Figure 2. Positive Sentiment for Hillary Clinton

4.2 Sentiment Analysis

According to our data, the trend for people who positively viewed Trump was very consistent with only a few variances near the end of the campaigning period. However, the trend for people who positively viewed Clinton depreciated as time went by. We hypothesize that this is because of the email scandal that she suffered.

Figures 1 and 2 above show the positive sentiment for both candidates. The average positive sentiment was 42.8% for Trump and 34.3% for Clinton; interestingly, the majority of users seemed to dislike both candidates.

The results in Figures 1 and 2 correlate with the results from a New York Times exit poll: 73% of the people who voted for Trump believed that Clinton was neither honest nor trustworthy, and 71% of Clinton voters thought the same of Trump [25]. In the same study, when asked if Clinton was more qualified to serve as president, 89% of Trump voters responded that she was not, with similar results for Clinton voters [25].

The data from Reddit reflects a similar trend, showing that both candidates had mostly negative comments written about them. The graph presented in Figure 2 demonstrates that Trump had the least positive comments on October 7th, 2016, the same day that the video of Trump bragging about groping women surfaced on the internet. At this point of the presidential election, FiveThirtyEight gave Trump an 18.2% chance of winning the election. After this day, Trumps positive sentiment rises until election day.

In Figure 2, Clinton hits her lowest point in positive sentiment on September 9th, which was when Clinton called Trump supporters deplorables. On the other hand, her highest point was on July 20th, the day Trump was announced as the Republican candidate at the RNC, even though she had not been officially announced as the Democratic candidate yet. However, Clintons positive sentiment declined when the DNC chair Wasserman Schultz resigned after an email leak on July 25th; afterwards, Clinton was unable to achieve increasing or constant positive sentiment. In the end, she trailed behind Trump by 11.1% the day before the election.

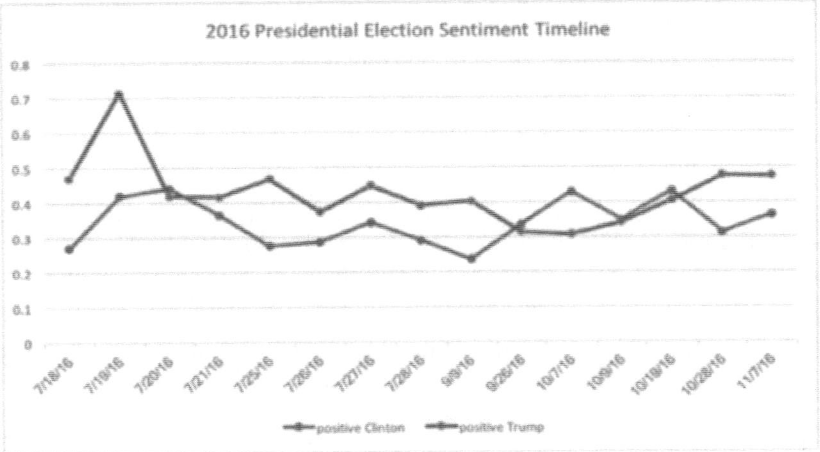

Figure 3. Combined Positive Sentiment for Both Candidates

5. CONCLUSION

Our research shows that the sentiment of relevant Reddit posts corresponded with results from election polls during the campaign season, which suggests that sentiment analysis is a viable avenue for predicting election results. We do, however, need to address some challenges if we are going to use sentiment analysis as a major tool for election prediction.

The first is that Reddit offers no location data, but location is an important part of the United States electoral college. Because the US does not elect presidents with the popular vote, who voted where matters. We also have no way of knowing if some geographical regions are overrepresented.

We also have to consider the prevalence of fake news, robots, and Russian interference. Fake accounts can corrupt data by misrepresenting the views of real people, and Russian interference, a heated topic during the election, can manipulate other people's thoughts. Russian interference was a significant problem for Twitter, which admitted that over 50,000 accounts were involved. Another source states that up to 45% of Trumps follower base could be made up of spam or fake accounts, which could have inflated his Reddit positive sentiment. Eliminating bias and filtering unwanted data is an important issue in sentiment analysis, but sentiment analysis is proving itself to be a successful way of gauging the publics view of presidential candidates. With improvement, sentiment analysis could be used during the election cycle to help understand how much the population likes a candidate, which seems to be the most important factor in winning an election.

REFERENCES

Beaumont, A. (2019). US election final results: how Trump won. Retrieved from http://theconversation.com/us-election-final-results-how-trump-won-69356

Bort, J. (2019). Twitter Has a Big Problem with Fake User Accounts. Retrieved from https://www.businessinsider.com/twitter-has-a-big-problem-with-fake-user-accounts-2012-8

Ceron, A., Curini, L., & Iacus, S. (2019). How pollsters could use social media data to improve election forecasts.

Retrieved from https://www.washingtonpost.com/news/monkey-cage/wp/2016/12/21/using-these-4-steps-pollsters-could-use-social-media-data-to-improve-election-forecasts/?noredirect=on&utm_term=.3a3779d0ed43

Evans, P. (2019). Can social media predict election results?. Retrieved from https://www.bbc.com/news/election-us-2016-37942842

Gayo-Avello, D., Metaxas, P., & Mustafaraj, E. (2019). Limits of Electoral Predictions using Twitter. *Proceedings of the Fifth International Conference On Weblogs and Social Media.*

Goyder, J., Warriner, K., & Miller, S. (2019). Evaluating Socioeconomic Status (SES) Bias in Survey Nonresponse. *Journal of Official Statistics.*

Hoffman, A. (2019). http://time.com. Retrieved from http://time.com/5268499/melania-trump-cyberbullying-humor/

Ingram, M. (2019). The Facebook Armageddon. Retrieved from https://www.cjr.org/special_report/facebook-media-buzzfeed.php

Kennedy, C., Blumenthal, M., Clement, S., Clinton, J., Durand, C., & Franklin, C. et al. (2019). An Evaluation of 2016 Election Polls in the U.S. - AAPOR. Retrieved from https://www.aapor.org/Education-Resources/Reports/An-Evaluation-of-2016-Election-Polls-in-the-U-S.aspx

Krombholz, K., Merkl, D., & Weippl, E. (2012). Fake identities in social media: A case study on the sustainability of the Facebook business model. *Journal Of Service Science Research*, *4*(2), 175-212. doi: 10.1007/s12927-012-0008-z

Matsa, K., & Shearer, E. (2019). News Use Across Social Media Platforms 2018. Retrieved from https://www.journalism.org/2018/09/10/news-use-across-social-media-platforms-2018/

Mitchell, A., Holcomb, J., Barthel, M., & Stocking, G. (2019). Reddit news users more likely to be male, young and digital in their news preferences. Retrieved from https://www.journalism.org/2016/02/25/reddit-news-users-more likely-to-be-male-young-and-digital-in-their-news-preferences/

The role of technology in the presidential election. (2019). Retrieved from https://www.economist.com/united-states/2016/11/20/the-role-of-technology-in-the-presidential-election

The role of technology in the presidential election. (2019). Retrieved from https://www.economist.com/united-states/2016/11/20/the-role-of-technology-in-the-presidential-election

Where polling failed, Facebook prevailed. (2019). Retrieved from https://www.economist.com/graphic-detail/2016/11/30/where-polling-failed-facebook-prevailed

Pardee, T. (2019). Infographic: How Obama, Romney (and Friends) Are Using Social Media. Retrieved from https://adage.com/article/campaign-trail/infographic-obama-romney-social-media/236798

Perez, S. (2019). Analysis of social media did a better job at predicting Trump's win than the polls –

TechCrunch. Retrieved from https://techcrunch.com/2016/11/10/social-media-did-a-better-job-at-predicting-trumps-win-than-the-polls/

RealClearPolitics - Election 2012 - General Election: Romney vs. Obama. (2019). Retrieved from https://www.realclearpolitics.com/epolls/2012/president/us/general_election_romney_vs_obama-1171.html

reddit.com Traffic Statistics. (2019). Retrieved from https://similarweb.com/website/reddit.com

Saru, N. (2019). What Is Twitter Doing about Fake News? - TechAcute. Retrieved from https://techacute.com/twitter-fake-news/

Syed, I. (2019). Retrieved from https://s3.amazonaws.com/app_usa_prod_eqffnyamdzrb/pdf6099%20%283%29.pdf

Tumasjan, A., Sprenger, T., Sandner, P., & Welpe, I. (2019). Predicting Elections with Twitter: What 140 Characters

Reveal about Political Sentiment. *Proceedings Of The Fourth International Conference On Weblogs And Social Media.*

Woolf, N. (2019). How to solve Facebook's fake news problem: experts pitch their ideas. Retrieved from https://www.theguardian.com/technology/2016/nov/29/facebook-fake-news-problem-experts-pitch-ideas-algorithms

Wortham, J. (2019). Presidential Campaign on Social Media. Retrieved from http://archive.nytimes.com/www.nytimes.com/interactive/2012/10/08/technology/campaign-social-media.html

Zurcher, A. (2019). Clinton emails - what's it all about?. Retrieved from https://www.bbc.com/news/world-us-canada-31806907

CLOUD AGNOSTIC STREAM ANALYTICS

Chandan Kumar
Ryerson University,
beCloudready, Toronto, Canada

ABSTRACT

As machine learning is getting more and more mainstream, increasing number of public cloud providers are providing machine learning related APIs such as Text Analytics, ANN, Auto ML (pretrained) APIs which are on one hand make life easier for many application developers, but on the other hand brings API management complexity in hybrid or multi cloud environment.

The current evolution of these ML (machine learning) APIs leads to more coherent integration with the current cloud provider and makes it harder to switch between the providers. These leads to a vendor locked in situation where it becomes difficult for application to easily switch the service provider.

A cloud agnostic framework has been proposed here which would allow to develop modern cloud-based data science, machine learning, AI applications using the proposed framework or similar approaches where the application provider could seamlessly switch between various cloud vendors as well as native OS level APIs painlessly and programmatically. As the subject of data science is so broad that we will focus only on one aspect of it to show case the proof of concept of the framework using sentiment analysis APIs to demonstrate stream analytics capabilities. Same approach could easily be applied on other APIs as well.

KEYWORDS

Bigdata, Stream Analytics, Cloud Agnostic, Sentiment Analytics

1. INTRODUCTION

There are two aspects need to be addressed, when it comes to building stream analytics data pipeline. One being the data science part (building the model, Algorithm), other being the data engineering part, which involves preparing the data and deploying it in production environment. Often deploying in production environment is time consuming, expensive and difficult to maintain due to the fact that deploying a good model into production has IT related complexity such as security, compliance, high availability and performance.

In this paper we are trying to solve both problems from the business use case and application standpoint rather than from a data scientist standpoint, which mean this paper will focus on effectively utilizing available solution to help rapid application development rather than creating brand new model we are doing so by using cloud native APIs.

We will be using Python as application development language. Although, Python has inbuild support for NPL and used heavily among the Python community members, the availability of cheap cloud APIs has made it very attractive and easy to use state of the art Algorithms when it comes to any kind of machine learning or sentiment analysis.

As already mentioned, we will be using publicly available social media data (tweets) to build a cloud agnostic sentiment analytics platform (stream analytics platform). As with any other data pipeline, before we could even use these libraries, the biggest challenge will be to parse the tweets and make sure they are ready to be consumed by the API. Few limitations are very common, especially when it comes to sentiment Analysis such as Language issues. Most sentiment analysis libraries only support small percentage of languages notably

In this paper we will be using sentiment analysis use case for demonstrating the stream analytics capabilities using Cloud (SaaS) APIs. The major application of sentiment analysis is applicable to product reviews, political opinions, movie reviews, and even health related trends.

As we are considering streaming the data rather than storing and analyzing it later, we have to do the data preparation on the fly (Huggani et al., 2014). Fortunately, Python has rich set of string manipulation libraries which could help us with these issues. There are plenty of sentiment analysis APIs and libraries available; however, later Cloud that provided APIs have become norm across multiple application to get the best possible outcome. I will be evaluating the following algorithms;

- Google Natural Language API
- Azure Text Analytics API
- AWS Comprehend

Hence our front end will be only a wrapper script which could either run on local machine or on the EC2 or even in AWS Lambda.

2. LITERATURE REVIEW

Vast majority of stream analytics-based research are done on IoT application, which involves stream of data being generated by sensors and which are analyzed on the edge device for certain time window to make quick prediction or trigger some alarm (Sikder et al., 2018). Some researchers such as Jayaraman et al., (2017) are also focused on building a multi-cloud analytics as service concept on semantically enabled hierarchical processing. Ari et al., (2014) implemented Pearson-Product Moment Correlation for analytics and Apriori & FPGrowth algorithms for stream mining inside a popular event stream processing engine called Espe, in which they used both correlation analysis and association rule mining (ARM) over streams. In this context, they used cloud as source of the data rather than destination. Cloud based solution often provides an alternative with no capital requirement where lot of Machine learning APIs are available as service. Huqqani et al., (2014) articulates that various cloud-based solution providers are able to provide cost efficient GPU based solution which outperforms traditional GPU based solution when it comes to performance. In the experiment they explained how various parallel execution on large data set could be used GPU based Cloud solution to achieve higher performance for neural networks. Twitter is a stream-based application where you get instantaneous information, hence the data need to be analyzed on the fly. Researchers in Japan developed real-time earthquake-monitoring systems based on Twitter using streaming API to generate live alerts (Ari et al., 2012). Yang (2017), articulated how streaming solution for IoT devices could be used in large dataset to investigate fog system in certain geographical region for monitoring and alerting system. Nair et al. (2018), introduced a real-time health status prediction system and the user communicate via Twitter. The Twitter data was used as input their Spark base ML libraries to create a predictive system (Sakaki et al., 2010).

3. DESIGN ARCHITECTURE

A text mining task has always been one of the challenging tasks in the field of data analytics simply because of unpredictability of the data source. The data source could come from hundreds of languages which possess another challenge to most of the NPL algorithms as most of them are designed and optimized for English language. Often non-Latin languages possess another challenge in terms of UTF encoding, where if the programmer is not careful, it can easily crash the application.

3.1 Data Ingestion

- Data ingestion is the key to any type of data pipeline or data warehousing solution. Well defined data ingestion method and strategy goes long way to ensure the right data is present in the system for required analytics work. In current implementation data ingestion is very simple which means pulling the tweets from tweeter rest API, but we will ensure that a common API is developed so that in future more data sources could be easily added.

3.2 Data Wrangling

- The concept and importance of data wrangling could not be better explained then the research paper done by Kandel et al., (2011). Later on, Kandel and Heer went on to create in 2012 a data wrangling company called Trifacta
- Data Wrangling mean preparing the data to be ready for analytics work. Simple example could be cleaning up the data by removing stem words, removing not supported languages or anything that deems not necessary for analytics purpose.
- Language detection (Python or Azure)

3.3 Data Analytics

Data analytics in case will involve two aspects.

- Sentiment Analysis.
- Aggregating the sentiment over time series.

Part one will be done by Cloud APIs such as Google Cloud NPL, AWS Comprehend and Azure Text Analytics. The sentiment would be recorded for each and every tweet and will be stored into a data frame/table. We can use either data frame or table in a SQL database to tabulate the time series data and to measure various descriptive statistical associated with the sentiment polarity and magnitude, so analyze what is the overall picture for the topic.

4. APPROACH

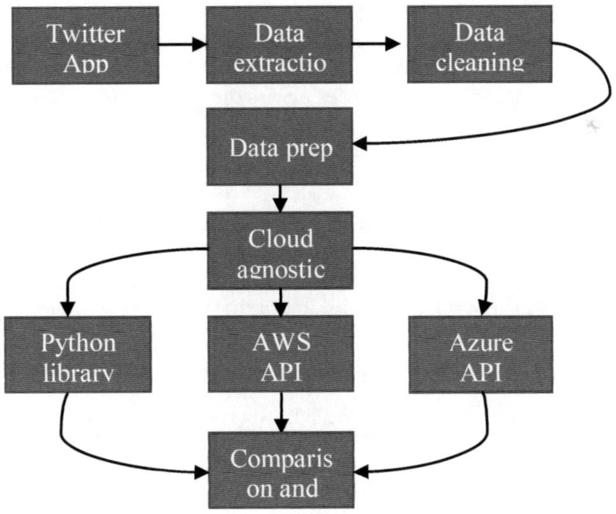

Figure 1. The data pipeline approach used for the application

4.1 Cloud Agnostic API Wrapper

One of the key goals of this project is to have a seamless integration and access to most, if not all, AI APIs in a unified, simplified and cost-efficient manner. While doing so, the project will try to provide a solution where users can avoid all pitfalls of being vendor locked-in. Lately getting vendor locked-in has become a concern among various enterprise. If you deploy your infrastructure in one vendor's public cloud, say Amazon AWS, what will you do if the service fails to meet your standards or if the prices increase? What if the features you need are no longer supported? Sure, there are a couple of other big public Cloud providers – Microsoft Azure and Google Cloud. More vendors are making sure that their technologies are supported across multiple public Clouds. But it can be complicated and time consuming to move your applications and data from one Cloud to another.

The software has been written in a modular fashion [Figure 1] by keeping each service provider, whether native Python libraries or any public cloud APIs. The data structure used to prepare the data, as discussed in data cleaning and data prep section, is Python Pandas data frame.

The project layout shown in the image above depicts the class layout of the application. At the current state of the project it only supports following providers

- AWS
- Azure
- Python text blob

Similarly, more providers could be incorporated.

5. APPLICATIONS

5.1 Small Business, Retail Customers

At the moment, getting access to good quality analytics tool is often expensive, time consuming, and in most cases out of reach for these businesses. This tool could leverage the free tier service provided by most of the Cloud service providers, which would allow them to have access to top quality analytics tool at reasonable price or even free by spreading the quarries across the various providers using the Cloud agnostic API wrapper.

5.2 Enterprises looking for a Cloud Agnostic AI API Service

Enterprises adoption to AI and analytics services have increased dramatically; however, their IT infrastructure to support such massive change has not grown to the same pace. On the other hand, onboarding cost of on-prem AI infrastructure and team is very costly and time consuming. This tool can help them to achieve vendor agnostic interface and implementation to their services and hence providing better flexibility.

5.3 Ability to choose the Best Model for Select Data Sets

With array of algorisms and cloud service providers, it is becoming increasingly difficult to identify which pre-trained model works best for certain data sets. This tool could help developers to archive some level of comparison of different libraries against the same data set.

REFERENCES

Ari, I., Olmezogullari, E., and Çelebi, O.F. (2012). Data stream analytics and mining in the cloud. 4th IEEE International Conference on Cloud Computing Technology and Science Proceedings, *Taipei.* p. 857-862. doi: 10.1109/CloudCom.2012.6427563

Huqqani, A. A., Schikuta, E., & Mann, E. (2014). Parallelized neural networks as a service. 2014 International Joint Conference on Neural Networks (IJCNN), 2282-2289. doi:10.1109/IJCNN.2014.6889742

Jayaraman, P. P., Perera, C., Georgakopoulos, D., Dustdar, S., Thakker, D., and Ranjan, R. (2017) Analytics-as-a-service in a multi-cloud environment through semantically enabled hierarchical data processing. *Softw. Pract. Exper., 47*: 1139– 1156. doi: 10.1002/spe.2432.

Kandel, S., Heer, J., Plaisant, C., Kennedy, J., Frank van Ham, Riche, N.H., Weaver, C., Lee, B., Brodbeck, D., Buono, P., (2011) Research directions in data wrangling: visualizations and transformations for usable and credible data. *Information Visualization, 10* (4), p.271-288. doi: 10.1177/1473871611415994.

Nair, L. R., Shetty, S. D., & Shetty, S. D. (2018). Applying spark-based machine learning model on streaming big data for health status prediction. *Computers and Electrical Engineering, 65*, 393–399.

Sakaki, T., Okazaki, M., and Matsuo. Y. (2010). Earthquake shakes Twitter users: real-time event detection by social sensors. Proceedings of the 19th international conference on World wide web. *ACM*, p. 851-860.

Sikder, A. K., Petracca, G., Aksu, H., Jaeger, T. and Uluagac, A. S. (2018). A survey on sensor-based threats to internet-of-things (IoT) devices and applications. *arXiv preprint arXiv:1802.02041.*

Yang, S. (2017). IoT stream processing and analytics in the fog. IEEE Communications Magazine, 55(8), 21-27. doi:10.1109/MCOM.2017.1600840

BIM CAPACITIES IMPROVED WITH VR TECHNOLOGY IN THE BUILDING PROJECT

Alcínia Zita Sampaio
University of Lisbon, IST, Dep. Civil Engineering
Av. Rovisco Pais, 1049-001 Lisbon, Portugal

ABSTRACT

The potential of Building Information Modelling (BIM) methodology to support a transformation of the processes of design and construction has been evident in the construction industry. A current topic that requires attention is the integration of BIM with Virtual Reality (VR) where the user visualizes a virtual world through interactive devices or a total immersion. By adding VR, the BIM solution can address retrieving and presenting information and increasing efficiency on communication and problem solving in an interactive and collaborative project. BIM + VR allow two main capacities: walkthrough and consulting data, and currently BIM tools allow links to VR plugins in order to achieve both capacities. The objective of the study is to report the improvement of BIM uses with the addition of interactive capacities allowed by VR technology.

KEYWORDS

BIM Methodology, VR Technology, VR+BIM Applications

1. INTRODUCTION

Building Information Modelling (BIM) methodology enables project stakeholders to create information-rich virtual models that help better visualize building projects. There is currently a shift in the AEC (Architecture, Engineering and Construction) industry to embrace BIM as a tool that can assist in integrating the fragmented industry by eliminating inefficiencies and redundancies, improving collaboration and communication, and enhancing overall productivity (Campbell, 2007). BIM is defined as the process of creating building information, stored in a centralized virtual model that can be managed allowing exchanging and sharing building data in an interoperable and reusable way (Azhar et al., 2008). BIM concerns the process of development of a computer generated model representing all disciplines of a building design, and its use in several tasks as design simulation, construction planning or facilities management. The resulting product, a Building Information Model, is a data-rich, intelligent and parametric digital representation of the building project. So, as a first perspective, the result of BIM methodology can be considered as a virtual representation of a building, an object-oriented three-dimensional (3D) model, but is also a repository of project data (Eadie, et al., 2013). The BIM data-model can be easily accessed, facilitating interoperability and exchange of project data with related software applications.

An actual BIM subject that requires research, practical application and software adaptation, is the integration of BIM with Virtual Reality (VR) technology. Current VR devices allow the user to visualize a virtual world and to interact with the virtual space and its components. The main objective, that has been reported, concerns the use of VR system combined with plugins in order to support BIM multiuse throughout the building lifecycle. As so, the VR environment integrates information systems and immersive environments. For that, VR requires devices for interaction with the virtual environment of the building and the construction space. The current target, concerning integrating VR and BIM, is the study of how to use or adapt those VR devices and how to establish links for the presentation of information contained in a BIM model. This is bringing BIM data into a VR environment. Visualizing virtual worlds and interacting with it, is essentially a VR aspect, and creating and manipulating design data, is the essence of BIM, so the link of these two strong capacities should be known and explored. Following this perspective, commercial software houses have been developing advanced BIM + VR products. The use of BIM technology on construction projects has the potential to improve the process by allowing all team members to collaborate in an accurate and efficient way. Unlimited extension of the use of BIM information combines BIM-based software with other advanced technologies (Chen and Luo, 2014). These advanced technologies link the digital to the physical entities and research has already been conducted to investigate the combination of BIM and other technologies. The present reflection involves the link of BIM to VR.

Concerning BIM training, the school has an important role in the education of young entrants in the industry and to equip them with BIM skills, including the additional knowledge about VR+BIM. Regarding current digital 3D modelling technologies, added to design information and provided in mobile equipment, students and professionals can use advanced capabilities of interaction like VR technology, improving the use BIM methodology. The objective of this text is to report some of the most important enhances of BIM uses, when interactive capacity allowed by VR technology is added. A research concerning technologic advances in VR software, as a complement to improve BIM environment's management, was made.

2. VR AND BIM CAPACITIES

Virtual Reality (VR) technology leads to a better communication for key players across the building sector, based on a greater design visualization, contributing to a better understanding of the project (Jiao et al., 2013). The knowledge about the different type of data that can be associated to the set of parameters that identifies each parametric object, base of the BIM modelling process, is of great importance when the team members wants to analyse problems and to discuss alternative solutions. Interacting with the BIM model, in order to visualize the geometry of the elements and to consult the parametric data, is an improvement in the development of a collaborative project. For instance, a VR tour can be applied over a BIM model in order to check, from a facility management perspective, the maintenance schedule (7D/BIM model), or from a project team view, the constructability review (4D/BIM model), supporting decisions making. VR technology can improve BIM methodology, as it allows interaction with 3D/BIM models in two essential ways:

- **Walkthrough** is the most popular as the user can view the 3D model in a virtual environment in real time from multiple perspectives of the building, from inside or outside;
- **Consulting data** concerns the possibility to retrieve information centralized in a BIM model, namely, data associated with parameters that compose the parametric objects used in the modelling process.

2.1 Walkthrough

VR technology allows the user to observe artificial world, by walking through outside and inside and see everything around, and also reach out touching objects in real time. The immersive VR spaces are created using a combination of computer graphics, wireless tracking technology, headsets, high-definition projectors, polarized glass and more, all working together to create interactive and real-life experiences (VRS, 2017). The world of 3D virtual design and engineering is a fast growing field and the current perspective is the use of VR applied over the BIM model improving the construction nD activity. VR technology has seen developments in recent years and has been applied in architectural, engineering and construction fields. Currently architects, engineers and other construction specialists are already exploring the length and breadth of the joint RV+BIM technology in a walkthrough base:

- **Oculus Rift** is a real-time viewer application with interactive capacities, developed by the Oculus Company, and can be implemented as a plug-in in Revit (Rift, 2017The device provides stereoscopic 3D view and includes a gyroscope, an accelerometer and a magnetometer to determine the orientation of the user's head in the real world. In the case of the Rift the stereoscopic 3D view is implemented by means of split-screen rendering, where the left half of the screen corresponds to the left eye, and vice versa (Figure 1);

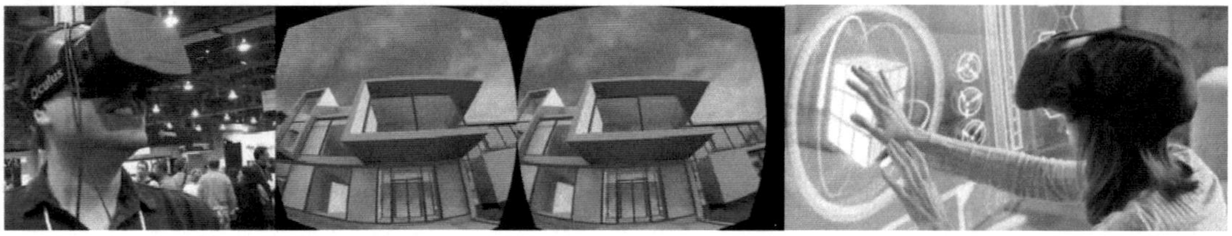

Figure 1. Left and right half of the screen corresponds to each eye [20] (Rift, 2017) and ttouchable holograms

- The use of **hologram projections** in the construction activity, enables the end user to experience different textures or choose from a variety of in-built texture formats the required aspect for the project (Cherian, 2016) (Figure 1). The Revit model can be manipulated using hologram projections supporting a building collaborative design;
- With the **Enscape** Revit plugin, the user is able to quickly explore different design options in projects t and so it has become a standard application in projects worldwide (Enscape3D, 2017). A walkthrough using Enscape for real-time visualization and rendering enables the project team to accurately communicate with engineering design, clients and stakeholders, improving the collaborative design. The ability to walkthrough inside BIM models and to regenerate design changes without leaving Revit is of a great importance and time saver (Figure 2);

Figure 2. Walkthrough capacity using Enscape Revit plugin and an igloo BIM cave

- **CAVE** (Cave Automatic Virtual Environment) platforms have been developed for immersive VR experience as they track user's head and control stick usually with 6 degrees of freedom, to navigate inside the virtual environment and interact with the contents of a 3D model including a 3D (BIM model (Nikolic, 2017). A CAVE takes normally the form of a cube-like space in which images are displayed by a series of projectors, but an Igloo BIM cave was recently developed (Figure 2).

2.2 Consulting Data

Once the model is inside the VR environment, things like materials, lighting, furniture and other small details that make the VR experience feel real, are added. This is the concept of walkthrough, but BIM contains data and it is convenient to explore BIM-data while walking inside a virtual model. VR can play an important role at all stages of the design-to-construction process, from evaluating design options and showcasing proposals, to designing out errors and ironing out construction and serviceability issues before breaking ground on site. Fully interactive VR software has extremely high performance demands, during a tour, but additional technology capacities concerning model-data retrieving is required when bringing BIM data into a VR environment.

The model is centrally hosted and access to project data is permissions-based, and it can be accessed by project teams anywhere. So, when collaborative projects are discussed between firms, they consult BIM data in models hosted on clouds. In addition, the capacity of consulting BIM data can be improved with VR devises applied directly over the BIM model. Several plugins or BIM viewer allows consulting data from the 3D/BIM model and now there is a new class of mobile apps available that let project teams experience building plans in 3D:

- Autodesk 360 allows the integration of the team in collaborative projects, as every modification in a BIM model is displayed in a handy timeline for everyone to see (Autodesk360, 2017). Along with showing the 3D model, Autodesk 360 display every sheet embedded in the uploaded Revit model (Figure 3). So all data can be consulted, analysed and changed, refining the project in a collaborative environment;

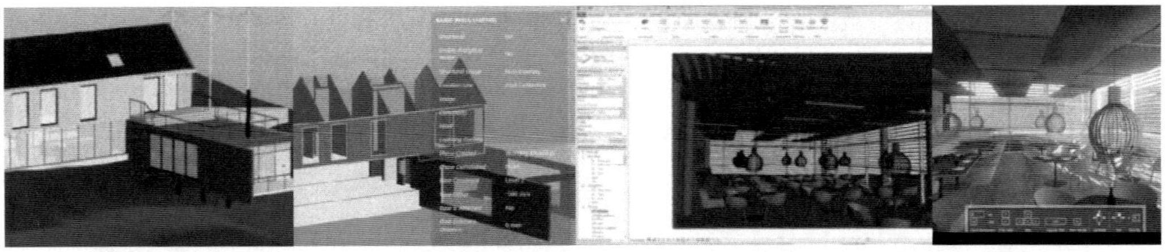

Figure 3. Using Autodesk 360 in a collaborative project and Enscape plugin of Revit to access data

An accessible high end visualization and virtual reality of a BIM model is obtain using the VR plugin of Revit, the **Enscape** (Enscape3D, 2017). It was previously mentioned just the walkthrough capacity, but Enscape also allows, together with Revit, to consult data. Inside Revit is possible to access the plugin Enscape and the user can observe both models in Revit and in Enscape (Figure 3). In Revit the user can consult the rich-data incorporated in the 3D/BIM model and in Enscape, can interact in a virtual space. So, all changes in Revit are immediately available to evaluate in Enscape.

- Combining BIM and VR, based in linking Revit with **Covise**, VR software (Covise, 2017), projects as well as data can be visualized in VR and reviewed 1:1 scale even in team meetings. Compared to various existing approaches, the new approach is to have bidirectional data exchange between the systems and as so, changes in Revit are directly reflected in Covise software and vice versa, continuously updating the model and its underlying database (Figure 4).

Figure 4. Interacting with Covise software and system coordination and constructability review using Web3D.

- Some progress has been made on VR techniques but only recently the link to BIM methodology has being made. A VR system should be combined with in-use applications to support multi-disciplinary users throughout construction lifecycle. Jiao et al. (2013) presents a pilot cloud framework regarding an environment utilizing **web3D**. It can be applied in several BIM uses supporting the AEC industry, namely, in system coordination and constructability review tasks (Figure 4). So technical solutions to key issues such as authoring, publishing, and composition are designed. The proposed environment is seamlessly integrated into in-use information systems and therefore enjoys greater usability.

The BIM includes semantics into the construction process (e.g., structure, air conditioning/ventilation, mechanical, electrical, plumbing, etc.) and data for simulation (materials/structure resistance, energy consumption, thermal calculations, lighting, acoustic simulations, etc.). These issues must be addressed throughout the construction project but mainly, at the beginning during the design phase to fulfil the customer's requirements, during the maintenance phase to control the building. Any BIM tool allows the consult of BIM data and so it support management and maintenance within a collaborative team.

VR+BIM enable architects and designers to better communicate design within the team members and with the client. The advantage to using VR is in the communication of ideas, concepts and the vision for the building. This enables all the parties to more quickly reach a full appreciation of the building plan and the distinct discipline projects. The BIM + VR topic require dissemination; application in real cases and pointed out, in reports, achievements and limitation; following the technologic advances that supports the BIM use and the visualization of data, in real time while the interacting with the model made possible by VR technology. BIM + VR provide an opportunity to analyze and explore BIM models within virtual environments.

In construction activity the use of VR capacities brings interesting potentials. Presenting BIM models of projects in VR environment redefines communication and collaboration in the field and in the office. BIM technology and VR have the ability to innovate the building industry. At a first perspective, many feel the benefits of using a BIM model with VR are only for improving the 3D model for visual aids, but taking a second perception at a BIM model it reveals diverse reasons to adopt BIM with VR. Collaboration in VR can be the future of VR BIM.

3. CONCLUSIONS

Introducing VR interactive capabilities into 3D/BIM models in the construction process is a main way to test virtually and correct a construction project before the realization, as the walkthrough is available as well the visualization of data linked to each parametric object, improving the necessity collaboration within the design team. So, BIM/VR applications can contribute to reduce costs due to the construction of a real mock-up, and to avoid mistakes on site that generates material wastes. Software houses have been demanding the integration of BIM with VR plugins in order to support the development of nD/BIM tasks. The fundamental base of BIM+VR concerns the collaboration as a first step, but the possibility of consult data while walking through the building, improves significantly the use of BIM in design, construction, maintenance and management.

REFERENCES

Autodesk360 (2017) https://bim42.com/2014/07/trying-out-autodesk-360/

Azhar S, Hein M, Sketo B (2013) Building information modelling (BIM): benefits, risks and challenges, http://ascpro.ascweb.org/chair/paper/CPGT182002008.pdf 2008

Campbell DA (2007) Building information modelling: the Web3D application for AEC, Web3D 2007, Italy, April 15–18, 2007, https://www.researchgate.net/scientific-contributions/69864924_Dace_A_Campbell

Chen LJ, Luo H (2012) A BIM-based construction quality management model and its applications, Automation in Construction, 46 (2014) 64–73 http://dx.doi.org/10.1016/j.autcon.2014.05.009

Cherian S (2016) Integrating BIM and Virtual Reality – The Next Big Thing?, https://www.linkedin.com/pulse/integrating-bim-virtual-reality-next-big-thing-sarita-cherian

Covise (2017) BIM goes virtual, https://thebimhub.com/2016/07/14/bim-goes-virtual/#.Wh8IvamqmaQ

Eadie R, Browne M, Odeyinka H, McNiff S (2013) BIM implementation throughout the UK construction project lifecycle: An analysis, Automation in Construction, 36 (2013) 145–151. http://dx.doi.org/10.1016/j.autcon.2013.09.001

Enscape3D (2017) Real-time rendering for Revit, Sketchup and Rhino, https://enscape3d.com/

Jiao Y, Zhang S, Li Y, Wang Y, Yang BM (2013) Towards cloud Augmented Reality for construction application by BIM and SNS integration, Automation in Construction, 33 (2013) 37–47. http://dx.doi.org/10.1016/j.autcon.2012.09.018

Nikolic D (2017) Headsets, Caves, AR and VR – what's the reality for construction?, http://www.bimplus.co.uk/technology/hea8dsets-cav6es-ar-and-vr-w7hats-reality/

Rift (2017) Oculus Rift, https://www.oculus.com/experiences/rift/

VRS - Virtual Reality Society (2017) How do virtual reality glasses work?, https://www.vrs.org.uk/virtual-reality-gear/glasses/how-do-they-work.html

ECG SIGNAL ANALYSIS OF EARLY AND LATE RISERS: A POPULATION BASED CASE CONTROL STUDY

Muhammad Hassan[a], Sami Ur Rahman[b] and Zhou You[a1]
[a]*College of Computer Science and Technology, Jilin University, China*
[b]*Department of Computer Science and Information Technology, University of Malakand, Khyberpakhtunkhwa, Pakistan*

ABSTRACT

This paper investigates the effect of early rising on heart rhythm. We have analyzed the ECG signals of early (or Controls) and late (or Cases) risers. In the study we obtained ECG signals of two hundred healthy humans having age range between twenty and thirty-five years. The twenty features of ECG signals were analyzed in the experiment. The significant difference in the two groups was reported based on the two features of the ECG signals i.e. QRS and QTc. Cases were associated with the variations in QRS complex and QTc features of their ECG signals. The QRS complex abnormal values were 76% for cases and 31% for controls. Similarly, the QTc was also found abnormal with 75% for cases and 33% for controls. The accumulative abnormal values of both QRS and QTc were found 75% and 48% for late and early risers respectively. There is a relative high occurrence of heart abnormalities in cases than controls. The probability of QRS and QTc abnormality is more for Cases as compared to Controls.

KEYWORDS

Electrocardiogram (ECG), Circadian Cycle, Heart Rhythm, Early Rising, Late Rising

1. INTRODUCTION

Heart is an amazing muscular organ in the human body and other animals that pumps blood continuously to the different organs using vessels (Venes). The heart related variations in energy in different states of body can be measured from ECG. Electrocardiogram (ECG) is a measure of the wave form of energy generated by the heart and represents an individual cardiac feature. ECG has been analyzed by different researchers for various diseases identification (Dubin, 2000, Golden Jr et al., 1973). ECG has been used for examining of many activities, behaviours and characteristics like sleep, loneliness, smoking and other lifestyle (Kesper et al., 2012, Devi et al., Hawkley et al., 2003, Sherwood et al., 1990). Sleep and Cardiovascular health are interconnected with each other. Cardiovascular health is also effected from many habitual activities like smoking (Devi et al.). ECG signal disorderness and differential activation are also associated with people spent much their time in loneliness (Hawkley et al., 2003). The habit of getting up in the morning varies from person to person. Getting up early in the morning has been advocated in all the times and many researchers have described its social, economic, and psychological benefits. In this paper, Psycho-physiological and behavioral effects on human heart is studied. For this purpose, the subjects are selected and classified into Cases and Controls. The ECG signals of both the Cases and Controls are investigated and analyzed with considering the total number of 19-features including (P, Q, R, S and T wave) as well as QRS(depolarization) and QTc(repolarization).

[1] Corresponding Author: *Zhou You, College of Computer Science and Technology, Jilin University, China*
Email-Address: zyou@jlu.edu.cn

2. RELATED WORK

Getting up early in the morning has been advocated in all the times and many researchers have described its social, economic, and psychological benefits (Franklin, 1855). They have investigated the positive effects of early rising on social, academic and professional life. In the study of correlation of morningness-eveningness, it has been investigated that those students who wakeup early in the morning have shown significant academic outcomes and achievements than the late risers (Randler and Frech, 2006, Laino, 2008).The performance of morning-type (MT) students is better in school as compared to evening-type (ET) students (Den, 2000). A study conducted in Texas University(Laino, 2008) shows that the early morning risers have received high score in their GPAs as compared to the late risers. It has also been investigated that the student's biological rhythm is varied with sleepiness and it affects performance during daytime in school schedule (Andrade and Menna-Barreto, 1996). Harvard biologist, Christoph Randler revealed that early risers are more proactive(Randler, 2009). Randler's research also discovered that "morning people" are more likely to anticipate problems which leads to more success in the business world. It has also been explored that early risers exhibit character traits like satisfaction, optimism, being agreeable and consciousness (Ravi, 2015). On the other hand, night owls are associated with creativity and intelligence while they are more likely to exhibit traits like pessimism, depression, and being neurotic. Benjamin Franklin appreciated to go early to bed and wakeup early in the morning (Franklin, 1855). In the study of sleep and biological rhythm, it is suggested that variation in sleep-time influences hippocampus volume (Kuperczko et al., 2015). Hippocampus is a part of the human brain located under the Cerebral-Cortex and its volume size is related to short and long term memory (Seifert, 1983). Hippocampus is found significantly smaller in volume for the students with late wakeup time as well as for shorter and longer sleepers. According to the sleep experts, if you go to bed early and get up early in the morning, your body will be more in tune with the earth's circadian rhythms (Randler, 2009).Circadian cycles (circadian rhythm) are the physical, mental and behavioural changes in the human body that occur during the 24-hour cycle. In addition, it has also been reported that an exposure to the light in the morning is effective for patients with depression and seasonal effective disorder (Goel et al., Terman et al., 1989). Circadian rhythm is considered effective on cardiovascular system and its pattern associated with cardiac related diseases like myocardial ischemia and acute myocardial infarct, and sudden cardiac death (Portaluppi et al.). The day-night patterns are significantly associated with atrial arrhythmias-premature beats, tachycardia, atrial fibrillation, and flutter. There is a strong evidence that cardiovascular system have shown variations with the intrinsic-circadian-clock and causes many cardiovascular diseases including arrhythmia and temporal trends(Chen, 2015). A review is also carried out regarding of human behaviours and their association with daily life activities both in ancient and modern perspectives (Rahman and Hassan, 2014, Hassan et al., 2016). In this study, the source population for study members involved people having variation in their rising habits. The objective is to determine the strength of association between various heart abnormalities in late risers.

3. METHODOLOGY

3.1 Selection of Cases and Controls

The case-control study conducted on participants having age between twenty and thirty-five years, from August 2016 to November 2016. The participants are healthy and have not any history of heart diseases. The sources population are all those participants who have variations in their occupations and activities. The ECG signals are obtained during 9:00 am-12:00 pm. The participants are categorized such that, in which 80 participants from cases and 120 participants from controls are included in the given population. For Cases identification, all participants admitted to cardiology ward. Cases are eligible if they have characteristics symptoms plus electrocardiogram changes indicative of heart abnormalities. The controls are those participants who have not experienced any heart diseases. They found normal in their ECG recordings. Similarly, the age and sex-matched controls found identical to those described for cases, with additional criterion that control have no previous diseases. About 58% controls are selected as hospital based and 42% are community-based or non-cardiac ward controls.

3.2 Study Questionnaires

Structured questionnaires were administered to ask case-participants and controls about locality, age, and smoking history, current and previous medication. Similarly, physical examinations were undertaken in the same manner in cases and controls. Information about demographic factors, socioeconomic status (education, income), lifestyle (smoking, leisure time and physical activity), personal and family history of cardiovascular disease, behaviours (early and late rising) and risk factors (hypertension, diabetes mellitus) were obtained. Psychosocial factors (depression, locus of control, perceived stress, and life events) were systematically recorded. Following steps were taken to perform the ECG acquisition, features extraction and their analysis for any chances of diseases. In addition, information was collected regarding diagnosis of general health conditions, including asthma, lung disease (defined as emphysema, chronic lung problems and/or chronic bronchitis), heart disease (defined as heart problems from birth, rheumatic heart disease, angina, heart attack, and/or heart failure excluding hypertension), diabetes (type I or II), other metabolic disorders, kidney disease (defined as kidney transplant, renal failure, and/or dialysis), liver disease, blood disorders (defined as sickle cell disease, thalassemia, or hemoglobin problems), mental health diagnoses, neurologic conditions (defined as conditions that involve muscles, nerves, or the brain), immune suppression (defined as cancer, HIV infection, or immunosuppressive medication), and obstructive sleep apnea.

3.3 ECG Acquisition

Before taking ECG of an individual, five to ten minutes were given to each subject for relaxation. In the experiments, ECG was taken from Cardio-Care2000 Bionet machine (Bionet, 2015). This machine is facilitated with 12-channel leads to find accurate heart's electro-magnetic field. During experiments, every subject was guided about their position and orientation. The machine enabled us to extract ECG print out in 3-Chanels, 6-Chanels and 12-Chanels as well as in soft form in the computer with 10 and 60 second duration. The EKG-Plus II software (Bionet, 2015) was used on PC to visualize the ECG in different formats.

3.4 Features Extraction

We used nineteen features for each subject's ECG. These features are heart beats variation (PBS), PR interval, QRS duration and amplitude, QT/QTc, P-axis, amplitude and duration, T and R axis, T amplitudes and durations, Q amplitudes and durations and ST amplitude (Hassan et al.). The peak values are computed with setting-up a threshold value. The identification of the peak (R locations) values are further used as a base to find more features including R-amplitude (highness) and duration (interval). Similarly, the skewness is measured by calculating the orientation of R-peaks. The RR interval is equal to one beat which is further multiplied with 60 seconds and it produces one beat per minute. Furthermore, the QRS-complex is the combination of Q, R and S wave (Figure 1). It is the most complicated and important part of ECG signal. The combination of all these points generates the QRS complex. The angles of P, R and T (skewness of P, R and T) wave along the axis are calculated as depicted in Figure 1 (Singh and Singh, 2011).

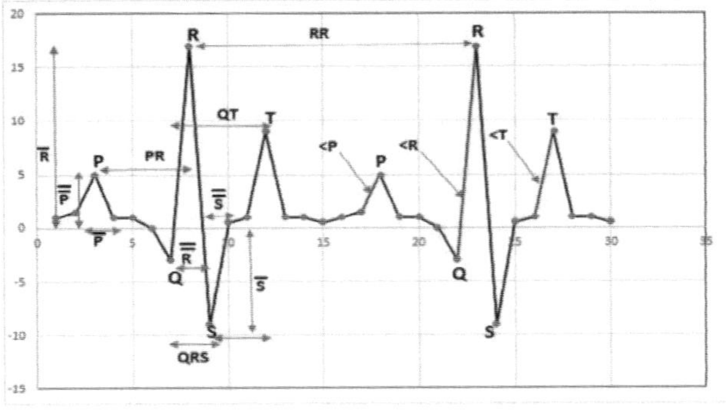

Figure 1. ECG signal with its intervals (QT, PR, $\bar{P}$, QRS, $\bar{\bar{R}}$, $\bar{\bar{S}}$, ST), amplitude ($\overline{R}$, $\bar{\bar{P}}$, $\overline{S}$, $\overline{Q}$) and Angle (<P,<R,<T)

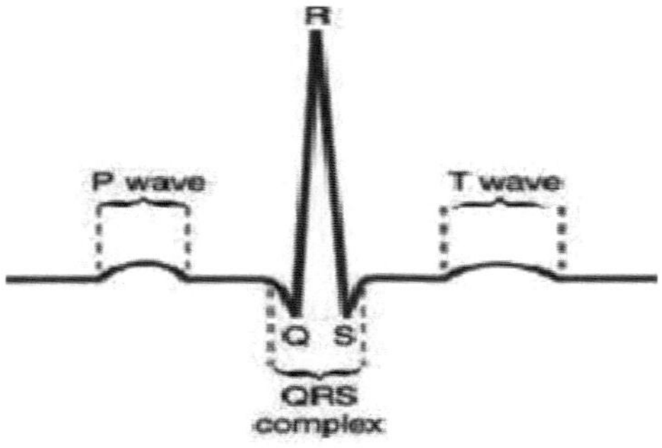

Figure 2. QRS Complex with Start and End Points

4. RESULTS ANALYSIS AND DISCUSSION

In the result analysis and discussion, we describe the morphology of 1) QRS-Complex and 2) QT/QTc as well as their 3) statistical analysis. 1) QRS-Complex is the combination of three graphical deflection points (Q, R and S) in normal ECG (Trahanias, 1993). It is the central and most obvious part of ECG signal which indicates depolarization. The QRS complex starts with Q wave and ends with S wave (Figure 1). Normal duration and range of QRS complex is 0.06-0.01 seconds or 1.5 to 3 boxes (Becker, 2006) for male subjects. The normal duration of QRS complex is about 0.06-0.01 seconds, where variations in its normal range cause many types of abnormalities. A prolonged QRS complex indicates abnormalities in LVEF (Murkofsky et al., 1998) as well as increased LV ESCs and LV EDCs (Murkofsky et al., 1998). Similarly QRS changes also cause Myocardial Infarction, LVH and Anterior (Wagner et al., 1982). In addition to these abnormalities, exceeding the normal duration of QRS also causes diseases like WPWS, Ventricular-Tachycardia and LBBB (Chung et al., 1965). 2) In the QT/QTc Morphology, QT-interval is the time from the start of QRS-wave to the end of the T-wave. It represents repolarisation and depolarization of ventricles in the heart. The length of QT has inverse relation with the heart rate. The duration of QT decreases at faster heart rate and increases at slower heart rate. QTc is the corrected value to estimate the QT value over different heart rate to improve an accurate detection of arrhythmias. Normal range of QTc for men is 350-450 ms and 350-460 ms for women. Abnormal prolonged QT is associated with risk factor of ventricular arrhythmia where short QT interval is related with ventricular fibrillation, paroxysmal and sudden cardiac death. Different types of syndromes such as Hypokalaemia and Hypomagnesaemia have prolong QTc (Ponte et al., 2010). 3) In the statistical analysis, the proportions of characteristics among case-patients and controls were compared, as shown in Table 1. The comparison and evaluation of cases and controls are also shown in Table 2 and Table 3 with significant P value. In Table 1, QRS and QTc were considered from the ECG signal of cases and controls. The cases exposed to risk factor for QRS and QTc were 76% and 75% respectively. On the other hand, for controls, it is 31% and 33% for QRS and QTc respectively. Similarly, further analysis of Odd Ratio (OR) can be read in *Interpretation of Odd Ratio.* The odds ratio is interpreted the same way as other ratio measures (risk ratio, rate ratio, etc.). The OR is 6.8 (more occurrences of QRS abnormal) and 1.5 based on QRS and QTc. A prolonged QRS complex indicates abnormalities in LVEF, LVESCs, LV EDCs (Murkofsky et al., 1998). Similarly, the OR for QTc also found greater than one (1), which indicates a high-risk factor of heart abnormalities in the cases. Abnormal prolonged and short QT is associated with risk factor of ventricular arrhythmia and ventricular fibrillation, paroxysmal, sudden cardiac death respectively while prolong QTc is associated with Hypokalaemia and Hypothermia (Ponte et al., 2010).

Table 1. Case controls study of early and late risers

	Cases		**Controls**	
	QRS	QTc	QRS	QTc
Exposed (late risers)	63	60	37	40
Non-Exposed (Early risers)	20	20	80	80
Total	83	80	117	120
%Exposed	63/83=76%	60/80=75%	37/117=31%	40/120=33%

Interpretation of Odd Ratios:

Odd Ratio=1 No Association | **Odd Ratio>1** Risk Factor | **Odd Ratio<1** Protective Factor

Odds ratio with respect to QRS=(63x80)/(20x37) = 6.8>1
Odds ratio with respect to QTc=(60x80)/(80x40) = 1.5>1

The OR values (6.8, 1.5) are greater than one (1) with respect to QRS complex and QTc, which indicates a high-risk factor of heart diseases in later risers.

Significance of the study: In order to determine whether the concerned features in the two groups (Cases and Controls) are showing significant variation or not, we have calculated ANOVA(ANOVA ($F(1, 49) = 10.875$, $p < 0.00001$)) is for QRS features which is significant. Similarly, the ANOVA for QTc is (ANOVA ($F(1, 49) = 13008.139$, $p < 0.00001$) which is also significant. Two variables have been declared, 1) assignment of two values, 1 and 2 to Controls and Cases respectively. 2) Storing the actual values of the QRS and QTc. The ANOVA for QRS and QTc have been statistically generated as shown in Table 2-3 respectively.

Table 2. Statistical Analysis of P value for QRS complex

VAR00001	Sum of Squares	Df	Means Square	F	Siq.
Between Groups	SST = 15.000	r-1 = 12	MST = 1.250	F = MST/MSE = 10.875	0.000
Within Groups	SSE = 10.000	n-r = 87	MSE = 0.115		
Total	SS = 25.000	n-1 = 99			

Table 3. Statistical Analysis of P value for QTc

VAR00002	Sum of Squares	Df	Means Square	F	Siq.
Between Groups	2419580.250	1	2419580.250	1.301E4	0.000
Within Groups	18228.500	98	186.005		
Total	2437808.750	99			

5. CONCLUSION

We investigated the effects of early and late rising on human heart using ECG signals. The significant difference found in the QRS complex and QTc interval among the participants of both groups. There are different diseases related to QRS complex abnormalities such as Left-Ventricular-Systolic-Dysfunctions and Left-Ventricular-Diastolic-Dysfunctions, Diastolic-Counts, Left Ventricular Hypertrophy, Wolf-Parkinson-White-Syndrome (WPWS), and Right-Left Buddle-Branch-Block. Moreover, QTc abnormalities are also associated with many diseases e.g. Hypokalaemia, Hypomagnesaemia, Hypothermia and Raised Intracranial Pressure. In the case-controls study, the Cases were found high risk of heart diseases compared to Controls. The statistical value of P and OR was significant which shows that the controls are healthier than cases.

ACKNOWLEDGEMENT

This research is supported by the National Natural Science Foundation of China (Grants No. 61772227, 61572227), the Science & Technology Development Foundation of Jilin Province (Grants No. 20180201045GX) and the Science Foundation of Education Department of GuangdongProvince (Grants No. 2017KQNCX251, 2018XJCQSQ026) and the Social Science Foundation of Education Department of Jilin Province (Grants No. JJKH20181315SK)

REFERENCES

Andrade, M., M & Menna-Barreto, L. (1996) *Diurnal variation in oral temperature, sleepiness, and performance of high school girls. Biological Rhythm Research,* 27, 336-342.

Becker, D. E. (2006) *Fundamentals of electrocardiography interpretation. Anesthesia progress,* 53, 53-64.

Bionet (2015) *CardioCare 2000.*

Chen, L. (2015) *Recent advances in circadian rhythms in cardiovascular system. Frontiers in pharmacology,* 6.

Chung, K.-Y., Walsh, T. J. & Massie, E. (1965) *Wolff-Parkinson-White syndrome. American heart journal,* 69, 116-133.

Den, W. V. (2000) *Time in bed, quality of sleep and school functioning of children. Journal of sleep research,* 9, 145-153.

Devi, M. R., Arvind, T. & Kumar, P. S. *ECG Changes in Smokers and Non Smokers-A Comparative Study. Journal of clinical and diagnostic research: JCDR,* 7, 824.

Dubin, D. (2000) *Rapid interpretation of EKG's: an interactive course,* Florida, United States, Cover Publishing Company.

Franklin, B. (1855) *Early to Bed, and Early to Rise, Makes a Man Healthy, Wealthy, and Wise, Or, Early Rising, a Natural, Social, and Religious Duty*, Theclassics US.

Goel, N., Basner, M., Rao, H. & Dinges, D. F. *Circadian rhythms, sleep deprivation, and human performance. Progress in molecular biology and translational science,* 119, 155.

Golden Jr, D. P., Wolthuis, R. A. & Hoffler, G. (1973) *A spectral analysis of the normal resting electrocardiogram. IEEE Transactions on Biomedical Engineering*, 366-372.

Hassan, M., Rahman, S. U., Alam, F., Ali, Z. & Alam, S. *Effect of Rising Habit on the Human Health Using ECG signals. Journal of Postgraduate Medical Institute (Peshawar-Pakistan),* 30.

Hassan, M., Rahman, S. U. & Rahman, A. U. (2016) *Heart's Role beyond a Blood Pumping Machine: A Literature Review in Modern Perspective.*

J. Appl. Environ. Biol. Sci, **1**, 197-210.

Hawkley, L. C., Burleson, M. H., Berntson, G. G. & Cacioppo, J. T. (2003) *Loneliness in everyday life: cardiovascular activity, psychosocial context, and health behaviors. Journal of personality and social psychology,* 85, 105.

Kesper, K., Canisius, S., Penzel, T., Ploch, T. & Cassel, W. (2012) *ECG signal analysis for the assessment of sleep-disordered breathing and sleep pattern. Medical & biological engineering & computing,* 50, 135-144.

Kuperczko, D., Perlaki, G., Faludi, B., Orsi, G., Altbacker, A., Kovacs, N., Doczi, T., Komoly, S., Schwarcz, A. & Clemens, Z. (2015) *Late bedtime is associated with decreased hippocampal volume in young healthy subjects. Sleep and Biological Rhythms,* **13**, 68-75.

Laino, C. (2008) *Early Birds Get Better Grades. Sleep Disorders Health* 1ed. sleep disorder center, Pomona Valley Hospital, California, WebMD News Archive.

Murkofsky, R. L., Dangas, G., Diamond, J. A., Mehta, D., Schaffer, A. & Ambrose, J. A. (1998) *A prolonged QRS duration on surface electrocardiogram is a specific indicator of left ventricular dysfunction. Journal of the American College of Cardiology,* **32**, 476-482.

Ponte, M. L., Keller, G. A. & Girolamo, G. D. (2010) *Mechanisms of drug induced QT interval prolongation. Current drug safety,* **5**, 44-53.

Portaluppi, F., Tiseo, R., Smolensky, M. H., Hermida, R. n. C., Ayala, D. E. & Fabbian, F. *Circadian rhythms and cardiovascular health. Sleep medicine reviews,* 16, 151-166.

Rahman, S. U. & Hassan, M. (2014) *Heart's Role in the Human Body: A Literature Review. Journal of Applied Environmental and Biological Science,* **4**, 199-208.

Randler, C. (2009) *Proactive People Are Morning People1. Journal of Applied Social Psychology,* **39**, 2787-2797.

Randler, C. & Frech, D. (2006) *Correlation between morningness-eveningness and final school leaving exams. Biological Rhythm Research,* 37, 233-239.

Ravi, R. (2015) *Why Even Night Owls Should Wake Up Early. Motivated Life.* Southern California, Los Angeles, Ravi Raman Enterprises, LLC.

Seifert, W. (1983) *Neurobiology of the Hippocampus,* United States of America, Cambridge, Academic Press.

Sherwood, A., Dolan, C. A. & Light, K. C. (1990) *Hemodynamics of blood pressure responses during active and passive coping. Psychophysiology,* 27, 656-668.

Singh, Y. N. & Singh, S. K. (2011) *Evaluation of electrocardiogram for biometric authentication.*

Terman, M., Terman, J., Quitkin, F. & McGrath, P. (1989) *Bright light therapy for winter depression: A review of efficacy. Neuropsychopharmacology,* **2**, 1-22.

Trahanias, P. (1993) *An approach to QRS complex detection using mathematical morphology. Biomedical Engineering, IEEE Transactions on,* **40**, 201-205.

Venes, D. *Taber's cyclopedic medical dictionary*, FA Davis.

Wagner, G., Freye, C., Palmeri, S., Roark, S., Stack, N., Harrell, F. & Selvester, R. (1982) *Evaluation of a QRS scoring system for estimating myocardial infarct size. I. Specificity and observer agreement. Circulation,* 65, 342-347.

AN OVERVIEW AND EVALUATION OF BLACK-BOX TESTING METHODS FOR SYSTEM TESTING

Anastasija Špakova and Marina Uhanova
Riga Technical University (RTU)
Riga, Latvia

ABSTRACT

The paper provides an overview of existing coverage-based functional black-box testing methods in order to choose testing method for checking student laboratory works in the study subject “Algorithmization and Programming of Solutions” at RTU Faculty of Computer Science and Information Technology. The aim is to increase the quality of the study subject and to automate student work checking process. It is needed to perform system type of testing in order to check student works. There are two similar testing methods that can help in checking works – scenario-based and domain testing. Nevertheless, the methods are similar and in theory should produce similar results, authors of the paper want to confirm if it is true or not. Practical application and evaluation of these methods will be presented in the paper.

KEYWORDS

Black-Box Testing Methods, Domain Testing Method, Scenario-Based Testing Method

1. INTRODUCTION

Testing can be described with five dimensions: testers, coverage, potential problems, activities and evaluation (Kaner et al. 2002). Each dimension gives tester direction for testing method selection. Testing methods can be involved in all five dimensions (Kaner et al. 2002). The focus of this paper is the two functional coverage-based testing methods which belong to coverage dimension: scenario-based and domain testing methods.

The system should be tested from customer’s perspective, and that appropriate test data to be selected for testing. Scenario-based testing checks the system from user perspective and domain testing helps to select appropriate test data. Both these methods are similar, thus in theory they should show similar results as well. Two metrics are used in order to clarify if this is true or not: number of defects and failure size – number of test cases in percentage in a set of test cases that have found a particular defect (Grindal et al. 2006).

The paper provides an insight about coverage-based testing methods. It will help to select appropriate testing method for student work checking in the study subject “Algorithmization and Programming of Solutions” in order to automate the checking process and to increase the quality of it.

The paper is organized as follows. Section 2 gives description of testing methods. Section 3 describes the testing program. Section 4 describes domain testing. Section 5 describes scenario-based testing. Section 6 gives examples of created test cases/test scenarios. Section 7 reviews the practical application of methods and summarizes the results. Section 8 includes conclusions and further research.

2. CLASSIFICATION OF COVERAGE-BASED TESTING METHODS

Several coverage-based testing methods are proposed in (Kaner et al. 2002):

- Function testing checks every feature or function which user can do in the system.
- Feature or function integration testing and scenario-based testing test several features or functions together in some combination.

- Use case testing checks the system on a transaction by transaction basis from start to finish (Tools QA).
- Menu tour tests all of the menus and dialogs in a GUI product (Kaner et al. 2011).
- Domain testing focuses on input/output values testing rather than the feature testing.
- Equivalence class analysis tests input or output data which are divided in equivalence classes where only one test value of each class must be tested (Dustin 2002; Black et al. 2012).
- Boundary testing tests input/output values that are located on equivalence class boundaries (Dustin 2002; Black et al. 2012).
- Combination testing tests two or more input or output values in combination with each other.
- Input field test catalogs test each type of input field.
- Map and test all the ways to edit a field.
- Logic testing tests logic or business rules. Input values have logical relationships in the system.
- State-based testing or state transition testing checks if a system moves from state to state correctly.
- Requirements-based testing checks if the system satisfies every requirement in a requirements document.
- Specification-based testing tests the product specification.

Coverage-based testing methods can be divided into three categories by their purpose (Table 1).

Table 1. Classification of coverage-based testing methods

Based on input/output values testing	Based on transactions testing (the sequence of actions)	Based on specific unit testing (system element or specific functionality)
• Domain testing • Equivalence class analysis • Boundary testing • Combination testing	• Feature or function integration testing • Scenario-based testing method • Use case testing • Logic testing (Cause-effect graphing and decision table testing techniques) • State-based testing or state transition testing	• Function testing • Menu tour tests • Input field test catalogs • Map and test all the ways to edit a field • Requirements-based testing • Specification-based testing

3. THE TESTING PROGRAM

State diagram is used for systematic test case creation. State diagram shows the states that a system can take and shows the events that cause and/or result from a change from one state to another (Black et al. 2012). In the case of domain testing, test cases are created by focusing on test data and in the case of scenario-based testing, test scenarios are created by focusing on various actions which are performed in the system. The program used for testing is one of the student's laboratory works written in Java. It is about order tracking for sewing manufactory. Program data: customer name/surname; date when ordered; order price; how much has already been paid. Program requirements: view file content; record order data; remove order data; adjust order data; order data by dates and surnames; find data about all customers who paid incompletely; calculate the total cost of all orders. The scheme of state diagram of task specification is shown in Figure 1.

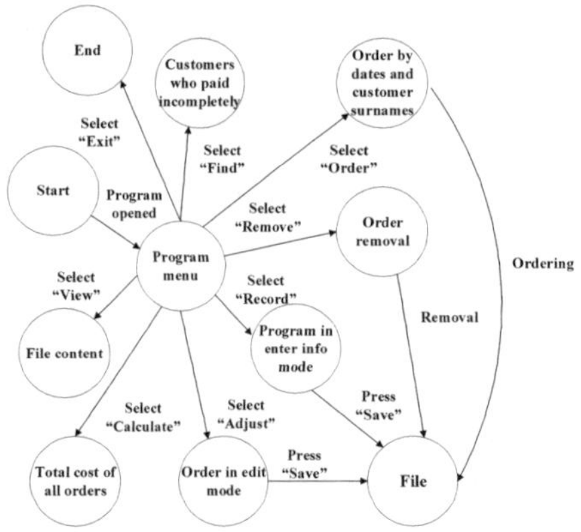

Figure 1. State diagram for the program

4. DOMAIN TESTING METHOD

Domain testing considers numeric input and output values of fields. It implies that input/output values are divided into input/output domains of values. A domain is a set of values that includes all possible values of a variable of a function or feature. Domains with values are partitioned into sub-domains (equivalence classes) and then values from each sub-domain are used (Kaner et al. 2002; Kaner et al. 2005; Kaner et al. 2010). Two testing methods are used for domain testing: boundary value analysis and equivalence class analysis.

The structure of the domain testing which is used for our program testing is: identify input values and output values; partition input and output values into equivalence classes; define boundary values. The scheme of input values is shown in Figure 2. User selects any menu option. If user selects "data about new order" or "data editing", then he needs to enter/change respective input data. Format and value type (numeric, non-numeric) should be checked. Output values are shown schematically in Figure 3. User selects any menu option and the result (output) of this option is saved in the file. File format and content should be checked. Equivalence partitions and boundary values of input/output values are shown in Table 2.

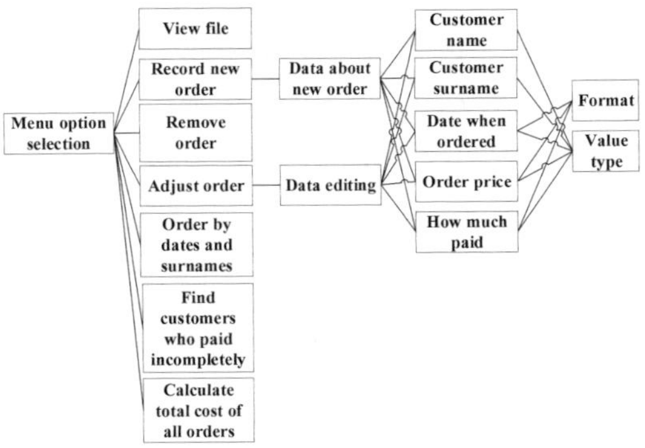

Figure 2. Input values of the program

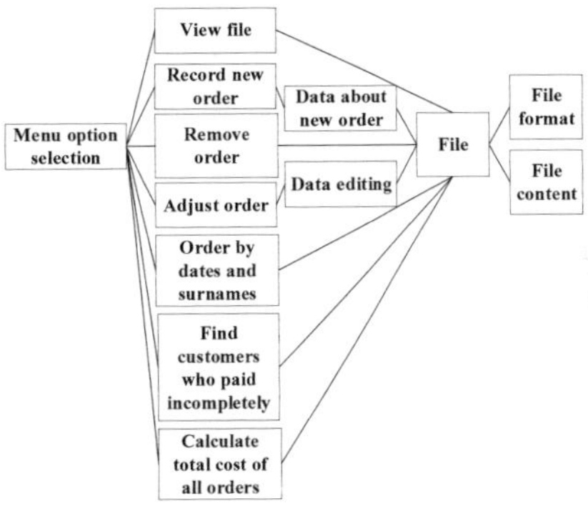

Figure 3. Output values of the program

Table 2. Equivalence partitions and boundaries of input and output values

Input/output values	Valid equivalence classes	Invalid equivalence classes	Valid boundaries	Invalid boundaries
Menu option selection (input)	Correctly selected	Incorrectly selected	Not applicable	Not applicable
Name (input)	Non-integer	Integer; empty	Not applicable	Not applicable
Surname (input)	Non-integer	Integer; empty	Not applicable	Not applicable
Date when ordered (input)	Correct format	Non-integer; incorrect format; date in the past; empty	1.06.2020; 15.12.2020	Not applicable
Order price (input)	0.00 – Max (infinity); integer; correct format; >how much has already been paid	<0.00; non-integer; incorrect format; empty; <how much has already been paid	0.00; 999.99; order price = how much has already been paid; order price = how much has already been paid + 0.01	– 0.01; order price = how much has already been paid – 0.01
How much has already been paid (input)	0.00 – Max (infinity); integer; correct format; <order price	<0.00; non-integer; incorrect format; empty; >order price	0.00; 999.99; how much has already been paid = order price; how much has already been paid = order price – 0.01	– 0.01; how much has already been paid = order price + 0.01
File output when removing data about order from the file	There are orders to remove	There are no orders to remove	Not applicable	Not applicable
File output when ordering by dates and customer surnames	Not applicable	Not applicable	01.01.2020; 15.12.2021; date + 1 day; date – 1 day; date 1 = date 2 (two identical); customer surname 1 = customer surname 2 (two identical)	Not applicable
File output when searching customers who paid incompletely	There are customers; there are no customers	Not applicable	Not applicable	Not applicable
File output when calculating total cost of all orders	0.00 (all orders); 1 order – Max	Not applicable	0, 1 and 2 orders	Not applicable
File format (created file is output)	Correct file format	Incorrect file format	Not applicable	Not applicable

5. SCENARIO-BASED TESTING METHOD

Scenario-based testing method deals with creation of test scenarios. Test scenario is based on a scenario that is a hypothetical story or situation about system use (Kaner et al. 2011). The structure of the scenario-based testing which is used for our program testing: identify all features which user can do in the system and identify all situations how user can use the feature. Feature and user actions are the following:

1. **View file content (option "View").** User views content when file is empty and when it contains orders.
2. **Record data about new order (option "Record").** User enters data about customer; records new order directly in the file; enters all fields incorrectly; adjusts one field incorrectly and other fields correctly.
3. **Remove data about order from the file (option "Remove").** User removes order; enters removed order once again and removes it; tries to remove order when no orders are in the file; adjusts all fields incorrectly; adjusts one field incorrectly and all other fields correctly.
4. **Adjust order data (option "Adjust").** User adjusts data about customer using option "Adjust"; adjusts data directly in the file; leaves one field empty and enters other fields correctly.
5. **Order data by dates and surnames (option "Order").** User orders by dates and surnames.
6. **Find data about all customers who paid incompletely (option "Find").** User searches customers who paid incompletely.
7. **Calculate total cost of orders (option "Calculate").** User calculates cost when there are 0, 1, 10 orders.
8. **Exit the program (option "Exit").** User selects menu option "Exit" after he opened a program; viewed the file content; recorded, removed and adjusted order; ordered data by dates and surnames; found data about all customers who paid incompletely for work; calculated the total cost of all orders.

6. CREATION OF TEST CASES AND TEST SCENARIOS

Domain and scenario-based testing methods can overlap. Boundary values/equivalence classes are used for test values selection in scenario-based testing method. For boundary values/equivalence classes selection in domain testing the tester must think about various user actions what user might want to do in the system. For example, one of user actions can be that he can enter new order correctly when order price is 999.99, and this is boundary value which is identified using domain testing. Examples are shown in Table 3 and Table 4.

Table 3. Test case "User enters new order incorrectly"

Precondition: The file should be empty.	
Steps	**Expected results**
1. Select menu option "Record".	The screen for data entering is shown.
2. Enter the following data: name = integer value; surname = integer value; date when ordered = 00:00; order price = – 0.01; how much has already been paid = – 0.01. Press "Save".	Error is shown that user entered data incorrectly.
3. Select menu option "View".	No data are shown.
4. Open created file and check if previously entered data are saved in the file.	Previously entered data are not saved in the file.

Table 4. Test scenario "User enters new order incorrectly"

Steps	**Expected results**
1. Select menu option "Record".	The screen is shown.
2. Select "Exit".	User exited the program.
3. Select menu option "Record".	The screen is shown.
4. Enter the following data: name = non-integer value; surname = non-integer value; date when ordered = 00:00; order price = 999.99; how much has already been paid = 0.01. Press "Save".	The data are saved.
5. Select menu option "View".	User can see the data.
6. Select "Exit".	User exited the program.
7. Open created file and check if previously entered data are saved in the file.	Data are saved in the file.

7. TEST EXECUTION AND RESULTS

21 test cases and 28 test scenarios were created. Test cases/test scenarios were executed manually. Domain testing and scenario-based testing found the same defects. 5 defects were found altogether.

The more test cases/scenarios find one and the same defect, the higher is possibility to find this defect (Grindal et al. 2006). Table 5 and Table 6 shows failure sizes. Test results show that the highest number of test cases/test scenarios that is unsuccessfully executed due to one and the same defect is 10 test cases and test scenarios for both testing methods. The 1st defect is found using domain testing method, but scenario-based testing did not find it. The probability to find the 5th defect is bigger for scenario-based testing than for domain testing. Conclusion can be made that both methods are good for finding defects and each method concentrates on specific aspect of testing. Both methods also can find one and the same defect.

Table 5. Failure size (Domain testing)

Defect No.	Number of test cases affected by the defect	Failure size
1.	1	4,76%
2.	10	47,62%
3.	1	4,76%
4.	2	9,52%
5.	2	9,52%

Table 6. Failure size (Scenario-based testing)

Defect No.	Number of test scenarios affected by the defect	Failure size
1.	0	0%
2.	10	35,71%
3.	1	3,57%
4.	2	7,14%
5.	4	14,29%

8. CONCLUSIONS AND FURTHER RESEARCH

Both evaluated methods – domain testing and scenario-based testing produce similar results and can find one and the same defects because the methods overlap. The statement that similar methods produce similar results is approved by the testing results. This means that there are no good or bad testing methods. Each method focuses on specific aspect of testing. Tester should decide what is relevant in the specific situation – to use only one method or to use combination of several methods. Both evaluated methods can be applied for student laboratory work checking and can effectively find defects. The authors of this paper suggest to use domain testing and scenario-based testing in combination in order to gain more thorough testing and possibly to find more defects.

The program tested was relatively small so futher practical evaluation of these two methods should be performed on more complex and bigger systems. The amount of test cases/scenarios depends on size of the system and it will increase in case of bigger system testing. Thus, automation of test cases/scenarios should be applied in that case. The further research is to create automatic tests using these or other functional black-box testing methods. For evaluation of these methods it is required to select structural testing test coverage criteria (e.g. statement, decision coverage) in order to know how much each method can cover the code.

REFERENCES

Black, R. et al, 2012. *Foundations of software testing: ISTQB certification*. 3rd Edition, Cengage Learning EMEA, Hampshire.

Dustin, E., 2002. *Effective Software Testing: 50 Specific Ways to Improve Your Testing*. Addison-Wesley.

Grindal, M., et al, 2006. *An Evaluation of Combination Strategies for Test Case Selection*. Available at: http://barbie.uta.edu/~mehra/54_An%20Evaluation%20of%20Combination%20Testing%20Strategies.pdf (Accessed: 31 March 2019).

Kaner, C. and Bach, J., 2005. *Black Box Software Testing 2005 Academic Edition Domain Testing*. Available at: http://testingeducation.org/BBST/domain/BBSTDomainTesting1.pdf (Accessed: 31 March 2019).

Kaner, C. and Fiedler, R.L., 2011. *Black Box Software Testing: Introduction to Test Design: A Survey of Test Techniques*. Available at: http://www.testingeducation.org/BBST/testdesign/BBSTTestDesign2011pfinal.pdf (Accessed: 31 March 2019).

Kaner, C. and Padmanabhan, S., 2010. *An introduction to the theory and practice of domain testing*. Available at: http://kaner.com/pdfs/kanerPadmanabhanVISTACONDomainTesting.pdf (Accessed: 31 March 2019).

Kaner, C., et al, 2002. *Lessons Learned in Software Testing: A Context-Driven Approach*. 1st Edition, John Wiley & Sons, Inc., New York.

Tools QA. Available at: http://toolsqa.com/software-testing/test-scenario/ (Accessed: 28 March 2019).

Posters

SENTIMENT SCORES OF SENTIMENT KEYWORDS: ANALYSIS OF HOTEL REVIEW DATA

Ye-Seul Jeon, Eun-Young Jang and Hwan-Seok Jang
Research Engineer in Daumsoft, Graduate school of applied statistics, Yonsei-University
97, Dokseodang-ro, Yongsan-gu, Seoul, South Korea

ABSTRACT

Utilizing hotel review data by analyzing specific keywords as either being positive or negative, it is possible to aid consumers in selecting a suitable hotel. For this purpose, we propose creating a Sentiment Score of each Sentiment Keyword. We first construct a Sentiment Lexicon by extracting Sentiment Keywords by natural language processing. Afterward, we formulate a coefficient between the Sentiment Keyword and the evaluation score through ridge regression. The coefficient is then normalized to arrive at the cumulative probability of normal distribution, ultimately employed as the Sentiment Score of the specific Sentiment Keyword. However, if the coefficient is considered to be insignificant, the Sentiment Score is replaced by the probability of the Sentiment Keyword as either being positive or negative by using label propagation with the *k*-Nearest Neighbor (*k*-NN) classifier. The data analyzed is focused on South Korean hotel reservation websites.

KEYWORDS

Sentiment Analysis, Ridge Regression, Label Propagation, Review Analysis, k -Nearest Neighbor

1. INTRODUCTION

In South Korea, many travelers utilize hotel reservation websites. Hotel reservation websites aid consumers in selecting the most suitable hotel by providing in-depth information such as their reviews. However, its shortcoming is that it requires users to spend excessive time reading the actual reviews to get a better idea of the hotel for a qualitative perspective. Previous studies endeavored to solve this issue by categorizing reviews as either positive, neutral, or negative (Kasper, W. and Vela, M., 2011). However, categorizing a single review to a single category may impair the specific ideas posed in the review. For this purpose, our study creates a Sentiment Score of each Sentiment Keyword that consumers deem important, thus complementing the conventional evaluation score.

2. METHODOLOGY

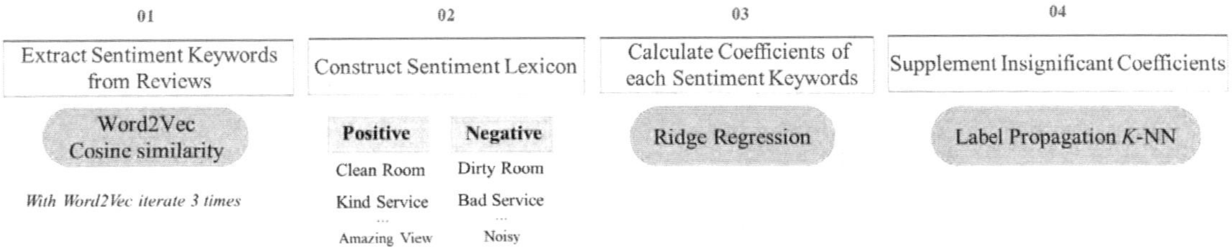

Figure 1. A framework of the proposed methodology

After collecting reviews from Korean hotel reservation websites, Sentiment Keyword candidates are extracted through natural language processing. Employing Word2Vec, a Sentiment Lexicon is then created by calculating the distance between each keyword by cosine similarity.

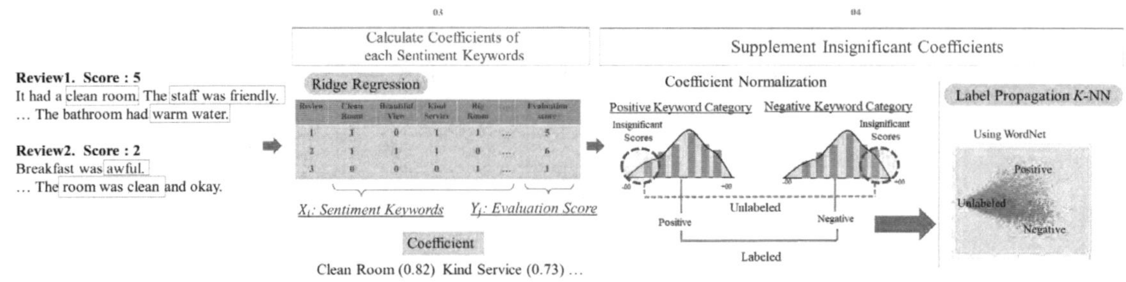

Figure 2. A process of calculating sentiment score

Figure 2. shows the process of extracting sentiment scores. We implemented ridge regression as the machine learning model to derive the coefficient between Sentiment Keywords (independent variable) and its evaluation score (dependent variable). The ridge regression shows better prediction when the predictor variables are highly correlated and it is stable to select variables (Donald W., 1975). We then normalize the coefficient of each positive and negative keyword. We equate the cumulative probability of each coefficient as its Sentiment Score for both positive and negative keyword categories, with the cumulative probability for the negative keyword category stated as $(-1) \times (1 - \text{Cumulative Probability})$. Meanwhile, in cases where the coefficient is considered as insignificant (i.e. Positive Keyword Category: Cumulative Probability < 40%, Negative Keyword Category: Cumulative Probability > 60%), the Sentiment Score of a Sentiment Keyword is substituted by the probability of the Sentiment Keyword as either being positive or negative. This is achieved through a semi-supervised method as according to k-NN(k=5) using label propagation after constructing a WordNet based on the Sentiment Lexicon (Rao D., 2009). In this study, there are two labels that one is positive and the other is negative. To do label propagation, insignificant keywords are unlabeled while significant keywords are labeled as either positive or negative. As a result, insignificant keywords are labeled according to their similar meanings of the keyword's label.

3. RESULTS

We collected approximately one million reviews of more than forty thousand hotels from five different websites, including Airbnb, Booking.com, Daily Hotels, and etc. A Sentiment Lexicon was constructed with approximately thirty-nine thousand Sentiment Keywords using Word2Vec. Through the Sentiment Lexicon, we analyzed a myriad of review data posted in Booking.com, containing approximately eleven thousand Sentiment Keywords. We conduct ridge regression by assigning lambda = 10 as a penalty. To calculate the accuracy of polarity resulted from ridge regression, we first assign keywords with a positive/negative coefficient as a positive/negative keyword (i.e. predict sentiment) after which we compare the accuracy between the predict sentiment and the actual sentiment from the lexicon. We conducted ridge regression and label propagation with the accuracy as shown in Table 1. Ridge regression resulted in an accuracy of 65.42% and complemented the model with label propagation, thus improving the overall level of accuracy to 81.44%. The trained Word2Vec for Label Propagation expresses each word in 256 dimensions and the size of vocabulary is 542,841.

Table 1. Model Accuracy

Ridge Regression	Ridge Regression + Label Propagation
65.42%	81.44% (Final Model)

Table 2. shows an example of Sentiment Keyword coefficients calculated by ridge regression and its cumulative probability after normalizing and the results for insignificant Sentiment Keywords using label propagation.

Table 2. Sentiment keywords and sentiment score

Polarity based on Lexicon	Sentiment Keyword	Ridge Regression Coefficient	Cumulative Probability	Label Propagation	Final Sentiment Score
Positive	Awesome View	0.0230	0.5092	Labeled	0.5092
Negative	Bad Service	-2.2054	0.0137	Labeled	-(1-0.0137) = -0.9863
Positive	Clean Bedsheets	-0.5367	Unlabeled	0.9167	0.9167
Negative	Unfriendly Staff	0.5942	Unlabeled	0.8989	-(0.8989)

Table 3. shows that Sentiment Scores of each Sentiment Keyword complement evaluation scores, thus aiding consumers to better understand the satisfaction level of the hotel. For instance, in cases where low/high evaluation scores were given despite being an overall positive/negative review, Sentiment Scores point out that the review also included a positive/negative opinion.

Table 3. Sentiment score of a sample review

Review	Sentiment Score	Evaluation Score
It had a small room. The staff was friendly. … The bathroom had warm water.	Small Room -0.58 /Staff Friendly 0.64 Clean Room 0.61 /Quiet 0.56 /Warm Water 0.62	**2.5**
The breakfast was awful. … The room was clean and okay.	Awful -0.77 / Clean 0.59	**9.6**

4. CONCLUSION & FUTURE WORK

Sentiment Scores are an effective quantifiable measurement tool that helps us grasp the essential meaning of specific Sentiment Keywords. We believe that Sentiment Scores can be a useful tool for consumers in selecting a suitable hotel that meets their needs and for hotel management in terms of selecting the right marketing strategy in ways to react to the right problems that hotel user face.

A similar study has used the product parse-paraphrase paradigm to calculate emotional scores. In this study, emotional scores were calculated using the frequency-based ratings of adjectives and adverbs in sentences (Liu, J., 2009). However, since the method using simple appearance frequency each sentiment keyword is affected by the frequency. It is unstable to calculate the exact score of sentiment keywords. In comparison, the method proposed in this study has the advantage that the emotion score can be calculated irrespective of the frequency with which the word appears in the review.

However, the methodology of Label Propagation that is used in this study also has limitations. It costs exhaustive computation to deal with such newly input samples. In order to overcome this limitation, it seems possible to continue the study to reduce the computational cost using Logistic Label Propagation (Kobayashi, T., 2012). Logistic Label Propagation is powerful when there are a lot of keywords or data to compute.

ACKNOWLEDGMENT

This research is supported by the Ministry of Culture, Sports and Tourism (MCST) and Korea Creative Content Agency(KOCCA) in 2019 program of Integrated and Convergence Service for Supporting Tourism Development.

REFERENCES

Kasper, W. and Vela, M., 2011.Sentiment Analysis for Hotel Reviews. Proceedings of the Computational Linguistics-Applications Conference, Jachrenka, Poland, pp. 45-52

Kobayashi, T., Watanabe, K., & Otsu, N. 2012. Logistic label propagation. *Pattern Recognition Letters*, Vol. 33, No. 5, pp. 580-588

Liu, J., & Seneff, S. 2009. Review sentiment scoring via a parse-and-paraphrase paradigm. *In Proceedings of the 2009 Conference on Empirical Methods in Natural Language Processing,* Vol. 1, pp. 161-169

Marquardt, D. W., & Snee, R. D. 1975. Ridge regression in practice. *The American Statistician*, Vol. 29, No. 3, pp. 3-20.

Rao D. and Ravichandran D., 2009. Semi-supervised polarity lexicon induction, *12th Conference of the European Chapter of the Association for Computational Linguistics*, Athens, Greece, pp. 675-682

EXPLAINING BLACK-BOX MACHINE LEARNING MODELS

Krzysztof Dzieciolowski
John Molson School of Business, Concordia University
Montreal, Canada

ABSTRACT

Despite the advances of Machine Learning (ML), the models are still being considered black-boxes that are difficult to explain. In order to address the need to interpret the ML models, I suggest the novel Input Prediction Association (IPA) plots which are based on the means of inputs and predictions, calculated in the model's prediction ranks. The resulting plots provide a model-agnostic method of visualizing associations between the inputs and predictions. The IPA plots can help detect inputs that are linearly correlated with predictions as well as help identify the pattern of their relationships. The IPA plots can also be used to establish inputs' thresholds that correspond to high predicted probabilities for the event of interest, thus extending the interpretation of the model inputs to an individual observation level. Such an approach can be applied in Customer Relationship Management since it suggests not only who to target but also it provides insights as to why to target specific individuals. We illustrate the IPA approach with an example from the field of home equity loan risk analysis in banking.

KEYWORDS

Machine Learning, Black-box models, Inputs, Predictions

1. INTRODUCTION

Predicting the probability of customer events is an important task in the application of machine learning (ML) models in the business environment. The ML models need not only to predict accurately and robustly which customers will, for example, likely purchase a product, but also explain why they would do it. In the paper, I suggest an Input Prediction Association (IPA) approach to plot model's ranks inputs means against the means of the predictions. The value of an IPA plots is that it may help discover the pattern of the relationship between the inputs and model predictions. IPA plot may also be used to customize individual recommendations in Customer Relationship Management (CRM) applications.

The discussion about the explanatory and predictive approaches to data-modelling initiated by Breinman (2001) and continued by Shmueli (2010) and others have helped create a focus on creating more accurate and robust predictive models. However, the machine learning models are still the black-boxes that cannot be easily interpreted. There has been growing interest in finding ways to interpret the models, most notably by Friedman (2001) who suggested the heuristic Partial Dependency Plots (PDP) and by Goldstein et al (2015) who proposed using Individual Conditional Expectation Expectations (ICE). Implementation of PDP and ICE plots in SAS software has been developed by Wright (2018). Zhao et al. (2019) have shown that these plots can help extract causal relationships from the black-box models. However, the PDP approach can work only when the variables of interest and non-interest are independent. Both PDP and ICE plots are also a subject to high variability, which may obscure the relationship between the inputs and predictions. In order to address this question, I suggest the Input Prediction Association (IPA) plots which provide the visual, model-agnostic approach of assessing the relationship between inputs and predictions. The IPA approach is different from PDP method in that, instead of integrating-out the inputs of no interest, the inputs of interest are conditioned on the prediction values. In section 2, I define the IPA approach and provide a heuristic algorithm for constructing IPA plots. An illustrative example of IPA plots for Home Equity Loans data is provided there too. Conclusions and recommendations for further research follow in section 3.

2. INTERPRETING BLACK-BOX MODEL WITH IPA PLOTS

In order to visualize the effect of a single input variable on model predictions, I suggest graphing the means of the inputs and predictions obtained from model ranks. The resulting plot is called an Input Prediction Association (IPA) plot. The novelty of the IPA plot is that it is obtained directly from the input variables and model predictions conditioned on the model ranks. The IPA plot helps to identify ranks-based "smoothed-out" relationships between the inputs and predictions. If the goal of the analysis is to extract linear relationships, then Pearson correlations can be calculated from the IPA plots. Here are the steps to obtain an IPA plot.

Step A. Construct a model to predict the target response Y using the inputs $X = (X_1, \ldots X_p)$. Rank-order the model predictions in k quantiles (e.g. k=20).

Step B. Calculate the k means for each of p input variables to get $\bar{X}_{ij}$ $(i \leq p,\ j \leq k)$ and for predicted values to get $\bar{Y}_j$ $(j \leq k)$. Plot $\bar{X}_{ij}$ versus $\bar{Y}_j$ in k-ranks $(j \leq k)$ to obtain an IPA plot for an ith input $(i \leq p)$.

Step C. For detecting a linear relationship between an ith input and predictions, calculate the Pearson correlation coefficient, $r_i = Corr(\bar{X}_i, \bar{Y})$ from k ranks. The inputs that are linearly associated with model predictions can be identified as having high values of r_i, $i \leq p$. In regression models, the slopes of IPA plots are proportional to its leverage of the "hat" projection matrix and corresponding regression coefficient. Let's assume a linear regression model, $y_m = \sum_{j=1}^{p}(\beta_0 + \beta_j x_{mj}) + \varepsilon_m$, where $m \leq n$, p is the number of inputs and n is the number of observations. In order to explain the effect of the input x_j on $\widehat{y_m}$, using the chain rule, we calculate the partial derivative of $\widehat{y_m}$ with respect to input x_j,

$$\frac{\partial \widehat{y_m}}{\partial x_j} = \frac{\partial \widehat{y_m}}{\partial y_m}\frac{\partial y_m}{\partial x_j} = h_{mm}\beta_j$$

where h_{mm} is an mth diagonal element of hat projection matrix $H = X(X'X)^{-1}X'$ and $\hat{y} = Hy$. Hence, in the linear regression model, an input x_j "influences" the prediction $\widehat{y_m}$ through m^{th} leverage and j^{th} slope.

3. EXAMPLE

We illustrate the construction of IPA plots defined in section 2 using the example of Home Equity Loan data (n=5960) from the library SAMPSIO of SAS® Enterprise Miner™ software.

Step A. Obtained a Gradient Boosting model to predict the likelihood of the binary response, "default or seriously delinquent" (bad=1), using10 inputs, as shown in Table 1.

Table 1. Inputs and IPA correlations for Bank Home Equity loan data

Input number	Input Description	IPA Rank Correlations (sorted)	Population Correlations	Gradient Boosting Importance
1	Number of major derogatory reports	0.98	0.44	1
2	Number of delinquent trade lines	0.95	0.60	10
3	Number of recent credit inquiries	0.95	0.31	5
4	Debt to income ratio	0.79	0.25	2
5	Age of oldest trade line in months	0.66	0.23	8
6	Amount due on existing mortgage	0.53	0.08	4
7	Amount of current loan request	0.47	0.09	3
8	Years on current job	0.35	0.08	7
9	Value of current property	0.30	0.05	6
10	Number of trade (credit) lines	0.05	0.01	9

Step B. Calculate means of inputs and predictions in (k=20) ranks and their Pearson correlation coefficients.

Note that, as shown in the Table 1, the input "Number of major derogatory reports" has the highest correlation, r_1=0.98, with predictions, followed by the "Number of delinquent trade lines", r_2= 0.95. Observe also, that correlations of the variables in the ranks are much higher than those in the population, due to variance reduction resulting from averaging the input and predictions in the ranks. Such noise-canceling approach helps to reveal the significant relationships. In addition, the IPA based inputs' importance is quite different from that of gradient boosting model. Hence IPA plots may detect important variables, not noticed by the model.

Step C. Construct Input Predictions Association (IPA) plots for Bank Home Equity Loans variables

The IPA plots for the three inputs from Step B are shown in Figure 1 where the means of inputs in the ranks are plotted against the corresponding means of predicted probabilities of loan default (bad=1). The high likelihood of defaulting on home equity loan suggests the high values of "Number of major derogatory reports" and "Number of delinquent trade lines". However, the "Value of current property" reveals a quadratic-like relationship with predictions. Using a high threshold value for the loan default prediction may help identify customers who satisfy the threshold value of the corresponding inputs. These inputs can be used to provide insights as recommendations for customer-facing agents in CRM applications.

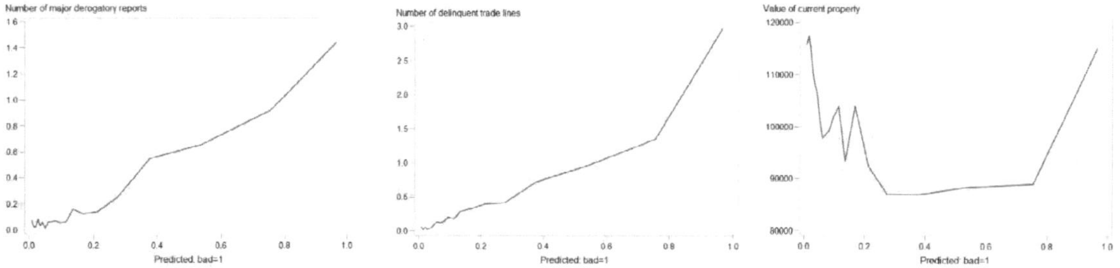

Figure 1. Input Prediction Association (IPA) plots for Home Equity Loans data (default on loan bad=1)

4. CONCLUSIONS

The IPA plot is a visual, model-agnostic tool to help reveal the nature of the relationship between inputs and predictions. In addition, the individual observations can be classified as satisfying input-based threshold criteria to be qualified for the targeted campaign. Hence, IPA plots may help understand black-box ML models both at the population and individual customer levels. It could be useful to find an optimal number of ranks, k, since as $k \rightarrow n$, IPA rank correlations between inputs and predictions converge to population correlations, which are not helpful. Addressing these questions would help explain ML black-box models and advance their applications in CRM applications.

ACKNOWLEDGEMENT

Author would like to thank Concordia University Part-Time Faculty Association (CUPFA) for the financial support of this research.

REFERENCES

Breiman, L. 2001, Statistical modeling: The two cultures. *Statistical Science, Vol. 16, 199–215.*

Friedman, J.H. (2001), Greedy Function Approximation: A Gradient Boosting Machine. *The Annals of Statistics, 29*

Goldstein, A., Kapelner, A., Bleich, J., and Pitkin, E. (2014). Peeking Inside the Black Box: Visualizing Statistical Learning with Plots of Individual Conditional Expectation. *arXiv:1309.6392v2.*

Shmueli G., 2010, To Explain or To Predict? *Statistical Science, Vol. 25, No. 3, 2010, 289–310*

Wright R., 2018. Interpreting Black-Box Machine Learning Models Using PDP and ICE Plots, *SAS Institute Inc.*

Zhao Q., Hastie T., 2019. Causal Interpretation of Black-Box Models. *Journal of Business and Economic Statistics*

DATA MINING FOR ENERGY MANAGEMENT IN A WATER DISTRIBUTION NETWORK

Hohyun Lee, Dae Wook Kim, Sung Taek Hong and Gang Wook Shin
K-water, Daejeon, Korea

ABSTRACT

In the water treatment process, it is important to predict the flow used by citizens and control valves for using large reservoir tanks maximally. In this study, flow predictions are proposed by applying several non-linear algorithms with recursive form to minimize additional learning. To control the valves properly, the target levels of each tank are determined based on flow prediction and genetic algorithms. A simple polynomial learning algorithm is also proposed to control the valves less frequently than a conventional feedback controller until the target tank levels can be reached, which also help not to break down the valves. The proposed method to maximize the usage of reservoir tanks is expected to reduce the electric fee and improve water quality.

KEYWORDS

Water, Reservoir Tank, Learning Algorithm, Electric Fee

1. INTRODUCTION

Unlike electricity, water can be stored in large tanks for more than a dozen hours and citizen's water demands have certain patterns which may be estimated by statistical approaches.

Most of the costs of sending treated water to citizens are attributed to electrical fees which are caused by pumping (Reynolds, 2010). The electric fee depends on the time and season, which is called a load shift. The policy was even applied to public water suppliers. In addition, a new optimization target, the on/off minimization of pumps, should be achieved not to degrade water quality. If input flow is suddenly increased to water treatment plants by the use of more pumps, more turbidity and particles will be supplied to the citizens, which can be minimized by the on/off minimization algorithm.

The optimization of both load shift and on/off minimization are based on the control level of the storage tanks, which needs to be controlled by their electric valves. But it is not easy to control because of a variety of constraints and non-linearity.

2. PROPOSED ALGORITHM

In statistics, predictions are possible about unknown parameters, when the number of measurements are larger than the number of unknown parameters and the measurement errors are normally distributed. The database for water treatment processing has already accumulated massive amounts of data to be analyzed. It is enough to estimate water data with non-linearity and time series. Many algorithms have been introduced and reviewed to estimate the short-term and long-term demands.

Multi-Layer Perceptron and adaptive neuro fuzzy inference systems are used frequently. While a single layer perceptron network cannot solve nonlinear problems, a multi-layer perceptron network gives a solution to the problems (Alpaydin, 2004). Figure 1 (a) describes the 3 layers of the perceptron to approximate flow demand, in which the estimation error is updated by a back-propagation algorithm (Rumelhart, Hinton, & Williams, 1985).

ANFIS stands for adaptive neuro fuzzy inference system, which was first proposed by Roger Jang. It can identify nonlinear components linearly in a control system and predict times series (Jang, 1993). The architecture of ANFIS is shown in Figure 1 (b).

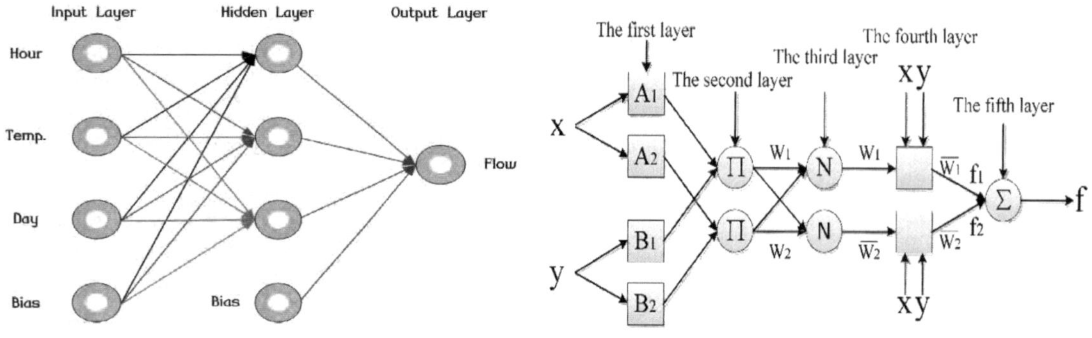

(a) (b)

Figure 1. Structure of a learning algorithm: (a) Basic structure of MLP, (b) Basic structure of ANFIS

3. EXPERIMENT

Flow prediction and optimal pump control are necessary to have all of the information of tank levels and flows, which also help to control electric valves. But the data and controlling valves are restricted to some of the large tanks. Prediction and control might be achieved under these conditions. At first, the main large tanks flow are estimated by ANFIS, and then the estimated flow will extend to all of tanks. The flow is compensated by a recursive algorithm that calculates the error between the estimated flow and real output for 24 hours. Then, the relation between valve position and flow can also be approximated by the polynomial regression algorithm as shown in Figure 2.

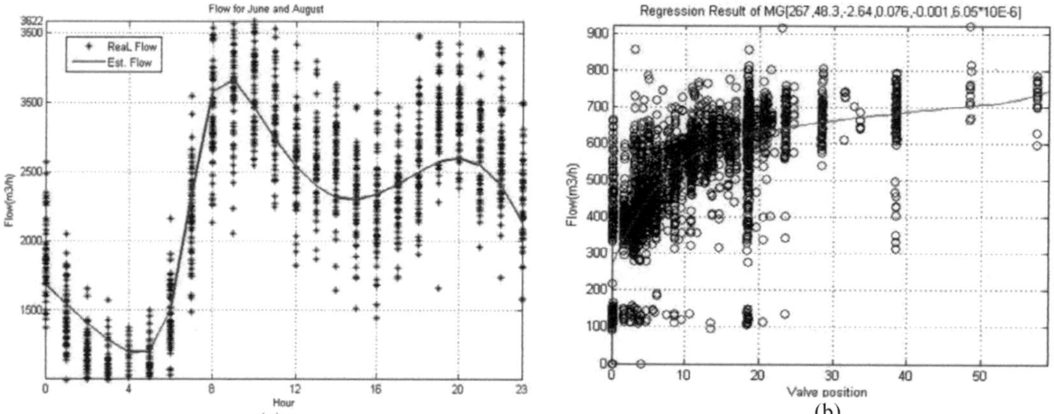

(a) (b)

Figure 2. (a) Flow prediction by ANFIS, (b) Basic structure of ANFIS

General algorithms such as regression, neural network and support vector machine are considered and their results are shown in Table 1. LR(Linear Regression) had the worst result, which means hourly flow doesn't have a linear trend. Other algorithms had almost the same results.

Table 1. Estimation result by each algorithm for flow prediction

Error		LR	Polynomial	MLP (Hidden 3)	MLP (Hidden 20)	ANFIS	LS_SVM
Train Error	MAPE	22.75	13.47	13.28	12.49	12.80	12.22
	MSE	178,050	77,787	78,993	68,841	71,856	67,186
Test Error	MAPE	22.67	13.72	13.42	12.87	12.95	12.54
	MSE	179,070	80,486	81,202	72,572	74,107	71,052
# of Parameter		4	12	4*3+4*1 =16	4*20+21*1 =101	14*4 =56	18950 (SV)

To control the valve, it should be decided to divide the target water flow to each tank. Supply water from WTP would be multiplied by each tank weight, which is calculated by the mean supply of water from each tank. Then, each flow is added or subtracted according to present and target levels.

$$\mathrm{F}_i^{target} = F^{tankin} \times \omega_i^f + Q_i^{level} = F^{in} \times \omega_i^f + \left(L_i^{target} - L_i^{present}\right) \times Q_i^{unit} \quad (1)$$

$$\text{Where } \omega_i^f = \frac{u_i^f}{\sum u_i^f}, u_i^f = \frac{1}{n}\sum_{j=1}^{n} F_j^{tankout},$$

$$F^{takin} = F^{wtp} \times \alpha + \Delta F_{i-1}^{wtp}, \Delta F_{i-1}^{wtp} = \Delta F_{i-2}^{wtp} + \left(F_{i-1}^{wtp} - F_{i-1}^{truewtp}\right) \quad (2)$$

Because their flows are bounded in certain areas, they should be saturated in minimum and maximum flow as follow.

$$\mathrm{F}_i^{target} = \max\left(F_i^{min}, F_i^{target}\right)\, and\ \mathrm{F}_i^{target} = \min\left(F_i^{max}, F_i^{target}\right) \quad (3)$$

If more than one of tank flow are over the limit, their burden must move to other spacious tanks as below.

$$\Delta F^{tank} = F^{tankin} - \sum F_i^{target}, \rightarrow Divide \Delta F^{tank}\ to\ spacious\ tanks \quad (4)$$

After the target flows are decided as above, the proposed valve controller should be working. Figure 3 shows that the target levels were reached.

(b)

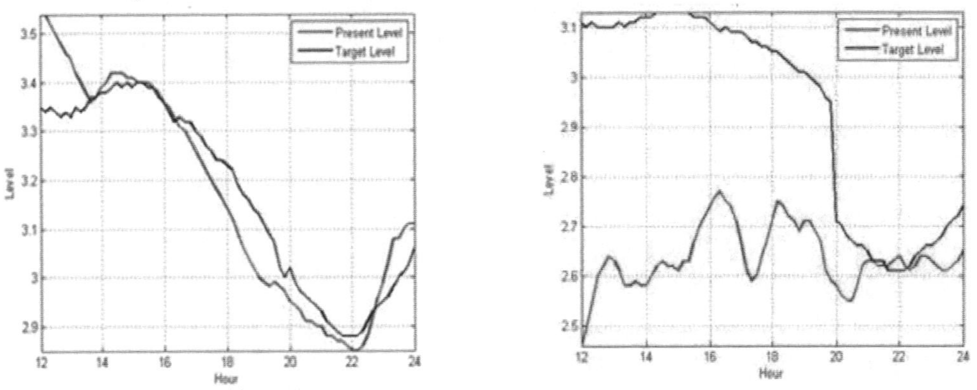

(a)

Figure 3. (a) Error comparison of JW tank level, (b) Error comparison of JM tank level

4. CONCLUSION

Flow predictions are estimated by learning algorithms with recursive form, which makes it possible to track the latest trends and it is not necessary to do any additional learning differently from existing methods. Then, optimal operation levels are determined to minimize costs based on flow prediction and genetic algorithm. The electric cost is different in a specific time and season, in which the tanks levels are estimated by the optimal algorithm. The number of operation pumps are calculated for 48 hours, by which target levels of each tanks are calculated according to load shift. While the target levels should be reached to reduce the operation costs, it was not easy to control the valves because there are many constraints such as low to high flow, level, and long operation intervals, which makes a normal PID controller useless. After modeled by simple polynomial learning algorithm, valves are controlled to use the least amount of time as possible and the constant level target in the WTP and equal distribution in the tanks can be reached. It is expected to maximize the usage of reservoir tanks, which is thought to reduce the electric fee and improve water quality.

REFERENCES

Alpaydin, E. (2004). "Introduction to machine learning", *The MIT Press*, 229-251

Jang, J.-S. R. (1993), ANFIS: Adaptive-Network-Based Fuzzy Inference System, *IEEE Transactions on System, Man and Cybernetics*, 23(3), 665-685

Reynolds, L. K. (2010). Improving energy efficiency of pumping systems through real-time scheduling systems. *Integrating Water System-Boxall and Maksimovic(eds) 2010 Taylor and Francis Group*, London, ISBN 978-0-415-54851-9

Rumelhart,D. E., Hinton, G. E., & Williams, R.J. (1985). Learning internal representations by error propagation, *Cognitive science*, 4-8.

STUDY ON DATA CLEANSING ALGORITHMS FOR OUTLIERS IN WATER SUPPLY SYSTEM

Jong Rib Kim, Gang Wook Shin, Sung Taek Hong and Dae Wook Kim
K-water, Daejeon, Korea

ABSTRACT

There has been systematically sharing data between government agencies, local governments and public organizations and more public organizations are encouraged to open public data in Korea. In the water industry, research on artificial intelligence using big data, a technology related to the fourth industrial revolution, is currently being carried out actively. As a result, quality control of acquired data is necessary to secure the reliability of data by developing algorithms of data cleansing to minimize outliers. In this paper, LSTM (Long Short Term Memory) for cleansing outliers and missing data is proposed to improve data quality management.

KEYWORDS

Outlier, Data Cleansing, Water Supply, LSTM

1. INTRODUCTION

The waterworks are composed of various data tags. Water quality, flow rate, pressure and water level are very important data in the operation side of water purification plants, and numerous data to operate pumps, valves, etc. are organically linked (Jang, Lee, Hong, & Chun, 2014). Unlike the relatively easy-to-detect missing data, it is difficult to detect inaccuracies in data. Therefore, various analysis studies have been conducted to clean abnormal data measured in the water treatment process such as the existing average imputation and the statistical method (correlation and regression) (Choi, Song, & Kang, 2016; Kim, & Lee, 2010). In research, quartiles and LSTM algorithms are studied to improve the reliability of cleaned data and try to implement them by open source.

2. PROPOSED ALGORITHM

The water industry is supposed to disclose major data to citizens and other relevant organization in Korea. Reliability is critical for these data, and the sensitive data to be corrected are selected in collaboration with manager and operational staff working in a plant. As shown in table 1,236 water data were selected for this research to develop the data cleansing to correct the outliers.

Table 1. List for Data Quality Management

Item	Data List
Public Open Data	Water Quality, Flow, Level, Pressure
Data for Water Quality Management	Turbidity, Residual Chlorine, pH
Data for Water Quantity Management	Flow, Level, Pressure, Chemical Dosage Rate
Linked Data to Other Organization	Effluent Flow, Level, Pressure

At first, correlation analysis between the data is performed using the Minitab program as shown in Figure 1. 100,000 data were used for modelling which were collected one minute data during two month period and the five most correlated tags with an absolute value of 0.5 or more were selected. It has been found that the data tag "Transmission flow rate of the water pump in circulation" as shown in Table 2, has a high relationship with BR effluent pressure and HS input flow rate.

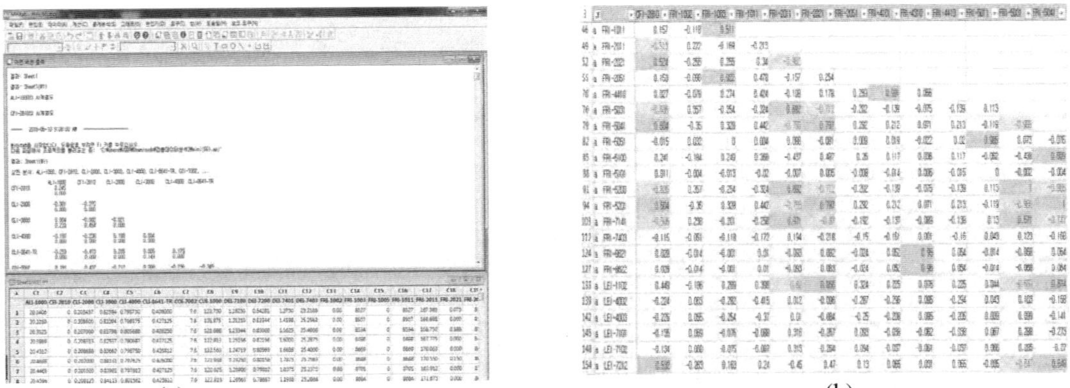

(a) (b)

Figure 1. (a) Correlation Analysis by Minitap, (b) Correlation Analysis by Excel

Table 2. Correlation Result between Effluent Flow and Relevant Data

Dependent Variable	No.	Independent Variable	Correlation Coefficient
Effluent flow rate in BR WTP	A	SC Pressure	0.617
	B	BR Effluent Pressure	0.686
	C	HS Pressure	-0.583
	D	CD Pressure	-0.598
	E	HS(P) Input Flow	0.602
	F	SS Input Flow	0.551
	G	HS Input Valve Position	0.564
	H	HS Input Flow	-0.623
	I	WC Pressure	-0.62
	J	SS Input Flow	0.525

The equation using the regression algorithm is derived from the target data on the left and the independent variables on the right, as shown in Table 3. In the event of wrong and missing data, the correction value is derived by the corresponding equation.

Table 3. Cleansing Equation using Regression Method

$$Y = 0.617 * A + 0.686 * B - 0.583 * C - 0.598 * D + 0.602 * E + 0.551 * F + 0.564 * G \\ -0.623 * H - 0.62 * I + 0.525 * J$$

Based on the correlation coefficient, the input variables are selected, and water quality data are corrected using the linear regression equation. It has an error of 2 to 30.9% depending on the input variables. Its disadvantage is that some highly correlated data can't be explained and water delay time is not considered. In addition, it is difficult to generalize a linear regression equation, which use different inputs to outlier and missing data. Thus, time series analysis needs to be considered to solve the delay time and generalize the algorithm.

We conduct outlier detection and imputation separately using artificial intelligence algorithm. First, the quantile method are proposed to detect the outlier as shown in Figure 2 (a), in which all of data is divided into five quantitation and the relevant data are grouped among them. One year data were used to make the quantile mapping. If it happen that new quantiled data don't belong to the existing mapping, LSTM proposes which value is replaced. Its structure is shown in Figure 2 (b). The algorithm use their own values as input{Y(t-1) to Y(t-360)} and output variables{Y(t)}, which are applied to the all of data imputations to consider the time series characteristic. LSTM was compared with moving average method because both algorithms can work as autoregressive model.

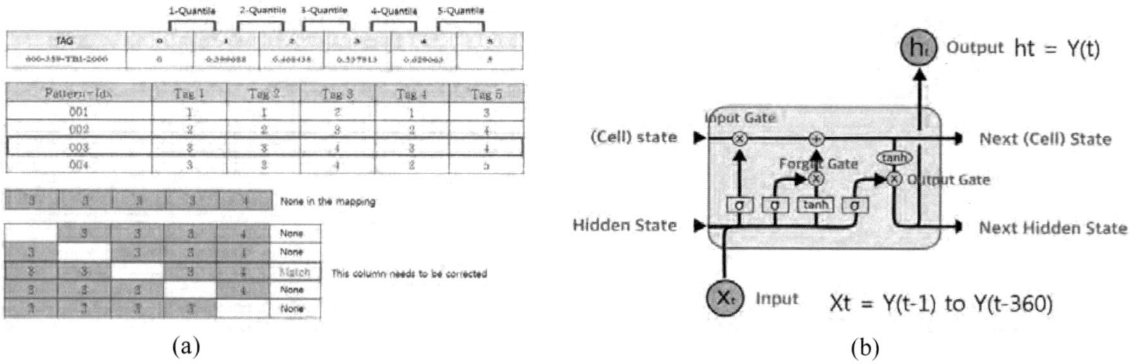

Figure 2. (a) Outlier Detection by Quantile Method, (b) Data imputation by LSTM

After the random outlier data from 20% to 100% of their true value is created for five target tags, the moving average (MA) and proposed methods were compared. Table 4 shows the difference of the existing Mean Imputation and LSTM method, in which it is shown that the error is improved by 5%.

Table 4. Prediction Error between Mean and LSTM Imputation

Imputation	Tag #001	Tag #002	Tag #003	Tag #004	Tag #005	Percentage Error
MA	5.376	20.147	22.433	6.923	16.624	14.3006
LSTM	2.619	11.376	13.682	1.377	16.085	9.0278

3. CONCLUSION

MA Imputation has the advantages of easy application and data correction by estimating missing values by the average of observed data values, but has the disadvantage of distorting statistical distributions in the wide range of missing data, which lead to the reduction of data reliability. LSTM is proposed to cope with those problem, which needs to be checked by the quantile method to detect abnormal data. Even though LSTM has a 5% less error than MA, there is still a 9% error and it is thought to be that further research is needed.

REFERENCES

Choi, G.-W., Song, K.-S., & Kang, J.. (2016). Understanding and policy assignment of R&D of deep learning. KISTEP, *Issue Paper* 2016-08, 1-51, https://www.kistep.re.kr/c3/sub3.jsp?brdType=R&bbIdx=10484

Jang, S.-B., Lee, H.-H., Hong, S.-T., & Chun, M.G.. (2014). Development of Smart Remote Unit of Water Treatment SCADA System. *Journal of the Korean Institute of Illuminating and Electrical Installation Engineers*, 28(2), 24-30.

Kim, S.-H., & Lee, C.-S. (2010). A Master Data Quality Management Framework. *Entrue Journal of Information Technology*, 9(2), 109-121.

A NOISE-TOLERANT EVOLUTIONARY ALGORITHM BASED ON ACCUMULATIVE SAMPLING

Jeongmin Kim, Steven Kurniawan and Kwang Ryel Ryu
Department of Electrical and Computer Engineering, Pusan National University
2, Busandaehak-ro 63beon-gil, Geumjeong-gu, Busan, 46241, Republic of Korea

ABSTRACT

This paper proposes an evolutionary algorithm that can efficiently solve noisy optimization problems for which the objective functions can be evaluated not accurately but only approximately. While the accuracy of evaluation may be improved by taking many samples of evaluation and taking the average, it can be computationally demanding. The proposed algorithm is an improvement over a previous work to achieve higher search efficiency by better allotting different number of samples to different candidate solutions in the population during the course of evolution. Experiments with a set of benchmark problems show that the proposed algorithm significantly outperforms the previous algorithm.

KEYWORDS

Noisy Optimization, Evolutionary Algorithm, Restricted Tournament Selection

1. INTRODUCTION

In this paper, we apply the idea of *accumulative sampling* (Park and Ryu, 2011) to solving *noisy optimization* problems by using an evolutionary algorithm called the *restricted tournament selection* (RTS) (Harik, 1995). Many real-world optimization problems are noisy in the sense that their objective functions cannot easily be evaluated accurately. A good example of such kinds can be seen when we have to conduct many simulations to obtain an accurate evaluation of a candidate solution. If we make the simulation simpler by reducing the simulation scenarios in an attempt to save the computation time, the resulting evaluation becomes inaccurate or noisy. A baseline approach to solving a noisy optimization problem would be to use what is called a simple *resampling* method that takes a large number of samples of fitness (i.e., objective evaluation) for every candidate solution to reduce the effect of noise. However, such an approach makes sense only for the problems that does not demand much computation time in obtaining each fitness sample. The accumulative sampling (AS), which can be considered as a kind of *dynamic resampling*, allots different number of samples to different candidate solutions during the course of evolution under the framework of an *overlapping-population* model or a generational model equipped with an *archive*. AS gives only a minimum number of samples when a solution is first generated, but then allots more samples to those that survive longer in the archive (Park and Ryu, 2011) or in the overlapped population (Jang et al., 2012), and updates the fitness by using both newly and previously sampled values to obtain a more reliable estimate. As the selection between the competitors is made *probabilistically*, estimates form larger samples result in more reliable decisions. Given a fixed number of total evaluations, using AS has been shown to search more efficiently under noisy environment by better utilizing the computational resources for evaluation.

The noisy optimization algorithm proposed in this paper is an extension of the algorithm called NTGA proposed by a previous work (Jang et al., 2012), which is basically an AS method implemented on top of Harik's RTS. The main difference between our algorithm and NTGA lies in the way additional samples are given to the individuals in the population. While NTGA unconditionally gives an additional sample to an individual whenever it becomes a competitor for survival selection against a newly born, our algorithm does so only when the result of probabilistic comparison between the two is not decisive. By allotting additional samples more conservatively, our algorithm makes use of the computational resources more efficiently and thus achieves better search performance for optimization under uncertain environment. Experiments with some benchmark functions show that the proposed algorithm outperforms NTGA significantly.

2. PROPOSED ALGORITHM

Figure 1 shows the pseudocode of our proposed algorithm named NT-RTS (noise-tolerant RTS). As is done in the original RTS, m offspring are generated from m random parents without reference to their fitness. Each offspring y is evaluated by sampling n_i times and then probabilistically compared with a competitor for a survival selection. As the competitor, t individuals are randomly selected from the population and then the one most similar to y is selected. Notice that the competitor x already has some fitness samples accumulated to it. If their average looks better or worse than that of y with a high confidence, the winner is decided right away. Otherwise, the comparison is done again after n_a additional samples are given to x to revise its evaluation. Then, the final winner (either x or y) replaces x in the population.

```
procedure NT-RTS
  P: population, M: mating pool, T: buffer pool, n_i: initial sample size, n_a: additional sample size,
  m: mating pool size, t: buffer pool size, p_t: confidence threshold to take additional samples

begin
  Randomly initialize population P
  for each individual s in P do
    f_s ← evaluate(s, n_i)  /* by averaging the results of n_i different evaluations */
  repeat
    M ← randomly selected m individuals from P
    M ← reproduce(M)  /* now filled with offspring */
    for each offspring y in M do
      f_y ← evaluate(y, n_i)
      T ← randomly selected t individuals from P
      x ← most_similar(y, T)  /* competitor for survival selection */
      p_c ← max(p(f_y < f_x), p(f_y > f_x))  /* confidence of probabilistic comparison */
      if p_c < p_t then f_x ← update_eval(x, n_a)  /* give additional samples to x only when not confident */
      if f_y <_p f_x then remove x from P and insert y into P  /* <_p denotes probabilistic comparison */
  until termination condition holds                /* lower fitness values are better (for minimization) */
end
```

Figure 1. Pseudocode of NT-RTS

3. RESULTS AND FUTURE WORKS

NT-RTS has been compared with the simple resampling method and NTGA using three benchmark functions: Ackley, Dropwave, and Alpine (Jang et al., 2012). The dimension of the functions are set to 30 and additive zero-mean Gaussian noise is added to make the problem noisy. The population size is set to 100, and the total number of evaluations (i.e., samples) is fixed to 100,000. Other parameter settings are $n_i = 2$, $n_a = 1$, $m = 2$, $t = 50$, and $p_t = 0.99$. The resampling method is set to constantly give 5 samples to each individual. Table 1 shows the results of paired t-test after running each case 50 times. More investigation shows that NT-RTS evaluates 5~6% more candidate solutions than NTGA by making an efficient use of the allowed 100,000 limit, which seems to be the main reason of the dominant performance by NT-RTS. Our future works include more experiments with more benchmark functions with more careful parameter tuning. We will also apply NT-RTS to some real world problems of simulation-based optimization.

Table 1. Results of paired t-test using benchmark functions ('+' indicates that NT-RTS is significantly better)

	Ackley			Dropwave			Alpine		
Noise level	Low	Medium	High	Low	Medium	High	Low	Medium	High
Resampling	+	+	+	+	+	+	+	+	+
NTGA	+	+	=	=	+	+	+	=	+

ACKNOWLEDGEMENT

This research was supported by the MSIT (Ministry of Science and ICT), Korea, under the ICT Consilience Creative program (IITP-2019-2016-0-00318) supervised by the IITP (Institute for Information & communications Technology Planning & Evaluation).

REFERENCES

Harik, G. R., 1995. Finding multimodal solutions using restricted tournament selection, *Proceedings of the Sixth International Conference on Genetic Algorithms*. San Francisco, CA, pp. 24-31.

Jang, H., Choe, R. and Ryu, K. R., 2012. Deriving a robust policy for container stacking using a noise-tolerant genetic algorithm. *Proceedings of the 2012 ACM Research in Applied Computation Symposium on - RACS '12*. New York, USA, pp. 31-36.

Park, T. and Ryu, K. R., 2011. Accumulative sampling for noisy evolutionary multi-objective optimization. *Proceedings of the 13th annual conference on Genetic and evolutionary computation - GECCO '11*. Dublin, Ireland, pp. 793-800.

Doctoral Consortium

RECOMMENDER SYSTEM USING UNSUPERVISED MACHINE LEARNING FOR SATISFACTION SURVEYS

Baba Mbaye
EFFET B company, France
Laboratory of ELLIADD, University of Franche-comtè, France

ABSTRACT

Satisfaction surveys are being used more and more by companies to improve their sales force. With the development of new technologies the piloting of these satisfaction surveys is digitized in a partial way.
Piloting these surveys often involves the expertise of a human agent in order to make a judgment on the results obtained from satisfaction surveys. This is a tedious task for the decision-maker, as it faces a huge and heterogeneous amount of data.
This problem may be mitigated by using a recommendation engine based on the unsupervised machine learning algorithm. This recommendation system (RS) will be oriented towards two axes: decision-making (DM) and machine learning (ML).
In our approach, we use RS for consistency between the user and the recommended items. ML will allow us to include in our list of recommendations, unexpected items, items that are not derived from the algorithmic logic of the recommendation system and to make the system partially autonomous on decision-making (to less involving the recommendation engine). Our approach is divided into a) the recommendation process for decision-making, b) unsupervised ML and c) partial "empowerment" for decision-making.

KEYWORDS

Recommender System, Unsupervised Machine Learning, Collaborative Filtering, Satisfaction Surveys

1. INTRODUCTION

Faced with the exponential growth of the amount of data from satisfaction surveys, experts are drowned in a mass of information that makes decision-making difficult in the face of a given problem. Various RS are often offered through research in various fields. The purpose of these RS is to help users find new items or services such as music, books or even people, based on user or item information (Abdi, H. 20007). These systems play a very important role in decision-making. Indeed, these allow us to maximize user profits (Chen, L. Et al, 2008) or to minimize risks (Bouneffouf et al, 2013).

These recommendation engines are built around a set of concepts and rules with results deductible most often by the human. By integrating ML algorithms, the system, over time, will allow us to obtain recommendations that we never thought (not deduction from the rules and concept from our recommendation engine).

In this paper we present a modeling of an RS using unsupervised ML. This recommendation system is of the collaborative filtering (CF) type.

In our approach the ML is used for the purpose of obtaining results that are not derived from the concepts and rules of SR. Indeed, the ML adapts to the environment of execution of the algorithms and generates the appropriate models.

Thus, in this document we will first explain our contribution, then review the literature and present our approach to modeling the system.

2. CONTRIBUTION

This work makes a significant contribution to the following fields of research: satisfaction surveys and SRs. First, we will review the literature on RSs, in their generalities and for satisfaction surveys. Then secondly, we will show the use of an unsupervised ML module combined with the RS module can generate more relevant, personalized and unintended recommendations. Thus our architecture will be composed of two parts : a motor part of recommendation and a second part which represents the module of ML a result, we will see how ML can improve cold start for a new user in a collaboratif filtering algorithm. We will also see how an ML system can be efficient and optimal by combining it with a recommendation engine. Finally, we show how unsupervised ML agorithms can lead us to obtain unexpected predictions. This study is applied with data from satisfaction surveys. A satisfaction survey is a process used by a company to evaluate the quality of its services.

3. RELATED WORK

3.1 RS for Satisfaction Surveys

The aim of an RS is to provide users with the resources required based on their credentials. The latter thus see their research time reduced, but also receive proposals from the system that they would not spontaneously pay attention to. The development of the web has greatly contributed to the establishment of such systems as in the field of e-commerce. RS can be viewed initially as a response to users who have difficulty making decisions in the context of using a "conventional" information retrieval system.

The research in information is based on a principle of indexing data in order to respond to requests from users. More specifically, documentary research, under the discipline of information retrieval, consists of querying a knowledge base through written queries in natural languages or in the form of key words (Joachim Schöpfel et al, 2017). These key words are then compared to all the indexes of the documents present in the database of the search engine when users redirect to a set of relevant results with their initial query (Hulusi Karagel et al 2014).

A satisfaction survey (mystery survey) is a point-of-sale visit by an investigator. The purpose of a visit to a point of sale is to measure the quality of the welcome, the quality of the advice and the respect of the sales instructions.(Yong Li et al, 2017).

These surveys are conducted by "fake" clients recruited and commissioned by companies to evaluate their sales network and are used in many economic sectors (e.g. Automotive, Banks, public energy regulators). They allow companies to acquire a concrete measure of the quality of a service offered in order to improve it, by modifying their offer or by offering training to their employees. Mystery surveys are complementary to satisfaction surveys that provide a measure of opinion as well as complaints denouncing possible malfunctions (AMF, 2011).

The purpose of these mystery visits is to reinforce preventive action in the area of savings protection by monitoring, in the field, the concrete conditions for marketing financial products accessible to the general public.

These mystery visits are a new tool enabling companies to identify as early as possible possible malfunctions in the marketing chain for financial products. The latter make it possible to highlight good and bad practices in the marketing of financial products and to detect the risks of abusive or inappropriate sales of financial products.

The recommendations made from satisfaction survey results are of the action plan type or of a personalized training list for the employees of the company that requested this survey.

3.2 RS for Decision-Making (DM)

According to (Woodman et al, 1976) "The decision is the best choice for a multitude of opinions in order to arrive at an optimal solution and a given problem". This definition reveals that decision-making is done in a collective way, from where it is necessary a good interaction between the different agents of the process.

Thus, the use of a CF type RS responds to this task. The CF is an approach based on the sharing of opinions between users. It reiterates the principle of "word of mouth" practiced by humans since always to build an opinion on a product or service they do not know (schafer et al., 2007). The principle of this method is that the opinions of other users are often used to provide a reasonable prediction of the active user's preference on an item he has not yet noted. These methods assume that if users have the same preferences on one set of items, then they will probably have the same preferences on another set of items they have not yet rated. Suppose for example that Mary's neighbors find that the new restaurant that is open in her neighborhood is a success, she may find it interesting to go try it. If, on the contrary, the majority of her neighbors feel that it is a failure, then she may decide to abstain from going. The techniques of CF therefore recommend to the current user, the items appreciated by the users with whom he shares the same tastes, we speak of similar users.

In our study, all items represent the list of action plans and training proposed by the system on confirmation of the expert. Indeed, the satisfaction survey allows the company that asked for it, first to obtain notes on the various vectors of satisfaction that it has set. These satisfaction vectors are modeled as questions that constitute the questionnaire of the satisfaction survey.

3.3 ML

Machine learning is increasingly used in intelligent software (Simon et al, 2018). It is a subfield of artificial intelligence that focuses on the development of models able to represent certain characteristics of the world around us, to learn some statistical properties of the distributions of the data they process, with the aim of accomplish a multitude of tasks (rem N. Ramkumar et al, 2018). Its link with intelligence is derived from the ability of these models to generalize, extract relevant information from data processed during an update process called "training" and to reuse them effectively on new data never previously encountered. A model is a decision function that in the case of supervised learning takes as input a value $x \in \mathbb{R}$ et $\{(x_i, y_i)\}^n_{i=1}$ where y_i is the target value associated with x_i and qui returns a prediction $f(x_i)$ mean of y_i. When the target is discrete, we are talking about a classification task (Yanxin Zhang et al 2019).

In unsupervised learning, there are no explicit targets. We can take an example of an estimate on the reading time of a document, for example, or the probability of rainfall.

In the case of recommendation systems, ML is a solution for predicting recommendations that the expert does not even think about. The data provided to the artificial intelligence system is not tagged or categorized, and the system's algorithms process the data without any prior training, the results obtained at the output depend on the algorithms implemented (Ezequiel López-Rubio et al, 2018). Unsupervised learning algorithms can perform more complex processing tasks than supervised learning systems, but they can also be unpredictable (Gangadhar Shobha et al , 2018).

Even if an unsupervised ML manages to sort out shirts and Tshirts for example, it can also add unexpected and unwanted categories to classify for example brands of unusual shirts and t-shirts creating confusion instead of putting on order.

Unsupervised machine learning algorithms organize the data into a group of clusters. It describes its structure and gives complex data a simple, organized look for analysis (Ezequiel López-Rubio et al, 2018).

Unsupervised learning occurs when you do not have labeled data for training. This is the basic type algorithm where you only have input data and no output variables that coincide. These are called this because there is no corresponding output for a particular input. Their problems can be grouped together in a cluster to discover the inherent clustering and association issues. Some popular examples of unsupervised learning algorithms are k-ways for grouping problems used in referral systems, customer segmentation, targeting marketing, and the dimensionality reduction problem for data visualization. bulky, feature development, structure discovery, etc (Ezequiel López-Rubio et al, 2018).

ML is a category of algorithms that allows applications to make accurate predictions without explicit programming.

3.4 RS using ML

Nowadays, RSs are used in many information-based companies, such as facebook (Tadlaoui, 2015), Google (Liu et al 2010), or Netflix (Steck at al, 2013). The field of SR came into being in the mid-1990s with the introduction of Tapestry (Goldberg et al, 1992), the first RS. As the RS field evolved, researchers studied the use of algorithms derived from machine learning (ML), an area of artificial intelligence (AI). Machine Learning has been studied since the late 1950s (Martens et al, 1959), with the emergence of the AI field. There is now a plethora of ML algorithms (k-nearest neighbor (Walid, 2018), clustering (Jinhong Huang et al,

2018), Bayes network (Friedman et al, 1997), to name just a few. some types, used in applications ranging from pattern recognition in images (Emiliano et al, 2019) to autonomous vehicles (Nynke et al, 2017). The potential application of ML algorithms is vast and the field looks very promising.

This ML can be of three types: supervised, unsupervised or reinforcement learning.

In the case of recommendation systems built on unsupervised learning personalize the delivery of online advertisements in real time. It's no coincidence that a search on amazon brings up shoe ads on other websites.

4. OUR APPROACH AND EMPOWERMENT OF DM

As a computer domain, machine learning is closely related to mathematical statistics; Having a through knowledge of statistics is useful for understanding and exploiting ML algorithms (Samuel Eisenberg et al 2018).

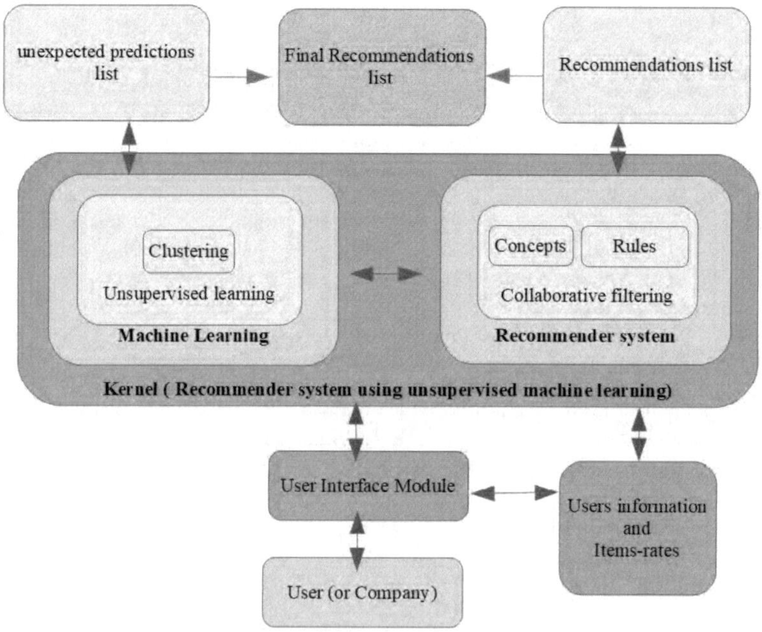

Figure 1. Kernel of recommender system using unsupervised machine learning

So in our recommendation system we use unsupervised learning algotrihms. These unsupervised ML algorithms will allow us to obtain unexpected predictions, ie recommendations that differ from those from a set of predefined rules and concepts in the recommendation engine.

Our architecture will consist of a core containing two modules. A first module representing our RS by collaborative filtering and a second module where ML algorithms will be modeled.

The idea here is to do at the same time, two preliminary recommendations process treatments, one by collaborative filtering based on a set of rules and concepts and the other by a machine learning engine. This learning engine will take into account the conditions that are not applicable to the predefined rules in the collaborative filtering algorithm. Indeed the unsupervised ML algorithms will take into account other additional factors for the construction of these models of recommendations. The factors are : the recommendation context, scalability, overall modeling, automation and iterative processes. The items from these two recommendations will be ranked in order of relevance according to user profile. To do this we apply these items in a Bayesian classification algorithm on a predefined model model.

For a new user (a new company in our case study), we assume that the ML can mitigate cold start. Indeed, by using a system with unsupervised learning, the system can build a model from the cold data of the user and the distance of similarity with the users who have already received recommendations in the past. As a result, from this model the new user will be recommended items of acceptable relevance.

This below, we present you, our system architecture of RS netwire by filtering collabotafi using the ML.

5. CONCLUSION

In this article we presented a modeling of a recommendation system using unsupervised machine learning for satisfaction surveys. We have shown in this paper the existing work around recommendation systems, especially on collaborative filtering and machine learning, specifically on unsupervised learning.

This research is a partial contribution of my thesis which is implementation course. The first results that will be obtained will be presented in the final paper.

REFERENCES

Abdi, H. (2007). The method of least squares. Encyclopedia of Measurement and Statistics. CA, USA: Thousand Oaks.

Bouneffouf, D., Bouzeghoub, A., & Ganarski, A. L. (2013, January). Risk-aware recommender systems. In Neural Information Processing (pp. 57-65). Springer Berlin Heidelberg.

Chen, L. S., Hsu, F. H., Chen, M. C., & Hsu, Y. C. (2008). Developing recommender systems with the consideration of product profitability for sellers. Information Sciences, 178(4), 1032-1048

Emiliano Noce, Alberto Dellacasa Bellingegni, Anna Lisa Ciancio, Rinaldo Sacchetti, Angelo Davalli, Eugenio Guglielmelli, Loredana Zollo, EMG and ENG-envelope pattern recognition for prosthetic hand control, Journal of Neuroscience Methods, Volume 311, 2019,Pages 38-46,ISSN 0165-0270,

Ezequiel López-Rubio, Esteban J. Palomo, Francisco Ortega-Zamorano, Unsupervised learning by cluster quality optimization, Information Sciences, Volumes 436–437, 2018, Pages 31-55, ISSN 0020-0255,

Friedman, N., Geiger, D., & Goldszmidt, M. (1997). Bayesian network classifiers. Machine learning, 29(2-3), 131-163.

Gangadhar Shobha, Shanta Rangaswamy, Chapter 8 - Machine Learning, Editor(s): Venkat N. Gudivada, C.R. Rao, Handbook of Statistics, Elsevier, Volume 38, 2018, Pages 197-228, ISSN 0169-7161, ISBN 9780444640420,

Hulusi Karagel, Döndü Üçeçam Karagel, Identification and Importance of Headings and Key Words in Research in the Framework of Geography Methodology, Procedia - Social and Behavioral Sciences, Volume 120, 2014, Pages 356-364, ISSN 1877-0428,

Goldberg, D., Nichols, D., Oki, B. M., & Terry, D.(1992). Using collaborative filtering to weave an information tapestry. Communications of the ACM, 35 (12), 61-70.

Jinhong Huang, Zhu Liang Yu, Zhenghui Gu, A clustering method based on extreme learning machine, Neurocomputing,Volume 277, 2018, Pages 108-119, ISSN 0925-2312,

Joachim Schöpfel, Hélène Prost, Violane Rebouillat, Research Data in Current Research Information Systems, Procedia Computer Science, Volume 106, 2017, Pages 305-320,ISSN 1877-0509,

Liu, J., Dolan, P., & Pedersen, E. R. (2010, February). Personalized news recommendation based on click behavior. In Proceedings of the 15th international conference on Intelligent user interfaces (pp. 31-40). ACM.

Martens, H. H. (1959). Two notes on machine “Learning”. Information and Control, 2(4), 364-379.

Mohammed Tadlaoui, Sébastien George, Karim Sehaba. Approche pour la recommandation de ressources pédagogiques basée sur les liens sociaux. Sébastien George, Gaëlle Molinari, Chihab Cherkaoui, Driss Mammas et Lahcen Oubahssi. 7ème Conférence sur les Environnements Infor- matiques pour l'Apprentissage Humain (EIAH 2015), Jun 2015, Agadir, Maroc. pp.192-203, 2015.

Nynke E. Vellinga, From the testing to the deployment of self-driving cars: Legal challenges to policymakers on the road ahead, Computer Law & Security Review, Volume 33, Issue 6,2017,Pages 847-863, ISSN 0267-3649,

Prem N. Ramkumar, Sergio M. Navarro, Heather S. Haeberle, Jaret M. Karnuta, Michael A. Mont, Joseph P. Iannotti, Brendan M. Patterson, Viktor E. Krebs, Development and Validation of a Machine Learning Algorithm After Primary Total Hip Arthroplasty: Applications to Length of Stay and Payment Models, The Journal of Arthroplasty, 2018, ISSN 0883-5403,

Samuel Eisenberg, Chapter 3 - Machine Learning for the Government: Challenges and Statistical Difficulties, Editor(s): Feras A. Batarseh, Ruixin Yang, Federal Data Science, Academic Press, 2018, Pages 29-40, ISBN 9780128124437,

Steck, H. (2013, October). Evaluation of recommendations: rating-prediction and ranking. In Proceedings of the 7th ACM Conference on Recommender Systems (pp. 213-220). ACM

Simon Willcock, Javier Martínez-López, Danny A.P. Hooftman, Kenneth J. Bagstad, Stefano Balbi, Alessia Marzo, Carlo Prato, Saverio Sciandrello, Giovanni Signorello, Brian Voigt, Ferdinando Villa, James M. Bullock, Ioannis N. Athanasiadis, Machine learning for ecosystem services, Ecosystem Services, Volume 33, Part B, 2018, Pages 165-174,ISSN 2212-0416,

Walid Cherif, Optimization of K-NN algorithm by clustering and reliability coefficients: application to breast-cancer diagnosis, Procedia Computer Science,Volume 127, 2018,Pages 293-299,ISSN 1877-0509,

Yanxin Zhang, Ye Ma, Application of supervised machine learning algorithms in the classification of sagittal gait patterns of cerebral palsy children with spastic diplegia, Computers in Biology and Medicine, Volume 106, 2019, Pages 33-39,ISSN 0010-4825,

Yong Li, Hui Huang, Validating the Job Satisfaction Survey in voluntary child welfare, Children and Youth Services Review, Volume 83, 2017, Pages 1-8, ISSN 0190-7409

AUTHOR INDEX

International Association for Development of the Information Society (IADIS)
Rua Sao Sebastiao Da Pedreira
No. 100, 30, 1050-209
Lisbon, Portugal

ISBN 978-1-5108-9238-5

CURRAN ASSOCIATES INC.
proceedings.com

9 781510 892385